Interests of State

Interests of State

The Politics of Language, Multiculturalism, and Feminism in Canada

LESLIE A. PAL

McGill-Queen's University Press
Montreal & Kingston • London • Buffalo

ISBN 0-7735-0974-7
Legal deposit second quarter 1993
Bibliothèque nationale du Québec

∞

Printed in Canada on acid-free paper

This book has been published with the help of a
grant from the Social Science Federation of Canada,
using funds provided by the Social Sciences and
Humanities Research Council of Canada.

Canadian Cataloguing in Publication Data

Pal, Leslie A. (Leslie Alexander), 1954–
    Interests of state: the politics of language, multicul-
turalism and feminism in Canada

    Includes bibliographical references and index.
    ISBN 0-7735-0974-7

    1. Canada. Dept. of the Secretary of State.
2. Citizenship – Canada. 3. Multiculturalism –
Canada. 4. Feminism – Canada. I. Title.

JL103.S33P35 1993   354.710685   C92-090726-1

This book was typeset by Typo Litho composition inc.
in 10/12 Baskerville.

To Mary, Matthew, and Michael

Contents

Tables

Acknowledgments

This book is about Canadian citizenship policy since the 1960s, principally about the relationship between the Department of Secretary of State and the various groups that it funds in the policy fields of official languages, multiculturalism, and feminism. It is a complex story of trying to pursue national unity through the encouragement of political advocacy and participation. For a brief period between 1968 and 1972, the federal government sought to create advocacy organizations that would promote a federal policy agenda. The result is that all of the significant citizen's organizations in these three crucial policy fields depend almost entirely on Ottawa for their funding. Whether this makes them mere ciphers or not is a major theme of this book, as is the question of the ultimate effect on the government itself and on the tenor of Canadian political debate.

Tracing three separate and distinct policy fields over a period of thirty years and examining in detail the state-group relations in each posed an interesting research challenge that I was able to meet only with the generous help and support of colleagues, activists, government officials, and institutions. Several dozen officials from government and interest groups kindly submitted to confidential interviews which provided indispensable detail and background information. Numerous colleagues provided advice and criticism as I shaped the argument and analysis: Michael Atkinson, Amy Bartholemew, James Bickerton, André Blais, Stephen Brooks, Sandra Burt, Alan Cairns, Marsha Chandler, Peter Clancy, William Coleman, Stéphane Dion, G. Bruce Doern, Thomas Flanagan, Alain-G. Gagnon, Roger Gibbins, Henry Jacek, Rainer Knopff, Guy Laforest, Ronald Manzer, Alan Maslove, Patrick McCartney, John Meisel, Denis Monière, F.L. Morton, Susan Phillips, Paul Pross, Greg Prycz, Davia Stasiulis, Ian Stewart, Gene Swimmer, David Taras, Hugh Thorburn, Glen Toner,

Carolyn Tuohy, Robert Young, and two anonymous readers. Colleagues at the John F. Kennedy Institute for North American Studies at the Free University of Berlin (where I was visiting professor in 1989) stimulated me to think about Canadian issues in broader political terms. I am also grateful to Dieter Rauch and Peter Wagner, then of the Wissenschaftzentrum in Berlin, for their help on the question of social movements.

I was fortunate to have several highly competent research assistants over the last several years. They included Catherine Bailey, Michel Burrowes, Goldy Hyder, Alex Ker, Michael Pretes, and Laureen Whyte. Generous and indispensable financial support was also provided by the University of Calgary's University Grants Committee, which provided me with a grant to investigate the potential for a large research project. A two-year Canadian Studies Writing Award from the Association for Canadian Studies was most helpful, as was a grant from the Social Sciences and Humanities Research Council. Carleton University's School of Public Administration gave me a visiting professorship in 1988–89 which made my stay in Ottawa that year both intellectually and socially stimulating. The University of Calgary also awarded me a Killam Resident Fellowship which permitted completion of the manuscript. I am grateful also to *Canadian Public Administration*, for permission to reproduce previously published material in chapters 3 and 4, and to Copp-Clark Pitman, for permission to reproduce parts of "Official Language Minorities and the State: Dual Dynamics in a Single Policy Network," from William Coleman and Grace Skogstad, eds., *Organized Interests and Public Policy* (1990), 170–90. Philip Cercone of McGill-Queen's University Press encouraged the project from its beginnings, and his active support and advice were indispensable to its completion. John Parry took a very sharp pencil indeed to the text and expertly clarified and enlivened it.

I cannot refrain from a personal note. This book began as a typical scholarly enterprise, seeking answers to theoretical questions such as the nature of the contemporary state. It soon became, for want of a better phrase, an exploration of Canada's soul, for these three programs and the issues and people that they touched have been crucial to Canadian political debates over the last twenty years. I have tried to be dispassionate throughout, but the evidence may persuade some readers that these programs were misguided, confused, biased, and ultimately ineffectual. Others of harder heart may conclude – though I do not think that my findings warrant this – that the programs did more harm than good. It is certainly easy to be sceptical about both the origins and evolution of the federal government's support to advocacy organizations. There is also a sad irony that twenty years after the origins of programs intended to foster citizenship, national unity, and linguistic, ethnic, and gender harmony, Canadian citizenship now seems more fragmented, national unity more elusive, language tensions more pronounced, and worries about racial and sexual discrimination more prevalent. Despite their imperfections, the programs represented Canada's quest for itself, for a political formula that would foster harmony through respect for and celebration of diversity. Whatever the success or failure of that formula and the political discourse that it encouraged, Canadians would do well to ponder the lessons of their experience.

Interests of State

Introduction

The idea for this book occurred to me some years ago as I worked on a study of Canadian unemployment insurance. One question I explored in that work was the influence of business and labour groups on policy development. As I reviewed the program's evolution in the 1970s, I noticed that women's organizations had mounted strong campaigns to end what they considered discriminatory provisions of the legislation, dealing principally with maternity benefits. I noticed also that many of these organizations were funded in one way or another by the same government that they were attacking. I thought this fact intriguing and made a mental note to find out more about government funding of advocacy organizations. After all, it seems peculiar for a government to fund its critics.

I should also confess that initially my preoccupation was almost obtusely intellectual. I was, and am, interested in the way in which the modern state shapes society. Much of the academic literature on interest groups is concerned with their influence on government, and I wished to explore arrows that ran in the other direction. Of course, the simple act of passing legislation and implementing public policy often changes society in some way. To return to unemployment insurance for a moment, it is clear that people behave differently in labour markets when such insurance is available than when it is not. So to say that the state affects society is, in one sense, banal. The problem becomes more intriguing if one adds several possibilities. The first is that state actions (and ultimately public policy) may have their source *within* the state itself – their roots, as it were, in some interior logic that is quite distinct from societal forces, or at least is not in any obvious way determined by those forces. An example of this, again to use unemployment insurance, is the actuarial ideology that governed the way in which the program was expanded and contained in the 1950s and 1960s. This ideology was an arcane science known in detail to only a few program administrators, but it so thoroughly imbued the legislation that it set the imaginative horizons of what were considered reasonable modifications to the program. A second possibility is that state institutions are a distinct forum for discussion of issues and the resolution of conflict. An interest group that presents its case before a parliamentary committee is likely to use different arguments, and perhaps even a different logic, than it might before the media or in an open debate with its adversaries. Thus, our tendency increasingly to address and resolve social issues within the context of certain political institutions (e.g., Parliament, committees, royal commissions, inquiries, and courts) may be altering outcomes. The final possibility comes closest to the original question that motivated this book. If the state were to fund interest organizations which, in the absence of that funding, either could not organize or would organize differently, would that not make a difference to the flow of political and social forces?

It was this final, somewhat arcane question that drove my initial reflections on government funding of interest groups. At first I thought that I would try to develop a full inventory of these efforts and groups, but I almost immediately discovered that the sheer scale of the enterprise (even at only one level of government) would bury me in archives and libraries for the better part of my adult life. I then decided to focus on only one federal department in its relations with three distinct types of organizations. The department was the Secretary of State of Canada (SOS). The SOS has a continuous history extending back to Confederation, and while its functions have varied widely over the decades, since the mid-1960s it has had the primary responsibility for citizenship development and providing assistance for advocacy and service organizations in the language, multicultural, and women's areas. These programs originated in 1969 (Official Language Minority Groups – OLMGs), 1971 (Multiculturalism), and 1974 (Women's Program), all within the SOS, and all within one section of that department, the Citizenship Branch. In 1987–88 the SOS provided over $50 million in grants to over 3,000 organizations in these three policy areas. By Ottawa standards, this is a small expenditure, and slightly more than half of it goes to projects sponsored by groups, not the groups themselves. However, the remainder is distributed in the form of core funding to assist organizations in their day-to-day operations. In the majority of cases, SOS grants are the primary source of funding for these organizations. In this way, the SOS supports some of the most visible and active advocacy organizations in Canadian politics: Alliance

Quebec, provincial francophone organizations, the Canadian Ethnocultural Council, the Women's Legal Education and Action Fund, the Canadian Day Care Advocacy Association, and the National Action Committee on the Status of Women. As advocacy organizations, these groups are active in areas that are vital to Canada's contemporary policy debates, such as linguistic rights, immigration and multiculturalism, and gender equality.

The sos has several other programs similar to the ones considered in this study, assisting groups for the disabled, human rights advocates, and native peoples. All three deserve separate treatment, and this was already a long book. I was reasonably confident, however, that the three areas that I selected captured the more prominent areas of the department's concerns and were at the core of its mandate for citizenship development. This rationale does not apply as well to the native area, where the sos has been providing core funding for native organizations since the 1970s. I was acutely aware, however, of the complexities of the native policy area and the long tradition among non-native academics simply to relegate native issues to footnotes or asides in their analyses of Canadian politics. An adequate analysis of sos funding of aboriginal organizations would have taken this book deep into questions concerning the Indian Act, the 1969 White Paper, land claims, and the complex structure of aboriginal communities and their representational forms. These are indeed vital issues and deserve detailed discussion, perhaps along the lines developed in this book.

While the sos is perhaps the most visible federal agency providing support of this type to non-governmental organizations (NGOs), it is not alone. There are no systematic data on the scope of government support, but anecdotal evidence (for 1987–88) provides some context. The Department of National Health and Welfare, for example, offers both sustaining and project grants to voluntary non-profit organizations for both health services/promotion and social services. Its grants to national voluntary organizations under these two categories amounted to $6.1 million in 1988. Its granting procedures are quite formal in comparison to the Department of Environment, which until 1986 relied on ad hoc requests for money on a project-by-project basis. After the criticisms from the Auditor General, Environment reorganized its grants systems into several categories. The Class Grants Fund ($150,000 in 1988) provides sustaining grants to environmental NGOs. In the first year of its operation, the program received 65 applications. One year later, it received over 500. Another category is the Canadian Environmental Network Contribution. The network is an umbrella organization consisting of over 1,500 environmental groups from across the country, and the department provides a core/sustaining grant of $250,000. In exchange, the network chairs an annual conference, organizes meetings between the minister and groups, compiles an inventory of environmental organizations, and provides advice as needed to the department. The Department of Agriculture supports 4-H Clubs across the country and also offers grants for the establishment and maintenance of producer co-operatives. The Department of Justice has three main funding pools. Human Rights provides no core funding but will support special projects with contributions up to $10,000. Access to Justice provides operational funding through cost-sharing arrangements with provinces for specific programs that promote access to justice (e.g., legal aid). The Consultation and Development Section of the Research and Development Directorate again offers no core funding but does support projects. The Solicitor General complements these funds through grants to NGOs in the criminal justice field.

An example of a department that delivers most of its policies and programs through grants to NGOs is Fitness and Amateur Sport. Sports Canada is a major sponsor of sports organizations. Its mandate includes provision of financial assistance for the development of Canadian sport, and it works closely with some 85 national sports organizations and a number of specialized agencies to create and support policies and programs. Sports Canada's budget in 1988 was $50 million, most of which was divided among national sports organizations, athletes, university researchers, sports scientists, and others. Its main funding vehicle is the Core Support Program, which in 1987–88 awarded almost $46 million in direct funding to client organizations. This was divided among single-sport national organizations ($27 million to 69 groups), multi-sport service organizations ($9 million to the National Sport and Recreation Centre), and multi-sport organizations (e.g., Canadian Interuniversity Athletic Union, the Canadian Olympic Association, and the Commonwealth Games Association). Other allocations include Participaction ($1 million), Youth Fitness (national organizations such as the Girl Guides of Canada and Cross Country Canada), the Disabled Program (for organizations encouraging participation by the disabled in sports), and Skills Program for Management Volunteers.

Virtually every important federal department government has some sort of funding program for NGOs, in the form of either sustaining grants or (more usually) project grants. The Canadian International Development Agency, which reports to External Affairs, has a Public Participation Program to assist groups, institutions, and communities in promoting awareness of international development issues. The Department of Consumer and Corporate Affairs awards project grants to national, regional, and local consumer groups and organizations offering education, information, advice, or representation. The Department of Indian Affairs and Northern Development has various programs for native groups, from the Indian Community Human Resource Strategies Program to support for research and negotiations of native claims. The Department of Fisheries and Oceans provides ad hoc support to groups on both coasts, and the Department of Labour provides project support to labour unions. Departments and agencies also spend millions of dollars each year on research that is sometimes conducted by client organizations.

In short, while no one has attempted to calculate the total costs of government support to NGOs, it is clear from the anecdotal evidence that at the federal level alone it would amount to millions, if not hundreds of millions, of dollars each year. The SOS programs are only a small part of this larger picture but have been explicitly harnessed to the larger goals of citizenship development and nation-building. Also, in contrast to most other departments (except perhaps Environment, Consumer and Corporate Affairs, and Indian Affairs and Northern Development), its programs have been directed at pure advocacy organizations.

Despite the pervasiveness of these programs, very little is known about them, even the more prominent ones considered in this book. Official languages policy, unfortunately, has been virtually ignored by political scientists and policy analysts. Perhaps understandably, demographers and sociologists have been more interested in the distribution of language communities and their patterns of linguistic retention. The most acerbic and informed discussions have come from the Official Languages Commissioner, but with a focus on program implementation rather than group funding. Multiculturalism has attracted good work by historians, sociologists, anthropologists, and economists, but once again the policy dimension has been undeveloped. This may result partly from a reigning prejudice that the entire policy framework is largely symbolic and therefore without much practical effect. The issue of group funding has come up in this literature but has been viewed primarily as a sordid patronage ploy. Women's studies have expanded in the last decade and produced much good work, but most of the authors in the field are *parti pris*, and so usually celebrate women's organizations for their struggles rather than critically analyse them. A recent book dealing directly with feminist organizing in Canada, Nancy Adamson, Linda

Briskin, and Margaret McPhail, *Feminist Organizing for Change: The Contemporary Women's Movement in Canada* (Toronto: Oxford University Press, 1988), devotes only a few paragraphs to funding. To understand the magnitude of this oversight, one need only remember that every key feminist advocacy organization in the country receives or has received funding through the sos Women's Program; moreover, this funding typically accounts for between 50 per cent and 80 per cent of the organization's budget. Proportions are similar for some ethnic organizations, but often higher for OLMGs.

The literature on government financing of advocacy organizations is not much better. Readers should be clear on the analytical distinction between advocacy and service, even though they often overlap in organizations. Service organizations meet some direct need of a designated community, usually on a volunteer basis or through third-party donations. Examples include hostels, church kitchens, food banks, and women's shelters. Canadian governments have supported efforts of this type for decades. Advocacy organizations may or may not provide a service, but their primary raison d'être is the political representation of a designated constituency in order to demand services, legislation, recognition, or rights from government. "Representation" should be understood broadly to embrace a continuum from initial mobilization of a constituency that may not be completely clear on its characteristics and its needs to articulation of demands from a well-defined and established community. Government support for such organizations – as opposed to service groups – is somewhat more problematic from several perspectives.

From the liberal perspective, which expects the state to be a neutral arbiter of competing societal interests, there seems to be an element of unfairness or bias in funding some organizations and not others. Why should the state fund women but not gay people, OLMGs but not "third-language" lobbyists, rape crisis centres but not anti-abortion counselling clinics? There are four responses to this. The first is that, in fact, virtually every person and every group in the modern state *does* get subsidized in one way or another. The subsidies may not be for advocacy per se but include tax concessions and exemptions, or the use of subsidized or regulated services such as telephones. This response is weak, of course, because it is precisely for their direct advocacy purposes that organizations wish funding. Understandably they are resentful when their good cause gets passed over in favour of others.

The second response is that every democratic state has a right to support and foster democratic institutions. It has no obligation to support those whose activities might eventually undermine those institutions. A distinguishing feature of liberal democracy in modern complex states is tolerance of other points of view and, more recently, other "life-styles." Presumably then, organizations that promote tolerance are worthy objects of support, and those whose aims may lead to intolerance can expect no help from the state, even while they should not be suppressed (as long as they remain peaceful). This is a good answer, and it has some empirical validity in the Canadian case because organizations in the three policy areas have couched their political agendas in terms of greater tolerance for minorities. Those people who would criticize official bilingualism, multiculturalism, and feminism may therefore be considered "intolerant." A good recent case of this logic was the REAL (Real, Equal, and Active for Life) Women imbroglio, where Secretary of State David Crombie refused to fund the organization because he deemed that its program did not accord with the department's vision of women's interests. The National Action Committee on the Status of Women (NAC) and other feminist organizations were quick to label REAL Women as intolerant on the issues of abortion (they oppose it), women working outside the home (they uphold "family values"), and indeed of feminism itself. The problem with this argument is its slippery terminology. NAC is "intolerant" of REAL Women, OLMGs are "intolerant" of those who would argue against official bilingualism, and ethnic Canadians are "intolerant" of those who propose a dualist vision (i.e., French/English) of the country. In some measure, every political interest is and must inevitably be "intolerant" of its opponents.

The third answer gets around this problem by simply rejecting the fiction that liberal democratic governments must be neutral arbiters of the public will. Presumably governments are elected to fulfil policy commitments made in their campaigns. In the case of bilingualism, multiculturalism, and feminism, the Liberal governments of the day had a responsibility as well as a right to develop policies to implement their vision of the country. The problem with this argument is that political parties rarely provide clear policy alternatives in elections, and outcomes in a three-party system usually mean that the majority of the electorate voted for someone other than the government. The mandate is therefore murky and ambivalent, if it exists at all. One might accept that bilingualism was sufficiently mooted in the 1968 federal election to warrant a mandate for the Official Languages Act, but this would not be true for Multiculturalism (introduced three-quarters of the way through the mandate in 1971) or the Women's Program, which was not directly discussed at all in the

1972 election. In any case, even if mandates were clear and unambiguous in one election, the continued force of that mandate would require continued support in subsequent elections.

A final response to liberal quibbles about government financing of advocacy organizations is that some types of interests are inherently more difficult to organize than others and therefore require some government support to compensate for their disadvantages. Business organizations, because they have few members and seek relatively clear and direct benefits, are relatively easy to organize. The interests of consumers, environmentalists, and women are not, because they are so extensive and because they often seek fundamental and far-reaching political change. Moreover, minorities by their nature have difficulty raising funds and support in the face of more entrenched groups and interests. True democracy lets all voices be heard, but circumstances often silence the weakest of those voices for organizational or financial debilities beyond their control. Political debate is thus impoverished and prevailing power structures are maintained. Government should act therefore to redress the balance by helping the weaker partners in a democratic system. The problem with this argument is less at the philosophical level than at the practical one. Government assistance presumably cannot be open-ended and freely given to each and every organization claiming to represent an interest; some criteria have to be set. But in establishing the criteria of bona fide organizations representing the interests of this or that constituency, the state must inevitably inject some bias. In other words, the full spectrum of organizations that might be legitimately representative of a larger constituency will almost always be wider than the funding criteria established by a government agency. In short, if the Women's Program is to fund "women," why did it not fund REAL Women, if that group reflects, as clearly it must, some part of the rich spectrum of women's thoughts on contemporary political questions? (In 1989, SOS did finally award a conference grant to REAL Women.) If it is because those thoughts offend the government, then we are back to the issue of bias again.

Government funding of advocacy organizations is also problematic, however, from the conservative and the left perspectives. From the conservative point of view, in Canada the National Citizen's Coalition and in the United States the Cato Institute have argued that the lion's share of government funding for advocacy organizations goes to anti-business, anti-capitalist, anti-family organizations. The reasons are either ideological ("pink" Liberal governments in Ottawa and Democratic governments in the United States), political (the organizations demand patronage in exchange for support or silence), or bureaucratic (aggrandizing officials launch programs to build constituencies that will then demand more programs and hence more officials). As well, since these organizations are typically staffed and supported by the well-educated middle class, public money ends up going to the economically privileged. These arguments influenced conservative politicians in the last decade. In 1980, after Ronald Reagan's election to the White House, the American right called for a concerted campaign to "de-fund the left," while in Prime Minister Brian Mulroney's second Conservative government, funds for women's organizations were capped and frozen in two consecutive budgets.

Predictably, the left sees the danger of government funding quite differently. There is a rich array of objections, but they tend to fall into two distinct categories. The first sees the primary danger as one of co-optation. It assumes that the organizations that receive funding are in fact pushing forward the real interests of their constituencies but that, in becoming dependent on government financing, they ultimately lose their élan as well as their radicalism. Money corrupts, officers and salaried personnel multiply, agitators become embroiled in debates over administrative detail, and reporting requirements sap resources. In short order, a vital social movement becomes another safe, mainstream institution. The second position rejects the assumption that funded groups in fact represent the core of a constituency's interests. In this view, government funding is deliberately directed at the tamer, less troublesome elements of a movement in an attempt to divide that movement, draw its community into an internecine fight over who got funding and who did not, and ultimately legitimize that portion of the movement least threatening to the social order. Some radical feminists, for example, have complained that the Women's Program supports "safe, middle-class" feminism so that when the interests of women have to be articulated they are spoken with an uptown accent.

This book tries to come to terms with these debates through a focused study of three key Canadian citizenship programs and the groups that they support.

It should be clear from the preceding pages, however, that how one analyses government funding for groups depends in part on how one understands the nature of interest groups, collective action in politics, and the state. Part 1 of the book therefore discusses these issues and establishes a framework for the study. Chapter 1 addresses the role of the state in supporting some species of collective action. The traditional literature simply assumed that it was rational for people to pursue their individual interests with others who shared those interests and that therefore the really interesting question was how much political influence those groups were able to exercise. Traditional interest-group theory tended to focus on economic groups (e.g., farm, labour, and business), but the turmoil of the 1960s spawned a host of "new social movements" that did not fit into the traditional categories. Ironically, the chief theoretical development in associational theory of the time – Olson's logic of collective action – argued that social movements or public interest groups should be weak and relatively insignificant because they were so large and diffuse that few people had rational incentives to join and support them. It was easier to "free ride."

The empirical analysis of the new social movements is just beginning, but the scattered evidence seems to suggest that organizations of this type – the same type as those studied in this book – survive with the help of government. Chapter 1 takes up this theme by exploring the three most influential approaches to the modern state: neo-Marxism, neo-institutionalism, and public choice. Rather than offering a full and detailed portrait of each theory, the chapter seeks to isolate their conceptualizations of the state, its autonomy, and the political effects of this autonomy. Without striving for some artificial consensus, the chapter concludes that there are some important points of agreement among the approaches. The state is a formal matrix of rules and normative order that is structurally autonomous from civil society. This makes it increasingly a target for collective action, even while the state itself, because of its autonomy, increasingly strives to construct a social order in its own image.

This somewhat abstract conclusion is fleshed out in chapter 2 through a review of existing empirical studies of state funding for advocacy organizations. While they contain some useful insights, on the whole they are too scattered and anecdotal to be of great help. The basic questions about government funding to groups in our three areas remain to be answered. Why were the programs undertaken in the first place? Why were they designed as they were, and what trajectories did they follow after being initiated? What were the effects for both the organizations and the state? These questions are answered in parts II and III of the book.

Part II contains four historical chapters that try to show the evolution of citizenship policy since the Second World War. Chapter 3 discusses the historical origins of sos and Ottawa's incipient interest in "managing" the voluntary sector for the war effort around 1942. At the time, Ottawa was most concerned about resident "aliens" from non-francophone and non-anglophone ethnic groups and established the Nationalities Branch to monitor and influence their activities. Chapter 4 shows how this wartime effort flowered into the Citizenship Branch after 1945 and a loose amalgam of programs to assist organizations in the citizenship field. The question of the proper relation of government to the voluntary sector was being asked quite early in this period, and the firm answer (from the government itself) was that there should be very little connection. With little support at the political level, the Citizenship Branch languished and was almost disbanded in 1966. Chapter 5 documents its remarkable revival under the first Trudeau government as it was harnessed to the interest in national unity. Citizenship became linked to unity, and in turn both were wedded to a vague idea of participation, and the Citizenship Branch suddenly found itself in the role of animateur sociale. The outlines of what were to become the three main programs were developed in this period, though by 1972 enthusiasm at the political level was waning. Quebec separatism seemed on the decline, the federal Liberals almost lost the 1972 election, and the advocacy organizations aided by sos were irritatingly effective critics of government policy. The programs could not simply be disbanded, however, and chapter 6 traces their subsequent history to 1989.

Part III shifts from the historical to the analytical. Each of the three programs is discussed in turn, first through a review of internal program evaluations done at various points in their development, second in terms of their detailed program guidelines and granting patterns, and finally through three case studies of prominent organizations that receive funding from sos. The evidence from these chapters shows that funding guidelines have been confused and vague from the beginning, that program administrators rarely know what they are supposed to be achieving through funding, and that groups are jealous of their rights and their funding, making program development very difficult. The cases studies in chapters 7, 8, and 9 are not meant to be representative in any statistical sense. The variety of groups funded in each of the three programs is so wide that it is doubtful that there is any such thing as a "typical" group. Given the limitations of space and the fact that sos concentrates group funding on national organizations, I decided to present detailed profiles of three groups, one from each program category, that would show the diversity of group support as well as the concrete results in terms of policy advocacy.

Part IV concludes the book with a chapter on citizenship policy and collective action and another on the nature of the state. Chapter 10 points out an important difference between Canadian and American government support for public interest groups: the Canadian pattern since the 1960s has been explicitly couched in terms of national unity and citizenship. Canada was the scene of many of the same social movements that appeared in other Western liberal states at the time, but those movements were channelled in particular ways in the Canadian context. The chapter also establishes that groups of this type grew exponentially after 1968, though with different rhythms in each of the three policy fields. By the mid-1980s, SOS was supporting some 3,500 organizations across the country, organizations that varied enormously in size and function. Despite this diversity, it is clear that even by the end of the 1970s it was impossible to conceive of these three policy fields without thinking about the government-funded advocacy organizations active in them. What effect did these groups have on Canadian politics? The chapter points out that the whole issue of government support of voluntary organizations in the mid-1960s was couched in terms of national unity, and consequently in terms of citizenship, identity, and participation. This in turn encouraged a political discourse of collective rights and equality. The chapter argues that SOS-funded groups have been effective constituencies demanding program expansion in their areas, as well as major contributors to the perpetual Canadian debate on "identity." While on balance I judge their contribution to Canadian political debate to have been one of fragmentation, the chapter also points to several "nationalizing" features of their practice.

Chapter 11 takes up the theoretical questions about the state raised in part I of the book. It points out that programs of the type discussed here fall under the category of "citizen mobilization," a technique of public policy implementation that has received less attention than it deserves. For most liberal-democratic states, the degree of mobilization is quite innocuous, but in Canada, with the concatenation in the late 1960s of the Quebec question and social movements, mobilization took a more vigorous form in citizenship participation programs, first for youth and then later for the groups described in this book. The commitment to vigorous mobilization was short-lived and more an artifact of circumstances than the result of fundamental shifts in the polity. This helps explain why political enthusiasm and support for the programs waned after 1972, even while the programs limped along year after year. The chapter considers the state's autonomy in three senses, as actor, as target, and as structure. The state as an actor refers to the scope for conscious decisions and choices made by officials and politicians. While the empirical record shows many instances of creative intervention, these were the exception rather than the rule. Indeed, once they were elaborated, the programs were often an irritant to politicians and officials. They survived in part because of the second dimension of the state's autonomy. The state as an institutional collection of powers is a target for societal actors who would use those powers for their own benefit. The final conceptualization of autonomy is the most abstract – autonomy as structure – and refers to the way in which the state can shape fundamental social processes and forms of political language.

My conclusions here are admittedly tentative, since it is impossible to make direct links between such large categories and the evidence that we have available to us. Nonetheless, I think that an objective reading of the material in chapters 2 through 9 clearly suggests that Ottawa's citizenship programs contributed to the peculiar emphasis on "identity" and "collective rights" in Canadian political discourse. My point is that this emphasis is not merely natural but has been amplified by political interventions made over the past twenty years. Our politics – with its puzzling stridency and its sensitivity to rights and identity – is in part a creature of our own making.

PART ONE

Theoretical Considerations

... my idea was to have it a department which would bring all voluntary organizations together and give them proper direction in the war effort ... I wanted the Minister to help mold public opinion.

W.L. Mackenzie King, Diary, 5 October 1942

You will also be asked to consider measures relating to Indians, to citizenship, to national symbols, to cultural agencies ... Some of these proposals involve the righting of wrongs and others the opening of opportunities long denied. Together they exemplify the essential connection between justice and national unity.

Speech from the Throne, Ottawa,
12 September 1968

A major activity of the department is to support voluntary organizations whose role in society is recognized and appreciated by the federal government. These groups of citizens provide the government with important public feedback that indicates the sectors in which government action may be required.

Voluntary groups touch nearly all aspects of society: health, education, human rights, social development, youth, women, Native citizens, the handicapped. Their preoccupations are in line with the ideal of social justice that the Department of the Secretary of State seeks to promote.

Secretary of State of Canada,
Annual Report 1981–82

The Department of the Secretary of State and Multiculturalism and Citizenship Canada have grants and contributions budgets to assist groups and organizations active in the areas of citizenship development and multiculturalism.

These budgets will be reduced by $23 million annually from planned levels in 1990–91 and 1991–92. The Secretary of State and Minister of State for Multiculturalism and Citizenship will provide further information on the implementation of these reductions.

Department of Finance, *The Budget*,
20 February 1990

CHAPTER ONE

The Problem of the State

COLLECTIVE ACTION, SOCIAL MOVEMENTS, AND THE STATE

One of the great political phenomena of the last twenty years has been the growth of social movements or public interest groups. In Canada, for example, as Khayyam Paltiel has noted, the "1960s were characterized by an explosion of self-awareness among consumers, students, women and native groups and ... by Québécois nationalism and ethnic group self-consciousness. These social movements were accompanied by a bursting forth of clientelist groups, created in response to the elaboration of the welfare state during the same period."[1]

Ironically, one of the most influential books on collective action in the 1960s predicted that groups and movements of this type would be insignificant. In *The Logic of Collective Action* (1965), Mancur Olson argued that small constituencies of interest that were seeking relatively concentrated benefits were likely to be the most effective in overcoming problems such as "free riders" (individuals that take the benefits of collective action without contributing to the costs). Widely spread interests, therefore, should not be successful. Olson noted that logically his theory should cover all groups but that in practice it "is not at all sufficient where philanthropic lobbies, that is, lobbies that voice concern about some group other than the group that supports the lobby, or religious lobbies, are concerned."[2] He added that the theory would not be very useful for groups characterized by a low degree of rationality or groups that fight for "lost causes." These are labours of love, since people make sacrifices that by definition will be ineffective. (In a bracketed comment, Olson asserted that the "insignificance of such groups is of course consistent with the theory.") As Sidney Tarrow has noted: "It is ironic that Olson's work – which has been used to demonstrate the unlikelihood of collective action – was published just as the western world was erupting in a paroxysm of protest, riot, rebellion, and increased political involvement."[3]

The pattern of interest-group politics changed substantially after the late 1960s. New bodies arose, labelled variously issue-oriented groups, attitude groups, expressive groups, public interest groups, and, most broadly, social movements.[4] In the United States, such organizations have come to be known as "public interest groups" (PIGs), "an organizational entity that purports to represent very broad, diffuse, non-commercial interests which traditionally have received little explicit or direct representation in the processes by which agencies, courts, and legislatures make public policy."[5] PIGs are organized around characteristics that define virtually everyone in the community: "consumer, citizen, taxpayer, member of the biosphere."[6]

While PIGs had been around for years at the community level, they emerged at the national level in American politics only after 1965. Various factors were responsible: evolution of the civil rights movement which largely excluded middle-class whites from leadership roles; an oppositional and protest Zeitgeist unleashed by the wars waged against poverty, discrimination, and Viet Nam; growth of an urban, educated middle class interested in reform principles; a growing commitment by foundations to funding of institutional innovation; and media interest.[7] McCarthy and Zald, for example, note that part of the sociological explanation for the rise of new American social movements in the 1960s hinges on changes in levels of affluence, leisure, discretionary income, and funding patterns of churches and foundations. They also observe, however, that the "government itself has been involved in the business of supporting social movement organizations. While the federal government may be rapidly withdrawing such support, it is clear that its support was crucial in the latter half of the 1960s."[8]

Goldstein's analysis of the Consumers' Association of Canada (CAC) provides another example of the state's encouragement of interest representation. The CAC was founded in 1947 from some women's organizations that had helped the Wartime Prices and Trade Board to control prices: "From its inception, the organization received the moral support and financial assistance of the federal government."[9] In 1961, the CAC's budget was $27,000, of which $10,000 came from Ottawa. In Goldstein's assessment, in its early years the CAC preferred non-confrontational, informal accommodation with government. From 1968 to 1977 it adopted a more activist role in presenting its views before regulatory agencies and government. Consumerism and "Naderism" in the United States, as well as inflation, stimulated a new advocacy politics. Although the CAC avoided Nader's tactics of public hearings, picketing, and boycotts, it did develop its "legal advocacy" – defence of consumer interests before royal commissions, regulatory agencies, and courts.[10] But another reason behind its new stance was the newly established Department of Consumer and Corporate Affairs (1968), with its mandate to encourage more consumer advocacy. The department gave the CAC $100,000 in 1973. This support reflected newly found enthusiasm among bureaucrats for "citizens' participation," wherein "every legitimate group within society should be encouraged to articulate its claims and grievances, thus integrating those groups within the body politic and allowing the government to adjudicate among competing interests."[11]

An important article in the same vein by Jack Walker acknowledged that the very groups that have been reasonably successful in affecting policy over the last twenty years – groups that have only a cause or an idea, rather than financial or organizational resources, and that represent the socially disadvantaged – are the ones that according to traditional theory should be moribund. In developing a data base of national voluntary associations, Walker concluded that "there are more interest groups operating in Washington today than in the years before World War II, and that citizen groups make up a much larger proportion of the total than ever before."[12] Walker claimed to find that these citizens' groups did not depend on either selective benefits or coercion to bind their members. Group leaders, rather than relying on coercion or selective benefits to keep the group going, have instead a strategy of finding new sources of funding. State agencies in particular helped support groups, principally those that supported more expansive government activity. Walker's evidence led him to conclude that government agencies were unlikely to sponsor "groups that do not share their fundamental political sympathies."[13] For groups involved in education, transport, and environmental protection, Walker argued that "the formation of new groups was one of the *consequences* of major new legislation, not one of the *causes* of its passage. A pressure model of the policymaking process in which an essentially passive legislature responds to petitions from groups of citizens who have spontaneously organized because of common social or economic concerns must yield to a model in which influences for change come as much from inside the government as from beyond its institutional boundaries."[14]

Recent theoretical work has arrived at much the same conclusion. Moe, in extending Olson's analysis of interest groups, tries for example to look more closely at the logic of their relations with state actors. Insofar as interest groups are in the business of pressuring the executive, it can be of tremendous advantage if they are recognized by officials as the legitimate representative of a sector. When this happens, "other groups from the same sector are effectively denied the perquisites that go along with being favored."[15] Even though Moe does not discuss anywhere in his book the possibility that state agencies might materially support certain groups with which they are sympathetic, he does understand that the state has an incentive to try to mould the associational system: "It is a short step to the conclusion that officials can use their positions to wield rewards and sanctions in their relationships with the [group] entrepreneur. As noted earlier, their assistance may be purchased in return for campaign contributions, information, technical assistance, and the like. But, clearly, they might also require certain entrepreneurial policy positions as their price. ... When this happens, group goals are not the outcome of internal processes of decision making, but of a wider bargaining process that includes the rewards and sanctions of public officials."[16]

Cairns and Williams, in discussing some Canadian social movements and the constitution, have noted how the collective action characteristic of language, ethnic, and gender movements has focused on rights claims – on demands centred around identity. They argue that the recent Canadian preoccupation with rights in effect involves making political claims against the state. "The state becomes the major instrument to facilitate or block changes. The resultant group politics of competitive affirmation politicizes newly emergent cleavages. Drawing on the rhetoric of rights, citizen groups seek to employ the state for their own advancement."[17] In their view as well, the state is central to explaining the nature of contemporary Canadian interest group politics: "The role of the modern state, in particular its key position as the major catalytic agent of social transformation, politicizes the group basis and cleavages of society and engenders an increasing resort to political action as competing groups play the political market in pursuit of their self-interest. The result is a mushrooming pluralism of specific demands."[18]

Public-interest organizations, linked to the broad social movements that swept most democratic states in the 1960s, should face the greatest difficulty in coherent collective action, and yet most observers agree that they have been surprisingly successful in forcing at least some items in their agenda onto the public stage. Scattered empirical evidence suggests that they overcome these problems by turning to the state, which appears as well to have an interest in providing support to these organizations. Moreover, the formation and practices of these organizations take place on the terrain of the state: they seek to pursue ends, establish rights, and promote identities through political means. In this sense, the problem of collective action resolves itself into the problem of the state.

As one authoritative review of the literature notes, "The state has once again become a central topic for research and theoretical reassessment."[19] Theda Skocpol, a partisan of "state-centric" approaches to public policy, has argued that the rediscovery of the state as a theoretical category indicates an "intellectual sea change" in contemporary political analysis.[20] Even David Easton, no friend of this shift, agrees that "state, a concept that many of us thought had been polished off a quarter of a century ago, has now risen from the grave to haunt us once again."[21] "Society-centred" approaches to politics, to use Nordlinger's phrase,[22] have been challenged by theoretical orientations that take the state and its institutional materiality more seriously.

This chapter reviews three key contemporary approaches to understanding the state: neo-Marxism, neo-institutionalism, and public choice. Each posits the state as autonomous, though each defines the mechanisms of autonomy in different ways. The concluding discussion tries, without imposing any artificial uniformity, to draw together their common points in order to develop a more general understanding of the nature of the contemporary state. This understanding will then permit development of a framework of analysis in chapter 2.

NEO-MARXISM: STRUCTURE, FUNCTION, CLASS, OR CONTRADICTION?

Neo-Marxism is a complex theoretical orientation of which the question of the state is only a part.[23] Most observers would agree that the contemporary neo-marxist debate on the state was initiated in the mid-1960s and early 1970s by Louis Althusser, Ralph Miliband, and Nicos Poulantzas. They were joined by Perry Anderson, James O'Connor, Ian Gough, E.P. Thompson, and Erik Olin Wright, and more recently by Claus Offe and Adam Prezworski. All of these leading theorists have been engaged in a debate with an older Marxist tradition. The classical Marxist tradition had an undeveloped theory of the state and politics in Marx and Engels's own work and conceptualized the state as a weak appendage of larger economic forces under capitalism. In his journalism, in longer treatises such as *The Eighteenth Brumaire of Louis Bonaparte*, and even in volume 1 of *Capital*, Marx offered interesting and perceptive analyses of politics. In the absence of detailed and disciplined theorization, however, the Marxist tradition was left to rely on several formulae that reduced the bourgeois state to a "committee" ruling in the interests of capital or a "superstructure" that simply reflected the contradictory requirements of a capitalist economic system.[24] Marxist theorizations of the state since the mid-1960s have tried to reconcile a degree of capitalist state autonomy with some form of ultimate or final determinacy of the state by its capitalist context. The intellectual manoeuvres undertaken to achieve this have been exceedingly subtle and challenging, but what unites them and defines them as Marxist is their continued allegiance to the idea that the state and its effects must, in the final analysis, reinforce and support the broad interests of the dominant class.

Beginning with Althusser, Miliband, and Poulantzas, through O'Connor and Gough and later Offe, there have been a variety of strategies to square this circle. In one form or another, they have all strived to develop the notion of "relative autonomy," even when they have not used precisely this term (it was popularized by Poulantzas and hence still has something of a structuralist flavour). Relative autonomy implies that the state is autonomous within limits and so naturally demands that we consider both the factors that create the autonomy and those that enforce the limits. In some formulations, the same factor creates both; in others, separate factors are at work.

Miliband offered the simplest and in some ways the most direct solution to the problem. In an early contribution he put forth the view, supported empirically, that "everywhere and in all its elements the state system has retained, socially speaking, a most markedly upper- and middle-class character."[25] The limits to the state's autonomy were thus set sociologically through an ideological and practical affinity between state functionaries and the capitalist class. Ownership of private property, profit, the essential justice of accumulation, and a lingering and unarticulated distrust of and unfamiliarity with the proletariat ensure that no matter what the personal, subjective views of recruits to positions of influence within the state, they can never collectively stray too far from the interests, or at least the assumptions, of their own class. "Social origins" is a sufficiently broad factor to permit autonomy, but firm enough to establish its limits. Miliband was also alive, however, to the impact of other factors, such as the "rules of the game" in parliamentary democracy, that could further insulate the state from direct influences by the capitalist class or the imperatives of the capitalist system.

The French structuralist movement, led by Althusser and Poulantzas, found Miliband's analysis dissatisfying. To them, it implied too much subjectivism in the state's actions, relied too much on conscious intentions, and was contaminated by too many non-Marxist concepts.[26] It looked like elite theory dressed up in Marxist rhetoric. For Poulantzas, in his early formulations, the fact that the capitalist state is capitalist has nothing to do with intentions or subjects. It has everything to do with structure. Poulantzas attempted an extensive theorization of the state and political power that would be more rigorous, pure, and non-subjectivist.[27] In calling Poulantzas a structuralist, I refer here to his non-subjectivism, his preference (at least in the early writings) to stress large, impersonal forces and structural relations which constrain actors. In fact, his solution to the problem of autonomy was functionalism. The state became, in Poulantzian terms, a relatively autonomous instance in the capitalist mode of production. Its autonomy is given by the nature of the capitalist relations of production, which through property relations create separate and antagonistic classes. The coexistence of free labour power, a politically disinterested dominant class, and a mode of production that creates class "fractions" within each primary economic class (e.g., finance capital, industrial capital) is the condition for a state that is removed from the immediate interests and direct control of the dominant classes (or "power bloc"). The relation between the state and the capitalist system within which it exists is therefore an objective relation, given by the system itself. The state is autonomous because the capitalist mode of production requires that the interests of dominant classes be organized (the classes cannot organize themselves) and that the interests of dominated classes be disorganized.

One of Poulantzas's central contributions was his insistence that the state not be seen in some external relation to classes. The state in his view was (and he used all of these terms) a crystallization, a condensation, an enscription, and an elaboration of class relations existing in the social formation. He meant that class relations were both reflected in and organized through the internal apparatus of the state. The finest Canadian example of this approach is Rianne Mahon's *The Politics of Industrial Restructuring: Canadian Textiles*, which argues that different state agencies represent different class interests and class hegemony (hegemonic classes get represented in hegemonic agencies). Policy outcomes are not given as such, since class interests and compromises must first be articulated within the state. The only given is that the final outcomes are functional for a system of class hegemony and the long-term interests of the hegemonic class bloc. In his empirical studies of fascism and dictatorships in Portugal, Spain, and Greece, and in some of his later work, Poulantzas moved away from his early functionalist moorings.[28] In those works he gave a much greater role to class conflict and explicitly criticized the functional determinacy of structuralists such as Althusser.

Class conflict can solve the autonomy problem in two ways. It can reject functionalism but posit that economic power will usually and over the long term be translated into political power. This allows any single conflict to be indeterminate in its outcomes (dominated classes might "win"), but the capitalist state as a whole over time will reflect capitalist interests. Ian Gough's *The Political Economy of the Welfare State* argues, for example, that the capitalist welfare state is both a concession won by workers' struggles and a functional necessity for the system: "The welfare state exhibits positive and negative features within a contradictory unity. ... It simultaneously embodies tendencies to enhance social welfare, to develop the powers of individuals, to exert social control over the blind play of market forces; and tendencies to repress and control people, to adapt them to the requirements of the capitalist economy."[29]

The other solution to the autonomy problem within a class-conflict approach is to accommodate a degree of functionalism by positing some systemic link between dominant classes and the state, but one sufficiently slack that it has some play in the face of struggles. The best examples of this approach stem from Gramsci's idea of hegemony.[30] Consciousness and ideology become the unifying instances in a capitalist formation, so that practices in the formation remain consistent within broad but determinate limits. The acceptance of everything from commodity production to the traditional form of the liberal-democratic state sets the boundaries of action. This approach can deal with conflicts and struggles that do not in themselves have any obvious or direct connection to economic power.

Structure, function, and class are three solutions to the problem of relative autonomy within neo-Marxism. They sometimes can coexist in the same analysis (Gough is an example), but despite their differences all three try to define a political space within which the state may autonomously manoeuvre but still be constrained to act in the interests of capital. Thus in varying degrees (less for functionalism, more for class conflict) the approaches can accept "non-class" factors as contributing to the state's autonomy. These might include organizational capacity, military power, or a monopoly of complex information. All three solutions continue to assume, however, some sort of political umbilical cord which, no matter how thinly stretched, binds the state to crucial features of capitalism. The ties between state and society are organic and primary.

Another solution to the problem proposes less an organic relation than a logical one, through analysis of the contradictions that capitalism produces and consequently the contradictory responses demanded from the state. A simple but fruitful example is James O'Connor's *The Fiscal Crisis of the State*. Capitalism is a system of economic accumulation par excellence. According to Marx, this accumulation occurs principally through exploitation of subordinate classes. The point of capitalism is accumulation, but accumulation is always threatened by subordinate classes. The system must somehow be legitimated in the eyes of these subordinate classes, while simultaneously allowing accumulation. By adding certain refinements concerning advanced capitalism and its investment requirements, one can then explain economic interventions, social policy and the welfare state, and the continued tension between classes and the role of the state.[31]

Despite use of the term "functions," this is not really a functionalist approach, since it relies primarily on mutual considerations of advantage by defined actors. State authorities, even if they do not have any allegiance whatsoever to capitalism, depend on tax revenue to maintain the state system. Without revenues, generated on the whole through economic activity strategically controlled by property owners, the state's life blood would dry up. Capitalists may or may not recognize that state economic and social intervention buys them social peace, but they exist (as a class) to accumulate and so can be expected to tolerate grudgingly instances in which the state ignores their agenda. Subordinate classes can be expected either to make a rational compromise with the system[32] or simply to be fooled by the state's social interventions.

The most sophisticated example of this approach may be found in Claus Offe's work.[33] His central thesis is that capitalist accumulation increasingly generates consequences that loom so large that they become the driving dynamic of the system and the state's attempts to deal with them. In other words, Offe uses a classic Marxist explanation — the primacy of economic forces — to argue that economic forces are becoming less primary: "The development of the internal social structure of the capitalist countries is also characterized by the appearance of phenomena which are functionally irrelevant or useless for capitalist growth. In order to maintain the stability of the system, priority must be given to minimizing the possible disruptive effects of these phenomena on the dominant system of surplus value creation."[34] For example, Offe argues that as capitalism has developed, its very productivity has made the relationship between wage-labour and capital less important for organizing societal labour markets. While there remains in all capitalist countries a "competitive sector" in which price competition plays its expected role, the "monopoly sector" is characterized by large unions and corporations that can to a large extent escape the discipline of the market, as can the "state sector."[35] Offe also describes what he calls the sector of "residual labour power" where "life is virtually 'decommodified': transfer payments to unemployed persons, invalids and old-age pensioners, the living conditions of school pupils, college students, drafted servicemen, full-time housewives and the occupants of prisons, hospitals and other 'total institutions' are determined directly by political or institutional means."[36] This "decommodification" of substantial portions of social life leads Offe to the paradoxical conclusion that "in late capitalist societies the processes of exchange-regulated capitalist accumulation are simultaneously dominant *and* 'recessive'."[37] Thus non–class-based forces become increasingly prominent in politics and policy: "Although exchange processes are decisive for the stability of the system as a whole, they have become increasingly obsolete as their potential to organize social life has been restricted to a small core area."[38]

In an essay entitled "The Attribution of Public Status to Interest Groups," Offe directly addresses the central question of this book. He notes that traditional pluralist theory tended to explain the existence and strength of groups in terms of "constitutive elements of organization" such as values, willingness to make sacrifices, and numbers. He emphasizes political factors instead, particularly in explaining the German case and the rise of corporatism, defined as an "axis of development" in the associational system wherein groups can bond more closely to formal political institutions by receiving either monetary support or formal rights of representation and consultation.[39] Using the explanatory manoeuvres described above, Offe proceeds to explain the growing centrality of corporatist arrangements (i.e. state-dominated relations with interest groups) in terms of developments in advanced capitalism. The core of the explanation consists of two points. First, political parties, in transforming themselves into mass representative organs, can no longer deal adequately with segmented or sectoral interests. Second, governments under advanced capitalism are increasingly driven to consider policy instruments that involve direct control over investment, consumption, or production. These are resisted by producer groups in the sectors in question, and so a solution is to delegate policy responsibilities to those groups in exchange for a measure of commitment to state goals.[40] The most obvious examples of this are self-regulation schemes delegated to professional groups such as physicians and accountants. Reflecting on the European experience, he sees these movements as developing outside the state and indeed rejecting the state in some measure. The corporatist arrangements that he describes in the essay concentrate on the role of the state in shaping the associational system, but largely with respect to producer groups.

Offe's solution to the problem of the state – a problem that may be defined as trying to understand both the state's autonomy and the limits of this autonomy set by capitalism – takes neo-Marxism as far as one might go and still remain within what might be termed a Marxist framework. While he maintains a formal connection between the nature of the state and the rhythms of capitalist (especially late capitalist) development, that connection is so tenuous and paradoxical (the dominance of capital makes it less dominant) that it comes extremely close to the position taken by Fred Block in an essay against Poulantzas: "State power is *sui generis*, not reducible to class power."[41] For Block, the complexities of how a divided business class gets its proposals on the public agenda forces a shift in attention to "processes within the state that mediate between business influence and policy outcomes."[42]

Block represents a variant of "post-Marxism," the essential logic of which insists on the irreducibility of politics.[43] It argues "that classes or any social groups are themselves constituted through political processes; social groupings and social mobilization are not an automatic consequence of social structure. Moreover political struggles have the potential to constantly reshape lines of political conflict or coalition; much political discourse can be understood as efforts to persuade people that their interests converge or diverge with those of certain others."[44] While class remains important, "many other collective actors organized around race, gender, age, sexual orientation, religious orientation, or shared views about the environment or the arms race."[45] A similar interest in ideology, the political struggle concerning identity, and the role of non-class actors may be seen in Jane Jenson's recent work, which draws its inspiration from the French "regulation school":

Politics in capitalist democracy involves representation, which is in part the social construction of collective identities. Actors bearing collective identities attempt to carve out a constituency for themselves. Out of this process comes the mobilization of interests, which are also social constructions. The politics of representation necessarily entails conflict because it involves disputes over which collective identities will achieve representation. Resolution of basic questions about who the main protagonists are to be, in turn, places broad limits on the definition of interests. Politics therefore involves the formation of collective identities as much as it entails conflict among groups and organizations over disputed claims about who gets what, when and how.

The terrain on which actors struggle for representation is the *universe of political discourse*, a space in which socially-constructed identities emerge in discursive struggle. As actors with a variety of collective identities co-exist in the universe of political discourse, their practices and meaning systems jostle with each other for social attention and legitimacy.[46]

When neo-Marxism goes this far, it abuts another, newly emerged orientation to the problem and nature of the state: neo-institutionalism.

NEO-INSTITUTIONALISM: THE POWER OF ORGANIZATION

Neo-institutional approaches to the state are as varied, if not more so, than neo-Marxist approaches. There is agreement on two issues, however: that the state is markedly more autonomous in its actions and its policies than has traditionally been assumed and that this autonomy is not linked in any obvious and certainly in no direct way with the development of advanced capitalism. Like Offe, but without the genuflection to "the forces of advanced capitalism," theorists in this tradition see the state and associated political phenomena increasingly as the driving motor of advanced societies. To illustrate this, I shall briefly review two leading theorists of this orientation, Eric Nordlinger and Theda Skocpol, and then provide some examples of Canadian neo-institutional analyses of the state.

Eric A. Nordlinger's *On the Autonomy of the Democratic State*, while certainly not the first attack on "society-centred" theories of politics, remains one of the most influential. Nordlinger's central thesis was that "the preferences of the state are at least as important as those of civil society in accounting for what the democratic state does and does not do."[47] Nordlinger opposed this view to one that he called "society-centred," in which powerful groups effectively controlled policy outcomes through their influence over the state. Nordlinger tried to establish that state preferences may converge, be compatible with, or be incompatible with societal preferences. Public officials invariably translate their own preferences into authoritative actions, and their preferences have at least as much explanatory value as societal wishes. Those officials have resources and powers that they may use to shift societal preferences over to their own.[48]

Nordlinger defined the state as "all those individuals who occupy offices that authorize them, and them alone, to make and apply decisions that are binding upon any and all segments of society."[49] Since the focus is on individuals, Nordlinger is driven to hinge his analysis on individual preferences. In itself, this might make it appear impossible for him to talk coherently about the "state," but he extricates himself from the difficulty by urging that the "state's preferences" consist of the balance of preferences of individuals competing within the state. With these conceptual foundations, Nordlinger was able to posit three types of autonomy – type I: state's and society's preferences diverge, but the state pursues its own preferences anyway; type II: state's and society's preferences diverge, and the state, over time, changes society's preferences; and type III: state's and society's preferences converge but have independent origins. The book explores the resources and strategies that state actors can use to manoeuvre around societal obstacles.

Critics have noted that Nordlinger, in arguing that state officials also have their own preferences and resources, succeeded only in stretching pluralist premises to their limit by giving those officials the same dignity as voters, economic elites, and organized interests.[50] Nordlinger's analysis is marred by the absence of any concept of structure or institutional capacity. However, his work is a good example of neo-institutionalism. While his lists of strategies and manoeuvres are somewhat numbing, when compared with the neo-Marxist approach to the problem of the state, his central themes emerge clearly. The state is not a captive of economic groups, its autonomy is based on unique sources of power, on the capacities and will of state officials. The result is a policy process driven by the logic of the state itself.[51]

Theda Skocpol has been another leading figure in what might be termed the neo-institutional revival. Like Nordlinger, Skocpol attacks the assumption that "political structure and struggles can somehow be reduced (at least 'in the last instance') to socio-economic forces and conflicts."[52] This assumption prevents analysis of the state as a structure with "a logic and interests of its own," or as an "organization-for-itself."[53] Thus, while many students of revolutions see them as "epiphenomenal reflections of societal strains or class contradictions," Skocpol, in her own study of the French, Russian, and Chinese revolutions, argued that political conflict over state structure has been a central, and autonomous, force in social revolutions. In her words, those revolutions were launched in large part as a consequence of "old regime crises" centred in state structures and situations.[54]

Skocpol has carried this perspective forward in various studies of the American New Deal.[55] For Skocpol, to claim that the state is autonomous is to assume that it can generate goals independently, not simply reflect the demands and interests of social groups. Once this assumption is granted, "one may then explore the 'capacities' of states to implement official goals, especially over the actual or potential opposition of powerful social groups or in the face of recalcitrant socioeconomic circumstances."[56] The bases of this independent goal formulation are varied but are linked both to crises in which the need to maintain order will be paramount and to more ordinary quotidian influences exercised by state officials. Skocpol's conclusion is that autonomy is itself therefore a variable feature, since its bases can vary over time and across systems.[57] She cautions that this autonomy may vary within the state as well, so that some agencies may be "strong" or autonomous even within a "weak" state system (like the American one): "One of the most important facts about the power of a state may be its *unevenness* across policy areas."[58]

Skocpol addresses the effects of the state on society. How should these be conceptualized? One way that flows logically from the view that the state is a collectivity of officials pursuing goals is to see effects in terms of the policy-specific differences that an autonomous state actor can make in a political process. The other – the one that Skocpol recommends – models itself on the nineteenth-century work of Alexis de Tocqueville: "In this perspective, states matter not simply because of the goal-oriented activities of state officials. They matter because their organizational configurations, along with their overall patterns of activity, affect political culture, encourage some kinds of group formation and collective political actions (but not others), and make possible the raising of certain political issues (but not others)."[59] This is what Skocpol calls "macroscopic" analysis, which stresses how states "unintentionally influence the formation of groups and the political capacities, ideas, and demands of various sectors of society."[60]

This conceptualization is novel, since it raises the stakes considerably in the debate over the problem of the state. If the state is only an actor, then its autonomy is that of only one actor among many. It would be absurd to claim that the state, in this sense of acting on preferences, has necessarily to win in every case or that its victories need be total. This is Nordlinger's approach, and it is perhaps deliberately cautious, since Nordlinger is trying to develop a theory of the autonomy of the democratic state. Skocpol's Tocquevillian perspective poses structural effects as well as actions and thereby invites us to see the shape of politics itself as a reflection, an outcome, an echo of the state.[61]

Canadian interest in neo-institutional state-centric theories of politics has been growing in recent years. Nossal points out that while a "statist" paradigm is not dominant in the study of Canadian foreign policy, a "modified statist paradigm" – wherein analysts accept some state autonomy balanced by some societal pressure – is reflected in the work of some leading students.[62] There are examples as well of analyses of domestic Canadian policies that have stressed state-centric explanations,[63] though others have sounded a more cautionary note about ignoring the "autonomy enhancing" capacities of societal actors vis-à-vis the state.[64] Most of this work has been within Nordlinger's idea of the state as an actor; less of it has focused on the effects of the state as a structure.

A leading example of neo-institutional state theory in Canada is offered by Alan Cairns. That component within it devoted explicitly to questions of the nature of the state sprang from a 1977 article, "The Governments and Societies of Canadian Federalism."[65] In his most recent formulations, Cairns refuses to make a hard distinction between state and civil society. Instead, he insists on the concept of "embededness" – a simultaneous process wherein the state increasingly penetrates and organizes civil society, even while this penetration binds the state ever more tightly and constrains its manoeuvrability.[66] Indeed, the distinction between civil society as an entity sui generis and the state as the artificial realm of politics strikes Cairns as specious: for him, civil society itself is increasingly the result of previous state actions, so that the state is embedded in society through the very effects of its policies. He argues that the state should be seen as "the sum total of the programs it administers" and thus that civil society is shaped by past decisions and old policies.[67]

Like Skocpol and Nordlinger, Cairns insists that the state not be reified as some single entity with a single purpose and consistent effects. The state is fragmented, particularly in the Canadian case, with its federal-provincial divisions, and this fact contributes to societal fragmentation. The unco-ordinated effects of policies on civil society reinforce and accentuate cleavages and differences, and as the state's influence and salience grow, more and more societal conflict is framed in political terms. "The overall Canadian federal state has become a sprawling diffuse assemblage of uncoordinated power and policies, while the society with which it interacts is increasingly plural, fragmented and multiple in its allegiances and identities. The more we relate to one another through the state, the more divided we seem to become."[68]

As Cairns stated in another of his essays, today's "developed western state is a sprawling, labyrinthine giant, with numerous dispersed power centres, a limited capacity for co-ordinated action, and a ubiquitous presence in the societies for which it plays a fragmented leadership role. It is a complex mix of historic institutional arrangements and evolving normative concerns."[69] In Cairns's view, the state's autonomy is attenuated because of this fragmentation. At best, the democratic state can exercise its limited autonomy at the margins: "State power in Canada is so widely dispersed and its application so fragmented that the state is incapable of achieving anything approximating total control of the citizenry."[70] And yet Cairns notes, in a way reminiscent of Skocpol's Tocquevillian approach, that the contemporary Canadian state is busy refashioning the collective identity of its citizens to reflect the changed ethnic realities of the Canadian polity.[71] This "societal role of the state" – management of an increasingly diverse, rights-conscious, and particularistic society based on ethnicity, gender, language, age, and race – will not abate in the future.

One of the prime reasons for this would appear to be Canada's constitutional culture, which is changing as a result of the Charter of Rights and Freedoms and increasingly encourages political demands framed as "rights." Another reason is the visibility of the modern, twentieth-century interventionist state: as citizens grasp its growing power to distribute advantages and disadvantages, they realize that status, prestige, income, and opportunity depend on manipulating the state.[72] Cairns is pointing to the global effects of a type of state, of a style of intervention. He is remarking less on the specific effects of single policies (though these are obviously important) than on the larger impact of the state on collective action and collective identity.

PUBLIC CHOICE: THE SUPPLY AND DEMAND OF POWER

The problem of the state in contemporary political theory concerns the bases of the state's autonomy, or its relations to configurations of power in civil society. In its most sophisticated forms, the neo-Marxist approach offers remarkable flexibility wherein the details of public policy are by no means a foregone conclusion. The neo-institutional approach prefers not to posit any essential relation between state and civil society. While the state is thus autonomous and distinct, and while it clearly will have the capacity to act independently, the degree of autonomy and the strength of that capacity will vary depending on historical context and conjunctural forces. But while these two theories differ substantially in their answers, they both assume that individual state actors/officials operate within structures or circumstances that are in some sense "given." In the case of neo-Marxism, the structures and circumstances are linked to advanced capitalism; in neo-institutionalism they reflect a host of factors from organizational context to availability of ideas for policy responses.

Recently another approach – rational choice or public choice – has arisen to offer its own answers. In fact, public choice theory is broad enough to purport to be a new theory of politics, not merely of the state. It takes its departure from the neo-classical economic assumption that individuals should be understood as being constantly engaged in maximizing their interests. As James Buchanan puts it, analysis of public and private choice should proceed on the assumption "that their fundamental laws of behaviour are the same under the two sets of institutions."[73] Combined with some simple assumptions about institutional environments, public choice theory tries to develop logical analyses of patterns of behaviour and the results, both intended and unintended, of those patterns. It is sufficiently abstract that it can be applied to different institutional contexts, from legislatures to state enterprises, but the following discussion focuses on the theory's answers to the problem of the state. The accumulation of research results done within this approach suggests that the state has a crucial and growing influence over the polity.[74]

Public choice theory applies the tools of economic analysis to non-market forms of allocations and as such is grounded in several key assumptions. First, since it emphasizes allocation, there must be some analysis of the things being allocated. Second, as in markets, there should be demand and supply in the allocation of public goods. In the context of democracies, this yields analyses of voting, party competition, and bureaucracy. Third, there should be some theorization of decision processes to make sense of how and why certain choices are made about allocation.[75]

Public choice analysis requires careful attention to the institutional framework within which citizens, politicians, and bureaucrats operate to "ultimately determine the allocation of resources in the public sector."[76] Breton argues that this institutional framework has three primary elements: societal decision rules (e.g., simple majority, plurality, unanimity), length of the period between elections, and variety of policies that a citizen chooses by voting for one representative or for one political party (i.e., the degree of formal decentralization or direct democracy in the polity).[77] The key to understanding public choice's answer to the problem of the state is to understand that these institutional rules, combined with a few other simple behavioural assumptions, are seen as insulators that protect public officials from citizens. In theory, one could generate a list of insulators, and the longer the list, the more "autonomous" the state: "Elected representatives can only retain the support of citizens if they supply the public policies desired by the latter. Each characteristic of the institutional framework separately and in combination makes it possible for politicians (and political parties) to neglect, for a time at least, the preferences of some citizens at no cost to themselves, that is without necessarily jeopardizing their own position as politicians."[78]

Citizens, of course, are presumed to create the demand for public goods and will in varying degrees try to influence politicians and bureaux both in and around elections.[79] Politicians, who can be assumed to have utility functions that include re-election (the pre-eminent utility, since without re-election the politician's other desires cannot be fulfilled, at least not as a politician), income, prestige, and fame, will logically adopt a variety of strategies to deal with this influence and manipulate preferences in their favour. For example, these functions will include hidden taxes (since all citizens can be presumed to dislike taxes but like services, the answer is to hide the pain and "hype" the gain) and policy cycles in which governing parties will enact unpopular policies at the beginning of a mandate and shift gradually toward offering more popular policies just before the election. They can also provide "discriminatory policies and private goods" tailored to specific individuals or groups.[80]

Of course, politicians are only one of the two main sets of actors supplying public goods. The other, in all developed democratic states, is bureaucracy, and it is in its analysis of bureaucracy that public choice theory has made perhaps some of its most notable contributions. The intuitive reasons for a focus on government bureaux are evident: compared to elected officials, their resources and their length of tenure should give them significant advantages. Public choice theory views bureaucrats as having, despite a modicum of democratic discipline, "a professional life of their own and a pattern of behavior unrelated to the preferences of citizens."[81] In an early treatment of the problem of bureaux, Gordon Tullock asserted that "every man is an individual with his own private ends and ambitions" and that bureaucrats could consequently be expected to be utility maximizers within their organizations.[82]

The most influential public choice analysis of bureaucracy comes from William Niskanen's *Bureaucracy and Representative Government* (1971). Niskanen argued that bureaux were "nonprofit organizations which are financed, at least in part, by a periodic appropriation or grant."[83] The bureau's relation with its sponsor is the key factor in its environment and, in Niskanen's eyes, distinguishes a bureau from others form of organization: "The sponsoring organization is usually dependent on a specific bureau to supply a given service, and the bureau usually does not have a comparable alternative source of financing."[84]

The central question in this analysis concerns what the bureau's head is trying to achieve, or alternatively what values he or she is trying to maximize. Niskanen offered the following utility function for bureaucrats: salary, perquisites of office, public reputation, power, patronage, output of bureau, ease of making changes, and ease of managing the bureau. All of these save the last two, it should be noted, are a positive and continuous function of the bureau's budget.[85] Anthony Downs, in another and slightly earlier public-choice treatment of bureaucracy, agreed that bureaucratic officials are motivated largely by self-interest: "Bureaucratic officials in general have a complex set of goals including power, income, prestige, security, convenience, loyalty (to an idea, an institution, or the nation), pride in excellent work, and desire to serve the public interest."[86]

To be sure, these are heroic assumptions, and Niskanen has been criticized for oversimplifying his portrait of bureaucratic behaviour. In a 1975 article, he refined his model by incorporating more explicit details about politicianss' utility functions (primarily re-election) and some institutional features in the budgetary process that might reduce the bureau's edge in negotiating with its sponsor.[87] The Niskanen model has been subjected to a range of tests and debate, leading to modification and development.[88]

The state's autonomy therefore rests on several factors: resources (organization and information), defined relationships (as between sponsor and bureau), imputed ends (for politicians, re-election; for bureaucrats, growth and budget), and insulation. From the public choice perspective, these factors in combination make for a policy process that is undemocratic in at least three senses. First, they imply a fairly high degree of coercion, even in nominally democratic polities. Whereas market mechanisms strive to meet private preferences and accommodate different tastes, the allocation of public goods usually requires coercion. Second, these factors combine to insulate the state (especially bureaux) from citizens' demands. Periodic elections and bureaucratic autonomy make it very difficult for citizens as a whole – or in smaller groups and organizations – to influence the state. Indeed, the state has at its disposal resources and advantages that allow it to manipulate its political environment. In Breton's words, "the governing party will allocate considerable money, time, and effort to advertising, that is, to an activity designed (or so the government hopes) to alter the preferences of citizens in such a way as to make them more homogeneous."[89] Third, as the size and influence of government grow, private actors are increasingly encouraged to pursue private gain through public action. Public choice has developed the idea of "rent-seeking" behaviour to describe this phenomenon. The economic definition of rent is "that part of the payment to an owner of resources over and above that which those resources could command in any alternative use."[90] The pursuit of profit is in this sense "rent-seeking," but public choice argues that in markets, these profits drive the system and are dissipated over time through competition. The scope of the modern state increases the incentives for individuals to "seek rents" by using the state's powers to capture benefits (e.g., artificially reduce supply, raise demand, or close entry through licences, quotas, and permits) that are too costly in relative terms to pursue in private markets.[91] Ironically, the best organized have the best chance of wresting such "rents" from the state, and thus public choice joins some left-wing analyses of the state to conclude that upper and middle classes benefit disproportionately from government largess.

DISCUSSION

The problem of the state as it has been posed in the contemporary political literature is really a problem with three facets. First, what is the state, and how should it be conceptualized? Second, given that the modern state is autonomous (all three approaches agree on this), how should this autonomy be conceptualized? Third, what are the main political consequences or effects of the modern state and its autonomy?

Benjamin and Duvall offer a two-fold answer to the first question. State 1 is "the continually operating (i.e., administering, regulating, etc.), relatively permanent institutional aggregate of public bureaucracy and administrative apparatus *as an organized whole*."[92] Their second definition, state 2, "is the more encompassing institutional-legal order, which is the enduring structure of governance and rule in society – the machinery and the means by which conflict is handled, society is ruled, and social relations are governed."[93] An example of the latter would be a constitution, which provides an overarching normative order for a society.

It is clear that these two formulations are more fruitful than trying to think of the state in purely relational terms. The matrix of institutions and apparatuses that we thus call the state has a separate organizational basis from society. It is this organizational dimension that Peter Hall highlights when he urges an institutionalist approach that focuses on "the formal rules, compliance procedures, and standard operating practices that structure the relationship between individuals in various units of the polity and economy."[94] It would be incorrect, however, to draw from this the conclusion that the matrix – the "organized whole," as Benjamin and Duvall put it – contains uniform flows of power or that it is a rational construction. All three of the major approaches reviewed above stress (though for different reasons) the fragmentation of the modern state, the variablity of power and capacity among sectors of the same state and certainly among states, and indeed the intrastate contradictions and inconsistencies that increasingly drive the system. The state, as an arrangement of institutions and as a normative order, is always an unstable compound.

This leads to a reformulation of the second facet of the problem of the state, that of relative autonomy. Most of the literature that explicitly addresses this issue does so in terms of the state's ability to contravene the interests of powerful (usually class) societal actors. Benjamin and Duvall join other observers in suggesting that one of the hallmarks of contemporary, developed Western economic systems is that they increasingly generate social categories that are more and more removed from the firm foundations of social class. This has immense repercussions for the way in which people organize politically, since they mobilize less on the grounds of objective economic interest than on "positional" goods – status, identity, and ideology. The state is thus autonomous both because of the new demands that are created in this environment and because the demands lead to structures and institutions that then develop interests of their own.

The neo-Marxist approach takes class power or the functional needs of capitalism as given. The state's autonomy is thus objective but "relative." The neo-institutional approach gives sections or segments of the state autonomy, depending on the possession of certain resources, but frames the issue as one of state against civil society. So, for Skocpol, the test of the state's (or some agency's) autonomy is the degree to which its project differs from that of powerful, economic interests. Public choice, as befits its more deductive and in some ways more ambitious approach, deals with generic democratic states and so argues that the forces and factors that it isolates are universal characteristics of the political. Autonomy arises from the largely unvarying mix of institutional rules and personal strategies. The problem with all three of these approaches is that they lack a dynamic character; the relations and qualities that they describe, at the theoretical level, are static.

The more fruitful approach is to acknowledge, with Benjamin and Duvall, that the modern capitalist state is autonmous as a structure in relation to traditional configurations of economic power. All three of the theories discussed above provide numerous ways of conceptualizing this structural autonomy: neo-Marxism in terms of contradictions, neo-institutionalism in terms of separate bases of power and Cairns's idea of embeddedness, public choice in the notion of "insulators." Within this structural autonomy, however, there will be instances where capital "wins" and other social forces seek to capture portions of the state or turn some of its interests to their advantage. Indeed, the very structural autonomy of the state, and the implications that that holds for the state's strategies in managing civil society, make it increasingly a target of organized interests. Compare, for example, Cairns's idea of societal conflict being channelled through the state with Buchanan's arguments about rent-seeking. They effectively point to the same phenomenon, one that would be incomprehensible unless we first acknowledge the state's increasing autonomy.

This brings us to the final facet of the problem of the state. If we may conceive of the state as an institutional matrix of power that provides society with broad normative order, and if the modern state is structurally autonomous from civil society, what consequences does this situation have for contemporary politics and for the logic of state action? The key consequence is that the state must be seen as the nodal point in an increasing number of contemporary political conflicts. Its growing structural autonomy gives it an enhanced interest in shaping civil society and deliberately constructing and regulating the normative order. This structural autonomy also and simultaneously makes it a target of an increasingly fragmented distribution of societal interests. Hence the ultimate and ironic paradox of autonomy: the more autonomous the state is, the more frequent will be the attempts to capture portions of it and use it in "non-autonomous" ways for special interests. It should be evident that this is not the same as saying that the state controls everything or that it always and everywhere has determining power. Indeed, at some points in a dynamic analysis, it may be quite the opposite. Once again, to cite Hall, "the institutional networks affecting state action extend well into society, in such a way as to expose the state again to societal influences. The state appears as a network of institutions associated with society and the economic system."[95]

It is in the evolution of these strategies and relations – always differing, depending on context – that we can see the ultimate consequences of an autonomous state in this sense. The politics of the 1970s and 1980s broke the mould of, or at least overlaid, the old configurations of conflict and debate. Social movements organized around a variety of issues, but most of these could be linked in one form or anther to the question of identity, of collective rights and obligations. Modern states, faced with the challenge, strove to contain and manage those movements through a variety of strategies whose global effect was either to reassert older patterns of collective identity or to formulate new patterns that could either be accommodated in the old ones or challenge them. In the Canadian case, the response was two-fold: development of modest programs to assist financially organizations that represented different facets of these movements, and a constitutional initiative, in which the aforementioned groups were major participants, that reconceptualized citizens' rights. Through these actions, the state shifted the contours of our public space; it helped redefine our political language and discourse; and these effects reach far beyond the narrower and more direct effects of specific policies.

CHAPTER TWO

Collective Action and the State

We saw in chapter 1 that Olsonian collective action theory predicts that "citizens' groups" or social movements will be weak and ineffectual. They do face problems with "free riders," but in fact have managed to be reasonably successful in both North America and Europe. One reason would appear to be the support that they sometimes receive from state agencies. There are three central questions to be addressed here. In what form does this support come? Why would groups seek and accept this support? Why would the state give it?

"Support" is an elastic term but may be organized around two vectors, positional and financial. Positional support means access for some groups and not others to information or to decision makers or to a formal or quasi-formal role in decision making. An advocacy organization for the elderly might receive, for example, advance notice of some new policy developments to facilitate its reaction and advice. Alternatively, it might be invited to participate in the early stages of policy development. If the group has been successful in pressing its claim to represent an important segment of its constituency, it will be invited to appear at later hearings. Usually, the organization will have had to establish its credibility before it is granted this positional support, but once such support is granted, its position vis-à-vis its competitors in the policy field is considerably enhanced.

Financial support comes in three principal forms: tax concessions, project funding, and core funding. The first is the grant of charitable or educational status, which releases the organization from tax liabilities that it would otherwise face on donations and other income (this factor was highlighted in Berry's analysis of PIGs). In return, the organization promises to be "non-political" and engage only in educational or charitable services. Charitable organizations of this type are not lobbies in the formal sense, though clearly they may pursue an educational agenda informed by a point of view that itself has political consequences. The Canadian Research Institute for the Advancement of Women and the Canadian Congress for Learning Opportunities for Women are both educational organizations that receive tax relief as a result of their status but nonetheless publish research broadly consistent with mainstream feminism. Project funding is a grant given for a limited purpose such as a film, research or travel, or some service – the permutations are almost endless. Core funding is a grant to an organization to help it meet a proportion of its operating costs.

The answer to the second question would seem obvious: groups want support, both positional and financial, in order to achieve their goals. With positional support they become "inside players" in the policy community and have an edge over other organizations competing to represent the same interests. Financial support gives them needed resources. But the issue is more complex. Many groups refuse support because, however benign it may be, they worry about co-optation and dependence. In a liberal-democratic state, we would expect some ideological reluctance to the state's providing support for groups, especially core support for advocacy organizations. Viewed from other perspectives, however, there are ample reasons why agencies might support organizations, even ones that appear to be critical of government policy. From a public choice perspective, support to groups and organizations is the same as creating allies outside the agency that can help when the agency is under attack.[1] Also, as Walker argued, organizations that demand more government intervention can become allies of state managers whose own interest lies in program expansion. For example, Alford and Friedland argue: "Each agency seeks to maximize its autonomy, to preserve its legitimacy, and to create a stable and broad constituency from clients, funding sources, and networks of influence with other bureaucratic agencies. The successful agencies expand, garnering more projects and larger budgets under their control. In this process of increasing the predictability of their specific environment, public bureaucracies incorporate external constituencies, blurring the boundary line between private and public sectors, as they establish powerful interest groups inside and outside the state with a stake in the preservation of the agency."[2]

Theodore Lowi has made much the same argument in his reflections on the nature of modern liberalism. In noting that the modern welfare state has gradually but significantly increased the scope of bureaucratic discretion over programs, he claims that "the secret to bureaucratic power is discretionary resources, resources that can be used to build supportive constituencies – whether they build a military-industrial complex or a welfare agency – welfare client complex."[3] Sabatier also observes that regulatory agencies can avoid "clientele capture" by creating policy constituencies through funding of third-party organizations. As a sidelight, this can be helpful for agencies whose mission includes pressing for policy changes within another jurisdiction.[4]

How much empirical support is there for these claims? The most extensive analysis of American "tax-funded" groups is contained in James Bennett and Thomas DiLorenzo's book entitled *Destroying Democracy*. They claim to demonstrate "how tax funds appropriated for social and other programs have been diverted on a massive scale to support political advocacy, that is, to help in the reelection campaigns of those who hold office and to expand the bureaucratic empires of public employees."[5] They estimate the amount of tax-funded support to groups to be in the hundreds of billions of dollars (e.g., $287 billion in 1982). They review what they call "anti-industry" groups (e.g., consumer advocates, environmentalists) and the financial support that they receive from public sources. These sources include tax-exempt status, project funds, intervenor grants for regulatory proceedings, and some core funding. The book also examines what Bennett and DiLorenzo call "tax-receiving independent non-government organizations" (TRINGOs) which advocate on behalf of the disadvantaged.

In their concluding chapter, Bennett and DiLorenzo attempt some explanations of what they have uncovered. They begin with the assertion: "Although government should respond to the desires of the electorate, it should not attempt to influence citizens' views on public policy issues. Government, however, has been making such attempts for decades; by supporting advocacy groups through grants and contracts, it inevitably promotes the propagation of a certain set of ideas that influences the course of public policy."[6] In their view, anti-capitalist organizations get most of the government support available to groups and have been remarkably successful in getting the programs that they demand.[7] But why would the state engage in this? Bennett and DiLorenzo's answer, much like Alford and Friedland and Lowi above, is that civil servants are entrepreneurs interested in income and prestige and thus have a strong incentive "to promote and stimulate a perceived need for their own activities."[8] "The funds flow to the groups on the left of the political spectrum because these groups favor an expansion of the role of government in the economy and of government programs and expenditures. By channeling taxpayers' dollars to left-wing organizations, the bureaucracy is merely rewarding its friends and providing support for those who will reciprocate by lobbying and campaigning for increased programs and budgets."[9] Politicians need help campaigning; groups can help them with money and volunteers and so in turn get rewarded. In the United States, congressional candidates can, within limits, keep surpluses of campaign contributions to cover personal expenses. They consequently have an incentive to get as many contributions as possible, even from these advocacy groups.[10]

President Reagan attempted to "defund the left" in 1983, a move that had its roots in efforts under President Carter in 1980, when the Office of Management and Budget (OMB) issued Circular A-122 – "Cost Principles for Nonprofit Organizations." The circular prohibited use of tax dollars for lobbying, but it was vague and consequently was ignored. On 24 January 1983, the OMB published a proposal in the *Federal Register* to tighten up A-122 by basically disallowing any funds for any form of advocacy (which it redefined broadly to go well beyond traditional lobbying). There was intense reaction, and finally the revised Circular A-122, issued in April 1984, allowed some lobbying. Bennett and DiLorenzo remain pessimistic about the prospects of limiting government funding to advocacy organizations.[11]

Despite the theoretical and, in Canada, the empirical importance of state funding of groups, there have been relatively few sustained analyses of the phenomenon by the left. One of the earliest was by Martin Loney, in an essay on Canadian citizen participation programs of the late 1960s. These programs were concentrated among native groups, the poor, and youth groups. Loney argued that their rapid growth was a function of social control, reflecting a "move to increasingly sophisticated strategies for reincorporating potentially dissident groups into the mainstream of society."[12] Citizens' participation kept discontented groups busy "without threatening the underlying stability or division of wealth and power in Canada."[13] Moreover, unlike Bennett and DiLorenzo, who claim that funding went to groups on the left of American mainstream politics, Loney concluded that "overall government funding and involvement in the voluntary sector must be seen as a conservatizing force. In most cases political activity which falls outside the conservative paradigm will not be funded."[14] The funding of clinics, tenants' and welfare rights organizations, the women's movement, community newspapers, and other organizations was, from Loney's perspective, a thinly disguised effort at "penetration of the voluntary sector" through a strategy of ideological hegemony.[15] Loney came to equally uncompromising, if opposite conclusions, to the ones drawn by Bennett and DiLorenzo: "In effect, the plethora of government funding becomes an instrument not for citizen control over government but for government control over citizens. Approved activities will be rewarded, and recipient groups will serve as poles of attraction for potential members. Favoured individuals will emerge through government funded groups to take their place on social planning councils as representatives of the poor or some worthy minority, and in the process will themselves cease to be poor."[16]

This view of the dynamics of government funding has been tempered in some recent work by Roxana Ng. Ng's study of a community, non-profit employment agency funded by Employment and Immigration Canada noted the co-opting effects of such funding but drew a different portrait of the early forces that led to creation of programs for citizenship participation: "I argue that it was a compromise arrived at by two opposing forces: the need to cope with the changing social and economic reality by the state on the one hand, and the increasing militancy of minority groups and their advocates demanding social programs to meet their needs on the other."[17] The changing social and economic reality that she refers to included the rediscovery in the late 1960s of poverty and inequality, Quebec's growing militancy, and immigration and its attendant racial tensions: "Viewed in this light, state funding to community groups can be seen as an inexpensive alternative to a coercive approach and a way of defusing criticisms directed at the welfare state while meeting the growing demand for social programs."[18]

Outside of Marxist analyses, sparse as they are, most of the work done on group funding has approached it as an example of patronage. Jeffrey Simpson's study of the Canadian politics of patronage links the modern instances of group funding by government agencies to the older pattern of blatant preferments: "In recent years the traditional reflections in the patronage mirror – partisan, religious, linguistic and regional interests – are no longer sufficient proof of the broadness of a political party. Now the mirror must also reflect the interests of women, native peoples, young Canadians, old Canadians and various multicultural groups. Their understandable desire for recognition accentuates the leader's frustration at the gap between the demands for reward or recognition and the supply of positions or preferment."[19] Simpson also argues, however, that the modern forms of patronage have undermined political parties, since they encourage multiple allegiances not to a larger community but to the segmented organizations that represent the interests of different groups: "The consequence for natives, women's groups, linguistic minorities – to name just a few examples – was that members channelled their energies and offered their allegiance not to the government that funded them, and the parties vying for control of that government, but to the organizations themselves."[20] His claim is that in these conditions, added to the impact of television and of large bureaucracies, "the mobilizing capabilities of patronage diminished."[21]

Clearly, the debate over the rationales and effects of grant programs must ultimately hinge on empirical research. Unfortunately, existing work is often scattered and anecdotal. Myrna Kostash's *Long Way from Home* (1980), for example, provides some glimpses into the formation of key Canadian social movement organizations in the 1960s: in sequence, peace movement, student movement, counterculture, feminism, and Quebec liberation. The first chronologically was the Combined Universities Campaign for Nuclear Disarmament (CUCND), which at its 1964 Regina meeting with New Democratic Youth, Quakers, young Communists, and others constituted itself as the Student Union for Peace Action (SUPA).[22] By 1967 the Company of Young Canadians (CYC, a government-sponsored youth corps) had absorbed most of SUPA's "Toronto-based leadership in staff or consultants' jobs, had hired half its project workers into its own volunteer groups, and had linked up with most of SUPA's extant projects. By the end of 1967, SUPA was dead and the chance to mature politically was forfeited."[23]

In a pioneering study for the Royal Commission on Bilingualism and Biculturalism, Meisel and Lemieux referred to how federal government grants in the mid-1960s had been used to "influence the structure of voluntary organizations."[24] In one case that they studied, Ottawa gave grants to associations with a "pan-Canadian orientation." But as Gwyn points out, the real surge in government funding for citizens' groups came after 1968, especially in 1970, with the appointment of Bernard Ostry and Michael McCabe to the Citizenship Branch of SOS.[25] While the CYC had been a Pearson initiative that gave unprecedented autonomy to an organization committed to social animation at the community level using youth volunteers,[26] the "Great Ottawa Grant Boom" occurred between 1970 and 1972.

The key programs at the time were youth employment initiatives, though these quickly became templates for other citizens' groups. As one observer at the time stated: "In political terms, the programs have created their own constituencies, and, it has to be added, their own dependents. In political terms, too, power is being decentralized, right down to community groups. These groups aren't likely to accept its ever being taken back."[27] Another analysis five years later drew a more pessimistic picture. While there had been a real surge in support and the opening of progressive possibilities in citizenship funding, by 1972–73 conservatism had once more settled on these programs, which, while they were still in place, were no longer facilitators of participatory democracy.[28]

There is some scattered empirical evidence to indicate that the government had a co-optive strategy in mind as it developed its programs to support various citizens' groups and constituencies. Milne, for example, argues that Pierre Trudeau's state-building initiatives involved the successful "use and incorporation of public interest groups and others in the private sector," especially charter supporters and civil liberties groups in the early 1980s.[29] Several studies of Canadian government funding of native organizations suggest the same deliberate use of the state to manage political processes. Weaver notes, for example, Ottawa's interest in supporting native groups after the failure of its White Paper on Indian Policy in 1969.[30] Hugh Faulkner, a former Liberal secretary of state, agrees that the Trudeau government's decision to permit public funding of interest groups was one of its "greatest innovations" and that consumers and natives have been principal beneficiaries.[31] Whereas Faulkner does not agree that this led to co-optation, Ponting and Gibbins argue that, for native groups, it created the possibility of what they call "socio-fiscal control": "That is, the provision of money is deemed to carry with it the right to specify how, for what, and by whom it will be spent. Other rights deemed to accompany the provision of money are the right to demand proof that the funds have been spent in accordance with the stipulations just cited, and the right to withdraw or terminate the funds."[32] The authors give several examples of this mode of control, which was sometimes used to curb deviance by organizations, to dispense money in ways to control factions on reserves, or even to sow disunity. Like Loney and Ng, they see public funding as a mechanism of social control, one that is not merely contingent but in fact embedded in program design.

The most extensive, if unsystematic, study of public funding of Canadian interest groups from a patronage perspective may be found in Paul Malvern's *Persuaders* (1985). He coins the term "reverse interest group" for organizations whose principal source of funds is government, and his analysis parallels those that find the logic of public funding to lie in social control. Reverse interest groups are, in his view, "mouthpieces" for the government.[33] Malvern's review of these organizations and different policy fields is largely anecdotal, and his consistent refrain is that government develops a symbiotic relationship with large organizations that are in fact not representative of the communities that they purport to champion. For example, he criticizes the National Action Committee on the Status of Women for being an upper class organization not connected to the grass roots.[34] The government's real influence is less in its direct control of these organizations than in its legitimation of feminist arguments through legitimation of the groups. The same argument about bias and differential access applies to multiculturalism, though Malvern argues that the program has come to be loved by politicians: "The politicians grew to love multiculturalism; it provided them with a new technique for social control and electoral success. The bureaucrats loved it; civil servants found in it new career paths and new ways of increasing the size and budgets of their departments and thus their power. The leaders of the various ethnic groups loved it; it gave them real importance for the first time, and with it, fabulous job and funding possibilities."[35]

In his review of what he deems to be the left-wing biases of government funding, Malvern concludes that these funding programs have four principal effects. They encourage excessive growth of government programs, demanded by groups supported by government; they lead to system overload, since as more groups get funded, the others inevitably will not be satisfied; they foster private selfishness at the expense of some sense of civic virtue; and they heighten social and political conflict, since groups have a vested interest in generating social problems that then will require government funding both for themselves and for the problems with which they are associated.

We can thus see that the general literature on Canadian federal government financing of interest groups tends to fall into three categories. First, from a perspective informed by Marxism, financing is profoundly conservative because it blunts radical and progressive forces in society and co-opts them through a series of mechanisms tied to funding (e.g., the necessity to file reports, meet grant guidelines, and so on). Public funding, as Loney says, is a means of social control. This view is challenged only modestly in Ng and some of the more contemporary work written within this perspective. Second, these funding programs are seen as refined, contemporary forms of traditional patronage, and so the emphasis is on the interest of politicians and bureaucrats in extending support. Social control is far less prominent, though it may be a byproduct. The prime motivator is the attraction of political support and the building of policy constituencies. Third, there is the "patronage/bias" school, represented by Malvern but echoed in some other analyses as well, which is upset by the apparent unfairness or selectivity of the funding programs.

The programs are interpreted as attempts at patronage, but with other instrumental dimensions beyond simple support. These might include helping groups that demand more government services or aiding organizations that happen to support the government's current stance on some issue. This position is distinct from the first, because while it certainly posits the state as an actor, it does not necessarily ascribe any larger ideological purpose to the manipulation of the groups. For example, Malvern notes how Ottawa aided language groups that supported Ottawa's vision of bilingualism.[36]

In addition to this general literature on the public financing of interest groups in Canada, there is some specific work on the three areas that have been selected for this study. With few exceptions, the analyses tend to fall into one of the categories mentioned above. In the case of language policy, for example, on which there is remarkably little written in Canada, Waddell notes how various "linguistic models" have been imposed from above by the state, and not particularly successfully.[37]

Most studies of the financing of women's organizations use the co-optation model. Conrad Winn's 1980 study of the sos, however, observed that in departmental budgetary allocations that fiscal year, women's organizations seemed to be clear winners, and it asked "about the extent to which the public purse should be used to assist bodies whose purpose is not mainly to provide services but rather to change society."[38] Steele, in the course of an anti-feminist diatribe, launches a heated, if scattered attack on what she claims is preferential funding for feminist organizations.[39] Most writers on Canadian feminism and the state, however, tend to share the critical assessment of Adamson, Briskin, and McPhail in *Feminist Organizing*. They qualify their criticism by stating that the state is contradictory and that while its support may weaken some women's organizations, sometimes "the government operates not in the interests of the capitalist ruling class, but in opposition to them. The gains are not to be underestimated: more funding for day-care, Secretary of State funding for women's projects, reform in sexual assault legislation, and so on."[40] They add, however: "Notwithstanding the optimism of this view, it is also important to recognize that the women's movement is changed by the form in which the government responds to us. The funding practices of the state, on which so many women's organizations depend; the establishment of advisory commissions and women's councils that demobilize change through bureaucracy; the language of legislation, which often limits the actual benefits accruing to women, have all molded and to some extent undermined the struggle of women to make change."[41]

Somewhat surprising, while Adamson, Briskin, and McPhail emphasize funding and the state's relation to feminist organizations, they fail to address the issue in their chapter on the practical aspects of feminist organizing.[42] Indeed, for a book devoted to feminist organization, the discussion of the nature of the state is jejune. The poverty of both empirical and theoretical work is reflected in a collection on feminist politics, edited by Angela Miles and Geraldine Finn: there is no discussion of the nature of the state.[43] The only exception is the careful work of Sandra Burt. She notes, for example, that "most women's groups rely heavily or exclusively on government funding. They are therefore subject to government guidelines and budget cuts, and this has sometimes restricted their flexibility and freedom to lobby."[44] Results of a 1984 survey of 144 women's groups showed that government grants were the largest source of income for 38 per cent, and the second largest source for another 10 per cent.[45] This fiscal dependence leaves the groups "at the mercy of government programs, places them under government control, and has restricted their freedom to act as lobbyists. The role of critic is compromised by this financial tie."[46] Her assessment is certainly supported by activists reflecting on the issue.[47]

Findlay's analysis of the Canadian women's movement and its relation to the federal state presents a more elaborate but similar accounting. She argues that from 1966 to 1979 the Canadian state was "engaged in organizing its formal response to women's demands for equality."[48] Her thesis is that the state is dominated by men and patriarchal perceptions and so resisted women's equality: what was accomplished was achieved for almost purely conjunctural reasons. She is sceptical of the institutional mechanisms established by the state in this period allegedly to represent women's interests in policy making. The one exception was the Women's Program in the sos. For a short time the program made a difference, principally because it was staffed by "feminists who had decided that the resources of the state could be used to support the development of the women's movement."[49] Grants to women's organizations were used strategically in consultation with the organizations themselves, and the program's administrators "held themselves accountable to the women's movement rather than to government priorities. All were defined as feminists and were largely drawn from feminist groups. Liaison with the women's movement was built into every aspect of the Program's work. A feminist perspective clearly determined the Program's development, and was reflected in project definition, staff recruitment, and the Program's organization and management."[50] The program's relative invisibility, rather than any real government commitment to feminism, explains these successes. In 1975, International

Women's Year, it received approximately $2.5 million and used it to good effect to support feminist organizations. At this point a (male) bureaucratic backlash occurred, and the program was gradually iso-lated, so that by 1979 it had lost a great deal of its energy.

The literature on multicultural policy has been split between those who see it as a mechanism of co-optation and social control and those who view it as a largely symbolic, ineffectual, or irrational re-sponse to political pressure. One partial exception is Raymond Breton, who posits that the program was important precisely be-cause it was symbolic but that nevertheless it has been heavily man-aged by the state. In tracing the roots of the policy, for example, he finds that there was relatively little public input and certainly no pre-cise sense within government of what support there was for the pro-gram. No official surveys were done before the 1970s, but in two that were published in 1976, there seemed to be a combination of broad support for multiculturalism without much knowledge of what the existing policy entailed.[51] After reviewing the evidence, Breton concludes that there was no grass-roots pressure behind multiculturalism in Canada: "The demand for a federal policy of multiculturalism seems to have come primarily from ethnic organi-zational elites and their supporters, from government agencies and their officers, and from political authorities."[52] Breton believes that the policy encouraged formation of organizations to represent eth-nic interests and indeed sometimes involved governmental authori-ties themselves in encouraging such organizations to facilitate communication.[53] While he concedes the multiculturalism has often been criticized for being simply a "song and dance" affair, he stresses the government's penetration of the associational system: "Third, in the implementation of a policy, there is always the risk of favouring or appearing to favour some ethnic groups over others and thus triggering processes of intergroup comparison and rivalry. Finally, through the allocation of subsidies, the government agency and its officials are drawn into the internal politics of the ethnic community. This may entail favouring or appearing to favour some organiza-tions over others (unless grants are given to all organizations)."[54]

In other pieces, Breton has developed the notion of the "symbolic order" as something wherein members of a political community wish to see themselves reflected and validated. In this respect, while both language and multicultural policy were certainly "symbolic," they were not so in the sense of being pure gestures without import. Bre-ton's argument is that struggles over the symbolic order are crucial to politics, since individuals expect "to recognize themselves in pub-lic institutions. They expect some consistency between their private identities and the symbolic contents upheld by public authorities, embedded in the societal institutions, and celebrated in public events."[55] Thus Breton might be interpreted as saying that policies such as bilingualism and multiculturalism reflect deep forces within society, even while the policy instruments that the government designs may co-opt some of the groups active in the areas.

The only other observer to give such a balanced assessment of multicultural policy is Buchignani. His position hinges less on the program's intrinsic importance than on its unanticipated consequences: "Overnight the program generated a legion of ethnic spokespersons and provided them with a forum to voice their opinions. It encouraged the creation of ethnic-based associations to the point where they are now endemic ... In a few years multiculturalism was beginning to look like something quite different than had been intended. In essence, it brought up for negotiation the very notion of what Canada was all about."[56]

Anderson and Frideres develop much the same sort of analysis as Breton's, although they see multicultural policy as being much more deeply implicated in the social relations of power in Canadian society. They believe that an interpretation of the policy purely in terms of vote gathering is simplistic and suggest that the effect of multicultural policy might in fact serve the interests of dominant classes, since it organizes and mobilizes along ethnic, as opposed to class lines. John Porter, in *The Vertical Mosaic*, held much the same view, although he thought that multicultural policies were a way for Anglo groups to keep all other Canadians in their place. Like Breton, Anderson and Frideres claim that, despite the small sums of money involved, multiculturalism policy has tremendous implications for state/society relations: "It is in the relationship of dependency established when an ethnic organization accepts funds from a government agency that one can observe the most serious effects of state intervention in ethnic community affairs."[57] This conclusion is shared by Bolaria and Li, who state baldly that "Because of their dependency on state funding, these private organizations often have to tailor their programs to the requirements and objectives of the funding bodies. Through the control of organizational grants, the state exercises a great influence over the way these private associations operate."[58]

The most ambitious attempt to analyse multicultural policy from a neo-Marxist perspective may be found in Stasiulis. In an article published in 1980, she argued that "the state plays a key role in restricting and structuring the alternatives of ethnic communities."[59] Her critique of grants and funding focused on several themes. The trend has been toward non-recurring project grants rather than core funding, and this works against smaller groups and to the advantage of established ones. These grants are short term and geared more to being visible than to being effective. The effort in applying for funds and accounting for them drains energy from leadership. The federal government funnels money to "national groups" in part to "foster structures which will further nationalist sentiments and feelings of gratification for the federal government."[60] The funding nexus reverberates through the community by articulating the state with only some segments and not others, by co-opting, and by generating battles over co-optation.

More recent analysis by Stasiulis supports this assessment of the global effects of multicultural funding for organizations: "In 1986–87, financial support was provided for sustaining the operations of approximately 50 organizations, with priority given to organizations representing visible minorities. As case studies have documented, however, the control exercised in the administration of grants has frequently served to depoliticize and constrain the activities of funded organizations. Funding through multiculturalism has also bolstered community factions that enjoyed little popular support in their communities, yet have been perceived as moderate, responsible and therefore acceptable to the funding agency."[61]

While this "state policy as state control"[62] interpretation has been prominent in discussions on multiculturalism, another, opposed tendency has argued that Canadian multicultural policy is a failure because it was badly organized and ill-conceived from the start[63] or that it emphasizes and celebrates differences that are merely ones of taste, not of real identity.[64] In support of this view, it must be recalled that the multicultural program in sos, especially that component devoted to group funding, has never had a large budget. Grants to groups are typically small (the majority between $5,000 and $20,000), and so it is hard to credit the view that the state is somehow vigorously managing the rhythms of ethnic politics with such anaemic instruments.

THE PERSPECTIVE OF THIS STUDY

Chapter 1 made it abundantly clear that there are severe and challenging problems in contemporary theorizations of collective action and the state. Some of the most important, visible, and apparently influential interest groups in modern politics are difficult to explain in terms of traditional theories, whether pluralist, Marxist, or public choice. The clues all lead, however, to the state. In reviewing contemporary analyses of the state, we saw that the trajectory of the most recent work has been to revalidate the state's autonomy and increasing impact on civil society. In turning to the Canadian case in this chapter, we saw that there are some fascinating examples of precisely the type of state/associational articulation suggested by the more theoretical literature: language, multicultural, and women's organizations are key social movements and collective actors in contemporary Canadian politics, and all of them receive strategic funding by the state through the Department of the Secretary of State. Though the phenomenon has not been widely studied in Canada, anecdotal evidence suggests that hundreds of interest groups at the federal and provincial levels in a wide range of policy fields receive both project and core funding from various state agencies. The sos programs are only the most visible of these.

Unfortunately, despite the empirical and theoretical importance of these groups and their relations to government, the available work on them, summarized earlier in this chapter, is flawed in at least five respects. First, apart from a few bits of anecdotal evidence, there is virtually no history of the development of public funding for interest groups. Most of the literature on the three policy areas cited above either simply ignores the question of when and why these programs were developed or addresses it in extremely broad and abstract functionalist terms (e.g., the need for social control or patronage). This papers over the important transformations that must have occurred to launch this style of policy making and this structure of relations between the state and civil society. Second, the same historical myopia has affected our understanding of program developments in the 1970s and 1980s. There is some good work on the evolution of multicultural policy, but the language and women's programs have been described in only the most abstract ways: we know nothing about how they evolved, what their structures are, how they are administered, what decisions were made (and why) about their administration, and how they compare with each other. Third, there are crucial gaps in the evidence adduced for the co-optation and patronage theses. At the simplest level, there is little attempt to develop a benchmark of how these groups might behave in the absence of funding, or to gauge the contribution of other factors to the alleged conservative (or radical) tendencies of the groups themselves. The patronage thesis makes claims about how politicians perceived the programs and what they thought they could get from them in terms of political benefits, but once again the evidence is either anecdotal or conjectural. Fourth, there is scant evidence of how important the funds are to the groups. Most of the evidence is aggregate, without much analysis of specific organizations and their activities and funding profiles over time. Fifth, and most surprising, there is virtually no analysis of the effect of these types of programs on the state. If indeed these programs reflect specific forms of interaction between state and civil society, there presumably must be some reverberations within the state itself, either in terms of program consistency or perhaps in terms of "colonization" attempts by outside interests.

Since the existing literature is less than helpful, we are forced back to asking the most basic questions. Why were these programs which provided public funding and support for advocacy organizations undertaken in the first place? Why did they take the shape and trajectories that they did? What were the effects or consequences both for the organizations and for the state? While the answers to these questions must be in part historical, they also will depend on some analytical model of the policy areas in question and of the state. Drawing on the discussion to this stage, the rest of this book will be informed by the following theses.

Thesis 1. The state in advanced capitalism is autonomous in five senses. (1) It has separate bases of power, such as physical force, knowledge, organization and authority. (2) It has separate structural goals, such as maintenance of its own integrity and some level of control of civil society. (3) It is made up of sectors differentiated in terms of their practices. (4) It is both a collection of apparatuses and the crucial instance of normative order, and this order always "lags" behind social forces and has an internal logic separate from those forces (e.g., legal precedents). (5) Both the state itself and civil society increasingly conduct themselves in relation to forces and factors generated from within the state.

Thesis 2. This autonomy of the state makes it a target for collective actors, whose basic practice involves the attempt to use the state's autonomy for their purposes. Economic associations seek benefits through the state, and the more contemporary social movements and public interest groups try to use both bureaucratic agencies and the courts to achieve their agendas.

Thesis 3. The state is consequently operating on three planes – as a structure generating vectors of consequences, as a target for societal actors, and as an agent in its own right, responding both to its own internal logic and to pressures from outside. This places the state squarely in the centre of collective action and political conflict, though it does not mean that the state can control all outcomes or indeed that it is all-powerful. Rather, collective action takes place within a tradition of state–civil society relations, is affected by the structural features and capacities of the state, and moulds itself to and is channelled by those features and capacities.

Thesis 4. The consequences that flow from this dynamic of state–civil society relations are indeterminate. There is no systemic constraint with which the vectors of consequences must in some sense be ultimately consistent. This is both because of the autonomy of the state itself, so that consequences at the level of the state have complex trajectories of their own, and because collective action has always to be articulated in political discourse, which itself attains a quasi-objective status and can in turn affect subsequent collective action.

How do these ideas guide the present study? Part II provides the historical context. The Canadian federal state, in the form of the SOS, evolved a set of practices and discourses around the notion of "citizenship" after the Second World War (chapter 3 and 4). This, along with the regime crisis of Quebec nationalism in the mid-1960s, created a terrain whereupon societal demands for participation and more open government were constructed and channelled as "citizenship participation" through public funding of advocacy organizations (chapter 5). The first and most committed efforts of this sort were directed at francophone organizations outside Quebec and were keyed directly to the regime crisis and the need to develop national unity on linguistic grounds. That program became a template, however, for others. The precipitating factors were thus structural, though political agents at the time saw opportunities in these programs for maintenance of their own power base. The structural rationale behind these programs explains why they were not carried further after 1972 (chapter 6), although state actors at the time also had to face the short-term problems of minority government, and so the programs were determined more by electoral logic than regime logic. The limited commitment and scope of these programs should not mislead us into thinking that they have been insignificant.

Part III analyses the administration of the programs (minority languages in chapter 7, multiculturalism in chapter 8, and women's program in chapter 9) and shows how they affected both internal state developments and the associational system. Evidence shows that the "co-optation" thesis is simplistic in the extreme, both because of the powers that organizations have over the state as a consequence of the programs and because of the role that state-funded groups play in contemporary politics. Part IV offers some reflections on the nature of the Canadian state and contemporary discussions of collective identity, which is the substantive issue behind these organizations and these programs.

PART TWO

Citizenship Policy
and Administration

CHAPTER THREE

Secretary of State, 1867–1945: Toward a Citizenship Role

1867–1939

The term "Secretary of State" can be traced back to the reign of Henry III of England (1216–72). At that point the position of "Our Principal Secretary of Estate" was a member of the king's household. By the time of Henry VIII, the principal secretary's position was confirmed by statute, and he retained a seat in Parliament and the council. Under Elizabeth I, the principal secretary was no longer attached to the household, thus marking the beginning of the development by which the sovereign's secretary became a minister of the crown. Until 1782 there were usually no more than two secretaries, known as "His Majesty's Principal Secretaries of State for Foreign Affairs." One was in charge of the Northern Department, handling correspondence with the northern powers of Europe, the other of the Southern Department, responsible for southern Europe, Switzerland, Turkey, and Irish and colonial business. In 1782 the Southern Department became the Home Office, and the Northern Department became the Foreign Office (the colonial secretaryship was abolished). In 1794 a secretary of state for war was added, and in 1858 the secretary of state for India was established.[1] The American secretary of state corresponds to the British foreign secretary[2] and to Canada's secretary of state for external affairs.

A dual principle may be discerned to have regulated development of secretaries of state in the British tradition – some position that requires substantial official correspondence from the sovereign or the sovereign's representative and some matter of large responsibility. In practice, these two coincided in the later designations of secretaries of war and of India; the earlier two secretaries simply divided up the jurisdictions of the sovereign's correspondence. As one authority states: "His Majesty's Principal Secretaries of State are heads of important government departments for whose administration they are responsible to Parliament, and constitutionally they also function as channels of communication between the Crown and its subjects."[3]

Canada is the only other country in the Commonwealth to designate a department Secretary of State.[4] The Secretary of State of Canada (sos) is one of the few federal departments that can trace an unbroken lineage back to Confederation.[5] It was originally accompanied by a Secretary of State for the Provinces, formed from the Canada West Branch of the Provincial Secretary's Office and then discontinued in 1873, when its correspondence functions were transferred to the sos. Reflecting its British origins, the sos was the keeper of the great seal of Canada and effectively designated as the office whereby the sovereign's (or governor-general's) correspondence would be managed. Correspondence with the provinces, for example, was held to occur between the governor-general and the lieutenant-governors. There also had to be some mechanism for the sovereign to communicate with his or her ministers in Canada. Again, this was effected through a somewhat cumbersome procedure which routed dispatches through the governor-general and then on to full cabinet.[6]

The clue to the core of the sos's responsibilities before the Second World War lies in its possession of the great seal: "The secretary of state is, as has been observed, the custodian of the great seal of Canada. The general rule governing the use of the great seal is that it should be put only to instruments the issue of which is authorized by statute or by the governor in council, and which bear the governor-general's signature or that of his duly authorized deputy. Commissions of appointment, Dominion land-grants, writs of election and proclamations, are among the documents that fulfil these conditions."[7] Accordingly, the sos in 1867 was given responsibility for handling all official government correspondence, registering all documents and charters, and managing Native Indian affairs (principally the purchase of land from the Indians). There was much departmental reorganization in the years immediately following Confederation, so that in 1887 a separate Indian Department was established, and the following year the Department of the Interior was set up to manage Dominion Lands and other responsibilities. For the next thirty years, the sos's mandate bristled with new and apparently unrelated administrative duties, but most of them were solidly anchored in its constitutional role as keeper of the seal and the evolution of the office under British traditions. In this respect, most of its new duties came under one of three principal functions: record keeping, registration, and correspondence. As record keeper, for example, the sos served as government archivist until 1903 (the Public Archives of Canada was set up as a separate department in 1912). Its registry function was enhanced in 1872 and 1874 with passage of new requirements for registration of trade unions and of local boards of trade. The Companies Act of 1902 authorized the sos to issue letters patent for the incorporation of companies, and this came to occupy a great deal of departmental energy.

Also beginning in 1902, the sos was required to maintain records of all naturalization certificates issued by provincial courts; in 1914 it had transferred to it authority to issue such certificates. Its responsibilities for naturalization in turn provided the sos with a logical claim to handle affairs pertaining to aliens, and so it was given initial responsibility in both world wars for censorship. Its other wartime activity was registration of war charities. At various times the sos also handled civil service examinations (the Board of Examiners reported through it from 1882 to 1908), the North West Mounted Police (1876–78), elections under the Canada Temperance Act (as of 1878), and reports under the Electoral Franchise Act (1893–97).

In one sense, the sos was a great bureaucratic garbage bin, into which odd or awkward pieces of legislation could be tossed while some more appropriate organizational vehicle was being developed. To see the sos entirely in these terms, however, would be to miss its significance and the governing principles that link its early activities with more recent ones (e.g., for multiculturalism). The British tradition had established the principle that the Secretary of State was a channel of communication between sovereign and populace, as well as official repository of the sovereign's seal. While the British case evolved considerably beyond this with a multiplication of secretaries, the Canadian approach was to develop but two (the office of secretary of state for external affairs was established in 1908). The sos therefore retained the broader sense of being the channel of communication for the government to civil society (this underlay its assumption of translation services in 1934), and of being the central registry of the "state's" recognition of formal bodies in civil society, such as trade unions, companies, and charities. This rationale helps explain the sos's responsibility for war charities during and after the First World War and the designation of the under-secretary of state as chair of the Voluntary Service Registration Bureau in 1940.

This registry function and the implications it was to hold for how the federal government related to non-governmental organizations (particularly among ethnics and immigrants) eventually led to a break in the SOS's history. From 1950 to 1966 it became largely an economic registry, with some of its traditional responsibilities intact (i.e., ceremonies and translation). Its citizenship functions were wedded more intimately to immigration, and so these were transferred to the new Department of Citizenship and Immigration. By the 1960s, as governments became more prepared to act in the cultural sphere and define citizenship more broadly than the training of immigrants, the SOS received a renewed mission and reclaimed its traditional mandate.

ONSET OF WAR

The Second World War and its aftermath put the SOS in a sort of suspended animation, at least with respect to mobilizing and overseeing the warp and woof of Canadian society. The SOS had always had responsibility for matters pertaining to the larger interests of the state, interests that could not be comfortably ensconced in one or another line department. In the broadest sense, the SOS was the department monitoring civil society, regulating relations between the "voluntary sector" and the state.

When Canada entered the Second World War, the informal sinews of Canadian society needed to be pressed to a much wider purpose. War is always extraordinary, and total war can be awe-inspiring; but war often exposes political relationships in a stark light not normally discerned in peacetime. That the state mobilized society in the Second World War is in some ways unsurprising; what is of note is that this mobilization function became embedded, admittedly at first in a timorous way, in the state's relations with civil society after 1945. This mobilization function came to reside in the Citizenship Branch of the Department of Citizenship and Immigration but grew out of the responsibilities that had been transferred from the SOS in 1940. They eventually came back to the SOS in 1966, with the branch's return migration. Thus the story of the Citizenship Branch is properly part of the history of the SOS, and together they form some of the earliest chapters in the articulation of "citizenship policy" – the official mobilization of collective identity.

The emergence of the field of "citizenship policy" during the Second World War must first be set against the backdrop of prevailing citizenship practice and the nature of Canada's wartime commitments and their reliance on the mobilization of loyalty. Until the passage of the 1946 Citizenship Act there was no legal concept of Canadian citizenship. Instead, legislation provided for "Canadian nationals" and "British subjects." One could achieve the former sta-

tus through birth in Canada or "naturalization" (five years' residence, with some additional conditions). All Canadian nationals
were British subjects. "Aliens," a concept derived from common law,
described all those outside these two categories. The political community was therefore conceptualized largely in terms of residence
and birth in Canada but allegiance and loyalty to Britain. The notion
of British loyalty faced obvious problems among French Canadians
and Canadians of non-British and non-Commonwealth origin.

These problems were compounded by the nature of Canada's war
commitment after 1939. At the start of the war, there was much less
of the pro-British jingoism that had marked Canada's wartime entry
in 1914. In Granatstein's words, the war "was not received with
cheers and enthusiasm."[8] It was this division in domestic opinion
over the war effort that lay behind Ottawa's initially modest commitments to Britain in 1939 and the pledge not to impose conscription.
The government did not shrink from harsh measures when it found
them necessary: Camillien Houde, mayor of Montreal, was uncere-
moniously thrown into an internment camp in 1940 for attacking
national registration, and 21,000 Japanese Canadians were evacu-
ated to camps.[9] Under the Defence of Canada regulations, "enemy
aliens" were forced to report to the Registrar of Enemy Aliens, who
kept track of their movements. But conscription was never debated
in terms of citizenship, and enemy aliens could be conveniently (if
not justly) excluded from the political community. The other question, which led to creation of the Nationalities Branch, was how to
enlist the support of non-enemy aliens and naturalized Canadians of
ethnic descent. The repressive measures of the previous war –
including the notorious 1917 Wartime Elections Act which disen-
franchised immigrants born in enemy countries and naturalized
since 1902 – would be of little use in the new circumstances of
1939–45.

This question antedated the Second World War. In 1938 a Committee on Enemy Aliens and Enemy Alien Property was formed, and
the RCMP was a zealous proponent of firm measures against "radicals" and "leftists," many of whom had roots in certain ethnic communities such as Ukrainian Canadians.[10] The Bureau of Public
Information had by 1940 taken a somewhat different line in addressing the issue of "aliens" by ensuring that foreign-language
translations of speeches and other propaganda were made for Canada's ethnic communities. Opening of the Western Front in May
1940, and rapid growth of Canada's war responsibilities, demanded
a more centralized and concerted domestic war effort. The war demanded, in short, that the government mobilize all of the country's

human and material resources, and so in June 1940 the Liberal government passed the National Resources Mobilization Act.[11] A bill to create a department to manage the act was introduced and passed on 12 July 1940. The new Department of National War Services was thus created, and its first minister was James G. Gardiner, also serving as minister of agriculture. Mr. Justice T.C. Davis was appointed associate deputy minister on 23 July 1940, although he was in effect deputy minister. The department was to see an extraordinary amount of flux and reorganization over the next four years, like many other departments and agencies in Ottawa during the war, shifting and jockeying as new responsibilities and fresh challenges made their appearance. It eventually became responsible for co-ordinating the "voluntary sector" and mobilizing consent for the war effort. Citizenship policy grew directly out of this logic.

The National Resources Mobilization Act had called for emergency powers in wartime to "permit the mobilization of all of the effective resources of the nation, both human and material, for the purpose of the defence and security of Canada," and so originally it was envisaged that the department and the minister would have very expansive powers indeed. The department was in charge of national registration of all citizens, organization and co-ordination of the different forms of voluntary assistance in order to make the "most effective use of personal services or material contributions for the prosecution of the war and the welfare of the nation," and co-ordination of "existing public information services."[12] Inevitably, these duties were so wide-ranging that some of them would be delegated elsewhere. National War Services originally served as an umbrella department, which explains some of its confusing history.

For example, the Division of Human Resources, principally responsible for national registration, was concerned with available supplies of civilian labour, and in September 1942 it, as well as responsibility for the administration of the National Resources Mobilization Act, were transferred to the Department of Labour.[13] The Division of Material Resources had a hopelessly wide mandate: "to conduct such surveys as are necessary to the mobilization of the material resources of the Nation, to aid and direct the development thereof, to aid in the co-ordination of the productive efforts of the industries of the Nation, to aid in the production, maintenance and distribution of the food supplies necessary to the successful prosecution of the war, to study the future industrial development of the Nation and to assist with information necessary to the proper location of industries so that the economy of Canada may be more evenly balanced."[14] These duties clearly infringed on activities within the purview of other departments, and so the division was disbanded in August 1941.

The core of the department was formed by divisions and services transferred in its first years from the SOS. The Division of Voluntary Services was formed out of the transfer from the SOS on 30 August 1940 of the administration of the War Charities Act. This division was responsible for assessing contributions of supplies and materials to Canadian war industries. The department assumed certain responsibilities with respect to the welfare of Canadian war prisoners (e.g., the Prisoners of War Next-of-Kin Division), in harmony with the SOS. In March 1941 it took over, from the SOS, the Voluntary Service Registration Bureau, which co-ordinated offers of voluntary assistance for the defence of Canada.[15] The Division of Publicity was the nucleus of what became the Citizenship Branch some years later (see below). It arose from the Cabinet Committee on Public Information set up in December 1939. With creation of the Department of National War Services came establishment of the Bureau of Public Information – essentially the government's war propaganda arm. It was much strengthened in June 1942 with assumption of control over the Canadian Broadcasting Act and the National Film Act.[16]

Ottawa was an administrative maelstrom in 1940–41, and as agencies and departments combined and recombined like great chains of administrative DNA, the Department of National War Services also underwent organizational change. In October 1941 the minister restructured the department into six rather than four divisions. Of particular interest was the new Women's Voluntary Services Division, an outgrowth of the Voluntary Services Registration Bureau. Just shortly before the war, a "Committee of ladies under the chairmanship of Miss Margaret Hyndman, K.C., Toronto," conducted a voluntary registration of Canadian women's potential contributions to the war effort. Thousands of cards were compiled and deposited with the Voluntary Services Registration Bureau. This was the first effort at the mobilization of Canadian women, but the division was transferred to the Department of Labour in March 1942.[17] To balance this reduction in responsibilities, the department established two new services, the Nationalities Division and the Corps of Canadian Fire Fighters for Service in the United Kingdom.

As a result of all these changes, the department was not really stabilized until 1943, when it had ten divisions, of which only the Division of Voluntary and Auxiliary Services was original to its establishment. Five of its divisions were identified with voluntary efforts, so that its original character – as a sort of omnibus co-ordinator of the domestic war effort – was partly preserved. As one departmental history noted, however, this had been implied in the prime minister's original remarks on the department's establishment. Nonetheless, the "supervision and regulation of voluntary effort [were] an unknown field" for officials and politicians, especially in face of "the will of the Canadian people to contribute money, materials and personal services ... borne out by the unprecedented success of the Victory Loan Campaigns, the appeals of the Canadian Red Cross Society and other organizations interested in relief to Allied countries, the work of the National War Auxiliary Services and of hundreds of citizen's organizations for the welfare of the men and women of the Armed Forces."[18] Before creation of the Department of National War Services, the SOS had had responsibility for the Voluntary Service Registration Bureau and the War Charities Act, but administration of the voluntary sector posed difficulties: "Further, the tremendous urge on the part of the Canadian people as a whole to do something personally toward winning the war had given an impetus to many newly established organizations which carried them in some instances to a point where co-ordination and control by the Government became imperative in the best interests of all."[19]

National War Services, in addition to dealing with an entirely new area – mobilization of voluntary assistance – had suffered several other handicaps. Its first minister, James G. Gardiner, was in charge of the large and complicated agriculture portfolio and so was unable to give it his complete attention. A full-time minister, J.T. Thorson, was not appointed until 11 June 1941, or almost a year after the department was founded. Upon Thorson's resignation in October 1942, to become president of the Exchequer Court of Canada, Major-General L.R. LaFleche, who had been associate deputy minister to that point, ran in a by-election, won, and was appointed minister. LaFleche was preoccupied with his election campaign that November, however, and on 5 November 1942 the other associate deputy minister, T.C. Davis, also resigned. A new associate deputy minister (in fact, since he was the only one, the deputy minister), C.H. Payne, was not appointed until 23 March 1943. The result? "During that hiatus the Department almost fell apart. Directors of Divisions, lacking direction due to the absence of the Minister, were in many instances framing policies according to their own ideas."[20]

National War Services had thus been badly organized from the start, was plagued by odd administrative procedures and some political neglect, and for a short period had to function without any effective administrative or political leadership at all. Some of these shortcomings attracted unfavourable publicity. By 1943, however, with the transfer of some responsibilities to more appropriate departments and agencies, a tighter administrative grip, and concentration on the voluntary sector, the department was able to steady itself. It had never been anything but a wartime organization, however, and so with the advent of peace, it was rapidly dismantled. Some functions were completely disbanded and discontinued (e.g., the Directorate of Censorship), while responsibilities such as the Canadian Broadcasting Corporation (CBC) were transferred to other departments. This is what happened to the Nationalities Branch, renamed the Citizenship Branch: it went to the SOS.

THE NATIONALITIES BRANCH

The Second World War, for Canada, centred in Europe, and a natural question for Canadian authorities was what the loyalties of recent European immigrants to this country would be. The RCMP had for years kept a close watch on various Communist organizations in Canada, the members of which were disproportionately from eastern and central Europe. Estimates at the time were that one-sixth of Canada's population was "derived from recent European stocks."[21] Government authorities were reasonably confident that the "loyalty of most ethnic groups was manifested by their large enlistment and cooperation generally in war work," but they still had some reservations about the Ukrainians (who, while on the whole supportive of the Canadian war effort, were divided) and Finns.[22] "Non-ethnic" Canadians were not receptive to recent immigrants, either: "It is now realised that the most important factor in the problem of securing keener participation in the war effort by minority groups was that of winning a greater sympathy from the larger English-speaking and French-speaking communities. To look for achievement in the way of national service from groups of recently European stock without a greater degree of appreciation of what the older stocks throughout the Dominion have done is a form of blind optimism which reckons without human nature. In brief, many English-speaking citizens expect the worst and are surprised when they learn that the best has been offered by these people of foreign descent."[23] The analysis continued: "It was evident that the tremendous upheaval in Europe was bound to react with special force on those Canadian citizens of recent European origin whose homelands were being subjected directly to the impact of war. How to bring these citizens into a united Canadian war effort, how to interpret for them the war situation in terms of Canadian and not merely European interests, how to make the British and French Canadians appreciate the part which other Canadians wished to play or were playing in the war effort, how to eliminate the discrimination which was sometimes shown amongst non-British Canadians who were not infrequently called 'foreigners,' – all these points were the objects of concern to the Government."[24]

By 1940, these concerns were being addressed by an informal interdepartmental committee on which National War Services was represented. Its Bureau of Public Information had already begun to monitor the foreign-language press and media in Canada, which could affect morale. The bureau, in co-operation with the CBC, therefore helped produce the radio series "Canadians All," aimed at new Canadians. In August 1941 the Cabinet War Committee reviewed the bureau's mandate, and Thorson appeared with a plan to develop a new "Foreign Language Section."[25] By October an informal group was called together under Professor G.W. Simpson, head of the History Department at the University of Saskatchewan, to conduct a study and make recommendations. Simpson eventually suggested establishment of an Advisory Committee on Co-operation in Canadian Citizenship (CCCC). Simpson himself was then appointed in December 1941 as senior adviser to the Bureau of Public Information,[26] together with Tracy Philipps, who was made European adviser.[27] The CCCC was not established until early 1942, and then simply by ministerial order rather than by order-in-council. This fact was to be important, since the CCCC thereby lacked the cabinet's imprimatur and effectively was an advisory body to the Bureau of Information. However, Simpson was made chair of the CCCC, and he, along with Philipps and a staff of one clerk and a stenographer, was transformed into the Nationalities Branch of the department. The mobilization function of the CCCC was clear from the minister's letter of invitation to join it: "This will involve bringing to the attention of the government points of view held by these citizens. It will also mean interpreting governmental policy to them as it develops ... Not only has the Department in mind the building up of a solid Canadian front in the war, but also the continued co-operation of all Canadian citizens in the peace time to come."[28] For much of the next year, the CCCC and the new branch were simply rumps to the Bureau of Public Information, but in September 1942 the bureau was absorbed by the Wartime Information Board, which reported directly to the prime minister, and the Nationalities Branch was able to function separately as part of the Department of National War Services.

The CCCC had three meetings in 1942: on 10 January, 11 March, and 23 September.[29] Its responsibility was to act as a link between the Canadian immigrant communities and the national government. It was to "maintain contact with Canadian citizens of non-British and non-French origin and to seek to interpret their points of view to the Government and to the Canadian public generally." As well, it was to "co-operate with the Director of the Bureau of Public Information in distributing news to the foreign-language press in Canada and in explaining public policy as it develops."[30] The most practical way for the Nationalities Branch and the CCCC to perform their mandate was to monitor and advise the foreign-language press. This was no mean feat: one estimate during the war was that Canada had 73 foreign-language publications, of which 16 were German and 14 were Ukrainian. By language groups, there were 31 Slavonic publications and 25 "Teutonic" ones.[31] Accordingly, an Editorial Section was established under Dr V.J. Kaye (he had only one editorial assistant and one stenographer), both to monitor these publications (many of which received foreign-language news directly from their countries of origin) and to prepare items for publication. While it was small, the editorial section's work was important: "In general, the responsibility of a foreign-language newspaper editor is far greater than that of an ordinary weekly newspaper editor. Frequently, those who subscribe to a foreign-language newspaper rely on it for all their information and knowledge. ... Most of the foreign-language editors have to be educators and mentors of the political life of their readers as well as disseminators of news. The majority came from and were educated in a country abroad and so retain strong ties with Europe. ... The wide freedom of the Canadian press, which was not curtailed even during the war, offered great temptation to outside factors to influence the opinion of the foreign-language groups through their press and thus bring pressure to bear on the Canadian Government."[32]

The Editorial Section conducted a survey of foreign-language publications in June 1942 and began to issue regular press releases as of 1 August that year. The enormity of the task for such a small group hampered the section's effectiveness, but several other events soon conspired to throw the whole organization of the Nationalities Branch and the CCCC into disarray. Professor Simpson, who had been a driving force behind establishment of the two agencies, was forced to resign as senior adviser and head of the Nationalities Branch for reasons of ill health in the autumn of 1942. He remained chair of the CCCC, but the committee was largely advisory in any case, without a real foothold in the slippery scree of bureaucratic Ottawa. On 9 September 1942 the Bureau of Public Information was absorbed by the Wartime Information Board, which did not wish to concern itself with the foreign-language press. Thus the Nationalities Branch was left with the Department of National Wartime Services. As noted earlier, this happened to coincide with a change of ministers (from J.T. Thorson to L.R. LaFleche) and the departure of the associate deputy minister, T.C. Davis, both of which occurred in October. A new deputy minister was not appointed for six months. Before leaving, however, Davis had suggested that the work of the Nationalities Branch had not been and could not be effectively carried forward with its current administration, and he recommended that the branch be abolished. LaFleche, as minister, decided otherwise: with all of the other transfers of responsibility from his department, his portfolio was losing its breadth, and without a deputy he had to be both political and administrative head of his department, leaving him little time to consider broad reorganization. LaFleche eventually decided the next year to increase the responsibilities and hence appropriations for the branch, and in going to the House of Commons to request it, he precipitated a three-hour debate on the meaning of the branch's activities and the nature of Canadian citizenship.

The problem with the Nationalities Branch had been only partly about resources, however. The larger difficulty had been with its personnel, and in particular the European adviser, Tracy Philipps. Philipps was British, had little experience of Canada, and approached the ethnic question not from a Canadian vantage point but from a European one. This had led him to propose positions to some ethnic groups and organizations which, while consistent with the stances taken by their European countries of origin, were at odds with Canadian government and Allied policy. With Simpson's resignation and the cabinet's failure to appoint a deputy minister, Philipps effectively took over administration of the branch. A British soldier and adventurer was thus in charge of a Canadian branch of government responsible for non-English and non-French nationalities. This was an "extraordinary situation of an Advisor who was not Canadian, and with a very limited knowledge of Canada, in charge of activities the purpose of which was to teach Canadian citizenship. Being familiar only with the European pattern, he placed his emphasis on the political problems in Europe rather than the cultural contribution of these groups to Canada."[33]

The Nationalities Branch fell into obscurity for almost a year (both Philipps and Kaye were seriously ill for periods in 1943, thus impairing work even more), until LaFleche asked his deputy and the cccc to advise him. The deputy minister's report on the Nationalities Branch catalogued with cold precision the branch's ailments: the disarray following Simpson's resignation, the difficulties encountered by Philipps as he tried to maintain personal contacts with ethnic communities across the country, and the weakness of the editorial division, which, because of Kaye's illness, was "only a shell of an organization which will not be able to continue even the routine work of preparing releases for the foreign press."[34]

The CCCC met on 25–26 November 1943 in Ottawa. A small executive committee of the CCCC met in Ottawa the following January to advise the minister further on the direction of the branch. It agreed that the best course would be to attract someone of experience and calibre to reorganize the branch, secure additional staff, and prepare for the transition from war to peacetime activities. This suggestion was taken up, and Robert England, who had resigned from the CCCC in 1943, was invited to conduct a review of the branch. He arrived on 1 April 1944 and immediately set about analysing the branch's history, activities, and future. He submitted his report on 12 June 1944. Between his appointment and the receipt of his report, events moved quickly. On 27 April, LaFleche appeared before the House of Commons to request an increase in the branch's appropriations and set off Canada's first modern debate about citizenship, multiculturalism, and the government's role in the policy field. Tracy Philipps resigned his post with the Nationalities Branch on 12 May 1944, to take up a position with the United Nations Relief and Rehabilitation Administration. In combination, the Commons debate and the England Report set the course of Canadian citizenship policy for the next few decades.

LaFleche's request to the Commons consisted of a budgetary increase for the CCCC from \$18,347 to \$46,367.[35] After the preliminary jousting over detail, debate focused on several themes. There were the usual questions of proliferating committees, distrust of bureaucracy, and picayune points about administration. The central debate, however, was over citizenship and over the relationship of the state to "national groups." Some members thought it absurd that the state should be involved in trying to foster citizenship in the sense of changing people's minds about how they felt toward each other and the country as a whole. Citizenship was a purely juridical concept, and Canadians would be citizens when they determined, as a country, to declare themselves Canadian citizens, not simply British subjects.

Members wondered about the intended effect of a citizenship-cum-multiculturalism policy and about its link to immigration policy. These issues were constants in the policy debates of the 1970s and 1980s. Some speakers argued that the purpose of citizenship policies was to integrate new immigrants into the mainstream, to assimilate disparate cultures and nationalities into something homogeneously Canadian. As Thomas Reid (Liberal – NewWestminster, BC) said: "I for one, however, do not see how we can ever become a united country, and a great nation if we allow certain groups within the country to live off by themselves, speak their own language and practically carry on as they did in the country they left."[36] This view, it must be said, was a minority one in the debate. Most participants allied themselves with a principle that was to guide Canadian citizenship/multicultural policy for the next thirty years: they wished simultaneously to celebrate ethnic and linguistic diversity while holding that this celebration in itself displayed a degree of tolerance and good will somehow uniquely expressive of the true Canadian character. Real "Canadian-ness" therefore would consist in maintaining one's ethnic identity beneath a lofty canopy of shared loyalties and aspirations.

LaFleche received his appropriations in the end, thereby saving the Nationalities Branch and placing it in a fiscal and organizational position to prosper under the proper conditions. These conditions arose as a consequence of the England Report in June 1944. The document gave tepid praise to the branch's activities during the war. Several key functions had not been addressed satisfactorily at all. The releases supplied by the branch had so little intrinsic appeal (e.g., an English version of a biography of Lord Strathcona) that many key foreign-language publications had no significant Canadian news content dealing with the war. England recommended that "the time has come when a determined and intelligent effort should be made to supply our foreign-language newspapers in the language of publication – current news, items of special interest to their readers, and bright feature articles which might be helpful to them in adjusting to the Canadian scene, and in encouraging Canadian attitudes."[37] England found preoccupation with the worries of Ukrainian, Polish, and Italian immigrants about possible communist takeovers of their homelands; a properly conceived Canadian war policy would emphasize the contributions that these groups were making to the war effort. There was also the question of racial or ethnic discrimination in Canadian society. England's arguments had a modern ring in pointing out that various ethnic groups had little or no representation in the professions or government service. Fighting this "racial prejudice" would be bolstered by greater celebration of the meaning of citizenship. Some 62,188 persons had been naturalized since 1939, but the government had not offered "these entrants to Canadian citizenship any opportunity to acquire a knowledge of our institutions and our way of life."[38]

England offered several other criticisms, but they all pointed to the central question of whether the branch should be continued, or disbanded as Davis had suggested two years earlier. England's answer was unequivocal:

Not only do we appear to be missing an opportunity to win from our present national concentration on the war effort a greater Canadian unity in the future but it cannot be said that we are developing as effective a participation in the war effort as we might do. The foreign-language press situation, the lack of a program in respect of naturalization, the ignorance of the general public as to the contribution of other races to the war effort, the gap that still exists between large ethnic group communities and Canadian life, the inability to exploit other media of reaching the public and determining attitudes in this regard through broadcasting, films, speakers, literature, art, music, drama, all indicate that a more vigorous and determined policy to win the utmost in collaboration from all groups should be inaugurated.[39]

England thus recommended that the Nationalities Branch be organized as a Division of Citizenship, with a program consisting of the following tasks:

1 research into the contributions of various ethnic groups to Canadian life, and dissemination to media;
2 news service on Canadian features for the foreign-language press;
3 co-operation with the CBC in radio broadcasts aimed at ethnic communities;
4 continued co-operation with the National Film Board in the preparation of documentaries on Canadian citizenship;
5 "More effective assistance to programs of the Canadian Handicraft Guild and Friendship Councils and other bodies dealing with cultural contribution in art, music and drama";
6 support for publication of literary classics of major groups;
7 "Co-operation with the Director of the Women's Voluntary Services Division with respect to promotion of women's activities designed to assist greater participation in the national war effort and in citizenship";
8 study of ways suitably to recognize families of servicemen, derived from groups, killed in action;
9 promotion of fitness programs, incorporating folk dancing;

10 development of a citizenship training program;

11 adopting the celebration of great Europeans of various communities as Canadian occasions;

12 co-operation to assist integration of returning servicemen of European origin into Canadian Legion branches;

13 supply of speakers of ethnic origin;

14 "Study of determining factors in racial discrimination so as to reduce the determining causes. Some research has been done in this field and the results of it ought to be developed in practice";

15 examination of discrimination resulting from the difficulty of pronouncing European family names;

16 assistance to various departments in the rehabilitation of discharged servicemen of European origin;

17 "Encouraging the widening of representation on voluntary committees to include representatives of ethnic groups";

18 co-operating in the reduction of racial discrimination in housing.[40]

England went into some detail on what he considered the most important of these items – development of a citizenship training program and some formal ceremony to recognize the achievement of citizenship. There was no such thing as separate Canadian citizenship; the Naturalization Act stipulated the means whereby someone could become "naturalized" and attain British subject status while being a resident of Canada. The England Report recommended a radically new concept of citizenship. It stressed the need to incorporate training in Canadian institutions as part of citizenship training, so that achievement of naturalization would rest on some degree of familiarity with this nation's history and institutions. The report looked to the future of ethnic communities in Canada, where, with the war's end, it would be a "measure of national wisdom to attach them closely to Canadian ideals and aspirations in the interests of their own peace of mind, and of the future welfare of their children."[41]

The report called for substantial reorganization and expansion of the Nationalities Branch and clearly assumed that at some point the new Division of Citizenship would be housed in the SOS. The report was accepted and implemented almost immediately. A new director, Frank Foulds, of the renamed division was appointed on 1 August 1944, and other staff members were hired as well. The new division claimed almost immediate success in mobilizing groups in the desired direction: "Through constant contact with ethnic groups and their organizations, it has been possible to discourage them from quarrelling amongst themselves over European issues and to persuade them that their main objective should be to further their establishment in Canada. In five major national groups cohesion had been induced between Left, Right and Centre sections whose differences were largely due to political conditions in their original homelands."[42] Indeed, the division's success and new organizational strength made a voluntary advisory committee superfluous, and so the cccc was disbanded in January 1945. As already mentioned, at the end of the war the Department of National War Services was terminated, and many of its functions were transferred to other agencies. The Citizenship Division (redesignated a branch) was transferred on 1 November 1945 to the sos, where it remained until 1950, when it became part of the new Department of Citizenship and Immigration.[43]

CHAPTER FOUR

The Citizenship Branch, 1945–1968

AT SECRETARY OF STATE, 1945–1950

Frank Foulds, the new director of the Canadian Citizenship Branch, drafted a memorandum on the functions of the branch as he saw them on the eve of its November 1945 transfer to the sos.[1] The practice of celebrating the cultural heritage of new immigrants, he wrote, often had the effect of "driving the various racial groups into closed section organizations rather than in inducing them to participate in general Canadian life. If people are going to cherish a loyalty to a way of life, they must first have a feeling of pride which evolves from an active participation in that way of life."[2] Foulds saw the branch's role as being a "liaison agency," fostering citizenship after the formal certificates and ceremonies were completed (the Citizenship Bill was before Parliament).

In striving for "assimilation of people into a better Canadian citizenship," the branch would work with government agencies such as the CBC and the National Film Board, but also with various voluntary agencies. The latter included the Canadian Association for Adult Education, the Canadian Council for Education in Citizenship (with membership consisting of the nine provincial departments of education), the Canadian Library Council, the Canadian Red Cross, and the Canadian Teachers' Federation, universities and other research organizations, the press (especially the foreign language press), the Canadian Folk Society (which Foulds favoured because it encouraged a "greater consciousness of being a Canadian people"), youth organizations, community centres, women's organizations, and United Nations educational and cultural organizations.[3] The old mission of the Nationalities Branch (especially as it had evolved under Tracy Philipps) – to mobilize Canadian ethnic communities around European issues – was explicitly eschewed. "Problems" of that type would be referred to the Department of External Affairs.[4]

The branch's visibility and responsibility were enhanced with the passage of the Canadian Citizenship Act in 1946. Until 1914, naturalization required simply three years' residence, good character, and an oath of loyalty to the crown. The Naturalization Act of 1914, after massive immigration had sparked a surge of nativism, required five years' residency and knowledge of either English or French.[5] The Second World War, and indeed the activities of the Nationalities Branch, heightened the sense of a distinct Canadian citizenship that should be recognized separately from the status of being a British subject. The first Citizenship Bill was introduced by Paul Martin (secretary of state) on 22 October 1945 but died on the order paper. He reintroduced a slightly modified version on 20 March 1946, noting that one of the bill's purposes was "to provide an underlying community of status for all our people in this country that will help to bind them together as Canadians."[6] Martin pointed out later that the bill would give the Citizenship Branch an opportunity "of dealing effectively and more fully not only with foreign language newspapers but with new Canadian groups."[7] The Citizenship Act was given royal assent on 27 June 1946 and took effect the following year.

Between 1945 and 1950, the Citizenship Branch struggled for a clear mandate in a policy field crowded with various, usually more powerful, agencies. Immigration was under the aegis of the Department of Mines and Resources, while foreign affairs and their connection to Canadian ethnic communities had now been assumed by External Affairs. The Citizenship Act had the advantage of giving the branch, in somewhat vague terms, a legislated mandate. Section 37 directed the sos to take measures to provide instructional facilities for applicants so that they might learn about the "responsibilities and privileges" of citizenship. A mark of how important this was to establishing bureaucratic credibility is that the branch was not even mentioned in departmental annual reports before 1949 (by contrast, the departmental library was always prominently described). This neglect may have been caused in part by the sos's evolution toward more of an economic department: by 1949, its main activities comprised incorporation of companies, registration of patents and copyrights, company registrations, and trademarks. The branch was increasingly anomalous within this range of responsibilities.

In light of its limited resources, the branch focused on those things that it could do cheaply, which amounted largely to writing and circulating short pamphlets and maintaining contacts with ethnic and other organizations. A memorandum in November 1949 clearly demonstrated the logic of this minimalist strategy. Since education came under provincial jurisdiction, the memo noted, the branch's contribution had been limited to supporting production of pamphlets and textbooks such as "The Canadian Scene" and the "Canadian Citizenship Series."[8] The branch's assimilationist bent was evident in its description of future pamphlets which would try to convey "our philosophy of life which is often referred to as 'the Canadian way of life'."

Limited staff resources forced the branch to work through voluntary groups, the majority of which fortunately "are joined together in provincial and national organizations."

These provide avenues for effective work. Outstanding amongst these are the youth organizations. The women's organizations accomplish a great deal and influence the whole community. The men's service clubs, Boards of Trade, Farm Federations, etc., constitute another group. One of the most effective places of contacting the newcomers is at their place of employment or through labour unions. The big majority of immigrants belong to ethnic groups where their own language is spoken, and they subscribe to newspapers in that language. Our liaison staff works constantly with these groups. In addition there are, of course, the church and school organizations. Our liaison staff working out of Ottawa and those at our Regional Offices will do our biggest job as they assist these voluntary organizations in conducting worthwhile citizenship programs.[9]

Try as it might, however, the branch found that its activities continued to grow more anomalous within the setting of the sos. It was fortunate then that in 1950 the government decided to shift the branch over to a newly created Department of Citizenship and Immigration. Ironically, however, the reorganization had little to do with the branch itself or the integrity of its programs. The rationale was rooted in larger considerations pertaining to the dismantling of the last vestiges of wartime government organization.

AT CITIZENSHIP AND IMMIGRATION, 1950–1966

In 1944 the government had established the Department of Reconstruction under C.D. Howe. The department was to manage some of the industrial policies that Ottawa had promised would achieve levels of high and steady employment in post-war Canada. By 1948 the department's original policy objectives (e.g., conversion of war-time industries to peacetime industries, restoration of railways and highways, public works, and housing) had been devolved to other ministries (Howe himself left to become minister of trade and commerce); all that remained were housing, public projects, and tourism. Tourism was its prominent function, and since the department had been always been conceived as a temporary one, by 1949 the government was looking for existing ministries to which these last responsibilities could be transferred. Mines and Resources seemed a natural choice, because of its responsibility for immigration, but as Prime Minister Louis St Laurent noted on introducing the parliamentary resolution: "That department, however, already was rather unwieldy, and the government concluded that it would not be reasonable simply to add further functions to that department."[10] St Laurent outlined the connection among the branch, immigration, and Native Indian affairs.

It has also been apparent for some time that the relationship between the citizenship branch, under my colleague the Secretary of State, and the immigration branch, under the jurisdiction of the Minister of Mines and Resources, should be as close as possible. The citizenship branch is designed to bring to full citizenship as many as possible of those who immigrate to this country. The scope of the citizenship branch has been expanded since the passing of the citizenship act. It was felt that uniformity of policy and treatment was more likely to be achieved if one minister had the responsibility for both immigration activities and the activities pursued by this branch of the government to bring those immigrants as quickly as could reasonably be expected to full citizenship ...

Once the decision had been reached to recommend the establishment of a Department of Citizenship and Immigration, it was considered that the minister responsible for this department should, in addition, be given the responsibility for the Indian affairs branch ... Having citizenship, immigration and Indian affairs in the one department would indicate that the purpose of the activities of that department was to make Canadian citizens of those who were born here of the original inhabitants of the territory, or those who migrated to this country.[11]

The branch was transferred, and the new department came into being on 18 January 1950. The immigration component was much larger and more visible than the Citizenship Branch, but the branch now had the comfort of at least being in an organizational environment more congenial to its activities. The department's first annual report, for example, described the branch's function glowingly as "to promote unity among all racial groups; to awaken in every Canadian, regardless of race or creed, a deep conviction of the worth of the individual and the principles of democracy; and to encourage a greater consciousness among our people of the achievements of the Canadian nation and the fact that all Canadians actively share in these achievements."[12]

Under its new auspices, the branch had three divisions: Liaison, Information, and Research. The Liaison Division was "concerned with the coordination of citizenship training programs sponsored by provincial departments of education and national organizations and societies." It maintained contact with voluntary educational bodies such as l'Association canadienne des éducateurs de langue française, the Canadian Association for Adult Education, the Canadian Citizenship Coucil, the Canadian Education Association, and la Société canadienne d'éducation post-scolaire. A youth liaison officer worked with organizations such as the Canadian Committee of Youth Services and the Co-ordinating Committee of Canadian Youth Corps. Liaison worked also with women's groups; the 1950 Annual Report noted that "in a large number of voluntary organizations dealing more particularly with Canadian problems and programs the membership is composed of women. They have exerted an enormous influence on ordinary Canadian matters and those dealing particularly with the immigrant." Organizations included the Canadian Federation of University Women, the Catholic Women's League, the Federation of Women's Institutes, the Imperial Order of Daughters of the Empire, and the National Council of Women.

The Information Division was "responsible for the preparation and distribution of material to the foreign language press, and to organizations and individuals requesting information of a general citizenship character." The division therefore produced a bulletin of Canadian news and information for foreign-language news editors in Canada. The Research Division was to produce citizenship training manuals and data relating to ethnic and cultural groups. It prepared booklets in the Canadian citizenship series (*Our Land, Our History, Our Government,* and *Our Resources*), and fifteen filmstrips on Canadian geography, history, and government; it compiled statistics relating to years of residence in Canada and ages of people filing declarations of intention to become citizens.

For a brief time in 1950, with the possibility of Korean hostilities looming, it seemed that the Citizenship Branch might once again wield some of its old wartime mobilization functions. On 8 September 1950 Foulds was asked to think about the branch's role in a possible wartime emergency. His written response to the deputy min-

ister observed that the "work that we are doing with women's organizations, youth groups, and especially with the foreign language
groups, will be even more valuable to the country in a time of emergency than in a period of peace. We have built up contacts with hundreds of voluntary agencies which will need co-ordination with one
another and with government agencies."[13] On 3 October, however,
Foulds had an indication that the deputy was contemplating a much
enhanced role for the branch, going well beyond simple liaison with
the foreign press and ethnic organizations:"At a meeting this morn-
ing the deputy minister went much further than he has before. He
asked me to submit recommendations whereby the work which we
are doing in Regional Offices might be done in a greater number of
centres. Apparently his thinking is that whereas in World War II
committees were set up under the Wartime Information Board,
Wartime Prices and Trade Board, and the Department of National
War Services to urge people not to hoard, to contribute to the war
effort, and generally to maintain a high morale, this work in a future
emergency might well be undertaken by the Citizenship Branch if
they can show that they are ready for it."[14]

Two weeks later Foulds made his case to the deputy minister in
outlining the virtues of allowing the branch to be the central co-
ordinating agency for mobilizing the Canadian, especially ethnic,
population during wartime. He argued that the way to encourage
the right attitude toward rationing versus hoarding was to reach individuals through groups in the community, something at which the
branch's liaison officers were already adept (though Foulds took the
opportunity to decry his staff shortages in this respect). Nothing but
chaos would arise if each department of government requiring public support for some program sent officers to contact voluntary
groups: "The constant contact of our Branch with voluntary agencies would adapt us to be the logical co-ordinating body. A unified
policy is essential to building morale."[15] The Korean hostilities,
while involving Canada, did not require mobilization on the scale of
the Second World War, and so the branch's brief grasp for some
greater glory was barren.

How did the branch understand itself on the threshold of the new
decade? What, in modern terms, was its corporate culture and its
bureaucratic ethos? A glimpse of this comes from the proceedings of
the branch's first annual conference, 20–25 August 1951.[16] In his
opening remarks to the small group, Frank Foulds, the branch's director, reminded participants that they preferred the term "integration" to "assimilation," because the adjustments involved in immigration took place on both sides, among "established" as well as

"new" Canadians. The branch was devoted to education and liaison, not social change or the more vigorous mobilization that had been characteristic of the war period. Indeed, Foulds drew a portrait of a rather cautious organization:

In our work as officials of the Canadian Citizenship Branch we must keep in mind certain factors of good judgment. As federal civil servants we must not voice our opinion on controversial matters, and we must not become too enthusiastic in the promotion of programs which are outside our scope. While it goes without saying that we must not play politics and must respect the political opinions of other people, we must include in our "don'ts" several other things that are "just not done." Tact and good judgment would assume that we respect the religious opinions and church affiliations of the persons on the committees with which we deal. We recognize that education is the prerogative of the Provinces, and that the organization of classes, even for immigrants, comes under the jurisdiction of the Provincial Departments of Education. While we look with favour on various members of the staff making personal contributions on school boards, club executives, etc., we should not place ourselves in a position where we are unacceptable to one or more groups because of our too evident enthusiasms as an office holder in another group. [17]

The minister, Walter Harris, attended the conference briefly and suggested that he and his cabinet colleagues would like to have a fresh statement of the branch's aims and objectives. Foulds responded within weeks with a short memo that wove together the various complex and colourful strands of the branch's activities. The branch's overriding purpose was to "foster good citizenship in all Canadians." [18] This general goal required that the public recognize several principles, the most prominent of which were: "(1) the individual citizen, regardless of his race, colour or religion, is invaluable to the nation. (2) the government of Canada, as in any true democracy, is elected to serve the interests of the people. (3) the responsibilities of the citizenship in Canada require the individual to be loyal to our democratic institutions; to accept public service readily if called upon to do so; to co-operate fully with his elected representatives and his fellow citizens in making Canada a better nation in which to live. (4) national unity is only possible through the close co-operation and ultimate integration of our various ethnic groups." [19]

The statement made only the most oblique reference to "supporting" voluntary organizations that were active in the citizenship field. Indeed, in 1951–52, for the first time, the branch provided grants totalling $20,000 to only four groups: Camp Laquemac, Macdonald College ($1,000), Canadian Association for Adult Education ($6,000), Canadian Citizenship Council ($10,000), and la Société canadienne d'enseignement ($3,000). As one history of the branch comments: "It is important to observe that the grants were not to be used for general purposes by the organizations concerned. Sustaining grants were frowned upon as tending to insulate the recipients against the need for public endorsation or support."[20] In 1952–53, these groups received identical amounts and were joined by the Faculty of Social Sciences, Laval University ($5,000), and by the University of Toronto ($5,000).[21] These latter were included because the branch had established an Economic and Social Research Division which, because of its small staff, contracted out much of its research.

The reason for the minimal number and size of the grants had to do with more than the normal budgetary constraints of a small agency in the federal bureaucracy. As Frank Foulds's admonishments at the branch's first annual conference and the statement of goals suggested, there was a philosophy that underlay and rationalized the branch's limited activities. Foulds's caution came from years of dealing with a wide variety of ethnic associations which would interpret overt support for one group as favouritism toward a given nationality. The stance of the branch's liaison officers was therefore to be helpful but neutral and to offer advice without judgment, direction without coercion, and support without favouritism. In a sense, the branch operated on a conceptual terrain where the "true" Canadian citizen (in a process of "becoming") lay somewhere between the raw ethnicity of newcomers and the smug complacency of "established" Canadians.

This was mobilization of a sort, but far less vigorous than what had been necessary during the war. It was also, in a paradoxical sense, the mobilization of passivity. The branch repeatedly made it clear that its concept of citizenship hinged on a pan-Canadianism that treasured some common "Canadian" history, had expunged any lingering prejudices, and was soberly aware of its responsibilities. Responsible citizenship was, in the branch's view, a matter of recognizing one's duties to one's country. In language that would perhaps strike the contemporary, Charter of Rights and Freedoms–conscious observer as peculiar, the branch never mentioned "rights." For all its talk of reaching individuals through their groups, the branch in fact operated with a quaintly organic view of society: its mission was to help groups weld together individuals in a common community cognizant of its duty to support responsible, democratic government. As we shall see shortly, the rhetoric of "citizen participation" of the late 1960s signalled a shift in the branch's view of the proper scope of mobilization from a passive to an active mode.

In the early 1950s it made no great sense to branch officials to offer grants to groups. Organizations would arise naturally among new nationalities arriving in Canada. The limited grants in those early years stand more as exceptions than as examples of accepted practice: the Canadian Citizenship Council absorbed almost half of the funds, and it was in effect an administrative adjunct to the department and the branch. Program philosophy and budgetary exigency thus encouraged the branch to see itself as a careful facilitator and educator, a helping hand drawing groups into the mainstream. As the 1952 annual report put it, "the branch continued to assist governmental or non-governmental agencies engaged in or interested in facilitating the adjustment and integration of newcomers and in making Canadians conscious of their privileges and responsibilities as citizens." The Liaison Division concentrated on the reception of newcomers by Canadians. The branch assisted in the organization of folk festivals and attempted "to bring the work of artists among the newcomers to the attention of the Canadian public and to introduce them to Canadian artists."

Provision of grants was nonetheless problematic for the branch.[22] From its inception as a department, Citizenship and Immigration had included some small provision in its estimates for "facilities for citizenship instruction." The Canadian Citizenship Council received most of the money.[23] Soon, however, the council was lobbying for support of overhead expenses rather than merely projects. Jean Boucher, special assistant to Laval Fortier, deputy minister of citizenship and immigration, wrote a memo on 19 December 1951 outlining some of the difficulties. He noted that the council "have a notion that they should provide us with a detailed statement of some of their expenses to which the Department would be willing to apply a grant."[24] The council would normally expect a grant of about $5,000, but Boucher noted that its incidental expenses (that is, after salaries, travel, housing, and financing) amounted to less than this.

Boucher was irritated with the council's method of calculation, calling it a "childish mathematical feat;" he could not discern why the department should pay for salaries of council staff and wondered about providing grants that the council itself would then control and distribute.[25] He concluded that the department had only two alternatives: "either to give the grant without check on its detailed application, or to make our own choice of certain suitable items out of a complete financial statement of expenditures (passed and prospective) which the Council would be willing to let us have."[26] The council's attitude was quite different; indeed, it had taken a somewhat proprietary view of the grants that it had received, writing at one point to the deputy minister and referring to the department's "appropriation earmarked for the Council." Laval Fortier replied stiffly: "I wish to say that we have no appropriation in our estimates earmarked for the Council. The amount of whatever grant is being paid to your Council is determined each year."[27]

By late 1953 the department was beginning to see an "increasing number of requests for financial assistance by organizations and agencies engaged in citizenship promotion" and decided that it needed a policy,[28] which was announced in December 1953. Apart from the normal platitudes about avoiding duplication and waste, the new directive stipulated that grants would have to be made "for a specific project or program" undertaken by the organization best suited to the function. Three clauses formed the heart of the directive:

(d) The organization or agency would be expected to submit a plan in sufficient detail that its value could be appraised and duplication avoided. The submission should suggest a plan which would have a definite conclusion, in a publication, report of research, or holding of conferences, etc.; or it might be used for a specific period to initiate a work which would be continued afterwards with public support once its value was proven;

(e) The plan would be submitted in advance so that provision can be made for the grant. The budget, which would accompany such a detailed plan, might include service costs and special salaries for the project, but not any part of the administrative expenses of the organization concerned. The Branch would not wish to control methods and management, beyond approval of the plan. This would be the responsibility of the organization concerned;

(f) A report would be expected within a reasonable time, on the conclusion of the project or on the progress of an on-going work, including a report on use of the money spent, since the Department must be prepared, at all times, to account for the funds so expended.[29]

Predictably, the groups that had enjoyed an unstructured relationship with the branch were displeased with this more formal approach. The new procedure was discussed at the 14 January 1954 meeting of the Canadian Citizenship Council. John Kidd, the executive director, apprised the meeting of the new policy and noted that it would require "planning 6 to 18 months ahead."[30] The definition of a "project" was vague, and in any case, service organizations like his spent a large portion of their funds on staff salaries.[31]

Later in the year, under continued pressure from both the council and other groups, the department had two further occasions to enunciate its grants policy. The stakes were higher than might have appeared from the number of funded groups or the amounts awarded (not over $10,000). In grasping the nettle of a grants policy, the department and branch were forced to consider the more philosophical question of the proper relation of the state to the voluntary sector. This was clear, for example, in a letter from Walter Harris to Frank Patton (the president of the Canadian Citizenship Council) on 16 July 1954, discussing funding. Harris claimed that the department had had extensive liaison over the years with various voluntary associations "without attempting in any way to influence the choice of programs of the organizations"[32]: "It is because it is sincerely believed that voluntary organizations should secure their primary support from private sources that it is considered desirable to provide financial assistance in support of specific activities rather than the whole program of any organization. ... In promoting responsible citizenship, the Department's grants should not be used purely for the general maintenance and administration of voluntary organizations. Practically all voluntary agencies are engaged in citizenship promotion in one form or another, and general support of voluntary agencies would lead to endless demands for financial support. In fact, it was evidence of such ever-widening demands that prompted, in some measure, the revision of the policy with respect to grants."[33]

The minister's letter intimated that other reasons, besides "ever-widening demands" for grants, had prompted the new policy. Eugene Bussière, director of the Citizenship Branch, articulated those other reasons in a memorandum to the deputy minister later that year. He pointed out that from an administrative point of view, project-based funding was less threatening to groups than core funding, since cuts in projects would not affect a group or organization that was otherwise healthy. This was an important consideration, since the Treasury Board was of the view that grants, once given to organizations, were withdrawn only with difficulty. "Moreover, the branch is interested in working closely with the organizations it supports and, if grants are given, the branch can more easily be associated in the planning and execution of these projects, when the grant is transmitted directly."[34] In short, the branch was loath simply to turn money over to "service" organizations that would then parcel it out to other groups, thereby getting credit without incurring cost.[35] The branch wished to maintain its own relations with groups and organizations through project-based funding.[36]

The irony of the branch's concerns about a proper grants policy is that it was in a very real sense a victim of its own success. With thin resources but robust ambitions, the branch relied on its contacts with groups. But most of the groups dedicated to development of Canadian citizenship did not exist before the branch did. Far from responding to swelling demand by organizations and groups, the branch, and the state in the larger sense as forger of the concept of Canadian citizenship, created a "space" – a new terrain of political practice – into which societal and organizational energies could flow. The groups were not creatures of the branch; but the branch had, in a direct and concrete way, given substance to a new range of organizational agendas – working for citizenship. It had also, through its promotional activities and ad hoc support for organizations such as the Canadian Citizenship Council, created a constituency that increasingly found the idea of "core funding" attractive.

These points are amply illustrated in a 1955 review of the branch's activities and its future plans. The minister had requested a "general statement on the background and record of the branch along with recommendations or proposals for its future development and growth" and so branch personnel obliged by producing a review of their activities.[37] By the mid-1950s the branch was increasingly occupied with the integration of immigrants, the numbers of which had surged dramatically since the war and would jump again in a year with the influx of Hungarians fleeing after the 1956 uprising. The report noted, however, that the "popular interest in citizenship came with the Canadian Citizenship Act."[38] "Most organizations inaugurated citizenship programs, appointed citizenship convenors and began to look to the branch, then under the Secretary of State, for suggestions, speakers, and materials in their program. Such organizations ranged from Chamber of Commerce, and service clubs, to the Home and School Associations, church groups, youth groups (including Scouts and Guides who have Citizenship Badgework) and a wide range of women's organizations."[39] Despite this view of its importance, the branch was not prepared to recommend anything but its standing practice of "careful attention to project grants with a definite policy of not providing permanent support."[40]

These claims of singular importance and general popularity might be expected from any bureau submitting a report to its superior. But the branch was in fact accurately describing the results of a complex coupling of state and societal interests. For example, by 1956 the branch had extended its services to the national and local offices of twenty-six separate ethnic groups in Canada: Armenian, Austrian, Chinese, Czech and Slovak, Danish, Doukhobor, Estonian, Finnish, German, Greek, Hungarian, Hutterite, Indian (Sikh), Italian, Japanese, Jewish, Latvian, Lithuanian, Mennonite, Negro, Netherlands, Norwegian, Polish, Swiss, Ukrainian, and Yugoslavian.[41] As the branch proudly proclaimed, it had "extended its services to a variety of non-ethnic voluntary organizations and interest groups across Canada, both to national offices and the numerous local organizations."[42] Table 4.1 shows just how far-flung the branch's connections were.

The scope of contacts reflected the practical and potential scope of the branch's activities. By the late 1950s the branch saw itself playing a role larger than the mere integration of immigrants. This role, though in practical terms the real basis for the branch's existence and rooted in a tradition that extended back to the Nationalities Branch in Second World War, was incidental to its larger purpose: "the ultimate goals had to do with national unity."[43] Citizenship and national unity were so broad a mandate that the branch had found itself drawn into much closer and wider contacts with voluntary associations than it had at first anticipated: "As this program developed it became clear that, after the first period of language training and adjustment, the program for integration and citizenship training of immigrants is not, in voluntary organizations, separated from other aspects of their citizenship activities."[44] In short, the dual focus on citizenship and integration had inexorably led the branch to project itself into wider and wider circles of societal activity. Assistance to newcomers was direct and reasonably constricted; "integration" had a broader logic.

As was noted earlier, the integration process was double-edged: immigrants had to develop a satisfactory sense of their obligations and attune themselves to Canadian-ness; established Canadians had to open themselves and their organizations to the newcomers. The concern with discrimination flowed directly from the concept of citizenship: true integration would mean treatment of the immigrant as a Canadian, and citizenship implied an equal place in a political community. The branch restrained itself on grants and deliberately clung to the view that voluntary agencies were the prime actors in the field. Its policy reflected, in short, an inchoate social theory. Citizenship policy assumed that integration, or the blending (if not eradication) of differences, was its ultimate goal. The logical policy instrument was education and the strategic support of projects that would eventually have an educational impact, both for immigrants and for "established Canadians." The branch was not out to change

Canadian society or mobilize against systemic prejudice or problems. Indeed, insofar as it thought about "the system," it saw it in largely benign terms.

This somewhat constrained and limited (in comparison to what arose in the late 1960s) matrix of assumptions did not of course foreclose expansion. It simply directed that expansion along a well-worn path. In the late 1950s, for instance, the branch became more involved with Native Indians and Métis as more of them began to leave reserves for urban areas. The branch could quite easily accommodate this new responsibility by conceiving of it as simply a matter of "internal migration," an analogue of overseas immigration. Thus the branch saw itself working to "encourage the integration of Indians into the Canadian community."[45] Its interest in immigration, refugees, and discrimination also made it a natural focus for the state's expertise on human rights and liaison with UN bodies. In 1955–56, the branch took over responsibility for payments of miscellaneous grants from the Department of Finance. While this was largely a technical transfer of minor administration, it signified the branch's expansion. The 1956 annual report noted that "the purpose of these grants is to assist in the promotion of citizenship." The branch also gave financial or other support to conferences on inter-group relations or leadership such as the Seminar on Human Relations, University of British Columbia; the Western Citizenship Conference for Young Adults, Banff School for Fine Arts, Alberta; the Intergroup Relations Conference, Lake Couchiching, Ontario; Laquemac – Lake Chapleau; and the Volunteer Training Institute, New Canadians Service Association of Ontario. By 1959 the branch had evolved a separate section entitled Assitance to Community Organizations.

This integrationist or assimilationist approach to citizenship was, at the end of the decade, broadly consistent with the tenor of high government policy. From the perspective of later years, when citizenship policy shifted to emphasize protection and preservation of minorities, the assimilationist approach might have appeared inconsistent, but it was grounded in the view that while cultural characteristics should indeed be respected, only individual rights should be protected. The philosophy undergirding Prime Minister John Diefenbaker's Canadian Bill of Rights of 1960 expressed this view perfectly. Diefenbaker had fought for a Bill of Rights since 1947 and introduced legislation to that effect in 1958. He saw the bill as negating what he called "hyphenated Canadianism" and ending "discrimination on a basis of race, creed, or colour."[46] He consistently defended his approach to human rights in terms of rejection of "second-class citizenship" grounded in the particularisms of race or

Table 4.1
Associations served by the Canadian Citizenship Branch, 1956

RELIGIOUS

Baptist churches of Canada
Canadian Council of Churches
− and local councils of Churches
− and in many cities the Church of All Nations
Catholic Women's Leagues
Presbyterian churches
Salvation Army
United Church of Canada

SERVICE CLUBS

B'nai B'rith
Chamber of Commerce and Junior Chamber of Commerce
Canadian Legion
Kiwanis Club
Lions Club
Rotary International Club

WELFARE, YOUTH, ADULT EDUCATION, IMMIGRANT SERVICES,
WOMEN'S GROUPS, ETC.

L'Accord
Boards of Trade
Boy Scouts
British and Foreign Bible Society
Business and professional women's clubs
Canadian Association for Adult Education
− and Joint Planning Commission and several provincial Joint
    Planning Commissions
Canadian Colonization Association
Canadian Council of Christians and Jews
Canadian Federation of Agriculture
− provincial and local federations of agriculture
Canadian Institute of Public Affairs
Canadian Mental Health Association
Canadian Welfare Council
− and provincial and local welfare councils
Caritas Canada
Children's Aid societies
Citizens' Forum
Citizenship councils
Community programme organizations
La Cordée
Councils of Friendship
Councils of social agencies
Ethnic press
Folk festival organizations
Folk schools

4H Clubs
Girl Guides
Home and school associations
Inter-ethnic councils
IODEs
Labour unions
Manitoba Historical Society
Mozart Centennial Committee (Edmonton)
National Farm Radio Forum
New Canada Press Club (Winnipeg)
Personnel divisions of many large companies and corporations
    such as Aluminum of Canada, Ltd
Public libraries
Radio and TV stations
Red Cross
Le service d'accueil aux voyageurs
Sisters of Service
Société d'aide aux immigrants
Société de St-Jean-Baptiste
United Co-Ops of Ontario
United Farmers of Alberta
Universities
– faculties
– extension departments
– international houses
– overseas student organizations
Victorian Order of Nurses
Women's Institutes and Homemaker Clubs
YMCA
YWCA

Source: National Archives of Canada, RG 6, Department of Secretary of State Files, ACC 86-87/ 319, file 1-1, R. Alex Sim (acting director, Citizenship Branch) to R.J. Nichols (Technical Services, Department of Citizenship and Immigration), 18 July 1956, 4–5.

ethnicity. A minor triumph was the insertion in the 1961 Census of the option to declare oneself simply "Canadian" rather than a member of some ethnic group.[47] The Bill of Rights was almost entirely Diefenbaker's invention and did not have passionate support in cabinet.[48] It received only a lukewarm reception in the legal community.[49] Most damaging, however, its approach to citizenship would ultimately clash with emerging Quebec sensibilities: "Diefenbaker's failure to understand French Canada was also illustrated by his Canadian Bill of Rights, which he considered the greatest achievement of his political career. In his Saskatchewan experience, ethnic minorities wanted to eliminate invidious distinctions and merge with the English-speaking majority. His bill reflected this experience by protecting all citizens against the exercise of arbitrary power by the federal government, regardless of their race or ethnic origin. ... But to

French-Canadians, Diefenbaker's emphasis on individual rights ignored their rigthts as a cultural group, and his ideal of "unhyphenated Canadianism" seemed to them to be a policy of assimilation."[50]

The Citizenship Branch had therefore operated with consistent regard for the prevailing wisdom on citizenship and integration since 1945. This consistency had given it a somewhat stodgy reputation with the Ottawa bureaucracy, but, more important, its connection to Citizenship and Immigration had meant that its activities would always be associated with and eclipsed by immigration matters in the department. Freda Hawkins notes that the relationship between the branch and the department had "not been very satisfactory."[51] The branch's involvement in essentially educational activities meant that it constantly trenched upon provincial jurisdiction and had to restrict itself to an advisory rather than to a managerial role. As Hawkins says: "But because its functions were largely advisory, because it was not integrated with the basic operations of the Immigration Branch, and because it received minimal government support for all its activities, the Citizenship Branch remained an appendage to the Department, a rather unimportant appendage with very limited resources."[52] Indeed, the branch's moves into the Native, human rights, citizenship development, and bilingualism areas, all features of the late 1950s and early 1960s, came as a result of encroachments from the larger departmental statutory responsibilities for immigration.

Initially, the small Citizenship Branch, with the Department of Citizenship and Immigration, concentrated its activities with a great deal of enthusiasm on immigrants and ethnic organizations in the Canadian community and related questions. But as the operations of the Immigration Branch expanded from 1950 onwards, its direct responsibility for immigrants, which the Citizenship Branch did not have, drew the Immigration Branch further into the settlement and integration areas. At the same time, the Citizenship Branch and its small Field Service, while they did not lose their interest in ethnic groups, became increasingly absorbed in the other activities for which they had become responsible: Indian integration, human rights, citizenship development and leadership training, and, later, bilingualism and biculturalism.[53]

The branch was lost in the labyrinthine bowels of a department whose responsibilities had grown steadily with the surge in immigration. A measure of the ease with which it could be overlooked in official Ottawa is the small squall that blew up over its participation in planning for the Centennial in 1967 of Canadian Confederation. Official committees were already being struck in 1959, and the branch had been asked to sit on those, but the pace picked up in 1963 with establishment of a senior committee entitled the Interdepartmental Committee on 1967 Celebrations. It was chaired by the commissioner of the Centennial Commission and had representation from key departments – all, that is, except Citizenship and Immigration. The acting director of the branch wrote testily to the deputy minister in October 1963 to protest the exclusion of his agency:

Additionally, however, I feel that I must again raise the question of departmental representation on the Interdepartmental Committee that has been established. As you know, the Citizenship Branch is the only agency of Government that is directly charged with promoting national unity and a greater degree of understanding and appreciation of Canadian institutions and traditions among all Canadians. ... While the present membership of the Committee is not questioned, the absence of a Member from this Department would unquestionably be the subject of comment among the agencies and groups that look to us for leadership and guidance in planning programs and projects in the field of citizenship and inhibit our effectiveness in sharing in the governmental effort toward ensuring the success of the Centennial.[54]

The branch and department won that battle,[55] but the fact that the skirmish had occurred at all suggested that the branch was far less visible in official Ottawa than it imagined itself to be throughout the voluntary sector in the country.

The branch's weaknesses were not lost on senior management in the department. The Liberal party won the 1963 federal election, prompting an evaluation of the various branches. One thrust was to bring in new personnel, and C.M. Isbister was appointed deputy minister. He was unhappy with the Citizenship Branch. He thought that the boundaries between it and the other branches in the department had been allowed to blur. "The personnel of the Citizenship Branch will have a far more concrete schedule of duties and priorities than in the past and will be increasingly in the position of providing services in response to expressed needs. They have gone too far in the direction of becoming a sort of generalized adult education and community service organization."[56] The history of the branch confirms this view: by the early 1960s the branch was involved in "attempting to solve problems that were inherent in today's complex way of life" and was orienting itself around the concept of "citizenship development." Community development and human rights also were claimed as areas of concern.[57]

In the next two years the Immigration, Citizenship Registration, and Indian Affairs branches were restructured to be more independent and less reliant on general departmental resources. This change raised the question of the role of the Citizenship Branch, which, as Isbister had noted, had become a generalized community service organization active in all three areas – immigration, registration, and Native affairs. As one branch memo candidly observed, the reorganization of the other branches necessitated a clear definition from the government as to its expectations for Citizenship. The agency, originally "commissioned to facilitate the integration of immigrants has become ... mainly involved in non-immigrant questions."[58]

The memorandum commented that one possible answer to the branch's dilemma was simply to disband its non-immigrant, non–Native Indian functions, leading to disbanding of the branch itself and incorporation of existing branch staff into other segments of Citizenship and Immigration. The document did not, however, recommend such radical measures:

The Branch would like not only to be confirmed in its non-immigrant, non-Indian role butto [sic] have that role become its main responsibility. The preference of the branch would be for a responsibility which could be defined as "helping all elements in the Canadian fabric contribute their full potential to society." ... A number of provinces have community programs and other forms of extension services designed to help in the leisure time activities of their citizens. The time has come for the federal government to commission a similar service on a national basis which would seek to involve people in voluntary projects not merely of a local and provincial nature, but mainly at the national and international level.

The specific areas of responsibility of this new agency would be very similar to those which the Citizenship Branch now has except for the quasi-staff role which the branch is playing vis-à-vis Immigration, Indian Affairs and Citizenship Registration. Its specific fields of responsibilities would be voluntary action, youth groups, intergroup relations, human rights, citizenship, community organization, research and experimental grants.[59]

The memo followed these promising phrases with a list of actions that might be undertaken under the various sub-headings. A close reading shows, however, that even at this point, with its survival imperilled, the branch had difficulty imagining a role much different from the one that it had been playing for the previous twenty years. Voluntary action, for example, included liaison with church groups, service clubs, and welfare and educational associations. Under human rights, the branch saw connections with civil liberties leagues, provision of educational materials, and Canadian application of international conventions and declarations. It was the comments on grants policy, however, that betrayed the full weight of tradition on the branch's thinking: *"Grant Program: –* in areas that are so close to the intimate aspirations of individual citizens, it would be ill-advised for a government agency to attempt to play more than an enabling and encouraging role. Each segment of the public would accept responsibility for its own programs but could rely on grants from the federal government much in the same way, though on a broader scale, as is being done under the present grant program of the Citizenship Branch."[60]

The review of the branch's role and its place in the department became enmeshed in a larger governmental reorganization that saw immigration matters being tied more directly to labour market considerations. In 1965, with the Government Organization Act, a new Department of Manpower and Immigration was created to fulfil this reconceptualization of the immigration field. It also led to an agreement, as the preceding memorandum suggested, to sever the immigration role from the Citizenship Branch and focus its energies on broader citizenship aspects. This could, of course, involve immigrants, but it would not be the "integration" role that had served as the branch's rationale at the end of the Second World War. The branch was thus moved out of the new department (with which it no longer had any logical or necessary connection) and back to the sos, where it had begun its organizational life in 1945.

By the 1960s, the sos had become little more than a repository for the higher symbols of state such as the great seal and a service bureau for the rest of the government through its translation facilities. It retained its vestigial responsibility for the state's relations with civil society, however, and so was a ripe candidate for enhancement when politicians began to cast about for a larger cultural and community role for the federal state. This was a result of the nationalist surge in Quebec after the election of Jean Lesage's Liberals in 1960. Since the war, Quebec's political and economic development had lagged behind the rest of Canada. Under Maurice Duplessis and the Union Nationale, Quebec society remained insular and distinctly traditional. With Duplessis's death in 1959 and the collapse of his party, the Liberals promised (somewhat ambiguously, it must be admitted) to bring Quebec firmly into the twentieth century. Frustrations so long repressed finally had an opportunity for expression, and Quebec began a long period of extraordinarily rapid change in every crevice and contour of its social and political structure.

Nationalist sentiments were inflamed and found a target in the province's apparent economic domination by Westmount's anglophones and political domination by Ottawa. A small but articulate group of anti-nationalists – Jean Marchand, Gérard Pelletier, and Pierre Trudeau among them – was concerned that nationalism could quickly transform into a political movement for separation. A strategy would have to be developed to demonstrate that Ottawa was not insensitive to Quebec's aspirations and to foster a stronger sense of allegiance to pan-Canadian institutions. The Royal Commission on Bilingualism and Biculturalism (the Laurendeau-Dunton Commission) and the Centennial celebrations were reflections of this strategy, and in 1965 the commission argued that the conflicts that it had investigated threatened the very fundamentals of the state itself. Gérard Pelletier recalls that "the Trudeau team's behaviour, the options before it, the goals it set for itself and the thrust of the action it took" must be set against the fact that the "Canadian federation was experiencing the most serious crisis in its history."[61]

In 1961 Lesage's government had established a Department of Cultural Affairs, as a counterweight to the Canada Council, which it saw in part as an instrument of Anglo-Canadian culture. In 1963 Lester Pearson's Liberal government also decided to pay more attention officially to culture and support for the arts. Maurice Lamontagne was made secretary of state and starting in 1963, received responsibility for the Board of Broadcast Governors (predecessor to the Canadian Radio-Television and Telecommunications Commission), the Canada Council, the CBC, the Centennial Commission, the National Film Board, the National Gallery, the National Library and Public Archives, National Museums, and the Queen's Printer. The Citizenship Branch was swept up in this new mandate for cultural development.

The simple grafting of one agency on to another, however, is not enough to give that agency a sense of mission. In 1966, the Citizenship Branch embarked on a two-year–long process of trying to redefine its objectives, make them consistent within the larger agenda of the SOS, and seek a firmer mandate from cabinet for its activities. The attempt to redefine its objectives had started some years earlier with developments within Citizenship and Immigration to clarify the boundaries between immigration and other matters. The process had almost to begin anew in the context of the SOS, since the issue was now justifying activities not vis-à-vis immigration but vis-à-vis culture. The branch's approach was to claim a distinction between "Culture" and "culture." "Large C" culture represented the arts and universal norms and aspirations. Culture with a small "c," in contrast, "tends to represent the adaptation of man to his universe and to represent purely regional or national norms and aspirations."[63] That such arcane considerations should be matters of discussion for bureaucratic memoranda is perhaps less noteworthy than the mention of the branch's possible abolition. The mere mention of abolition meant that the branch's fortunes were at low ebb, lost in what appeared to be the much more attractive and vibrant agenda of the development of cultural agencies. The distinction between small "c" and large "C" culture was specious at best – a transparent attempt to spruce up the frayed, old-fashioned, and somehow quaintly earnest work of "community development" that the branch had carved out for itself.

Specious and transparent though they were, the arguments were part of a clear plan to save the branch from extinction and give it a firmer foothold on the slippery battlements of bureaucratic Ottawa. Part of the strategy entailed getting the branch a new name, because of the overlap and confusion with the Citizenship Registration Branch and to acquire a more contemporary veneer. For several months officials peppered each other with memoranda about appropriate names: at one point in 1966, the list included Social Affairs, Social Programmes, Social and Cultural Affairs, Canadian Affairs, Community Planning, Community Programmes, Community Development, Community Relations, Community Affairs, Community Services, and Social Development.[64] The branch's preference, Social Development, was meant to parallel the sos's growing reputation as the agency responsible for Canada's cultural development. It also echoed a cautiously more proactive approach on the agency's part: it saw itself less as a salve than as a prod in the country's process of coming to terms with new problems and issues at the community level.

The ultimate goal of the exercise was a memorandum to cabinet which would, for the first time, give the branch a clear and unambiguous mandate. A draft, dated February 1968, sought "Cabinet confirmation of the goals and policies of the Canadian Citizenship Branch of the Secretary of State, namely, that of seeking to foster and sustain national consciousness, to strengthen national unity and to enrich the quality of life in Canada."[65] Noting that the branch's activities all had to do with culture with a small "c," the document defended the branch's apparent incursion into provincial jurisdiction as an effort to promote national unity and purpose. It also asked that its name be changed to Social Development, and that it receive more resources.

In his comments on the draft, G.G.E. Steele, under-secretary of state, commented that the most important point to put before cabinet was the rationale for having a branch of this sort at all: "Why the branch at all? It is surely because there is an entity called 'Canada' which is greater than the sum of the various provinces. I do not think that culture is provincial, although, as used by Jean Noël Tremblay, there is a case to be made that culture in Quebec is provincial because they are defining a recognizable set of values. The question is, are they doing this for all of the French-speaking people of Canada? I doubt it. The federal government must emphasize the national significance of cultural programs. Somehow or other, we have to bring this to the foreground as the main concern of your Branch."[66]

The memorandum encountered difficulty in the Prime Minister's Office as well. J.S. Hodgson, the prime minister's principal secretary, found the timing unfortunate, "because austerity will doubtless overhang any attempt to develop this field."[67] Hodgson thought the memorandum unconvincing in part because the rationale was weak. Instead of establishing the branch's right to existence in its history, Hodgson recommended a legal approach that would ground the branch's activities in the federal government's constitutional duties toward citizenship. "This responsibility is exclusively federal and represents a potentially vast field of activity, but not necessarily a major expense. In these days of social, political and economic crisis, it would be hard to find a field that might have greater significance to national unity (and against Separatism for example) than that of citizenship."[68] Hodgson also suggested that the designation of "Citizenship Branch" be retained in preference to "Social Development Branch," since the former was a "more fundamental objective" than the latter. The 1968 election intervened, and the memorandum died.

By 1968, therefore, the Citizenship Branch had failed to establish itself firmly with the sos. It had not been able to pursue its agenda of expansion or of "social development." It remained obscure and indeed shunned notoriety, since it viewed its function as that of gentle liaison with traditional community groups. And yet, within two years, the Citizenship Branch and with it the sos were to be the hot core of "citizen participation" programs in Pierre Trudeau's brave new world of government devoted to achieving a "Just Society." How could this have happened?

CHAPTER FIVE

The Rise and Fall of "Citizen Participation": 1968–1974

DEVELOPING THE ADMINISTRATIVE MANDATE, 1968–1970

The explanation for the sos's sudden change in fortune in 1968 hinges on several unco-ordinated events that catapulted the Citizenship Branch, at first quite unwillingly, into the forefront of youth, linguistic, ethnic, and women's politics. The two keys were the importance of national unity for the Trudeau government in its challenge to Quebec nationalism and the rising tide of "citizen participation."

Official Languages and Social Action

On the first score, the previous chapter noted how Quebec's rumblings in the mid-1960s had persuaded the Pearson government to demonstrate that Ottawa was the government of all Canadians and that it was as interested in cultural matters as was Quebec City. That was the original backdrop for giving the sos control over cultural institutions and development of a national cultural strategy. The Citizenship Branch, once it was transferred to the sos, was ensnared in this agenda, with a possible role in fostering national unity. As early as 1965, the senior liaison officers in the branch collectively agreed that Canadian unity was to be the "central concern of the branch from which all our other work should be derived."[1]

As mentioned in the previous chapter, this concern with national unity led Prime Minister Pearson to establish the Royal Commission on Bilingualism and Biculturalism (1963–69). The six books of the Laurendeau-Dunton Commission's final report were issued over four years (the last two in 1970) and helped shape the political discourse that underlay the Official Languages Act of 1969. Despite the contemporary significance of governmental support for linguistic advocacy groups, the antecedents to the 1969 act did not emphasize this policy instrument. The commission, for example, was virtually silent on the question of official language minority groups (OLMGs, as they came to be known), although it did touch obliquely on community representation and the voluntary sector. With few exceptions, whenever the royal commission discussed the linguistic minorities, it spoke of them as communities, not through the lens of the organizations that might represent and lobby on behalf of them. Nowhere in its report did it recommend support for the groups that represented and sustained the linguistic minorities. This may simply have reflected the way in which the linguistic communities had represented themselves to the commission. For example, of 404 individuals, associations, and organizations that presented briefs to the commission, only 71 could be counted as francophone. More important, most of those were private companies (e.g., radio stations), educational institutions, and chambers of commerce.[2] While the commission did not completely ignore voluntary associations, it clearly did not want to treat these bodies as just another transmission belt of government policy.[3]

Canada's first Official Languages Act was passed in 1969 and closely followed most of Laurendeau-Dunton's recommendations. At its 29 May 1969 meeting, the federal cabinet approved new spending proposals for the Social Action Branch of the SOS, and by 31 July the Treasury Board had authorized an allocation of $1.3 million under this program, to be chargeable to the Official Languages Programme.[4] The Social Action Branch was to spend this money in support of associations and organizations representing the interests of linguistic minorities, but as the program's title suggested, this was intended less for the traditional type of community-based linguistic or cultural group than it was for the new ideal of "social animation." This was the genesis of the core funding program for OLMGs, which eventually set the pattern for all other such initiatives coming from the SOS, particularly those in the Citizenship Branch. But the Commission itself had not referred to core funding, and indeed had held to the classical liberal idea that voluntary associations were almost purely private, even though their activities had public effects. The Social Action Programme itself noted: "No article in the Report of the Royal Commission on Bilingualism and Biculturalism explicitly recommends the setting up of an official languages program or, for that matter, the Social Action Branch of which it is a part."[5] From where did the idea of "social action" on the linguistic front come? The answer hangs on the nature of the SOS at the end of the 1960s, particularly of its Citizenship Branch, the national unity crisis to which the Commission was a response, and the decade's atmosphere of "social animation" and participatory democracy.

In 1969 the SOS received responsibility for the official languages program, creating four new branches that reported to the assistant under-secretary of state: Bilingualism Programs, Social Action, Language Administration, and Research and Planning. The objectives of Social Action were: "(1) to ensure that official language minorities continue to flourish and to encourage their participation in Canadian society without the risk of losing their identity; and (2) to promote a better understanding between the two official language communities."[6]

The Social Action Branch came into operation in August 1969 and immediately launched programs in several provinces. The annual report commented that "an attempt is being made to meet the needs of associations and agencies whose objectives correspond to those of the government as defined above. Organizations and groups receiving grants must play a part in carrying out their own projects."[7] In addition to offering sustaining funds, the branch was prepared to make money available for such things as cultural exchanges, social animation, seminars, youth activities, and "special or national projects designed to assist national and ethnic organizations."[8] During fiscal 1969–70, 109 grants were approved, for a total of $1,015,680 (though this included Citizenship Branch grants before the Social Action Branch was established). Under the sustaining grants component, provincial associations received $115,600 in direct aid. The social animation component gave eight provincial associations grants amounting to $312,621.[9] The director's 1970 report on the Social Action Branch described the latter as "a program which, by utilizing the services of professionally trained community development officers, attempted an in-depth attack on mass apathy and, concentrated, during the past months, on sensitizing and preparing confirmed or potential leaders through group dynamic sessions and leadership training courses."[10] The report claimed that over 20,000 people at the community level had been involved in such sessions.

"Social action" – deliberate mobilization of social sentiment in desired directions – was indeed an appropriate rubric for the program. It assumed a need for "better understanding between the two official linguistic communities,"[11] based on tolerance toward minorities within each of these communities. "In some cases, this involves consolidating an existing situation and in others, bringing about a change in attitude among the majority."[12] At the same time, however, the branch would ensure that all "activities are carried out in co-operation with organizations formed by citizens themselves. In this way the branch does not become a substitute for local initiative but rather encourages and promotes activities undertaken by local, regional, provincial or national groups."[13] The social animation program, for example, was described in the following terms:

Social animation, as related to the purposes of the branch's Programme, is a method of *encouraging* official language minority groups to identify and resolve their own social and cultural problems ... Social animation of a minority will encourage its development and enable it to combat the major causes of cultural assimilation, apathy and indifference. To these ends, the Social Action Branch Programme makes funds available, under certain conditions, to provincial organizations wishing to undertake this type of action but unable to do so owing to a lack of material resources and personnel. The first step in such a program is to train "animateurs" capable of encouraging the groups concerned to make decisions independently, ensuring cohesion among those involved, providing guidance to leaders and organizers and, finally, stimulating both individual and collective participation.[14]

This might suggest that the branch was taking a strong lead in shaping the associational system, reaching out to stimulate interest and assist groups to form and lobby. The program's guiding principles did indeed reflect an activist orientation of statism but were hedged by incantations of traditional liberal ideas of the autonomy of social actors in the voluntary sector. In this sense the program was assumed to be both proactive and reactive. For example, while the branch saw itself as "non-directive," where "organizations or programs do not exist that can respond to specific social and cultural needs the Social Action Branch may initiate action on its own."[15]

This reflected the ambivalence at the heart not just of the OLMG program but of the other citizenship development programs that were operating at the time or would emerge shortly to support youth, women, ethnic minorities, and community groups. The prevailing Canadian tradition of state–civil society relations in respect of the associational system had, until the late 1960s, been grounded in classical liberal principles of the autonomy of the voluntary sector. Faced with a regime crisis in the form of Quebec's Quiet Revolution, as well as emerging, new ideas about the stimulative role of the state vis-à-vis social change, programs were developed that involved a much more direct state presence and, for the first time, a widespread practice of sustaining grants for advocacy organizations.

Citizen Participation

In October 1969, Robert Stanbury was appointed minister without portfolio responsible for Citizenship and Information Canada, and he launched a comprehensive review of citizenship policy. In May 1970, the cabinet approved five new broad objectives as the mandate of the Citizenship Branch within the SOS: "reinforce Canadian identity and unity," "encourage cultural diversity within a bilingual framework," "preserve human rights and fundamental freedoms," "increase and improve citizenship participation," and "develop meaningful symbols of Canadian Sovereignty."[16] Bernard Ostry was appointed assistant under-secretary of state for citizenship in January 1970 and was encouraged by the prime minister himself to "shake up" the branch and expand its role in promoting national unity.[17]

A simple focus on national unity would not in itself have been enough to shift the branch into a more activist stance, particularly in group funding. For this to happen there had to be a redefinition of the meaning of citizenship and a new articulation of the proper role and relationship of government to voluntary organizations. As we saw in the last chapter, this redefinition had been gradually developing since the early 1960s but was given a great boost with the idea of citizens' participation. Indeed, Pierre Trudeau was able to capitalize on this with his famous 1968 campaign proposal that the role of government was to foster a "Just Society."

The citizens' participation movement antedated the Trudeau regime, within both the Liberal party and administrative practice. The roots of the party's evolution toward more participation – or at least openness – lay in the Liberal government's defeat in 1957. The defeat was widely ascribed to an ossified party structure, and so proposals soon circulated to give the grass roots more influence.[18] An informal group known as "Cell 13" (members included Keith Davey, Royce Frith, and Richard Stanbury)[19] lobbied within the party against the Liberals' traditionally close ties to big business and constituency control by small-time party bosses. It achieved some prominence in the Ontario Liberal party after 1959 but as an organized force had faded by 1963.[20] Nonetheless, the party apparatus was gradually modernized in the early 1960s with introduction of polling, centralized operations, new fundraising techniques, and better riding organizations. Modernization carried the cachet of openness, less bureaucracy, and, above all, more participation. As McCall-Newman notes, "If you were modern, you were urban, educated, reform-minded, adept at dropping words like 'participation' and 'communication' into every other sentence, and, above all, hard-nosed."[21] When Pierre Trudeau became leader of the party in 1968, Senator Richard Stanbury became its president. Stanbury had a keen interest in the broadest sense of participation – that is, a movement of reform within the party as well as creation of new channels of communication between the public and the government.[22] His influence was readily seen in the restructuring of the SOS and the cabinet's 1970 policy statement on national unity and citizenship.[23]

The idea of citizens' participation emerged early at the administrative level, as well. As we saw earlier, the Citizenship Branch itself was timidly trying to put on the robes of "social development" in 1965–66. There was much talk in those days of community development and social action, building principally on the American civil rights and students movements. The focus was not language, ethnic groups, or women, but the poor, urban renewal, students, and Native Indians.[24] In the American context, the links among poverty, class, race, and urban power were easy to make, because of the civil rights movement's concentration on the problems of poor blacks in inner cities. The first wave of community development and citizens' participation that came to Canada consequently also focused on youth and poverty and local control.[25]

These were also the years in which the Pearson government launched the Company of Young Canadians (CYC), an organization with remarkable autonomy modelled on the US Peace Corps but aimed at facilitating social change in Canada. One sympathetic observer commented that Canadian youth played only a minor role in its establishment and that "the government took the revolutionary spirit upon itself and became bold."[26] The CYC was important less for what it accomplished as an organization than for the entrée that it gave activists to government and the support that it gave to the idea of participation and direct action. Stewart Goodings, for example, was for a time an acting director of the CYC and later joined the Citizenship Branch. He and Cam Mackie were responsible for designing what eventually became the Opportunities for Youth Programme. In Sandra Gwyn's assessment, "the erstwhile radicals of the CYC have, to an extraordinary extent, stayed around to become Ottawa operators, in Manpower, Health and Welfare, the CBC, Secretary of State (Citizenship), even Information Canada."[27] In 1968, while Mackie was still with the CYC, he and Goodings wrote a paper proposing a $1-million student-run summer employment project called YES (Youth Employment Service). While it was not immediately accepted, the plan was "on the shelf" when Gérard Pelletier and Bernard Ostry were ready after 1970 to move on the youth employment issue. Ostry brought Michael McCabe into the Citizenship Branch as his director of program development, and, according to Gwyn, "the pair turned Citizenship into a flamboyant, freespending *animateur sociale.* Traditional, father-knows-best groups were upstaged. Instead, massive grants went out to militant native groups, tenants' associations and other putative aliens of the 1970s."[28]

The sos of course was the logical home for this new effort, at least insofar as it involved government funding of voluntary organizations that would in turn try to animate society. The Citizenship Branch in the sos represented a "state capacity," in Skocpol's terms, for this sort of activity. In the 1950s, funding had been undertaken gingerly and reluctantly, even by politicians who might have been expected to see some political gain in it. However, year by year, grant requests grew, as did the number and amount of grants. The branch's view always was that it preferred to give project rather than core funding, and for the most part it held to this commitment.

By fiscal 1966, for example, the branch was dispensing $250,000 in grants to organizations and groups; one-quarter of it went to Native friendship centres. Only two organizations received sustaining grants (the Canadian Citizenship Council and the Indian-Eskimo Association each got $15,000); these sustaining grants had been authorized by the Treasury Board on 31 October 1963. The remainder was distributed through supporting grants among twenty-seven organizations (exclusive of groups involved in Native issues) that were active in citizenship promotion and human relations.[29] Grants under this category had been approved by the Treasury Board in August 1962. Table 5.1 lists the groups and the amounts voted for each. The branch, in short, was active in the granting area but had expanded its efforts cautiously, in part because of the constant pressure it received from the Treasury Board about spending monies that were not strictly authorized by statute. Another factor that enhanced the branch's "capacity" to undertake the new participation initiatives was its increasing role in funding youth organizations.[30]

In mid-1969, the branch conducted a review of its granting policies in connection with two grants that had been awarded for inner-city development projects in Vancouver and Toronto. Both projects were heavily financed by the United Church of Canada's Board of Home Missions, and both were intended as a "training and sensitizing process of university students who may be involved either directly or as future decision-makers for the center town area."[31] The review recommended that the branch should not give grants to welfare programs, "symbolic participation-content programs," or areas

Table 5.1
Grants for citizenship promotion, as of 15 March 1966

	$ voted
SUSTAINING GRANTS	
Canadian Citizenship Council	15,000
Indian-Eskimo Association	15,000
CITIZENSHIP PROMOTION	
International Institute of Metro Toronto	4,000
NIC	3,000
Costi	6,000
L'Accord	1,000
Acelf	5,000
National Council of Women of Canada	850
Canadian Association for Adult Education	25,000
L'institut canadien d'éducation des adultes	25,000
Canadian Camping Association	2,000
UNA of Canada	800
Canadian Ethnic Press Club	500
HUMAN RELATIONS	
British Columbia	1,900
CAAE – BC Division	
Vancouver Citizenship Council	
Trial District Council of Women	
Prairies	1,500
Calgary Citizenship Council	
U. of Sask. Training Institute	
Banff Slavic Conference	
Farm W.U. of Alberta	
Group Proc. Institute	
w&c Cit. Comm. Regina	
Edmonton Welfare Council	
Ontario	1,800
Ontario Welfare Council Centre – Sudbury	
Ontario JC Hamilton	
Quebec	4,200
La Société Saint-Jean-Baptiste	
ICAP	
Maritimes	1,500
La Société nationale des Acadiens	

Source: National Archives of Canada, RG 6, Department of Secretary of State, vol. 661, file 2-4-8, vol. 1, memorandum from Jean H. Lagassé to C.A. Lussier, 23 March 1966.

that came directly under the aegis of other departments. There were eight permissible bases for grants:

(1) increase participation by people in the affairs of society and that decrease alienation. Participation assumes the potential for behavioural change in the persons concerned.

(2) make persons more socially aware in the sense of what happens to people.

(3) provide a voice for people who have not had a voice in their affairs.

(4) increase self-help, i.e., grass roots programs for grass roots people by grass roots people.

(5) are concerned with the values of human life and dignity (quality of life).

(6) that articulate the reality of the developmental process toward participation.

(7) that have a research component built in (Action-research).

(8) stimulate the emergence of local community leaders.[32]

Gérard Pelletier, secretary of state in the new government, wanted to apply the doctrines of the "Just Society" and "participatory democracy" to the cultural scene.[33] As Bernard Ostry describes it: "The Branch was supposed to develop and strengthen a sense of Canadian citizenship, chiefly through programs that would aid participation and assuage feelings of social injustice. Indian, Métis and Inuit political, social and cultural organizations were established and funded in the teeth of opposition from the Department of Indian Affairs; a women's bureau was set up before the government had commented on the Royal Commission's Report on the Status of Women; Opportunities for Youth, travel and exchange and hostel programs were undertaken without the blessing of the Manpower, Welfare or Justice departments, and millions of dollars were made available to the branch to ensure justice and fairness to every ethnic group that wished to preserve and celebrate its cultural heritage."[34]

Thus by January 1970 the sos, and in particular the Citizenship and Social Action branches, had a clear mandate to mobilize Canadian society on the linguistic and broader participatory front. In principle, virtually any social group or category could be eligible for help and guidance, though the mandate referred vaguely to the disadvantaged, which clearly included the core constituencies that the branch had cultivated and connected with over the years: immigrants, Natives, youth, and, most recently, official-language communities. But it could embrace the elderly, women, and virtually any group or organization struggling to participate in the political process either for the first time or against what then was referred to as "the establishment." And this is precisely what happened.

DESIGNING THE "ANIMATION" MACHINE, 1970–1972

For many social activists in the 1960s, the Citizenship Branch of the sos had appeared to be "the only part of government that seemed human."[35] It had modestly assisted the voluntary sector (most visibly through its grants to the Canadian Citizenship Council) and by 1969, as the preceding section suggests, had a clear mandate as well as the leadership to forge new policies in the area of citizen participation. One problem, however, was that the new orientation and mandate of the branch and the department departed significantly from the older administrative style of the previous decade. New approaches demanded new ideas and, in some measure, new people and new procedures. In 1969, when the prime minister and cabinet gave the sos its new role and its new minister, the department was a bit of a backwater in official Ottawa, lacking the sort of dynamism required by the challenges of the time.[36] The social program side of the branch's staff had a social-work orientation, and the grafting on of new programs required a good deal of "stretching and contorting."[37] However, by 1970–71 there was ferment in the branch, and an agenda had been developed to support Natives, women, ethnic groups, human rights, and citizenship organizations more broadly – largely the doing of Bernard Ostry after he became assistant undersecretary of state for citizenship. He accomplished this by bringing in his own people, such as Stewart Goodings, Michael McCabe, and Robert Nichols, and by launching a reorganization and reorientation of the branch.

As mentioned earlier, Ostry's (and Pelletier's) authority came from cabinet itself, which in May 1970 approved five objectives for a new citizenship policy,[38] including preparation of a new citizenship bill, to replace the existing Citizenship Act, and of a new citizenship promotion campaign. Bernard Ostry struck a committee to recommend how this mandate might be translated into a course of action, and the Bureau of Management Consulting (a branch of the Department of Supply and Services) was asked to help develop an organizational proposal. The bureau recommended establishment of three key roles within the branch: strategic planning, "deciding specifically what it is that the organization is going to accomplish";

program development, "determining how to go about doing those things"; and operations, which would be charged with carrying out programs.[39] This reorganization was accepted by Treasury Board in September 1970, after which the Bureau of Management Consulting was asked to help implement it.

To do this, the bureau first had to conduct a detailed study of the existing organization. Its report gives a fascinating snapshot of the Citizenship Branch on the threshold of its reorganization. At the time, it consisted of two parts, Citizenship Registration (responsible for Citizenship Courts and general administration of the Citizenship Act) and Citizenship Development. The latter was the direct heir to the programs discussed in the previous chapter:

The Branch implements policies of promoting good citizenship and orienting immigrants to the Canadian way of life, and has also undertaken programs in the areas of Travel and Exchange, Indian participation, Human rights, Immigrants participation and Citizenship development. It offers to agencies, organizations and groups services such as: information on available resources, provisions of educational and program materials, consultative assistance on projects and programs, technical assistance for conferences, training sessions and meetings. Through agreements with the provincial governments, free textbooks are provided, as well as financial support toward the teaching costs of language instruction for immigrants. The research section stores information on ethnic groups and their contributions to Canadian life, material for promotion of citizenship programs, and descriptive reports on voluntary agencies and groups in Canada. Field offices support all activities mentioned above in addition to the activities of the social action branch which is under the bilingual development program's organization.[40]

The bureau painted a bleak picture of the "prevailing situation." Interviews revealed that field personnel felt isolated and frustrated by what they perceived as headquarters' lack of understanding of their role. At headquarters, there was "an apparent lack of discipline."[41] The heads of programs were frustrated by "the lack of governmental guidelines and policies in the field of social development and the seeming lack of interest in the programs shown by former departmental senior officers."[42] The changes in upper management, combined with the pressures of the new mandate, had rendered the organization "unstable," so that there was little explanation to staff as to new directions and extensive reliance on outside contractors and ad hoc measures to get things done. "Employees are concerned and insecure. They interpret the arrival of new employees in senior positions as a vote of non-confidence in all employees who have been associated with the former management."[43]

With the bureau's recommendations in hand, Ostry asked the Canada Consulting Group to help design the management systems required in the new organizational structure of three directorates (Strategic Planning, Operations, and Programs). Its report also noted, as background, that the Citizenship Branch was at the centre of a revitalized federal commitment to fostering national unity. The branch's budget, for example, had almost doubled between 1969–70 and 1970–71 (from $4.6 million to $8.1 million) and increased five-fold in 1971–72 (to $44 million): "As a result, Citizenship has now become the single most important federal agency in the funding of voluntary organizations ... Because of this rapid growth of Branch responsibilities and the enormous pressures for immediate action, new programs were funded and rushed into execution without a fully staffed organization, detailed division of responsibilities, required management systems or adequate administrative support. Not surprisingly, the branch has sometimes looked inept, and its performance has not lived up to the expectations and targets of its own management."[44]

The report highlighted problems in the branch's grants administration which demanded attention because grants were a key means of meeting citizenship goals, as well as the most visible of the branch's "outputs." The report estimated that the branch had made 500 awards to organizations in 1970–71, totalling $3 million. In 1972–73 the number was expected to increase to 3,000, with a total expenditure of $21 million. However, the consultants found that the branch's casual procedures for awarding grants were inadequate to ensure administrative control. Three different grants systems were in operation (one for Opportunities for Youth, one for Travel and Exchange, and one for all other programs, known together as Social Development), and as a result management did not know "with any degree of certainty the total support being given to organizations by the Citizenship Branch."[45] Information was often not available in files, processing of grants was often delayed and certainly inconsistent, and granting criteria were loose. Decisions on grants were not "fact-based." Favourable decisions thus depended on personal advocacy of an organization's application in the bureaucracy, the political acceptability of the group or project, or (unspecified) external pressures. These uncertainties had led to a "constant stream of complaints from field, operations staff, and program heads."[46] Ostry's reorganization was meant in part to deal with this problem, though it was also supposed to enhance the policy capacity of the branch as well as facilitate development of new programs with a stronger emphasis on citizens' participation.

The reorganization took a year to accomplish (1971–72). The branch's old structure of Travel and Exchange, Ethnic Participation, Human Rights, and Native Citizens Development was replaced with three divisions: Strategic Planning, Program Development, and Operations. (Ironically, this reorganization itself only lasted for two years, as the Citizenship Branch was drawn into larger departmental reorganizations.) Before we start considering the implications of these changes, however, we should look at two broader developments in the federal government's policy environment, since they had a major effect on the branch's fortunes. These were the Report of the Royal Commission on the Status of Women and the government's announcement of an official policy of multiculturalism.

Most students of the Canadian women's movement distinguish between its "first wave," to 1960, and its "second wave" thereafter.[47] The beginning of the second wave is usually dated to establishment of an anti-war group called the Voice of Women (vow).[48] vow was formed in July 1960 after the failure of the Paris Summit Conference on disarmament in May. By fall 1961 it claimed a membership of over 5,000.[49] The group split when Prime Minister Pearson agreed to place nuclear weapons on Canadian soil, and many Liberal women who had been members of vow left the party. In 1966 Laura Sabia, then president of the Canadian Federation of University Women, called together representatives of thirty women's organizations, and they formed the Committee on Equality for Women.[50] In July 1966 she launched the call for a royal commission on women. At first the Pearson government ignored the request, and Sabia then threatened to march two million women on Parliament hill. The NDP, which held the balance of power in a minority situation in Parliament, and which was sympathetic to a commission, attacked the Liberals for not going ahead with it.[51] The government finally relented and in 1967 announced formation of a Royal Commission on the Status of Women, to be chaired by Florence Bird.[52]

This is not the place for a detailed discussion of the royal commission's report. We need note only that it was a remarkably prescient document which helped set the decade's agenda for mainstream Canadian feminism. In the course of its analysis, however, it had occasion to discuss the nature of women's organizations and to recommend that they receive financial support from the state. The report praised the past work of women's voluntary associations, notably their contribution to the success of equal pay legislation, but future tasks would be increasingly complex. The government, however, should not do anything to "interfere with the autonomy of volunteer work."[53] Women's organizations provided valuable services not only to women but to the community at large and deserved government support. Accordingly, the report's third recommendation suggested increased financial support for women's voluntary organizations.[54]

The other change in the sos's and Citizenship Branch's environment came with Ottawa's announcement that Canada was henceforth to be considered as officially multicultural. Observers are virtually unanimous in agreeing that Canadian ethnic groups were politicized in the 1960s by the Royal Commission on Bilingualism and Biculturalism. These groups were mobilized in an effort to ward off what they considered an essentially dualist vision of the country that underlay both the commission's analysis and the policies of the Liberal government of Pierre Trudeau.[55] The ethnic reaction was not well co-ordinated and lacked a clearly articulated alternative vision of the country. This general weakness was caused by the relatively small size and hence limited resources of most ethnic groups and their associations, and by the logic of ethnic cultural representation.

Each group, from the Chinese to the Germans, had organized itself on the tacit principle of cultural preservation and distinct ethnic representation. Unlike the women's movement, which was able to organize broadly around the concept of the general oppression of all women, there never was an "ethnic" theory of oppression or a government attack on benefits around which sentiment could be mobilized. The consequence was that policy makers, after noting ethnic dissatisfaction with dualism, had a free hand in moulding policy to respond to that dissatisfaction. Breton points out that the government did no surveys in that period to gauge the level of support for its eventual policy of multiculturalism, and that while there was ethnic protest, this "does not suggest a widespread mobilization across groups."[56] He sees no broad movement behind the policy; its motive forces were elite support from ethnic organizational leaders, politicians, and government agencies.

Canada's multiculturalism policy was announced by the prime minister in Parliament on 8 October 1971, two years after the release by the Laurendeau-Dunton Commission of an originally unplanned volume drafted partly to placate ethnic opposition to its main recommendations. Prime Minister Trudeau's remarks were the sole basis of Canada's policy of multiculturalism until the recent passage of separate legislation to that effect. The prime minister said: "A policy of multiculturalism within a bilingual framework commends itself to the government as the most suitable means of assuring the cultural freedom of Canadians. Such a policy should help break down discriminatory attitudes and cultural jealousies. National unity if it is to mean anything in the deeply personal sense, must be founded on confidence in one's own individual identity; out of this can grow respect for that of others and a willingness to share ideas, attitudes and assumptions. A vigorous policy of multiculturalism will help create this initial confidence. It can form the base of a society which is based on fair play for all."[57]

There were to be four guiding principles, the first of which had the greatest relevance to the SOS: "First, resources permitting, the government will seek to assist all Canadian cultural groups that have demonstrated a desire and effort to continue to develop a capacity to grow and contribute to Canada, and a clear need for assistance, the small and weak groups no less than the strong and highly organized."[58] The 1971 policy affirmed in essence that while Canada would be officially bilingual it would never be merely bicultural and that it valued its multicultural character. The statement referred to a variety of government initiatives to support multiculturalism, most of which had been tried in one form or another by the old, pre-1969 Citizenship Branch. The only substantially new program turned out to be core funding support to ethnic associations, on the model pioneered by the Social Action Branch and its support for OLMGs. While on the surface the policy seemed to contradict the government's emphasis on bilingualism, it actually was complementary. The prime minister and his senior advisers were well aware that a suggestion of official cultural duality would play directly into the hands of nationalist forces in Quebec. The combination of bilingualism and multiculturalism seemed to balance the need to accommodate Quebec without implying that there were simply two peoples – French and English – in Canada.[59]

The sudden force of women's and multicultural issues in 1971 had a dramatic impact on the Citizenship Branch, since in addition to other policy initiatives, the government had committed itself to providing support for voluntary organizations in each sector. We saw earlier that Ostry had restructured the branch into three divisions, Strategic Planning, Operations, and Program Development. In theory this would allow better control of the organization and enhanced capacity to develop new, innovative programs. Program Development, for example, now comprised five "areas": Native citizens,

citizens' rights and freedoms, citizenship promotion, citizens' cultures, and citizens' organizations. The last two were quite new and reflected the effect of multiculturalism and the new emphasis on broad citizen participation, particularly among the disadvantaged.

In 1971 the cabinet issued a memorandum on voluntarism, which in turn encouraged an SOS proposal to expand the old Citizenship Participation Program to embrace a wider spectrum of groups. The Treasury Board approved this proposal on 23 December 1971. The citizens' organizations area was described as follows: "The purpose of this program group is to strengthen the voluntary sector to enable citizens to participate more effectively in the decisions that affect the quality of their lives. Financial and technical support is given to a wide variety of citizen's organizations, with emphasis on low-income and disadvantaged citizens' groups."[60] The SOS's 1972 annual report described the citizens' culture program as trying "to encourage the development of a society in which individuals and groups have an equal chance to develop and express their cultural identity as an integral part of Canadian life."[61] The Operations Division received the old travel and exchange programs, hostels, and Opportunities for Youth (introduced in the summer of 1971 and moved to Manpower and Immigration in 1973 because of its employment component).

In 1973 the Citizenship Branch conducted an evaluation of its "Citizenship Participation Activities" which clearly showed the role of external developments such as multiculturalism and feminism and the branch's attempts to keep pace. It examined project and core grants awarded to citizens' organizations between December 1971 and December 1972, a critical transition year at the SOS. At this point the Social Action Branch was also offering grants to OLMGs and so was not considered in the evaluation report. Payments by the Citizenship Branch to organizations in this period added up to $1,040,274 over 157 grants.[62] In fiscal 1971 the Social Action Branch gave out 183 grants worth $1,822,314, with an average value of $9,958, as follows: 4 (totalling $23,968) for international conferences; 9 ($150,000) to provincial associations representing OLMGs; 10 ($571,050) for social animation to encourage further participation by groups in their own cultural development; 20 ($84,503) for seminars and conferences; 23 ($169,714) for cultural exchanges among groups; 27 ($129,167) for youth; 44 ($208,109) miscellaneous; and 48 ($309,339) for cultural centres.[63]

The report noted that at the start of the new fiscal year 1972, the branch had undertaken program analysis of its grants policy. Several factors necessitated a revision of programming strategy, including "the increasing number of new citizens' groups which appeared to be forming, often around a single issue, but with a potential for longer-term effective operation," and "the growth of new women's organizations and the more explicit focus of many established women's groups on the rights of women who were reacting to and building on the Report of the Royal Commission on the Status of Women."[64] Citizens' information and referral centres were emerging. The branch decided to focus its grants in three areas for the next year: new and emerging groups, established groups, and information and referral centres. A special priority was given to women's groups: "This priority was in part a response to the considerable interest and activity shown by women's groups toward the recommendations of the Royal Commission on the Status of Women, and in part to the Commission's Recommendation 3, which called for increased support to women's voluntary associations engaged in projects of public interest, and voluntary associations working in fields of particular interest to women. It also reflected the fact that women are in many respects a disadvantaged group in terms of participation in the decision-making processes of society."[65]

The momentum behind the citizens' organizations program carried through into 1973–74. Strong demand from women's organizations and the branch's perception that this area required special expertise of staff members familiar with such groupes led to creation of a separate Women's Program.[66] The new program had six objectives: to help in establishment of community-based Women's Centres; to provide women's services; to assist in investigation of areas where women's participation was restricted (e.g., the media); to assist in formation of new women's groups; to help mount projects addressing the status of women; and to assist in co-ordinating activities through conferences, workshops, and newsletters.[67]

In the same year, a separate Multiculturalism Program was set up to target funds directly to organizations representing the interests of Canada's ethnic groups, and the group support programs of the Social Action Branch were transferred to the Citizenship Branch under the new rubric of Official Language Minority Groups.[68] While the sos and the branch were to undergo various organizational changes over the next decade, by 1973 the basic division of grants programs within the branch had taken shape: women, OLMGs, multicultural organizations, and Natives. From time to time, various smaller programs were grafted on or lopped off (e.g., assistance to community groups, youth programs), but they did not affect the core mandate. Moreover, in the early years (1970–72) the emphasis in granting policy was still on projects rather than on core support.

It was the OLMG and Women's programs that took what at the time was considered the slightly unusual step of deliberately fostering organizations through core funding.[69] It is ironic then that just as the programs sorted themselves out, the enthusiasm and verve behind the idea of citizen participation waned.

WANING ENTHUSIASM, 1972–1974

The years (1970–72) described in the previous section were confused and complex ones for the SOS and the Citizenship Branch. They were also exciting times. The cluster of major policy initiatives undertaken in such a short time is quite impressive: bilingualism, multiculturalism, national unity, and improvement in the status of women. All of these were reflections of Prime Minister Trudeau's famous catch phrase of a "Just Society." This implied a new and more balanced justice for Canada's ethnic and linguistic minorities, for women, for natives, for youth, and for that great, general category – the "disadvantaged." The SOS was involved with and central to most of these initiatives. But in Bernard Ostry's words, the government woke up "with the hangover of a minority administration – in 1972. And the money flow dried up. Participation was dead; only the inelegant words democratization and decentralization remained."[70]

Indeed, in Ostry's estimation, an almost deliberate hostility developed to the idea of citizens' participation, to the point that the government was determined after 1972 "to refuse support to programs related to the philosophy of participatory democracy."[71] Opportunities for Youth went from being a progressive instrument of social change to just another employment program run by Manpower and Immigration. Multiculturalism was given its own minister of state in 1972 (Dr. Stanley Haidasz), but in Ostry's view this simply hived off the area with a minister not "associated with the Secretary of State Department." Money had flowed in during the heyday, to the extent that the branch's budget increased five-fold in the period; now budget allocations were stabilized and there was little growth. What happened?

Ostry is certainly correct in highlighting the effect of the 1972 election. The Liberal party lost 46 seats (going from 155 in 1968 to 109). Its proportion of the vote dropped from 45 per cent to 38 per cent. The opposition Conservatives had won 107 seats (with 35 per cent of the vote), and the NDP, holding the balance of power, won

18 per cent of the vote and 31 seats (up from 21 in 1968). In contrast to the "Trudeau-mania" of the 1968 campaign, the prime minister seemed distant and aloof. His philosophical musings during the campaign further alienated the electorate. Thus the mood in the Liberal party on regaining its precarious hold on power was both sobered and more focused. Party insiders, particularly the leader's office, asserted even greater control in the face of "the need to achieve a majority in the next election."[72] The sense of intense excitement and, among some officials and politicians, idealism, that had dominated the 1968–72 "Just Society" phase, evaporated. The citizens had indeed participated in 1972, but in a strikingly ungrateful way. It was unsurprising then that the government would look somewhat more carefully at the notion of social animation.

The multicultural program had not been established with narrow partisan purposes in mind, but the election changed that, too. The Liberals lost almost half their seats in Ontario (down from 64 to 36), and defeated candidates (in particular John Roberts, who found his way to the PMO) urged more aggressive use of the policy to garner ethnic support. Shortly afterward, a new Ministry of State for Multiculturalism was established, with Dr. Stanley Haidasz as its first incumbent. Oddly, the ministry was grafted on to the Citizenship Branch, so that while it was only one program in that branch it had its own minister. This organizational confusion led to friction between Haidasz and Ostry, still at this stage assistant under-secretary of state for citizenship. In May 1973 Haidasz announced several new multicultural programs as well as enhancements of existing ones. Funding was to increase by two and a half times over a single year (from $4 million to $10 million). The multicultural grants program alone was to increase by $1.1 million.[73] The emphasis on grants, as well as increased support for the ethnic press, left the minister open to charges of favouritism and political bias. As well, the Canadian Consultative Council on Multiculturalism, originally comprising between 12 and 15 members when first proposed, was established after the 1972 election with 101 members, many of whom had clear connections to the Liberal party.

Another factor lessening enthusiasm for participation was the dawning realization that citizens' groups funded and supported by the state might become a third pillar of critics of government programs and policies, joining the opposition parties and the media. This was clearest with some of the women's groups, especially the National Action Committee on the Status of Women (NAC), but the general principle had already been demonstrated with the Company of Young Canadians some years earlier. Indeed, within three years, sos-supported organizations in the women's and language areas would become among the government's most articulate adversaries.

These changes were linked to, and perhaps part of the cause for, major changes of personnel. Gérard Pelletier, reputed to be close to the prime minister and thus respected, left the sos after the 1972 election to become minister of communications (he left government service in 1975). He had had genuine sympathy for the sos's work, but without his personal commitment, as well as his connections to the prime minister, the programs were left exposed. He was replaced by Hugh Faulkner, who was less enthusiastic about participation. The Treasury Board had never been comfortable with the Citizenship Branch's exciting new ideas, because they conflicted with traditional government funding practices for the voluntary sector and because the programs then, as now, were never clear enough in terms of objectives to be adequately monitored and evaluated.[74] Jules Léger, under-secretary of state during Pelletier's tenure as minister, also left in 1973 (he became governor-general in 1974) and was replaced by Jean Boucher, whose forte was more financial management than social animation.[75] Ostry had had several battles with Treasury Board officials, and now with Pelletier and Léger gone, he was vulnerable. He left the sos in January 1974, as did many of his protégés, such as Michael McCabe. Jean Boucher had been director of the Citizenship Branch from 1956 to 1964 and so had less of a personal stake in participatory programs and perhaps a bias for the old methods pioneered in the branch in the 1950s. He was also engaged in "damage control" vis-à-vis the Treasury Board. The troika of Pelletier, Léger, and Ostry had had the influence and the nerve simply to establish programs whether the Treasury Board liked them or not. Opportunities for Youth was a case in point; while it may have been a splendid instrument of social animation, it was also wildly uncontrolled in terms of standard government financial practice.[76]

A final factor that helps explain the fall from grace of citizens' participation in 1973 is national unity. The Social Action Branch had been founded in response to the recommendations of the Royal Commission on Bilingualism and Biculturalism. The 1969 cabinet mandate for the sos and its new citizenship programs had also been rooted in the idea that the federal government must be more "proactive" in the development of Canadian identity. These measures have to be set against the background of Quebec's rising assertiveness in the 1960s and its actions, under the Liberal premier Jean Lesage (1960–66) and the Union Nationale's Daniel Johnson (1966–68) and Jean-Jacques Bertrand (1968–70), to enhance its powers and defend its culture. Concern with national unity peaked with the October crisis in 1970 – the kidnapping by FLQ terrorists of British diplomat James Cross and the murder of provincial cabinet minister Pierre Laporte.

A new Liberal government was in power in Quebec City, under Robert Bourassa, and it made no bones about its federalist sympathies. In 1971, during constitutional talks in Victoria, it seemed for a moment that Quebec, Ottawa, and the other provinces might agree on patriation and an amending formula. Even though Bourassa ultimately turned down the agreement in the face of nationalist criticism in Quebec, it at least seemed possible that Quebec and the rest of Canada could negotiate. The Parti Québécois (PQ) had been formed in 1968 under René Lévesque, but its results in the 1970 provincial election were unimpressive. All of this came together to create a sense that the worst tensions with Quebec were over. Certainly the PQ was a worrisome factor, but by 1973 the need actively to foster national identity and national unity seemed less pressing.

As the next chapter will show, the 1976 election of the PQ changed all that and placed national unity once more at the centre of the federal government's policy agenda. But even then, its approach was more deliberate and less idealistic. By 1973, and certainly by 1976, the federal Liberals thought that they had learned a lesson: attachment to *la patrie* cannot be fostered through abstract slogans or symbols, or indeed through generalized support for random forms of participation. The likeliest result of the latter is not identification but opposition: people and groups will be mobilized, not for love of country but for criticism of government. Allegiance and identification come through a more prosaic sense of benefit.

This realization helps explain the new form of politicization that infused these programs after 1973. Of course, the programs had always been politicized, but in a particular way. Contrary to the expectations of those in the "patronage" and "co-optation" schools described in chapter 2, the evidence seems to suggest that politicians and officials did not want to make these programs into vote-buying machines. There certainly was a political logic behind them, but it was more complicated than mere patronage. One rationale clearly was response to unrest, but in a distinctive manner. In Canada, the march of social movements always followed slightly behind American and European developments. The US civil rights movement had no parallel here, and so policy makers could assess the impact of a mass movement demanding equality and having ultimately to engage in violence to get it. The second-wave women's movement, while it had its own community roots in Canada, lagged by three years behind the American one, if the founding of the National Action Committee (1972) and that of the National Organization of Women (1966) are taken as benchmarks. Even the youth and the community development movements were started in the United States.

This delay allowed policy makers in Canada to observe what social movements might do if ignored. A contributing factor to this attitude was the political complexion of the Canadian government at the time. In the United States, for example, the Great Society programs and the social movements that grew around them were products of Lyndon Johnson's adminstration in the mid-1960s. When Richard Nixon moved into the White House in 1969 he undertook a deliberate campaign to reverse the support that the Democrats had given to the movements. In Europe, students and the New Left faced either right-of-centre governments or, as in West Germany, "grand coalitions" that effectively blocked any normal political avenues whereby they might register grievances. The evolution of political terrorism in Europe has been linked to this blockage of opportunity in the late 1960s.

Canadian policy makers had advantages and used them, but co-optation cannot explain the full story. The state's strategy in this period was very clearly a political one, but it was organized within a macro-political framework. The key threat was to national unity, and the main motives were directed to development of a citizenry attached to a single identity through their differences, vibrant and clashing though these might be. Some politicians, such as Pelletier, and some officials, such as Ostry, were pursuing what must plainly be called a social democratic agenda: they wanted to empower the people. The moment was right, and they seized it: in doing so they pursued simultaneously personal, political, and state agendas. When the moment passed, so did their aspirations, and they moved on. The programs, however, remained. For the people who had been mobilized, who had participated, who had talked and written and conferred and travelled and filmed and raised consciousness – these programs were vital in a way that the politicians and officials could only have dimly realized. Some groups limped and slipped and eventually lost their edge – students and youth, for example – but others, once their fingers and toes gripped the crevices of Ottawa's funding edifice, refused to let go. The programs, originally intended simply to enhance participation, became the foundations upon which key segments of Canadian society defined their identity:

women, OLMGs, and ethnics. The state, pursuing an eminently statist strategy, had been ensnared by the fruits of its efforts. While the Citizenship Branch thereafter lost some of its élan, and the government as a whole lost interest, the roots of "citizen participation" among groups and organizations themselves were now firmly established.

CHAPTER SIX

Program Evolution and Change, 1974–1989

The complex and dynamic changes in the Citizenship Branch of the sos between 1968 and 1974 ultimately left a legacy of three key programs: Official Language Minority Groups (olmgs), Multiculturalism, and the Women's Program. From 1970 to 1972, their design and development were part of a larger initiative known as "citizen participation." As we saw in the last chapter, official enthusiasm for participation waned considerably after 1973, to the point where it virtually disappeared as an organizing conceptual framework for government policy. The partisans of participation drifted away to other things or, if they stayed, were marginalized in a department rededicated to a more prosaic agenda.

But the programs could not simply be abandoned. Each, for its own reasons, was important to the government's agenda, and each soon developed a solid political constituency. As noted earlier, after the 1972 election there was a clear shift in the style of politicization of the multiculturalism program so that it was used quite deliberately to get support from key ethnic groups, particularly in the Toronto area. mps lobbied for group grants, and even though the sums were usually small, the sitting member could get some credit for his or her support. Most of the money "ended up in church basements" to support folkloric activities, but in political terms this was almost an asset for Liberal politicians.[1] The Women's Program, by contrast, was not developed at the political level at all but instead emerged from a bureaucratic initiative to stimulate "new and emergent groups." The olmg Program was the most central to the Liberal government's larger political agenda on bilingualism, enjoyed the support of French-Canadian cabinet ministers, and moreover supported organizations whose main lobbying efforts were aimed at the provincial governments for education and other services.

While the three programs were indeed under one roof – the sos – they had had quite different patterns of emergence from within the Citizenship Branch and quite different evolutions afterward. They shared certain features, but they were distinct in terms of design, clientele, and the way in which they articulated with their constituencies. The formative events that shaped them also were different: in OLMG, for example, the election of the PQ in 1976; for the Women's Program, the celebration of International Women's Year in 1975 and later, in 1981–82, constitutional negotiations.

In order to provide a perspective on the simultaneous evolution of these three programs from 1974 to 1989, this chapter is divided into two sections. The first gives an overview of general developments in the citizenship sector and the sos; the second provides a general narrative of each of the three programs. A more detailed analysis of funding levels and grant categories is offered in part III, chapters 7–9.

GENERAL PROGRAM EVOLUTION, 1974–1989

Before considering the programs singly, we should look at some general developments in the sos. In 1974, the Programs Branch of what was now called the "Citizenship Sector" consisted of "directorates" in the following areas: Citizens' Participation, Multiculturalism, Native Citizens. Official Language Minority Groups, and Women's Programs.

The Citizens' Participation Directorate was itself broken down into three new program areas. The first was Assistance to Community Groups: "Grants were provided to community groups to encourage the exchange and sharing of information and resources among organizations; to encourage organizations to develop democratic structures and programs and to assist them to acquire the necessary skills, resources and information; to increase the exchange of information between government and citizens; and, through the Student Community Service Program, to channel the energy and imagination of youth into the voluntary sector." It spent $697,986 on 197 grants; the Student Community Service Program received $3,627,262.[2] The second area was Social Communications: it financed travel, hostels, and exchanges among youth. The third was Group Understanding and Human Rights: "This division promoted and assisted intergroup understanding and the enjoyment of human rights and fundamental freedoms." It spent $1,388,395 on 30 grants.[3] In 1975, as well, the Citizenship Sector was further decentralized, in keeping with policy initiatives first undertaken in 1973.

There were no significant changes in departmental structure until 1977, when OLMG was once more moved from Citizenship back to Cultural Affairs. Like some unwanted orphan, however, OLMG stayed there for only one year, until in 1978 it was shifted back to Citizenship and that whole sector was renamed the Citizenship and Bilingualism Development Sector. The Citizenship Participation Directorate added a new program in 1977 clearly linked to the PQ's victory the year before. It was called "Consultation on Canada's Future" and gave out 75 grants totalling $1.1 million. "The Consultation on Canada's Future was designed to help citizens have a direct and positive impact on the public debate about the future shape of Canadian Confederation."[4] In 1978 the "Citizenship and Bilingualism Development Sector" was rechristened "Citizenship and Official Languages."

Changes over the next two years were minor, except for the temporary addition of Fitness and Amateur Sport in 1979–80 (transferred in September 1981 back to the SOS, where it remained until November 1982, when it was transferred to the Department of Health and Welfare). Citizenship Participation by 1981 had only four programs, two of which were the Women's Program and OLMG (the other two were voluntary action and youth participation). This in itself showed how the larger ideals of citizens' participation had evaporated in favour of ongoing, routinized programming.

However, 1980–81 was also, because of the Quebec referendum and the constitutional negotiations, a year of soul-searching for the department. It developed a mission statement and a new set of Strategic Objectives which formed the basis of a proposal to the Treasury Board on 20 September 1982 for a major restructuring. The 1980–81 annual report thus tried to set out the department's self-understanding.[5] It placed the SOS's activities in the context of the "major sociocultural objectives pursued by the Canadian government," and it noted that one of the "government's priorities is to foster a sense of belonging to Canada." The department was to encourage "full participation of citizens," and its programs were "designed to help the largest possible number of citizens to understand and appreciate the advantages, rights and responsibilities associated with full participation in Canadian society." This sentiment was reinforced the following year, when the SOS's annual report stated: "A major activity of the department is to support voluntary organizations whose role in society is recognized and appreciated by the federal government. These groups of citizens provide the government with important public feedback that indicates the sectors in which government action may be required. Voluntary groups touch nearly all aspects of society: health, education, human rights, social development, youth, women, Native citizens, the handicapped. Their preoccupations are in line with the ideal of social justice that the Department of the Secretary of State seeks to promote."[6]

The September 1982 submission to the Treasury Board was accepted, and changes were implemented in the next year.[7] In 1982, Citizenship Participation was disbanded, with its several components reporting directly to the assistant under-secretary of state for citizenship. The organizational expression of the participatory ideal had long outlived the ideal itself, but over the years its distinctive programs had been reduced and discontinued, until, when it had only a handful left, a separate designation seemed redundant. Bigger changes were in the offing, however. In 1983 four program areas were radically restructured: Administration and Regional Operations, Citizenship and Culture (with subdivisions of Canadian Culture, Citizenship Development – covering women and youth and disabled, Citizenship Registration, Human Rights, and Multiculturalism), Education Support, and Official Languages (which now had something called Promotion of Official Languages, and OLMG was renamed Official Language Communities). Indeed, usage changed, and there was reference now not to "sectors" but to "programs." So Citizenship and Culture was now called one of the four main programs of the SOS, but Citizenship Development was a sector in this program. The last major set of changes came in 1986–87. Citizenship replaced Citizenship and Culture and comprised Citizenship Development, (including disabled persons, Native citizens, voluntary action, women, and youth participation), Citizenship Registration, Human Rights, and Policy and Administrative Support. Multiculturalism was on its own, but Official Language Communities was still under Official Languages.

This catalogue of administrative changes is tedious, to be sure, but illustrates several important things. First, despite all the pulling and hauling and reorganizations, these programs continued to have a family resemblance that drew them together. Second, and quite the opposite, despite this family resemblance, clear differences made them virtually separate fiefdoms. Third, in very general terms, the importance of these programs to the government's agenda waxed and waned according to external developments. The PQ's election in 1976 and the 1980 referendum made the OLMG program crucial in the fight for national unity. The Women's Program languished throughout most of this period but received a sudden and dramatic boost around the time of the constitutional negotiations in 1980–81, as Ottawa sought allies in its fight to patriate the constitution and include with it a Charter of Rights and Freedoms. Fourth, the sos was in tremendous flux through most of this period. From 1969 to 1988 there were eleven different secretaries of state,[8] eleven ministers of state responsible for multiculturalism,[9] and three ministers of state for youth. Between 1977 and 1982, there were four assistant under-secretaries of state for citizenship. The entire organization was in turmoil, and so, unsurprising, it had little clear direction, no strong sense of priorities and objectives, and comparatively little political will to make major program changes. Under these conditions, programs' evolution was ad hoc and unco-ordinated. They were consequently ripe targets for MPs who could show constituents, through their tenacious sponsorship of grant applications, how well they were doing their jobs.

THE THREE PROGRAMS

Official Language Minority Groups

In the early 1970s it clearly appeared as though Ottawa, through the Social Action Branch of sos, was taking a strong lead in shaping the associational system, reaching out to stimulate interest and assist groups to form and lobby. When the sos received responsibility for the Official Languages program in 1969, it established four new branches that reported to the assistant under-secretary of state: Bilingualism Programs, Social Action, Language Administration, and Research and Planning. In its statement of policies and regulations governing the awarding of grants under the program, the Social Action Branch described itself as seeking: "a) to reinforce and to promote the linguistic and cultural development of the official language communities in areas where they are established as minorities; b) to help Canada's two official language communities to live and work together harmoniously in the pursuit of national goals by providing opportunities for the Canadian public to understand and accept the French-English fact and its implications for different spheres of national activities."[10] The branch delivered its services through eight distinct programs: cultural centres, cultural exchanges, international participation, seminars and workshops, social animation, special and national projects, sustaining grants to provincial federations, and youth activities. The two programs of greatest interest were social animation and sustaining grants to provincial federations.

The definition of the sustaining grants program is sufficiently important to warrant full citation:

In most provinces there exists a Federation (Association, Society) which serves as the official representative and spokesman for the minority in its province. It is largely through these organizations that a federal social action program can best reach the people and has the best chance of finding acceptance for its policies and projects. Experience has shown that, because of their minority situation, such organizations seldom achieve the necessary dynamism to attain their objectives if they are left to struggle along with no more than their own meager resources.

Traditionally, a high percentage of their time and energies are consumed in trying to sustain themselves, e.g., by fund raising for the operation of a permanent secretariat. Sustaining grants, applied to the operational budget of these organizations, will, by looking after some of their general overhead, allow them to channel more of their energies into productive activities.

Government action in the promotion of its bilingual and bicultural objectives, must not substitute itself for local initiative and effort; its action must support and stimulate popular involvement, but never replace it.[11]

The specific grant regulations under this sub-program stipulated that normally only one organization in each province would be recognized as the "official federation, association or society representing the official minority in its province."[12] Annual operating grants could go toward salaries, office rental, supplies, publications, utilities, and staff travel, but they were not to exceed 50 per cent of approved costs for any of these categories, and in no case would an organization receive a sustaining grant in excess of $20,000.[13]

The social animation program was firmly rooted in the citizen participation paradigm, as its title might imply. Once again the description of the program warrants a lengthy citation:

The purpose of social animation is to involve the people at the grass-roots level in the processes of problem-identification, decision-making, and action-taking. It is based on the conviction that each individual and each group, regardless of the level of development, is capable of autonomous creativity. Its goal is that of setting into action, in the most effective way, the creative potentialities that are unrecognized and dormant in those individuals or groups.

Applied to official language minority groups, social animation can become an effective tool against apathy, against assimilation and against the slow but relentless disappearance of one of Canada's cultural heritages. Much more effectively than propaganda, it can, by grass-roots stock-taking and popular involvement, bring about a pride ine [sic] one's heritage, a more positive appreciation of its assets, and a collective desire to preserve and strengthen it.

Since social animation addresses itself to the masses and is not revenue-bearing as such, the need for outside financial assistance becomes essential.[14]

Grants under this category would be made in consultation with the "official" provincial association. With the exception of the youth program, which was designed to help the establishment of OLMG youth organizations in each province, grants were not mutually exclusive. Thus, a provincial association with a sustaining grant could simultaneously apply for grants for cultural centres, cultural exchanges, seminars, and social animation. Indeed, under the logic of the program itself, this was very likely to happen, since the "official" provincial association would now, with the help of sustaining grants, have an organizational capacity superior to most other linguistic minority associations.

During fiscal 1969–70, 109 grants were approved, for a total of $1,015680 (though this included Citizenship Branch grants before the Social Action Branch was established). Under the sustaining grants component, provincial associations received $115,600 in direct aid. The social animation component gave eight provincial associations $312,621.[15] The 1970 report on the Social Action Branch described the latter as "a program which, by utilizing the services of professionally trained community development officers, attempted an in-depth attack on mass apathy and, concentrated, during the past months, on sensitizing and preparing confirmed or potential leaders through group dynamic sessions and leadership training courses." The report claimed that the branch had involved over 20,000 people at the community level in such sessions.[16] The following year the branch gave out 183 grants totalling $1,822,314, and its budget grew incrementally until by 1975 it was spending almost $3 million per year in grants. The original 1969 allocation to the program had been $1.3 million (of which only $1 million was spent), and so over six years the budget had barely tripled. To put this into perspective, in 1975 the Multiculturalism Directorate spent $2.2 million, and the SOS allocated $3.6 million to the Student Community Service Program.[17]

This apparent drift and the low priority given to OLMGs was reversed to some extent in the next five years. There were two key stimulants. The first was the PQ's provincial election victory on 15 November 1976. A separatist government in Quebec raised the question of national unity once more, and Ottawa realized the advantages of a strategy of fostering linguistic minority communities. The other stimulant came from the client groups themselves. It would have been surprising, even with the few resources devoted to social animation, if sustaining grants to provincial OLMGs and leadership training had not had some mobilizing effect. The Official Languages Act and the federal policy of bilingualism had created a policy commitment that could be criticized and had helped to institutionalize the critics by supporting groups whose main purpose lay in seeing expansions in the program. As Keith Spicer, the official languages commissioner, noted in his 1976 annual report: "Federal policy and funding have also enabled the provincial associations to emerge as more useful pressure groups. In Ontario, New Brunswick and Manitoba, to cite only the strongest, these groups now command attention from press and government, even if their views must always be fought for. In 1976, on advice from the report *C'est le temps ou jamais* (It's Now or Never) commissioned by the Secretary of State, the Government encouraged creation of a national common-front body called the Fédération des francophones hors Québec (FFHQ). This body, with extremely limited means, is already doing its job well by shaking up quite a few people in Ottawa."[18]

The FFHQ, in a press release on 5 January, 1977, said: "Quebec has decided to pursue actively its own destiny ... Its attitude is exemplary and francophones outside Quebec respect it and are inspired by it."[19] The FFHQ as a result demanded more direct funding for OLMG organizations as well as local community services in French. Another pressure on Ottawa to respond to these demands was the PQ's promise in April 1977 to support francophone communities outside the province.[20] As well, the official languages commissioner's annual report for 1977 severely criticized the SOS, calling it "Characters in Search of an Author": "After eight years of dealing with the official languages and official language minority groups, it appears that the Secretary of State's Department is still wondering where it is going and how it will get there."[21] The commissioner commented acerbically that "present misunderstandings result in considerable measure from a virtual breakdown of reasonable human intercourse between a government agency and a group it is designed to serve."[22]

The government responded in several ways to the new situation and criticisms. First, the Throne Speech in 1977 noted the crisis in national unity and promised a "comprehensive policy for official language minorities."[23] Second, on 27 October, the secretary of state, John Roberts, announced that resources available each year for linguistic minorities would increase from \$30 million to \$75 million over the next five years. For the first time, the program committed financial support to Quebec's anglophone organizations. The minister acknowledged that some of this money might help anglophone Quebecers fight the province's new language legislation (Bill 101) and campaign in the referendum that was expected on independence.[24] He made it abundantly clear that enhanced support for OLMGs was rooted in the government's larger national unity agenda: "We will succeed in staying the forces working for separation only if we can honestly say to French Canadians that one of our ultimate goals is to see to it that throughout Canada a climate proper to the development of French language and culture will prevail."[25]

Third, the SOS established a consultative mechanism to communicate with OLMGs. An interdepartmental committee, chaired by the assistant under-secretary of state, would report twice a year to the secretary of state. Regional officers were designated to act as channels of communication for the OLMGs.[26] This arrangement was in part a response to criticism by the OLMGs themselves, in particular by the FFHQ, in its report *Les héritiers de Durham*, which complained about lack of co-ordination in the program and specifically in the distribution of grants.[27]

Over the next three years, the OLMG program shifted among various sectors and branches of the SOS, to settle finally as Citizenship and Official Languages in 1981. In 1984, Official Languages, split into Promotion and Official Language Communities, was established as a separate concern, and OLMGs were redesignated Official Language Communities. (The sub-programs' titles were altered slightly in 1988, but without any change in substance.) In 1979 the program assisted in formation of the Council of Quebec Minorities, which in 1982 came together with other groups to form Alliance Quebec.[28] In 1980 the FFHQ received pilot money to found, through training sessions, new francophone associations, and the next year it received the right of regular meetings with the SOS.[29] Despite these efforts, a Departmental Task Force in 1980 noted that "some Sector staff questions its [the program's] *raison d'être*, its underlying philosophy."[30] In his 1980 annual report, the official languages commissioner characterized the SOS's activities in the OLMG areas as a "mixed bag of piecemeal reactions to community pressures interspersed with heavy insinuations that father knows best."[31]

The problem was linked to the success of the OLMG program itself, as illustrated in the fortunes of the FFHQ. Passage of the Official Languages Act and establishment of the Social Action Program in 1969 had refocused OLMG's energies and directed them to the national level. The FFHQ itself said that, with Ottawa's involvement, the provincial associations gained both the confidence and the resources to tackle a range of problems including communications, community development, the economy, education, and social policy. It was possible, in short, to begin to elaborate "une stratégie globale."[32] Provincial lobbying by OLMGs led the SOS to establish a Working Group on linguistic minorities which in 1975 released the report *C'est le temps ou jamais*. The recommendations suggested better consultative structures between the OLMGs and the SOS, and in November the FFHQ, as an umbrella association for the nine provincial associations, was set up.

The FFHQ took it upon itself to follow through on the other recommendations of the Working Group's report, but it was clearly intended to change the contours of the policy field in two ways. First, as indicated in the preceding quotation, it would press for "global" strategies on the language issue. This implied a concerted and broader approach that would integrate all elements of community life around language and culture, rather than isolating them as discrete components that might be addressed by other means. In practical terms, this meant principally seeking control over education and adoption of French as an official language in each of the provinces. More generally, the FFHQ was at the forefront of defining the linguistic issue in terms of fundamental rights rather than simply a technical matter of services. Any government service, whether it be education or community development, must be grounded in the "fundamental guarantees" of individual and collective rights inscribed in the constitution.[33] Second, the FFHQ was designed to loosen the paternalism of the SOS and develop direct consultative mechanisms wherein the provincial associations and the FFHQ would become partners in policy development. In practical terms, this approach has meant demands for regular meetings at senior levels and ultimately for some form of tripartism involving politicians, senior administrators, and OLMG representatives.

Secretary of State's *Grants and Contributions Manual, 1988* makes it clear that the Official Language Communities (OLC) program is intended to be proactive, to help change institutions and attitudes, and not simply to deliver services. The instruments for achieving this goal are to be, in part, advocacy organizations that happen to agree with the government's policy vision. The manual poses the following as the overriding objective of the OLC program: "To make Canadians aware of the country's linguistic duality and to help non-federal public administrations and the private sector set up and deliver adequate services to minority official language communities."[34] Along with assistance for the "creation, development and maintenance" of institutions, the manual envisages assistance "to organizations for lobbying activities." Eligible applicants are non-profit organizations, non-governmental institutions (established, non-profit, and not under the control of any government), provincial/territorial/municipal governments, and individuals.

The section on lobby groups shows that the program is prepared to encourage a broad range of activities.

Financial assistance will be provided for activities whose aims include:
a) access to or improvements in minority language education from pre-school to post-secondary institutions and minority community control over primary and secondary education services;
b) the passing and implementation of legislation recognizing the equal status of the two official languages;
c) access to improvements in social, judicial, economic and cultural as well as health, sports and recreation services in the minority language;
d) access to or improvements in telecommunications services, including the print media, radio and television and data information systems such as Telidon.[35]

This list consists almost exclusively of items in provincial jurisdiction. One of the less appreciated aspects of Canada's federal policy of bilingualism is how much of it must be directed at provincial services such as education; the policy aims at provision of bilingual services by the federal government throughout the country and the nurturing of linguistic communities. The former can be achieved with institutional changes and development of services by federal agencies; the latter depends on creating a supportive economic, social, and linguistic environment at the local level. The conflicts between francophone minorities and western provincial governments, as well as the more recent battle over Bill 178 in Quebec, illustrate the problem. In all these cases the linguistic minorities, with the aid of Ottawa, were targeting provincial language policies that they claimed made it difficult, if not impossible, for them to thrive as communities.

These program developments raise the issue of the effectiveness of the OLMG policy. Associations in this policy area exist to serve their respective communities and so can be understood only in terms of the history and current distribution of those communities. History would take us too far afield; it is enough to note that each province has a linguistic minority of long standing. The English in Quebec can trace an organized community of British origins back to

1763, and Acadians in the Maritimes and French-speaking minorities in Ontario and the west have roots in the earliest French settlements and explorations connected with the fur trade. According to the 1986 census, out of a total of 25 million Canadians, 15 million list English as their mother tongue and 6 million list French. Of those 6 million francophones, however, only about 838,000, or 14 per cent, live outside Quebec. The largest numbers of francophones outside Quebec live in Ontario (422,770, or 4.6 per cent of the provincial population) and New Brunswick (223,675, or 31.8 per cent of the province's population). In the other provinces, they range from a low of 0.3 per cent in Newfoundland to a high of 4.2 per cent in Manitoba. Anglophones in Quebec account for 8.9 per cent of the provincial population, but three-quarters of them live in Montreal, where they make up almost 20 per cent of the city's population. These statistics are based on mother tongue, but the 1986 census also provided information on language spoken at home. By this measure, the official-language minority groups outside Quebec are even smaller, dropping in some cases (e.g., Saskatchewan and Alberta) by more than half.[36]

The associational system built around these communities may be divided into three tiers.[37] The first is nation-wide umbrella groups, consisting principally of la Fédération des communautés francophones et acadienne du Canada (which in 1991 succeeded the FFHQ), la Fédération des jeunes canadiens-français, la Fédération nationale des femmes canadiennes-françaises, la Fédération culturelle des canadiens-français, and l'Association de la presse francophone hors Québec. The second tier consists of province-wide organizations that represent the minority language communities. These ten organizations are: la Fédération des francophones de Terre-Neuve et du Labrador, la Société Saint-Thomas d'Aquin, la Fédération acadienne de la Nouvelle-Écosse, la Société des Acadiens du Nouveau-Brunswick, Alliance Quebec, l'Association canadienne-française de l'Ontario, la Société franco-manitobaine, l'Association culturelle canadienne-française de la Saskatchewan, l'Association canadienne-française de l'Alberta, and la Fédération des Franco-Colombiens. The third tier is virtually uncountable and consists of hundreds of community-based organizations such as daycare centres, festivals, home-school associations, and youth clubs. These primarily service organizations are actors in the policy network.

Many of the organizations in the first and second tiers have long histories, though the character of their political activity has changed in the last twenty years. L'Association canadienne-française de l'Ontario, for example, can trace a continuous organizational history back to 1910, when its forerunner was set up to fight for francophone educational rights. Education was also the original core concern of la Société franco-manitobaine (established 1916) and l'Association canadienne-française de l'Alberta (1926). Other organizations are of more recent vintage. Alliance Quebec was created only in 1982, through amalgamation of several anglophone organizations. The FFHQ was formed in the mid-1970s to provide national representation for provincial francophone minorities.

Multiculturalism[38]

Within a year of its formal announcement, the Multiculturalism program could boast nine sub-programs. They included Canadian Identities (song and dance), Ethnic Group Liaison, Ethnic Press Analysis Service, Immigrant Orientation, Multicultural Centres, Multiculturalism Studies Program, and Non-Official Language Teaching Aids. The key element was Multicultural Projects Grants: "During the fiscal year 1974–75, the Citizenship Sector adopted a decentralized granting system. Under this new system 611 multicultural projects were supported at both regional and national levels for a total of $2,258,701."[39]

In May 1973, Stanley Haidasz, the minister of state for multiculturalism, announced several of these new programs but emphasized grants and left himself open to charges of favouritism and bias.[40] Also, the Canadian Consultative Council on Multiculturalism, when originally discussed in 1970, was supposed to have had 12–15 members. When it was finally set up after the 1972 election, it had 101, many of them Liberal supporters.[41] After the 1974 election, in which the Liberals managed to win a majority, John Munro became minister of state for multiculturalism, concurrent with his portfolio as minister of labour. Munro had trouble keeping his attention on the portfolio because Labour kept him so busy, but by mid-1975 it was time for a policy review of multiculturalism, and so an outside consultant did a review in late 1975, and a reorientation of policy was prepared in late 1975.

John Munro took a close interest in this process and even helped draft the proposals. In Munro's view too many of the grants under multiculturalism funded repetitive celebrations of folklore: groups would lose creativity and become dependent. He also worried that some larger groups (such as Ukrainians) had enough expertise to use the grants system better than smaller groups. The solution seemed clear: encourage groups to get some outside funding and reallocate funds so as to "place a higher priority on support for the visible minorities and disadvantaged groups who did not possess a well-developed organizational infrastructure, and who were particularly likely to be the victims of discrimination."[42] These changes represented a major shift away from the prime minister's 1971 statement that the program was oriented toward cultural and group survival; the new priority would be "group understanding" and tolerance. The new targets would be what Munro called the country's "real minorities": blacks, Portuguese, people from the Caribbean, India, or Pakistan.

Traditional ethnic organizations reacted unfavourably to this reorientation, however.[43] Julius Koteles, national chair of the Canadian Consultative Council on Multiculturalism, said that John Munro's plan was "incompatible with the multiculturalism program" and later attacked the minister so viciously that in November 1976 Munro asked him to resign. It is not difficult to understand resentment by the older ethnic groups. At the symbolic level, when multiculturalism had been mooted in the late 1960s, it had been conceived as a program to help "Third Force" Canadians claim their rightful place beside Canadians of English and French background. The entire emphasis had been on cultural sharing, against the backdrop of bilingualism. By 1980, the groups would lobby successfully to have non-official languages recognized and supported in some way through the program, arguing that the prime minister's statement of October 1971 had seriously erred in separating culture and language. But by the mid- and late 1970s, Canada's immigrant population was changing dramatically. Asian, African, and Caribbean peoples were accounting for the bulk of new immigrants, and they were less interested in celebrating their cultures than in battling discrimination and racism. These problems, to be sure, had plagued the earlier ethnic groups to some extent, but for the most part in the past and without the same force. Some officials thought that trying to address the needs of both sectors through one program was inadvisable, but no changes were made at this time.[44]

However, the very demographic changes under way in Canada in this period meant that eventually there would have to be some response within the Multiculturalism program. In 1980, for example, "emerging communities," such as the National Black Coalition of Canada and the National Association of Canadians of Origins in India, received funds.[45] In 1981, there were eight key programs under Multiculturalism: Canadian Ethnic Studies (for scholarly research, $500,000 plus $300,000 for a chair at Moncton in Acadian studies); Cultural Integration (immigrant integration, $1.3 million);

Cultural Enrichment ($1.4 million for heritage languages); Group Development ($2.5 million to organizations for projects of a general nature – for example, conferences); Intercultural Communications ($1.2 million for core funding for groups that worked together); Operation Support ($205,000 for core funding for voluntary organizations representing the interests of ethnics); and Writing and Publications, Performing and Visual Arts. In addition there were "initiative programs" – ad hoc programs to support, for example, conferences for immigrant women and a pilot project on race relations in Toronto.[46]

Policy was thus reoriented in 1981. The key shift was from "cultural retention" to a focus on social issues, and in particular, racism. According to Stasiulis, pressure was coming from the visible minority communities in the early 1980s, and the Liberals needed something to get their support in the coming election.[47] James Fleming, the minister of state for multiculturalism, was also concerned with the outbreak of some racist events (e.g., evidence of the Ku Klux Klan in Ontario and British Columbia). That led to establishment of a House of Commons Special Committee on Participation of Visible Minorities in May 1983; it issued its report, *Equality Now!*, in March 1984. The report made over eighty recommendations. It suggested tax incentives for businesses that offered opportunities to visible minorities, contract-compliance mechanisms to enforce affirmative action programs, stronger laws against hate literature, and compensation of Japanese Canadians for losses during their internment in the Second World War.

The minister tabled his response on 20 June 1984. While the government did not wish to proceed as far as the committee had recommended, it argued that three recent initiatives in multiculturalism reflected the desired reorientation of policy. First, in the previous year a Race Relations Unit had been started "because of indications of increasing racial tension in Canada."[48] Second, a new focus on multiculturalism in education had led to establishment and funding of the Canadian Council for Multicultural and Intercultural Education. The council had representation from provinces to facilitate curriculum development and projects related to intercultural understanding. Third, there was a new thrust to identify and meet the needs of immigrant women. (Another initiative that year saw changes in the Canadian Consultative Council on Multiculturalism – a reduction in number of members, more research money, and a higher profile.) The government rejected the committee's recommendation of a new Ministry of Multiculturalism and offered instead to pass a Multiculturalism Act that would outline the principles of the policy and Canada's commitment to it.[49]

Major developments occurred again in 1985–86: the first federal-provincial Conference on Multiculturalism in Winnipeg in May 1985, creation of a House of Commons Standing Committee on Multiculturalism, a comprehensive review of multicultural policy, a federally sponsored conference in April 1986 entitled "Multiculturalism Means Business," release by the prime minister on 21 March 1986 of a Proclamation on the Second Decade for Action to Combat Racism and Racial Discrimination, and tabling by the government on the same day of its progress report outlining actions taken to address the recommendations in *Equality Now!*[50]

In 1987 the new Standing Committee on Multiculturalism issued its first report, *Multiculturalism: Building the Canadian Mosaic*. The committee had heard from various ethnic groups and associations, and a consistent refrain in their presentations had been the demand for separate legislation, a multiculturalism commissioner (to parallel the official languages commissioner), and stricter enforcement of government policy in the private sector. The committee's final report showed how far the discourse on multicultural policy had advanced in fifteen years. The committee's view was that policy had evolved over the years from a dedication to cultural preservation to the attempt to ensure social, economic, and political equality for all Canadians. The report agreed with the idea of separate legislation and a separate department (with a budget of over $300 million, consisting of programs drawn from the SOS, Employment and Immigration, and Communications). Continued grants to organizations were also strongly supported.[51]

On 1 December 1987, David Crombie, secretary of state and minister responsible for multiculturalism, tabled a bill with a list of rights and principles. It was coolly received by multicultural organizations because the principles had no effective means of enforcement. As Dr. Peter Hlibowych, president of the Ukrainian Canadian Committee (Ontario Council) stated: "Nothing's new. A full ministry would have given multiculturalism the necessary power. It would give ethnics more status, a higher profile in Canadian society."[52] The legislation received royal assent on 21 July 1988.

The Canadian Multiculturalism Act placed the government's policy commitment to multiculturalism in a legislative, as opposed to merely programmatic, context. The policy entails ten separate commitments that may be assembled into several categories. The first category includes recognition – of "cultural and racial diversity" and of multiculturalism as a "fundamental characteristic of the Canadian heritage and identity." The second category covers general promotion of such things as the multicultural character of the country itself, the "full and equitable participation of individuals and communities of all origins" in Canadian society, and the understanding and general appreciation of the contribution of diverse cultures. The third category covers specific institutional promotion such as equal treatment and protection (while recognizing diversity) under the law, the use of "languages other than English and French," and a range of programs to put into practice the previous sets of commitments.

The legislation also tries to elaborate the specific ministerial mandate to accomplish all these goals. This list consists largely of platitudes, but for two clauses. The first says that the minister may "encourage and assist individuals, organizations and institutions to project the multicultural reality of Canada in their activities in Canada and abroad."[53] This is essentially a statement of the existing grants policy. The second is the commitment to "facilitate the acquisition, retention and use of all languages that contribute to the multicultural heritage of Canada." Finally, the legislation calls for an Advisory Committee to be appointed on the advice of "such organizations representing multicultural interests as the Minister deems appropriate." The legislation, while vague, is not merely symbolic. It articulates certain policy commitments which, however qualified, ratify the practices of the past, particularly support to and consultation with a range of organizations representing Canada's ethnic communities.

In May 1988 the federal government announced that it would spend an additional $62 million over five years on multiculturalism, and in July the House of Commons unanimously passed the new multiculturalism bill.[54] Not without coincidence, perhaps, a federal election was widely expected that year, and some critics argued that the government was simply shoring up its support among ethnic voters. The federal budget of 20 February 1990, however, reduced grant expenditures under the multiculturalism program (and the Women's Program) by $23 million.

Women's Program

As noted in chapter 5, the Women's Program emerged slightly later than either the OLMG or the Multicultural areas. The Royal Commission on the Status of Women in its 1970 report had recommended that women's organizations receive public funding, and the release of the report was itself a stimulus for fledgling women's groups to form both for the provision of special services for women and for more effective lobbying. The National Action Committee on the Status of Women (NAC), Canada's largest and most important women's organization, grew out of an Ad Hoc Committee on the Status of Women explicitly designed to monitor implementation of the royal commission's recommendations.

When the government seemed reluctant to move quickly on the commission's proposals, the Committee on Equality for Women (formed by Doris Anderson and Laura Sabia to pressure the Pearson government to appoint a royal commission on women's issues) turned itself into the National Ad Hoc Committee on the Status of Women in Canada. It met for the first time in 1971, and several radical feminist organizations joined it (e.g., Toronto Women's Liberation and New Feminists, also from Toronto). In 1972 it turned itself into NAC: "NAC dropped the optimistic 'ad hoc' from its title because the government would not fund ad hoc groups, and money was wanted, first for 'Strategy for Change,' the national conference which inaugurated NAC in the spring of 1972, and then for continuing funding (on which NAC still depends, its constituent groups making only token contributions)."[55]

Thus in 1971–72 the number of applications to the Citizens' Organizations program grew steadily, and, as chapter 5 showed, this led Citizenship Branch officials in 1973 to designate women as a special focus of the program. In 1974 the priority given to women's organizations was strengthened by development of a separate Women's Program.[56] The previous year, the government had established the Canadian Advisory Council on the Status of Women (Katie Cooke was its first chair) and designated a minister responsible for the status of women. Advisers on women's issues were also appointed in many departments, particularly Justice, National Health and Welfare, and Employment and Immigration. These served to supplement pre-existing networks of organizations such as the Women's Bureau in the Department of Labour, the Office of Equal Opportunity in the Public Service Commission, and the Office of the Coordinator of the Status of Women in the Privy Council Office.

Sue Findlay has provided the most detailed discussion of the Women's Program and was its director for a time. She argues that while many new advisory agencies and offices were created in the 1972–75 period, there was still substantial resistance to feminism in the state bureaucracy. Many of the women appointed were not feminists, but merely female bureaucrats, and this reduced their impact. Few feminist ideas got into the policy process, but even when they did they were met with ridicule. The Women's Program was an exception, however. "Organized by feminists who had decided that the resources of the state could be used to support the development of the women's movement and located in a department that had a history of creating programs for the 'disadvantaged,' the Women's Program was for a time able to present a feminist challenge to bureaucratic attempts to subordinate and incorporate demands for equality."[57]

In 1972 Findlay was hired on a short-term contract to document funding needs for women under the Citizen Participation program in the Citizenship Branch. She became the adviser on grants in 1973 and established contacts with feminist groups across the country. The program initially had only $200,000, but the grants were used strategically and in close consultation with local organizations. In 1974–75, this money was spread out over 79 organizations. Findlay argues that the women working in what became the Women's Program in 1974 "held themselves accountable to the women's movement rather than to government priorities. All were defined as feminists and were largely drawn from feminist groups. Liaison with the women's movement was built into every aspect of the Program's work. A feminist perspective clearly determined the Program's development, and was reflected in project definition, staff recruitment, and the Program's organization and management."[58]

On 18 December 1972, the General Assembly of the United Nations declared 1975 International Women's Year (IWY), giving a substantial boost to the Women's Program. Ottawa established an Interdepartmental Committee on the IWY, co-chaired by officials from the Privy Council Office and External Affairs. The Women's Program received $2.5 million out of a total of $5 million for the IWY program. Two-thirds of that amount ($1.6 million) went out in grants to women's organizations, while the rest was used to defray administrative costs and provide special activities as well as promote the program.[59] The grants did not go for projects or for core support, but instead for conferences and information resources, while approximately one-quarter of the grants were given to women's centres. As a mobilizing strategy the program seemed to be reasonably successful. An internal evaluation conducted in 1976 concluded that the "special program did stimulate the voluntary sector to organize for action on women's issues on a much wider basis than previously."[60] Approximately 500 groups received support from IWY grant funds, and one-third of these were what the evaluation called "ad hoc and emerging" – rather than established – groups.[61] The centrepiece of the IWY was the Interchange '75 series – nine seminars on subjects touching on women's concerns.[62]

Some IWY-supported projects continued into 1976, but the program was by definition limited and so did not permanently increase the resources allotted to the Women's Program. In 1978, for example, the program was able to award the NAC only $37,000 (up from $17,500 the previous year); it gave out in total only $500,000 in grants, the same as the previous year. In 1980, the program total was up to only $700,000, but in the next year it was almost doubled, to $1.2 million. In 1982, the Women's Program was increased dramatically again: it was almost tripled to $3.2 million. Though the sums are not in themselves large, the proportional increases far exceeded increases to other programs. The Liberal government's largess seems peculiar, because in 1981 Lloyd Axworthy, minister responsible for the status of women, became embroiled in a controversy with the Canadian Advisory Council on the Status of Women. Axworthy had tried to stop a council-sponsored national conference on the constitution because it might embarrass the government, and Doris Anderson, the council's chair, resigned, as did several researchers and board members.

Relations between the government and the women's movement at that stage were quite cool, but women's organizations (many of them funded by Ottawa) actually turned out to be valuable allies in Ottawa's struggle to win over the provinces and the populace to the patriation of the constitution. While feminists lobbied hard and successfully for stronger equality provisions in the Charter of Rights and Freedoms, they also were strongly in favour of the general principle of a Charter and did their best to lobby provincial governments.[63] Ottawa may have been rewarding its allies with the increased funds for the Women's Program. Alternatively, it may have been preparing the ground for the 1984 election, since in January of that year it announced yet another major increase, quadrupling the program's funds over four years to more than $15 million. As well, the government launched creation of five women's studies chairs at Canadian universities. The first was set up at Mount Saint Vincent University in Halifax in March 1984.

Ironically, just as the Women's Program was growing, one of its main opponents was being created. In the fall of 1983, a new, non-feminist women's organization was incorporated, calling itself REAL Women (Realistic, Equal, and Active for Life). The group originally claimed that it had 10,000 members, but this figure was soon discredited.[64] Its anti-abortion stand was perhaps its most visible position, but it also rejected equal pay for work of equal value, universal publicly funded daycare, and easier divorce provisions. The REAL Women funding case deserves detailed attention because it was a rare public battle over the objectives of the Women's Program, and also because it led to a parliamentary committee's reviewing the program.

REAL Women was formed on 3 September 1983 in Ontario by a group of women who had been active in the "pro-life" movement[65] and who were dissatisfied with the way in which "women's issues" were being championed by mainstream feminist organizations. In a 1984 letter to Serge Joyal, secretary of state, the president of REAL Women, Grace Petrasek, argued that for too long "radical feminist groups have had a monopoly on speaking for women" and argued that an alternative voice was required, one that would stress the importance of the family and would not assume that all women think the same way on issues such as pay equity legislation or daycare.[66] In August 1984, REAL Women applied to the Women's Program for two grants. The first was for a $17,250 project grant to mount a conference entitled "Women of Tomorrow: Positive Options for Women in a Changing World." The second was for a $93,400 sustaining grant to assist in administrative overhead. In September the file was forwarded to Ottawa and the attention of the director of the Women's program, Lyse Blanchard. In October the program wrote to Petrasek asking for details about the organization's founding and functions. Petrasek responded with a letter on 9 November 1984, detailing the group's national aspirations, its constitution, and its activities. She also mentioned that REAL now saw that it in fact needed as much as $185,000 annually for its operations.[67]

On 14 December 1984, Blanchard wrote to Petrasek and turned down both applications. She reminded Petrasek of the government's 1979 endorsation of three basic principles as part of its commitment to the World Plan of Action adopted by the United Nations that year. The principles were: that all persons should enjoy equal rights, opportunities, and responsibilities; that both women and men should be free to make life-style choices, and that therefore neither law nor society should impose sex-stereotyped roles on women or men; and that with the exception of maternity and short-term remedial measures to reduce or eliminate past disadvantages, there would be no special treatment on the basis of sex.[68] Blanchard's letter continued: "The purpose of R.E.A.L. Women, as clearly stated in your constitution and newsletter, is the promotion of the nurturing role of women within the traditional family structure. Your organization is therefore dedicated to supporting a particular way of life as reflected in the traditional family model. While there is no doubt that women's work in the home certainly represents a worthy and valuable contribution to society, the promotion of a particular family model is not within the spirit of the objectives of the Program. The Program concentrates on supporting groups who are working to explore all options for women as they work toward equality in a society that is changing rapidly."[69]

REAL responded with a letter to the prime minister (with a copy to Walter McLean, secretary of state) castigating the program for supporting radical feminists such as those in NAC. The letter emphasized the leitmotif of REAL by arguing that NAC did not represent the full spectrum of opinion among Canadian women, pointedly reminding him that while NA endorsed the NPD in the 1984 election, only 18 per cent of Canadian women actually voted for that party (30 per cent voted Liberal; 49 per cent voted Conservative). REAL also organized a letter-writing campaign that sent 300 complaints to the secretary of state. In April 1985, REAL succeeded in having a meeting with McLean, where the department's refusal to fund it was once more reiterated. In June, REAL met with approximately thirty members of the Progressive Conservative caucus, and tax treatment of women in the home and Women's Program funding were raised. On July 4, REAL met with the under-secretary of state, Robert Rabinovitch, and officials from Status of Women Canada, and once more the department's position not to fund it was stated.

REAL tried to resubmit its proposal once more in November 1985. It asked for an application form, which officials balked at,[70] because the usual procedure was to submit a proposal for review and development before receiving an application form. On 28 November 1985, however, Blanchard sent REAL another form, which was returned on 9 December 1985 with a request for a sustaining grant of $1,138,500.[71] The sum alone would have elicited more than a simple "yes/no" from the program, but in any case the normal procedure required prior submission of a proposal with more details than the application itself could convey. Unsurprising, therefore, the program wrote back to REAL in December requesting answers to a series of questions on past accomplishments, goals and objectives, links with "other equality seeking groups," structure and membership, decision making, and the specific projects to be funded.[72] This application was also turned down, but REAL met again with the secretary of state (by now it was Benoît Bouchard) in February 1986, and the minister advised the group to resubmit an application with more information. The rest of the year was occupied with this application, as officials requested more information and the REAL executive denied that the minister had suggested that more information was necessary. Finally, on 6 October 1986, Gwen Landolt (REAL's legal counsel) forwarded more information about the organization to support the application.

On 6 December 1986, REAL revised its application and asked for operational funding of $566,620. This request was turned down personally by the secretary of state, David Crombie, in a letter dated 4 January 1987. He admitted that treatment of REAL's original application had at times been incompetent and uncourteous, and he pointed out that the whole question of funding of women's organizations was now under review by the House of Commons Standing Committee of Secretary of State. His main defence of the rejection, however, rested on technical grounds. The program had only once (in the case of Media Watch, an organization with a proven record) given a group operating funding at the outset. The usual procedure was to fund only projects for a period of time to assess the group's viability and then, under certain circumstances, to give operational grants. He referred to the program's record of funding diverse projects, from quality daycare and equal pay to improved pensions and maternity leave. These projects all reflected approaches to equality that REAL did not share. REAL was on record as opposing abortion for any reason, universal daycare, no-fault divorce, equal pay for work of equal value, and affirmative action.

In January 1987, REAL began the application process all over again, this time applying (as it had originally) for project funding. By April, it had submitted a proposal to conduct research on why women worked outside the home, at a cost of $37,000.[73] In May, the program requested more precise cost estimates for the survey component of the proposal. At this point, however, the organization was already in some trouble. The Standing Committee of Secretary of State, chaired by MP Geoff Scott, started in December 1986 to review the Women's Program, in large part because of the REAL issue and the organization's public complaints of bias. The committee held hearings in St John's, Halifax, Ottawa, Winnipeg, and Vancouver, listening to testimony from 144 witnesses. In addition, it received 265 written briefs. The result of this avalanche of representation was a nineteen-page report in April 1987, one month after hearings had been completed.

Clearly the committee could not have had time to digest the information, let alone give a considered view on the nature of the Women's Program and the problem of funding advocacy organizations. The recommendations were all technical, dealing with minor adjustments to administration that in many cases were already in practical effect. The committee's only substantial recommendation was that funding should be directed to groups that supported the definition of women's equality contained in the Charter, *Dimensions of Equality: A Federal Government Work Plan for Women*, and the UN Convention for the Elimination of All Forms of Discrimination against Women.[74] Indeed, the report was so bland that the government was able to agree with all of its recommendations (save perhaps the suggestion that funding might be increased).[75]

Most of the groups appearing before the committee were affiliates of NAC, which had little more than contempt for REAL. The absence of any serious consideration of the meaning of equality in the committee's report meant a resounding defeat for REAL that crippled the organization. Petrasek resigned the presidency in 1986 and was replaced by Lynne Scime. Scime and her faction were interested less in attacking feminism and its agenda than in championing family values and linking REAL more explicitly with the anti-abortion movement.[76] According to Gwen Landolt, REAL had been run for most of its life by a small core of activists, who, without the benefit of SOS funding, were simply exhausted. They recruited new people who wanted to change REAL's direction from lobbying to education, and who also wanted to ally it with the Christian Heritage Party. There was therefore a split in the organization for some time that was resolved only in the 1988 annual meeting. Landolt and the original activists regained control.[77] By the end of 1988, Landolt and Lettie Morse were once more, on behalf of REAL, applying for a project grant to mount a conference on the theme of equality. The organization asked for $119,720 but was granted only $21,000 for a conference that it eventually held in April 1989.[78] The sum was less significant than the fact that any money at all was going to an organization that by its own admission opposed virtually everything that women's organizations funded by the Women's Program had stood for over the past fifteen years. However, the support for REAL had to be set against the larger canvas of the government's approach to women's organizations.

In the February 1989 budget, the government froze the Women's Program for three years.[79] The Conservative caucus, despite David Crombie's rejection of REAL funding the previous year, had been quite sympathetic to REAL Women and had become even more so when NAC supported the NDP against the Canada–United States Free Trade Agreement in the 1988 election.[80] In May 1989, Tory ministers declined a fifteen-year tradition of meeting with NAC for a lobby session.[81] In the budget of February 1990, the government announced actual cuts to the Women's Program which called for elimination of financing for three women's magazines (*Canadian Women's Studies Journal, Health Sharing,* and *Resources for Feminist Research*) and 20 per cent reductions in support for five feminist action groups (Canadian Association for the Advancement of Women in Sports, Canadian Congress for Learning Opportunities for Women, Canadian Research Institute for the Advancement of Women, Nouveau départ, and the Woman's Research Centre). Core financing for eighty women's centres was eliminated. As one NAC spokesperson put it: "It's just an awful day for women's groups. They didn't know this was coming. There hasn't been another cut like it. ... This goes to the bone of the movement."[82]

CONCLUSION

More detailed analysis of the three granting programs, their funding characteristics, and some of the key groups that they have supported over the years will be provided in the next three chapters. This chapter has sought only to give a broad sense of developments in the period 1974–89, which opened with Liberal party indifference and closed with barely disguised Conservative hostility. Several key points emerge from this review.

First, even though the programs all stemmed from the same sources described in the last chapter (the Quebec crisis, the new Liberal agenda in 1968, and the rise of movements seeking fundamental social and political change), and even though they were for some time grouped under the same rubric of "citizenship," they very rapidly developed their own characteristics and dynamics. This was in part because of the different social forces that each tried to harness. French OLMGs, outside Ontario and New Brunswick, were thinly scattered and weak. Isolated communities continued to exist in some provinces, and there was a strong will to survive, but they faced all but irresistible pressures to assimilate. Women were both more numerous and clearly preoccupied with an agenda conceived on an entirely different conceptual plane. The problem of sexism was arguably so pervasive that it forced a radical rethinking of women's political and social action that went far beyond anything addressed in the OLMG sector. Multicultural groups, by contrast, were often rooted in ethnic communities that had shown tremendous capacity for self-support as well as highly developed social structures such as churches, businesses, and various clubs. Moreover, whereas among OLMGs there was always an imperative (because of low numbers) to consolidate and unite, the ethnic associations were established precisely to celebrate separate identities. Program characteristics inevitably had to reflect these different constituencies.

Second, it is also clear that these programs had different rhythms, driven in large part by the external forces to which they were addressed. OLMG and Multiculturalism were bound in an uncomfortable alliance from the very beginning for reasons discussed in the previous chapter, and some observers have alleged that there has always been a tension between the dualist vision of the one and the pluralist vision of the other. In any case, Multiculturalism remained fairly stable throughout the period, despite the attempt to shift focus toward discrimination and rights after 1981. OLMG, however, was buffeted by every ill wind that blew across Quebec's political landscape. Conceived as an instrument of national unity in dealing with the Quebec question, it was dragooned in 1976 and once again in the early 1980s to support Ottawa's stand on bilingualism as well as tolerance for linguistic minorities. The Women's Program has perhaps had the most distant stimuli, with UN declarations figuring prominently.

Third, it is difficult to find evidence of any broad, strategic thinking on the part of elected or appointed officials with regard to these programs. Chapter 2 reviewed the literature on government subventions and support to interest groups, which tends to emphasize the political gains that might accrue to policy makers from these programs. The gains may be narrow in the sense of garnering support from the groups, or broad in the sense of stemming social unrest, but the literature as a whole, whether Marxist or public choice, assumes that the gains are necessary and sufficient rationales for the genesis and continuance of the programs. This chapter and the previous one show a more complex picture: strategic considerations certainly came into play with the OLMG Program and to a lesser extent with Multiculturalism, but, while visible, they were least important in the establishment of the Women's Program. Supplementing strategic considerations were genuine attempts to change the system, supported at the highest levels (e.g., Gérard Pelletier as minister and Bernard Ostry as assistant under-secretary). This factor was most prominent in the Women's Program, where feminists "captured" the state apparatus and then used it successfully – at least for a short time – to promote groups that supported their own ideological preferences. Once the programs were established, however, they tended to drift until stirred by external forces. In other words, while strategic considerations certainly lay behind creation of the programs, their continuation was a matter as much of inertia as of commitment. As the next chapters will show, these programs, once set up, did in fact help create constituencies that then in turn championed them.

Fourth, all three of the programs started as efforts at citizenship development but evolved toward promotion of social justice through the pursuit of political rights. Previous chapters have shown how initially, with the Nationalities Branch, citizenship was rarely if ever conceived as a matter of rights. Official policy in the 1950s highlighted the benefits and responsibilities of citizenship. By the 1960s, the discourse of citizenship was powerfully altered in Canada as a result of the national debate over Quebec and bilingualism and the surge in social movements (principally the peace, student, and women's movements). Issues surrounding Quebec and "social justice" resolved themselves into questions of rights, and so in the early citizenship development programs after 1969 the intent was to help community-based organizations claim their rights within a system that had previously ignored or denied them. In an interesting twist, the groups and constituencies supported by the federal government were "identity" constituencies: their raison d'être was to protect and promote linguistic, ethnic, or gender identity and thereby stimulate understanding and tolerance.

The final observation is linked to the previous ones. Throughout this period, the sos was in disarray. The turnover of ministers has already been cited, but to that must be added the almost constant flux in organizational and program authority, low morale, and even grudging disagreement with the entire concept of supporting grants for advocacy organizations.[83] As the following chapters will show, various evaluations done of each of the three programs over the years revealed substantial confusion over goals and procedures, and often high levels of frustration among program staff. Without clear goals or objectives, or indeed accepted standards by which to measure success, officials often did not know what they were doing. Again, this portrait is different from that offered in much of the theoretical literature. Instead of a state firmly shaping the social and political terrain, the picture that emerges here is one of confusion. The state was at least as much a captive of these programs as were its purported clients.

PART THREE

Programs and Organizations

CHAPTER SEVEN

Social Action and Official Language Minority Groups

PROGRAM EVALUATIONS

The Social Action Branch of the sos had a mandate of social animation aimed at cultural preservation and renaissance of linguistic minorities in Canada. The social animation component would stimulate the formation of groups and development of projects and
would also support OLMGs in presenting their case to governments,
both federal and provincial. As noted in chapters 5 and 6, its grants
were not large and indeed reflected the fact that the branch and its
support of OLMGs ran counter to the larger logic of the Official Languages Act of 1969 and the federal government's bilingualism policy, which was driven by concern for institutional and individual
bilingualism.

This apparent contradiction in terms was founded on two ideas.
The first was that all individual members of OLMGs, no matter where
they lived in Canada, should have access to federal institutions in
their language. Demographic realities meant that the federal government's services in Quebec, Ontario, and New Brunswick had to
be effectively bilingual. The second idea was that a policy of federal
support to provincial governments for second-language training
might eventually encourage some individual Canadians (and again
because of demography, outside Quebec this implied non-fran-
cophones) to learn the other official language. Language policy, in
other words, was not tied to group characteristics, since that would
have connected the program to demographically declining and in
some cases minuscule minority communities in provinces outside
Quebec. Moreover, had Ottawa's bilingualism policy hinged on
group characteristics, it might have encouraged Québécois to see

themselves as a distinct group or collectivity, with all the nationalist consequences that that might bring in train.

The federal government conducted an evaluation of OLMG grants in 1983, and it provides an interesting and detailed perspective.[1] The OLMG program was to have had its "sunset year" in 1982–83, and SOS policy also required that all major programs be reviewed at least once every five years. Planning for the evaluation started in September 1981. The program evaluation team was assisted by an advisory committee on which sat several academic advisers, government officials, and representatives of Alliance Quebec and la Fédération des francophones hors Québec (FFHQ).[2] The evaluation had three major questions. The first was how and why resources were deployed in the program and involved analysis of financial data and examination of selected program files (a random sample was abandoned because of incomplete files). The second question concerned the achievement of objectives, through determining whether "the situation of the minorities had changed and whether the majorities were more aware of the needs and aspirations of the minorities."[3] Qualitative analyses were conducted of government studies and reports as well as of publications by minority groups, academics, and the press. The third question pertained to the program's future – whether it should be renewed and improved.

Government evaluations, particularly ones that are publicly released and guided by advisory committees made up of "stakeholders," are unlikely to develop any major criticisms. Not surprising, therefore, the evaluation found that the program was important and largely successful and that it should continue with some minor changes. However, some of the detailed findings are of interest for our analysis in the next section. The report noted, for example, how the OLMG program "operates *from* the department and *through* the minority group associations and organizations. That is, it has one aspect internal to the Department of the Secretary of State and another external to it."[4] The link between the external and internal aspects was through social development officers (SDOs), or what in the pre-1969 Citizenship Branch had been known as liaison officers. "The role of the social development officer is, essentially, to interact with the minority group organizations of the region on grant or contribution applications or in regard to technical and professional matters connected with funded projects. Although these officers sometimes engage in community animation, particularly where there has been no organizational development, the bulk of their efforts is directed toward responding to requests."[5]

Despite what by 1982 had become a fairly routinized process of awarding grants, the report found it difficult to assess accurately the results of such funding – granting files "are sometimes cluttered with redundant material and are somewhat disorganized."[6] There was no filing protocol to control what information went into grant files, application forms were often completed by hand, were sometimes illegible, and lacked "quality and quantity of information."[7] Audits of grants did not have detailed information but rather only broad expenditure categories without uniform standards of definition. Nonetheless, beyond these occasional and limited audits, "the program has no feedback mechanism for describing the results of the funding in terms of where the money is actually spent."[8]

In 1977 the OLMG program officially stopped providing core funding in favour of project funding. As the report discovered, however, "many of these projects are providing for the ongoing operation of the associations, a fact freely admitted by the associations."[9] This fuzziness about program structure and operation disturbed the evaluation team. It wondered, for example, about the logical coherence of the program's objectives: "Some, like advocacy which in its militant form seems opposed to cooperation, appear somewhat contradictory."[10] As a result, the OLMG directorate had no indicators of success, and was unable to set priorities or develop selection criteria for grants, and its existing granting categories "bear little relation either to what the associations actually do or to its own objectives."[11] This lack of clarity and direction was not caused by incompetence but in fact reflected some key assumptions in the program, the most important being that "the minority groups must be agents of their own development, expressing their own aspirations and addressing their own needs."[12] OLMG funding could therefore be only a catalyst and would by definition be driven by the associations' demands and definitions of their needs.

The report also reviewed financial trends. The pattern had been one of slow growth in expenditures (from a base of $1.2 million) from 1969 to 1972, when they stabilized. In 1977–78 there was a surge of funding, so that in the period from 1977–78 to 1981–82, the program grew six-fold (see Table 7.1). But what effect did these expenditures have on the OLMGs? One measure is the extent to which the program stimulated creation of groups. The report found that of a sample of 325 organizations that submitted applications in 1981–82, fully 72 per cent had been established during the life of the program (since 1970) and that 40 per cent of these had been set up in the preceding five years.[13] The role of grants could be assessed

Table 7.1
Annual distribution (%) of OLMG grants and contributions by province, 1970–71 to 1981–82

| Province | Fiscal year | | | | | | | | | | | | Total |
	70–71	71–72	72–73	73–74	74–75	75–76	76–77	77–78	78–79	79–80	80–81	81–82	($ million)
Nfld	0.4	0.5	0.3	0.3	0.7	1.0	2.2	2.3	2.8	2.5	3.5	3.5	2.5 / 1.6
PEI	2.2	0.4	1.7	1.3	2.0	2.4	2.7	3.7	4.0	4.3	4.2	4.3	3.6 / 2.2
NS	9.1	6.8	4.2	11.0	4.7	4.8	5.2	6.1	6.6	6.8	6.9	7.0	6.6 / 4.1
NB	4.9	5.4	13.7	13.6	17.5	15.1	14.7	15.5	16.9	16.6	15.3	13.4	14.8 / 9.1
Que.	14.2	10.6	11.5	15.4	12.0	11.8	5.3	4.8	6.0	7.1	7.7	7.7	8.1 / 4.9
Ont.	26.2	44.2	30.7	28.8	36.1	30.5	30.2	25.7	27.1	26.6	27.5	28.0	28.2 / 17.4
Man.	17.6	13.7	10.9	12.1	13.3	12.8	13.0	13.4	11.2	10.3	9.8	10.5	11.3 / 6.9
Sask.	9.4	7.5	14.9	6.0	6.7	7.1	7.3	8.3	7.2	7.7	7.4	7.5	7.8 / 4.8
Alta	10.4	7.0	8.4	6.8	6.7	8.5	8.2	8.8	8.8	8.5	8.4	8.6	8.4 / 5.2
BC	5.6	3.8	3.7	4.7	4.8	6.2	11.2	11.5	9.4	9.6	9.3	9.4	8.7 / 5.4
Subtotal ($ million)	1.2	1.6	2.4	2.4	2.3	2.4	2.9	4.4	7.3	9.7	11.9	13.1	61.6
	100	100	100	100	100	100	100	100	100	100	100	100	100
National, special, and regional (%)	0.4	0.3	0.1	0.1	0.6	0.6	0.6	1.4	1.6	2.0	3.0	3.9	— / 14.6
Operating budget (%)	0.1	0.1	0.6*	0.3*	0.7*	0.3*	0.3	0.3	0.4	0.5	0.5	0.6	— / 4.7
Total ($ million)	1.7	2.0	3.1	0.8	3.6	3.3	3.8	6.1	9.3	12.2	15.4	17.6	— / 80.9

Source: Canada, Secretary of State, Program Evaluation Directorate, "Evaluation Reports of the Official Language Minority Groups (OLMG), 1970–82" (Ottawa, 1983), Table 2 at p. 59.

* The figures may differ from data from other sources.

Table 7.2
Proportion of OLMG funding to total project cost, 1976–77 to 1981–82

Year	OLMG funding* ($)	(%)	Other sources† of funding ($)	(%)	Total cost ($)	(%)
1976–77	3,528,396	24.6	10,843,534	75.4	14,371,930	100
1977–78	5,793,375	35.4	10,590,337	64.6	16,383,712	100
1978–79	8,917,568	42.2	12,207,368	57.8	21,124,936	100
1979–80	11,674,917	46.6	13,402,389	53.4	25,077,306	100
1980–81	14,983,077	50.1	14,914,451	49.9	29,897,528	100
1981–82	16,897,437	48.4	18,033,011	51.6	34,930,448	100
Total	61,794,770	43.6	79,991,090	56.4	141,785,860	100

Source: Canada, Secretary of State, Program Evaluation Directorate, "Evaluation Report of the Official Language Minority Groups Program (OLMG), 1970–82" (Ottawa: 1983), Table 7 at p. 70.
* Includes grants and contributions to provincial and national organizations.
† *Source*: OLMG financial data, 1976–77 to 1981–82.

also in terms of the proportion of the program's contribution to the total costs of projects. From 1970 to 1977, grants contributed 25 per cent of the funds required to implement projects. For the next six years, however, that proportion rose to 50 per cent. Project funding was also, in practice, core funding, and the pattern was repeated for national, provincial, and other organizations (see Tables 7.2 and 7.3).[14]

For provincial and national projects, the proportion of grants going toward paying salaries increased substantially. For provincial grants, the proportion rose from 28 per cent in 1976–77 to 51 per cent in 1981–82. For national projects, the increase was from 11 per cent to 37 per cent in the same period.[15] This should be placed in perspective, however. Over the period of the evaluation (1970–82) the program awarded $76 million, of which approximately one-fifth went to national projects. By 1982 the number of recipient organizations had almost doubled, to 370, and the majority of associations received less than $5,900 in grants and contributions annually.[16]

In addition to doing its own analyses, the evaluation team sought the views of francophone-minority group leaders. Among the leaders' recommendations were better feedback mechanisms to monitor the effect of the program on communities, recognition of the priorities established by the communities themselves, and acceptance that the first priority was education. "A large majority of the respondents

Table 7.3
Proportion of funding to total project cost and by type of organization, 1976–77 to 1981–82

Fiscal year*	National organizations†			Provincial associations‡			Other organizations§		
	OLMG funding	Other sources	Total	OLMG funding	Other sources	Total	OLMG funding	Other sources	Total
1976–77 ($000)	193.5	191.1	384.6	1,444.6	3,038.4	4,483.0	1,425.7	6,316.4	7,742.1
(%)	50	50	100	32	68	100	18	82	100
1977–78 ($000)	468.7	619.3	1,088.0	2,191.1	2,687.9	4,879.0	2,193.2	4,765.1	6,958.3
(%)	43	57	100	45	55	100	31	69	100
1978–79 ($000)	789.0	907.1	1,696.1	3,555.0	5,294.0	8,849.0	3,738.2	4,831.3	8,569.5
(%)	47	53	100	40	60	100	44	56	100
1981–82 ($000)	1,603.3	429.8	2,033.1	6,358.7	2,733.0	9,091.7	6,683.6	12,324.8	19,008.4
(%)	79	21	100	70	30	100	35	65	100

Source: Canada, Secretary of State, Program Evaluation Directorate, "Evaluation Report of the Official Language Minority Groups Program (OLMG), 1970–82" (Ottawa: 1983), Table 8 at p. 71.

* Data for fiscal years 1979–80 and 1980–81 are not available.

† The only grants and contributions counted are those to la Fédération des francophones hors Québec, la Fédération des jeunes Canadiens-français, la Fédération des femmes canadiennes-françaises, and la Fédération culturelle canadienne-française.

‡ Other national projects are not included in this table, which explains the difference in the totals from Table 6.

§ This category includes la Fédération des francophones de Terre-Neuve et du Labrador; la Société Saint-Thomas d'Aquin (PEI); la Fédération des Acadiens de la Nouvelle-Écosse; la Société des Acadiens du Nouveau-Brunswick; Alliance Québec; Association canadienne-française de l'Ontario; la Société franco-manitobaine; l'Association culturelle franco-canadienne de la Saskatchewan; l'Association canadienne-française de l'Alberta; la Fédération franco-colombienne; et la Fédération des francophones des Territoires du Nord-Ouest.

believe that *grants and contributions remain the best method* of assisting official language minority communities. The resource base should be increased."[17] At the same time, the leaders wished less interference in client organizations, a more simplified and shortened awards process, and multi-year financing.

As noted earlier, the evaluation concluded that the OLMG program was valuable and unique. The report discerned three primary objectives to the program: improved intragroup relations between official language communities, promotion and encouragement of the development and growth of official language minorities, and improved relations between OLMGs and surrounding majority communities. The report concluded that the first two objectives had also been met but that the third, in terms of real increased tolerance of majorities to their minorities, had not.[18]

PROGRAM GUIDELINES AND GRANTING PATTERNS

In 1988 the two bases of support for minority-language organizations were the programs Official Language Communities (OLC) and Promotion of Official Languages (POL). The SOS *Grants and Contributions Manual* stated that the OLC's objective was "to make Canadians aware of the country's linguistic duality and to help non-federal public administrations and the private sector set up and deliver adequate services to minority official language groups."[19] Voluntary organizations therefore received technical and financial assistance to "promote and call for recognition of the language rights of minority official language communities" and to establish institutions and offer services in their own langauge that would otherwise not be available. Eligible applicants under the OLC were non-profit organizations; non-governmental institutions; provincial, territorial, or municipal governments; and individuals.

There were three categories of eligible activities. The first was financial assistance for institutionalization. "Priority will be given to activities aimed at maintaining, expanding or establishing institutions or permanent educational, social, cultural and economic services and at achieving official recognition, through legislative or constitutional reform, of the rights of official language communities to permanent services."[20] Immediately after this statement in the *Grants and Contributions Manual*, however, comes another that appears to contradict it: "Institutional development does not include activities in support of demands that permanent services be established or expanded." The OLC program would not itself actually provide permanent services but only support activities to that end.

The second eligible category was financial assistance for bilingualization and access to services. Grants and contributions were directed at lobby groups and service organizations. Eligible activities included those aimed at "access to or improvements in minority language education"; "the passing and implementation of legislation recognizing the equal status of the two official languages"; "access to improvements in social, judicial, economic and cultural as well as health, sports and recreation services in the minority language"; and "access to or improvements in telecommunications services."[21] The third eligible category was technical assistance and involved the loan of resource persons to non-profit organizations needing specialists in order to carry out a large-scale project or service.

The Promotion of Official Languages (POL) program had an objective similar to that of the OLC: "To make Canadians aware of the country's linguistic duality and to help non-federal public administrations and the private sector set up and deliver adequate services to minority official languages communities."[22] The key operational objective was to make Canadians aware of the equal status of the two official languages "by means of financial and technical assistance to groups that encourage acquisition of the second official language and associations working to promote the equal status of the two official languages and to promote Canada's official languages policy abroad."[23] Grants would be provided to groups "promoting awareness," as well as to a broad range of private-sector and voluntary organizations for specific interpretation or translation projects. Eligible applicants were non-profit organizations, non-governmental institutions, professional associations, and provincial, territorial, and municipal governments.

SOS's *Grants and Contributions Manual, 1988* sketches the administrative guidelines for OLC and POL, but a more precise sense of how these grant programs operated requires analysis of how the money was actually spent. Using 1987–88 statistics, the POL (component 2210) gave roughly up to $20,000 (average $3,000 per grant) for translation services. Examples included the Alzheimer Society of Canada, the Canadian Meat Council, and the Fraternity of Canadian Astrologers: all got small grants for the translation of conference proceedings. However, Canadian Parents for French (CPF) received over $132,000 in 1987–88. OLC (component 2220) provided the basic operational funding for non-governmental organizations. There were four sub-categories of grants at the national level (under both components 2210 and 2220), and then regional grants under each of POL and OLC. The way to visualize this is as follows:

Component 2210 POL: Responsibility Centre 0654 National
            Projects
            Regional Projects
Component 2210 OLC: Responsibility Centre 0656 National
            Projects
            Responsibility Centre 0657 Special
            Projects
            Responsibility Centre 0658 Inter-Regional
            Projects
            Regional Projects

In fiscal 1987–88, the POL (National Projects) funded 360 separate projects, for a total approved amount of $7,389,636. The bulk of these projects were for translation services for conferences and exhibitions and bilingualism development plans. Several large grants went to provincial/territorial governments for bilingual program development: for example, British Columbia ($105,005); Manitoba ($315,521); Northwest Territories ($1,533,690); Nova Scotia ($171,805); Ontario ($800,000); Prince Edward Island ($4,500); and Saskatchewan ($42,500). These transfers totalled $2,973,021, or 40.2 per cent of all the money spent under the program. The only group to receive operational funding, as opposed to project funding for implementation of a bilingualism program or translation of a conference, was CPF. It got $132,525 in operational funding for 1987–88, plus $39,525 in supplementary grants, for a total of $172,050. This amount accounted for only 2.3 per cent of the money spent under the program. If provincial transfers are excluded, the proportion is still only 3.8 per cent.

The picture changes quite dramatically, however, when one considers the regional projects under the POL. CPF received federal funding in every province except Quebec. Table 7.4 shows the proportion in each region accounted for by CPF. Once again, in almost all cases, provincial governments received substantial sums of money that skew the granting profile. Table 7.4 shows both the total for each region and the total minus grants to provincial governments.

The table clearly shows the pre-eminence of CPF in the POL program. In five regions (Newfoundland, Nova Scotia, Saskatchewan, Alberta, and British Columbia/Yukon), the organization is a key player on a short list of recipients. Once the total grants are adjusted to exclude transfers to governments, it is the recipient of between one-half and all grants to non-governmental organizations. In some cases (Nova Scotia, Saskatchewan, and British Columbia/Yukon), it

Table 7.4
Regional funding under Promotion of Official Languages, fiscal 1987–88

Region	A Grants	B Total ($)	C Total provincial ($)	D CPF ($)	D/B (%)	D/C (%)
Nfld	3	103,920	45,995	33,670	32.40	73.20
NS	4	217,130	30,880	30,880	14.22	100.0
NB/PEI	51	993,393	181,345	50,940	5.13	28.09
Que.	30	62,837	62,837	0	0.00	0.00
Ont.	30	1,425,089	1,085,064	104,120	˙ 7.31	9.60
Man.	4	735,400	35,400	31,400	4.27	88.70
Sask.	3	137,038	37,000	37,000	27.00	100.00
Alta	5	95,814	95,814	56,400	58.86	58.86
BC/Yuk.	3	82,740	82,740	82,740	100.00	100.00
Total	133	3,853,361	1,657,075	427,150	11.09	25.78

Source: Secretary of State, Grants and Contributions, Fiscal Year 1987–88.
Note: Calculations made on basis of recommended grants and contributions.

is the only recipient in this category. This forces the conclusion that POL is largely the funding vehicle of CPF. The data show also that CPF is more prominent (measured by its proportion of grants) outside Quebec and Ontario. If Ontario and Quebec are excluded from the calculations, the proportion of non-governmental grants accounted for by CPF rises from 9.87 per cent to 63.44 per cent. That the group has no profile in Quebec is understandable; its low profile in Ontario is more puzzling. Ontario's francophone organizations may carry the standard for more educational services in French – a hypothesis corroborated by CPF's relatively low profile in New Brunswick, the other province in the "bilingual belt."

Once again, in the case of the four categories of programs under OLC, our interest is in the groups that received operational funding. Special and Inter-Regional Projects do not contain grants of this type and so will be passed over in this study (though recipients in these categories often appeared in the other two). Table 7.5 provides an overview of the four categories under OLC.

Almost three-quarters (73.3 per cent) of all the money spent under the three programs was expended through the regional grants. The other three categories together mustered only about one-quarter of the total spending. Nonetheless, the category of National Projects was significant in both the amounts spent and the number of groups/projects supported. As we shall see with the Women's Program, however, spending was heavily concentrated among just a handful of groups. Table 7.6 shows that five groups took 60.25 per

Table 7.5
Grants and contributions under the Official Language Communities program,
fiscal 1987–88

	No. of groups	No. of grants	Total ($)
National projects	40	52	3,435,985
Special projects	50	63	1,958,847
Inter-regional projects	5	5	183,192
Subtotal	95	120	5,578,024
Regional			
Nfld	8	11	499,705
NS	16	19	1,037,013
NB/PEI	45	61	2,395,350
Que.	18	35	2,220,000
Ont.	74	118	3,793,729
Man.	35	37	1,666,600
Sask.	39	52	1,121,200
Alta	29	43	1,488,287
BC/Yuk.	19	25	1,149,545
Subtotal	283	401	15,371,429
Total	378	521	20,949,453

Source: Secretary of State, Grants and Contributions, Fiscal Year 1987–88. Calculations made on basis of recommended grants and contributions.

Note: Multiple listings of groups were calculated as follows: groups designated by a general title followed by a district or regional affiliation (e.g., Alliance Quebec – Baie Comeau Chapter, Alliance Quebec – St. Maurice Chapter) were counted as one organization; if the organization's official title included a regional designation without mention of "chapter" or "district" (e.g., Centre Culturel Artem Inc. and Centre Culturel Le Chenai Inc.) it was counted as distinct organization.

Table 7.6
Proportion of grants and contributions, Official Language Communities, national
projects, fiscal 1987–88

Group	Grant ($)	% of total
Association de la presse francophone hors Québec	233,000	6.78
Fédération culturelle des Canadiens-français	332,650	9.68
Fédération des francophones hors Québec, Inc.	643,287	18.72
Fédération des jeunes Canadiens-français Inc.	544,924	15.86
Fédération nationale des femmes canadiennes-françaises	316,406	9.21
Total	2,070,267	60.25

Source: Secretary of State, Grants and Contributions, Fiscal Year 1987–88.
Note: Calculations made on basis of recommended grants and contributions.

cent of all grants and contributions in this program category. The figure for Fédération des jeunes Canadiens-français slightly misrepresents the group's significance, since it includes $225,000 in project grants that the other organizations did not have in this grant category. In terms of simple operational funding, the Fédération captured only 9.3 per cent of total grants. This makes the FFHQ the most prominent recipient of grants, receiving almost one-fifth of the total in this category.

Finally, the regional category of OLC also showed concentration among a few groups (see Table 7.7). The eleven groups receiving the largest single sums of money accounted for 38 per cent of total expenditures under the category. The concentration of the program was even greater than this might suggest, however, since in many provinces the second- and third-largest groups also got large proportions of the funds. For example, in the case of New Brunswick and Prince Edward Island, if one were to add the grants awarded to just two other (out of 61 files) organizations – Société Saint-Thomas d'Aquin ($432,600) and Fédération des jeunes francophones du Nouveau-Brunswick ($199,500) – the proportion of grants accounted for by these three organizations for this region rises to 47.2 per cent.

In one sense these findings should not be surprising. The concentration of funding, particularly under the OLC component, reflects the prominence of the relatively few organizations that have traditionally represented the official-language minority communities provincially and, since the mid-1970s, nationally. Of course, both POL and OLC support hundreds of groups and projects throughout the country each year. Project grants, however, are tiny in comparison with core funding for lobby groups, and in a political sense less significant. A review of these funding programs does suggest this somewhat surprising conclusion: Ottawa spends millions of dollars each year supporting organizations whose aims include lobbying provincial and federal agencies, pursuing a political agenda of bilingualism, and advocating changes in public policy. As we saw in the previous chapter, this has not always been a comfortable situation for the federal government, since the very groups that it supports through these programs often are the sternest critics of federal and provincial language policies. In any event, the key organizations supported by the programs have emerged as the recognized representatives of their communities, so that for example in the national debate over the Meech Lake Accord, linguistic minority positions were staked out by provincial associations but in particular by Alliance Quebec and the FFHQ.

Table 7.7
Regional distribution of grants and proportion given to leading grantee, Official
Language Communities, regional grants, fiscal 1987–88

Province/group	$ (prov.)	$ (group)	% total
NEWFOUNDLAND			
Association francophone du Labrador	499,705	100,000	20.01
Fédération des francophones de Terre-Neuve et du Labrador		180,000	36.02
NOVA SCOTIA			
Fédération acadienne de la Nouvelle-Écosse	1,037,013	777,964	75.02
NEW BRUNSWICK/PRINCE EDWARD ISLAND			
Société des Acadiens et Acadiennes du Nouveau-Brunswick	2,395,350	498,750	20.82
QUEBEC			
Alliance Quebec	2,220,000	1,100,000	49.55
ONTARIO			
Association canadienne-française de l'Ontario	3,793,729	1,218,000	32.11
MANITOBA			
Société franco-manitobaine	1,666,600	590,000	35.40
SASKATCHEWAN			
Association culturelle franco-canadienne de la Saskatchewan	1,121,200	461,533	41.16
ALBERTA			
Association canadienne-française de l'Alberta	1,488,287	315,000	21.17
BRITISH COLUMBIA/YUKON			
Association des Franco-Yukonnais	1,149,545	92,000	8.00
Fédération des Franco-Colombiens		486,875	42.35
Total	15,371,429	5,820,122	37.86

Source: Secretary of State, Grants and Contributions Approved, Fiscal Year 1987–88.
Note: Calculations based on total recommended grants and contributions. The group grants are
calculated on the basis of operational, not project funding. In most cases operational funding is
all that these organizations received under this program, but in a few others, small project grants
also accompained the operational funding. These sums are insignificant, however. Also, only the
main operational grant to the central body of the organization was counted. In the case of Quebec
(Alliance Quebec) and Ontario (Association canadienne-française de l'Ontario), district chapters
also received monies. In both cases, this made little difference. Alliance Quebec's proportion of
funding would rise from 49.5 per cent of regional total to 53 per cent, while that of the Association
canadienne-française de l'Ontario would rise from 32.1 per cent to 34.5 per cent.

To this point this chapter has presented aggregate data about the
programs and their operation. The following section will shift focus
and present three case studies of key organizations supported by
OLC and POL: CPF, the FFHQ, and Alliance Quebec.

ORGANIZATIONAL PROFILES

Canadian Parents for French

CPF was founded in 1977. It is a national organization of parents interested in French-language education for their children. There are chapters in every province and territory (almost 300 in total), and much of the group's activities are focused on the local school board or provincial level, since education is a responsibility of the provinces. Since 1970, however, Ottawa has had an interest in financially supporting bilingualism in education and has signed agreements with provincial authorities to that effect. CPF therefore has a national mandate as well, both to encourage the federal government in its efforts and to ensure that the concept of bilingual education enjoys broad public support.

In 1988–89, the national office of CPF had total revenues of $606,205, of which $391,713, or 65 per cent, came from the SOS. Membership fees of $61,175 accounted for 10 per cent of revenues.[24] CPF's financial dependence on the SOS has decreased over time. In 1982–83, for example, SOS grants accounted for 76 per cent of total revenues ($154,450 out of $202,950).[25] The difference can be explained by a slight increase in the proportion of membership fees and donations from corporations and foundations ($25,000, or 4 per cent) and a special grant from the CRB Foundation ($77,952, or 13 per cent). In July 1989, CPF had 17,887 members, 22 per cent more than the figure for 1986.

CPF was established as a result of an Ottawa conference entitled "Parents Conference on French Language and Exchange Opportunities," organized and paid for by the commissioner of official languages, Keith Spicer. As he stated in his opening remarks: "I haven't been able to find a way of getting through the Byzantine universe of federal/provincial jurisdictions and so, after talking to a lot of parents over the last couple of years and particularly in the last six months, the idea came that maybe we could do a little bit of constructive subversion and simply invite to a conference parents who have no particular title except enthusiasm, concern for their kids and a sense of imagination."[26] Spicer made it clear that the commissioner's office would be able to offer only moral and intellectual, not financial, support for anything that the parents might decide to do. Nonetheless, his intervention was designed to mobilize parents interested in bilingual education to develop proposals aimed at both the federal and provincial governments. His oblique reference to jurisdictional confusion referred to a crucial problem in Canada's official languages policy: if bilingualism were to flourish, it would have to be encouraged in education, which is a provincial responsibility. In effect, a national policy depended in large part on provincial delivery.

After two days of sessions, the group passed a set of recommendations, the first of which concerned the establishment of a national association of parents with three goals: "to promote the best possible types of French language learning opportunities; to assist in ensuring that each Canadian child have the opportunity to acquire as great a knowledge of French language and culture as he or she is willing and able to attain; more specifically, to establish and maintain effective communication between interested parents and educational and government authorities concerned with the provision of French language learning opportunities."[27] A provisional executive committee was created to organize a national conference later in the year. It also set out to produce a dossier of resources (publications, relevant research, and case studies), a directory of resource people, programs, and organizations, and a bibliography of research pertaining to the new association's goals. The emphasis on research and resources may seem surprising, given what should have been a national commitment to bilingual education, but the jurisdictional division of powers in education meant that there was very little national co-ordination. Even the concept of immersion education, widely accepted today as the best method for teaching a second language in a normal school setting, was little more than a decade old. Research on its efficacy and socio-cultural effects was just beginning to yield confident results.

CPF's first national conference was held in Ottawa on 14–16 October 1977 and coincided with the meetings there of the Canadian Association of Immersion Teachers. It attracted some 60 delegates (approximately 35 people had been at the founding in March). The conference was funded by the SOS, and Keith Spicer (by then retired as official languages commissioner) spoke to the group again, urging the importance of a parents' lobby which would educate politicians by "scaring the hell out of them."[28] Most of the proceedings were devoted to exchanges of information about successful programs in different parts of the country and recent research findings, but CPF was already harnessing its educational goals to the broader national agenda. Its January 1978 *Newsletter*, for example, contained an article with the title "French Second Language Programs and National Unity": "Our best hope is to start our children off with positive attitudes in the first place. Surely if they acquire an interest in, and understanding of, their fellow Canadians during their school years, they are unlikely to become ignorant, mean and sour as adults. Our belief is that proper teaching of our country's other official language, along with the culture that accompanies it, can make a real difference. It will not, in itself, save the country, but it is a useful step that English-speaking parents and their provincial education systems can take."[29]

For its first two years, CPF's expenses were met entirely by the SOS, which supported its twice-yearly newsletter, its small national office, and its first and second national conferences. Because the support was extended on a project basis, CPF had no guarantee of year-to-year funding to cover overhead expenses. By 1979 it had boosted its membership to 5,000 (there was no membership fee) and had developed a national network of chapters, ties with the research community, and a preliminary bank of resources for use by parents in local lobbying. At this point it became clear, however, that to develop further it would have to set up a paying membership base and begin to lobby more vigorously at the national level. Indeed, the 1979 national conference seemed to mark a turning point for CPF. Rather than concentrating on local efforts through provision of information, it set its sights on provincial ministries of education and the federal government. It also, for the first time in its published material, emphasized that bilingual education should be considered a right: "In addition, we must take our cause to our Ministers of Education. Whether formalized in a constitution or not, language rights in education will only become a reality if the provincial governments are committed to the idea. Our message will be that we want language rights for the majority as well as the minority, and that a child should have the right to be educated in either official language regardless of his origins."[30]

The shift in orientation coincided with two other events. The first was the renegotiation of the funding arrangements between Ottawa and the provinces for instruction in the second official language. The initial agreements had been signed in January 1970 and renewed without any changes in 1975. Ottawa's contributions to the provinces were divided into formula payments, in support of bilingual education at elementary, secondary, and post-secondary levels, and non-formula, or special grants, for special projects, such as bursaries and language training centres. The formula grants were percentages of average annual per student costs paid to provinces for each student studying in the minority language. From 1970–71 to 1976–77, Ottawa had transferred over $647 million for bilingual education to the provinces, most of that ($491 million) in formula payments. Negotiations on new arrangements began in 1977, and the SOS gave notice that the federal government wished gradually to phase out as much as 20 per cent of the monies being transferred through formula payments and redirect them to special projects grants. Ottawa received virtually no information from the provinces on the disposition of formula payments, and as a consequence had no idea of whether provincial ministries of education and local school boards were supporting bilingual education to the full extent possible. CPF feared that local boards, often reluctant to launch expensive immersion programs, would use the uncertainty surrounding Ottawa's proposal as an excuse to delay their plans.

The other major event in 1979 was the first commitment of long-term funding from the SOS to CPF. To this point, CPF had received financial assistance on strictly a project basis, but now it was guaranteed three years of funding in connection with an information-retrieval project. The support was still tied to a project, but the multi-year commitment gave CPF considerably more flexibility. The 1979 amount was $46,500.[31] It was not until 1981 that CPF began to receive core funding from the SOS.[32] In 1982, SOS began to fund provincial branches directly, through negotiation between CPF groups and regional offices of the department (see above for funding details in 1988). Within several years, therefore, the stream of support was going to both local and national levels.

In strict terms, this support was to be directed to non-political activities, since CPF was and is a charitable organization under the terms of the Income Tax Act and is therefore prohibited from engaging in what National Revenue defines as "lobbying." CPF's chair advised local chapters on what this meant but also made it clear that National Revenue's definitions did not unduly restrict the organization's capacity to make representations on public policy. As he pointed out, "An objective is 'political' if its ultimate intention is to influence the policy making process (as opposed to the administrative process) of any level of government. Ie., we can't be promoting a change in the law."[33] A CPF member was still permitted, however, to write to ministers, senior administrators, and his or her own elected representatives. CPF members could lobby directly, support candidates for office, and urge changes in legislation, as long as they did so as individuals.

The lobbying question was important to CPF because of the stalemate in negotiations over federal funding of provincial second-language programs. Talks between the two levels stalled in 1979, as Ottawa demanded that its monies be used in more innovative and accountable ways (through special projects rather than formula funding) and the provinces balked at having to report on policies and programs undertaken in an area of provincial jurisdiction. The Bilingualism in Education Program officially expired in March 1979 without formal renewal. Instead, an interim agreement provided for continuation of non-formula payments for a year, and this was renewed again for 1981–82. Negotiations on formula payments continued without result for the next two years, and an agreement was not signed until December 1983. During that period, CPF actively lobbied both federal and provincial authorities to sign a multi-year agreement on formula payments. It lobbied, for example, other federal ministers who sat with the secretary of state on the Social Development Committee of Cabinet in order to bolster the SOS's claim on funds for the program. It did this through meetings with officials in late 1980[34] and again a year later in direct correspondence with ministers.[35]

CPF sent a brief to the Council of Ministers of Education, Canada (CMEC), in January 1981 and received an invitation to meet with the members at its June meeting in Toronto. In March 1981, CPF sent a position paper to both levels of government, attempting in effect to mediate. CPF's position took a careful middle road between the federal government and the CMEC but did strongly urge that some sort of agreement be arrived at soon. It asked for at least two more five-year agreements to allow for the rational development of second-language training in education, a firm commitment by Ottawa as to the levels of future funding, and an equally firm commitment that this funding would not be tied to other policy objectives, notably fiscal constraint, but would reflect a national obligation to ensure that all children have the opportunity to be educated in the second official language.[36] At the same time, CPF agreed that the provinces should provide more detailed information to Ottawa on disbursement of federal funds in the program, give credit for federal support, and better co-ordinate their efforts. A novel recommendation was "the creation of an independent body to act as a buffer between the two levels of government and to make recommendations for long-term funding agreements and the implementation of bilingualism in education programs."[37] This "Language Council" would be composed of administrators, trustees, parents, and teachers.

Funding for Bilingualism in Education had been a testing ground for CPF's emergence on the national scene as the key organization promoting enhanced French-language training in schools. How much of an impact, if any, did CPF have on the negotiations? Poyen, who was involved in part of them, suggests that the organization did play a mediating role and moreover that its efforts enhanced its own credibility with Ottawa and the provinces. "It could make available information about provincial activities that federal officials could not access without intruding into provincial jurisdiction. As taxpayers, CPF members had a right to information on how the provincial governments were spending the federal grants."[38]

CPF's prominence in the SOS funding lists shows how successful it has been in the last decade in attracting financial support from Ottawa. Unlike the other two groups (Alliance Quebec and the FFHQ) discussed below, however, CPF was not established primarily as a lobby group. It was and is a national organization of parents interested in sharing information, developing certain service programs for its members, and on occasion presenting its views to government on issues related to education in the second official language. The funding issues in 1979–83 were so central to its mission that CPF had no choice but carefully to enter the fray and lobby. CPF also passed a resolution in 1981 supporting Canadian children's constitutional right to education in either official language (what eventually came to be section 23 of the Charter). Local chapters have occasionally presented briefs on larger constitutional issues (e.g., the Alberta chapter against the Meech Lake Accord in 1987–88). CPF has contacts with other organizations with similar objectives: Alliance Quebec, the Canadian Association of Second Language Teachers, and the FFHQ, among them. Perhaps its most distinctive feature is its strong support for official bilingualism and the fact that it is a national organization receiving federal funding to press for services that are delivered within provincial jurisdiction (if partly paid for by Ottawa).

Alliance Quebec (AQ)

In 1990, AQ (formally launched in 1982) was organized into 22 member chapters and regional groups, as well as 30 member organizations. Its head office in Montreal had ten senior staff members, five clerks, and eight "animators" responsible for community organizing. Each of the other organizations federated with it employs only one or two people. AQ claims to have 40,000 members.[39] Its budget in 1990 was $1.7 million, of which $1.5 million (88 per cent) came from Ottawa – $1.2 million of it in the form of core funding from the SOS.[40]

AQ had its roots in the Quebec election of 15 November 1976 and the PQ's victory. Within days, a group of anglophone Montrealers met informally to discuss the situation. Most were young professionals, and a few had been involved in student and anti-war protests in the 1960s. They were accustomed to community activism and were

convinced that, as a result of the PQ's victory, Quebec's anglophones
would have to organize and articulate their interests more effectively. Michael Goldbloom, later a president of AQ, attended the informal 1976 meeting and notes that the people at this occasion were
perhaps the first generation of English-speaking Quebecers who
were at home in the French language and identified directly with the
French character of their province. Over the next weeks the group
agreed to found a new organization called Participation Quebec.[41]
Another group that formed virtually at the same time was the Positive Action Committee, led by Alex Patterson (a well-known Montreal lawyer) and Storrs McCall (a professor at McGill). This
organization, while it paralleled Participation Quebec, was made up
of the more traditional leadership of English Montreal. Simultaneously in the Eastern Townships, the Townshippers Association was
being established.

The next major catalyst for AQ was the PQ's language legislation,
Bill 101 (originally introduced as Bill 1). Eric Maldoff, AQ's first president, and a founding member of Participation Quebec, remembers
its impact: "I can still vividly recollect the National Assembly hearings that were held on Bill 1. Over 30 groups, organizations and institutions from our community paraded down to Quebec city in June
and July of 1977. Each with its own brief and presentation. No two
briefs were the same and each organization claimed to be speaking
on behalf of our community. The scene was a dream come true for
the good Doctor Laurin and a nightmare, with an enduring legacy,
for our community. Through our weakness born of our division, the
government was able to enact Bill 101, virtually without amendment."[42] Accordingly, one of the first challenges for these nascent
groups was to develop some unity and co-ordination. In effect, this
meant the laborious construction of an identity or allegiance for
"English Quebec." As Maldoff recollects, "English-speaking Quebecers" did not know themselves or each other under that rubric. Quebec's anglophones had traditionally been less impressed by their
common linguistic identity than by their different religious, class, or
ethnic backgrounds. In Maldoff's words: "Clearly, the challenge of
bringing the communities together was even greater than imagined.
We would have to build a concept of an English-speaking community."[43]

Participation Quebec focused on developing a more accommodat-
ing approach to political problems in Quebec. For example, it conducted seminars to move "toward rapprochement." It published a
guide to available courses in French as a second language. It soon

became clear, however, that Participation Quebec and the Positive Action Committee were taking similar positions on issues and were criticizing not the right of the PQ to pass legislation such as Bill 101 but the specific implementation of some of its provisions on signs, education, and restrictions of the use of English in the legislature and the courts. It was also clear that the two groups needed the broadest possible coalition of English Quebecers because strength would come only with numbers and cohesion, and so they reached out to other minorities in the anglophone community. They sought as well to avoid identification of "anglophones" simply with Montreal, which permitted the PQ to dismiss them as a localized and relatively privileged group. The political base of the "minority" presence in Quebec had to be broadened, with an eye eventually to organizing that presence along a linguistic axis. The vehicle for this new effort was the Council of Quebec Minorities, established in November 1978 under the leadership of Eric Maldoff. As a federation of some twenty-five organizations and institutions, it forged the first broad, provincial alliance of non-francophone groups. But its federated character meant that its decision-making processes were cumbersome and often too slow.

The defeat of the "Oui" side in the 1980 referendum gave momentary rise to confidence, but the 1981 re-election of the PQ dashed any hopes that René Lévesque's government and strong Quebec nationalism had been merely a historical aberration. The referendum battle, moreover, had forced all the "Non" forces under one umbrella, leaving members of Participation Quebec again feeling that they lacked an effective vehicle for representing the special concerns of the province's English-speaking minority. Talks once more ensued, and steps were taken to forge what came to be known as Alliance Quebec. According to Goldbloom, there "was an understanding with the Secretary of State that the money would be forthcoming before we got established." Initially, AQ was formed out of a coalition of organizations formerly part of the Council of Quebec Minorities. This group announced provisional establishment of AQ through publication of a statement of principles in daily newspapers across the province. It then held a founding convention in May 1982, with delegates from provincial chapters of the fledgling organization and other associations and institutions. This was a deliberate strategy, since the leaders felt that the English-speaking community in Quebec was seen stereotypically by francophones as a Westmount enclave of self-appointed spokespersons for an elitist interest. It was vitally important to establish the group's democratic credentials. The convention itself was carefully designed to evoke some key Quebec symbols: the organization's colours were blue and white, as were the province's, and the entire meeting was held on a university campus, using yellow voting cards, as was the practice at the PQ's conventions.

In spring 1982, before the founding convention, AQ's leaders visited René Lévesque, and they met again with him after the founding convention in the summer. They presented six matters of concern to the premier, the same list that would guide AQ's action in the next decade: control and management of the community's health and educational institutions, permission for the optional use of second languages on commercial signs, elimination of French tests for Quebec-trained professionals, the right to use English as the langage of communication within the community's institutions, access to English-language schools for all of Quebec's English-speaking people, and fair representation on government boards and commissions and affirmative-action hiring programs in the public sector.[44] The premier was initally sympathetic to these six demands, but the government's official response some months later rejected them. The AQ then worked hard to get the Quebec press, both francophone and anglophone, on its side. In this it was largely successful, because the government appeared to be ignoring a democratic organization and because of the policy positions that AQ had shrewdly adopted from its inception.

AQ's most crucial strategic choice was its pan-Quebecism. While it lobbies on behalf of anglophones, it does so on the assumption that anglophones are a historical community within the province, part of its social character, and moreover that they share certain entitlements with other Quebecers. AQ has also appropriated minority discourse as a way of framing its demands. Historically, the English in Quebec had been identified with well-heeled Westmount, and so the use of minoritarian arguments did not initially strike a responsive chord in Quebec. But over time, AQ has successfully linked its minority status with disadvantages that require remedy. It has, for example, called for more opportunities for its members to acquire French and has urged community economic development policies to address the exodus of English-speaking youth from the province.

These strategies provide the foundation for AQ's provincial and national interventions. AQ's May 1989 document, "A Policy for the English-Speaking Community in Quebec," is divided into six sections. The first deals with employment and business, although the principal issue there, as elsewhere, is language. The section begins with the assertion: "French is the predominant language of work in

Quebec, but the continuing ability to do business in English as well as French is crucial for the future prosperity of Quebec."[45] Language testing for professions has been an extremely contentious issue under Bill 101, and AQ consistently lobbied for more lenient interpretation of the bill's regulations. Its position was two-fold. Quebecers, whether anglophones or francophones, educated in the province's secondary school system, were required to have competence in French before graduation, and so additional language tests were discriminatory. (This was recognized in 1983, and Bill 101 was amended.) Professionals wishing to be accredited in Quebec but who have not received their secondary education in the province should be subjected to tests of linguistic competence only where these are relevant to their work.

In large part because of AQ's lobbying, various sections of Bill 101 have been repealed or modified. For example, the act now recognizes the importance and distinctive character of Quebec's English institutions and no longer demands "full francization" or that all persons hired by those institutions know French, as long as these institutions are capable of providing services in French. On education, AQ recognizes that the government of Quebec has the right to set general goals and standards but claims that this right is consistent with a system of schools, school boards, colleges, universities, and adult education centres serving the anglophone community. The core of AQ's position is that the anglophone community must have access to, as well as control and management of, a system of primary and secondary, collegial, and university education. AQ also demands, however, that the Ministry of Education provide better opportunities and resources for instruction in French as a second language and also permit school boards to introduce instruction in the second official language at any level, in line with the wishes of parents. (This last point, of course, would allow French schools to offer more courses in English, a contentious issue in Quebec.)

AQ's policy on health and social services is straightforward. There must be access to services in English throughout the province wherever there is an anglophone population, English-language institutions should be supported by the provincial government, and anglophones should be adequately represented on the boards of these institutions as well as community and regional management boards.[46] Two basic principles guide AQ's policy position on culture and communications. First, AQ insists on the cultural distinctiveness of the anglophone community: the "heritage resources of the English-speaking community are an indispensable part of the history of Quebec, and as such must be fully recognized and their maintenance and preservation be appropriately funded by the public and private sectors and by the community."[47] Second, AQ is insistent that anglophone cultural institutions and organizations receive an equitable share of financial support from each level of government.

Thus the core of AQ's activities is focused on provincial policies and programs. From the beginning, however, this emphasis was coupled with action at the national level. Traditionally, Quebec's anglophone community had looked to Ottawa as its protector against unpalatable provincial laws. AQ was determined to shift energies to the provincial field, but it had to recognize (indeed, its almost exclusive reliance on federal funding forced it to do so) that the anglophone community had a champion in the federal government and federal institutions. But national developments, particularly with regard to the constitution, official languages policy, and the rights of francophone minorities in the rest of Canada, were of crucial significance to AQ.[48] AQ has little choice but to embrace a bilingual vision of the country. As a minority united by its use of one of Canada's official languages, it has every incentive to encourage a Trudeauesque policy on official languages: they are equal, and all citizens have the right to demand services from the federal, and to some extent provincial, governments in the language of their choice. Moreover, as representing a linguistic minority, AQ has every interest in ensuring that other (francophone) minorities be treated generously by their provincial governments. If they are not, then Quebec's government will feel justified in harsher measures toward the province's anglophones. As well, the continued existence and viability of francophone communities outside Quebec are a sociological foundation of official bilingualism; without them, the policy – and hence support for anglophone Quebecers – loses much of its rationale. As AQ puts it, "A victory for a linguistic minority anywhere in Canada, is a victory for all of us."[49] Not surprising, AQ was almost from its inception a strong supporter of an expanded and invigorated federal Official Languages Act.

While the federal Official Languages Act has been a focus of AQ's energies, constitutional issues have remained paramount: the "protection for minority language rights must reside in the most secure home available in a democratic society – in the Constitution where those rights are beyond the reach of any single majority."[50] The Canadian Charter of Rights and Freedoms contains several clauses crucial to continued survival of linguistic minorities. One of the most significant is section 23, Minority Language Education Rights:

23. (1) Citizens of Canada
     (a) whose first language learned and still understood is that of the English or French linguistic minority population of the province in which they reside, or
     (b) who have received their primary school instruction in Canada in English or French and reside in a province where the language in which they received that instruction is the language of the English or French linguistic minority population of the province,
     have the right to have their children receive primary and secondary school instruction in that language in that province.
    (2) Citizens of Canada of whom any child has received or is receiving primary or secondary school instruction in English or French in Canada, have the right to have all their children receive primary and secondary school instruction in the same language.
    (3) The rights of citizens of Canada under subsections (1) and (2) to have their children receive primary and secondary school instruction in the language of the English or French linguistic minority population of a province
     (a) applies wherever in the province the number of children of citizens who have such a right is sufficient to warrant the provision to them out of public funds of minority language instruction; and
     (b) includes, where the number of those children so warrants, the right to have them receive that instruction in minority language educational facilities provided out of public funds.

AQ's position is that section 23 should be interpreted in the broadest possible sense. It should apply not only to citizens but to permanent residents (an important consideration given Quebec's reliance on immigration). According to section 59 of the Constitution Act, 1982, section 23(1)(a) will come into force in Quebec only when the legislative assembly authorizes it. AQ demands that the assembly do so. It also demands that section 23(1)(b), the so-called Canada clause, be expanded to include parents who have been educated in English outside Canada and that the right to minority language education be extended to the descendants of the children in question. Finally, the section does not define the meaning of "minority-language educational facilities." AQ holds (and this has been supported in recent judicial rulings) that linguistic minorities must be able to control and manage their school systems in their respective provinces. AQ has consistently practised what it has preached by joining francophone minority groups in Manitoba and New Brunswick lobbying for enhanced provincial minority-language services. In 1983, for example, representatives of AQ travelled to Winnipeg to present a brief commending Howard Pawley's government for arriving at a negotiated agreement with the Société franco-manitobaine and the federal government on amendments to the Manitoba Act to restore some basic rights to the francophone minority that had been denied since 1890.[51]

AQ played an active role in connection with the failed Meech Lake Accord (1987–90). AQ from the beginning had accepted the provincial government's right to protect French language and culture, while it demanded accommodation for the anglophone minority. Indeed, AQ supported a bilingual Canada *and* a distinct Quebec: "We are, however, Alliance *Québec*, and as Quebecers we feel with great immediacy the uniqueness of our society. We know that, within the context of respecting fundamental rights, it is both legitimate and necessary for the National Assembly to take positive measures to protect the French language and to promote the distinctiveness of our province. We also know, however, that the unique character of Quebec is, in part, the result of our presence and our involvement."[52] AQ proposed amendments to the accord and supported the need to reconcile Quebec to the 1982 constitution and the provision that Quebec was a distinct society. Its detailed recommendations, however, effectively placed it in opposition to the Quebec government – for example, in strengthening the language affirming the existence of French-speaking people throughout and not merely elsewhere in Canada, urging that all governments be enjoined to preserve and promote Canada's fundamental characteristic of linguistic dualism, that all Charter rights be unaffected by the accord, and that section 33 of the Charter (the notwithstanding clause) be repealed.

AQ's fundamental positions on these linguistic policy issues have thus remained remarkably consistent over the last decade. Its founding principle is one of linguistic duality as a cornerstone of the nation. It is a firm supporter of the Charter of Rights and Freedoms but accepts that those universal rights might be applied or implemented somewhat differently in different parts of the country (to accommodate Quebec's concerns about preservation of French). It has worked with some success to develop an "English-speaking identity" in Quebec and has become the recognized representative of anglophones in that province. It has won significant victories at the provincial level and has been a visible presence on linguistic issues not only in Ottawa, but in other provinces, in co-operation with francophone minority groups.

In all this time, through all these accomplishments, AQ relied almost totally on SOS funding. It was to Ottawa's advantage to have a

Quebec-based organization advancing bilingualism. The SOS supported AQ's predecessors, and working relations between SOS officials in Quebec and the Positive Action Committee and Participation Quebec were quite close.[53] From the SOS's perspective, AQ's approach to the language question was the most compatible with the federal government's view of the proper way to proceed in the Quebec situation. AQ's support for official bilingualism before legislative committees in Manitoba and New Brunswick, along with litigation that it initiated to roll back some of the more draconian elements of Bill 101, obviously buttressed Ottawa's policies. At the same time, however, AQ lobbied vigorously against some elements of Ottawa's Official Languages Act and the Meech Lake Accord. On the Quebec front, the organization had to guard jealously its autonomy to avoid being dismissed as the national government's stooge.

*La fédération des francophones hors Québec
(FFHQ)*

The FFHQ (which in 1991 became the Fédération des communautés francophones et acadiennes du Canada) was formed in 1975 as the national federation of provincial and other francophone organizations across Canada. In 1990 it boasted fifteen members: la Fédération des Franco-Colombiens, l'Association canadienne-française de l'Alberta, l'Association culturelle franco-canadienne de la Saskatchewan, la Société franco-manitobaine, l'Association canadienne-française de l'Ontario, la Société des Acadiens du Nouveau-Brunswick, la Fédération acadienne de la Nouvelle-Écosse, la Société Saint-Thomas d'Aquin, and la Fédération des francophones de Terre-Neuve et du Labrador, as well as l'Association culturelle franco-ténoise, l'Association des franco-yukonnais, la Fédération des jeunes canadiens-français, la Fédération des femmes canadiennes-françaises, la Fédération culturelle canadienne-française, and l'Association des presses francophones.

The FFHQ's base operating budget in 1986–87 consisted of revenues of $599,534, of which $500,185 (83 per cent) came from SOS core funding. Member associations contributed $58,478 (10 per cent), and the Quebec government gave $6,559.[54] The FFHQ also received another $182,320 from the SOS for special projects and studies.

Its establishment in 1975 demonstrates the state's impact on the associational system. The FFHQ notes that after funding of OLMGs "les associations provinciales reprirent confiance en la possibilité d'attaquer de front l'ensemble des problèmes des communautés.

Économie, éducation, développement communautaire, culture, communications, affaires sociales – enfin, il semblait possible d'élaborer
une stratégie globale."[55] In 1971 Canada's nine provincial francophone associations began to meet to discuss common concerns.
They feared a growing anglophone backlash against bilingualism
and believed that the federal government was subtly reducing its
commitment to official bilingualism through its new emphasis on
multiculturalism and its restructuring of some administrative components of sos.[56] The associations demanded a policy review from
the sos, and so the minister, Hugh Faulkner, agreed in December
1974 to establish a Task Force on French Language minorities. The
group released its report in November 1975: *C'est le temps ou jamais*
made a series of recommendations to strengthen both the Official
Languages Act and the prospects of francophone minorities outside
Quebec. The FFHQ was formed, in part, to press for implementation
of the recommendations.

C'est le temps ou jamais articulated, perhaps for the first time, a truly
national agenda for Canada's francophone minorities. That agenda
was grounded in assumptions somewhat at odds with those that had
guided Canada's official languages policy. Perhaps because of this,
the document had a sense of urgency and passion that, by the
mid-1970s, had all but disappeared from the sos's administration of
language programs. The most critical assumption made by the Task
Force on French Language Minorities was this: that the Official
Languages Act was "only meaningful because there were French-
speaking minorities outside Quebec and because these minorities
had and must have a real future."[57] As argued in the previous chapters, support for official-language minorities had not in fact been
central to either the (Laurendeau-Dunton) Royal Commission on Bilingualism and Biculturalism or the Official Languages Act. Ottawa's
policy obviously understood and respected the existence of official
language minorities outside Quebec, but it also held out a vision of
language as divorced from culture and community, as a means of
communication that could be used and learned by all Canadians.
Federal institutions could therefore respond in either official language depending on individual preferences.

The OLMGs, however, and the task force that carried their banner,
could not countenance a purely individualist approach to language.
They could not and would not divorce language from the living
communities within which it is fostered and preserved. Government
policy supporting bilingualism would first and foremost have to assist and revitalize the OLMGs.[58] The indictments in *C'est le temps ou
jamais* of federal policy since 1969 were unequivocal. While creation

of the Social Action Branch of the SOS and passage of the Official Languages Act did indeed mark a new commitment by Ottawa to the OLMGs, they encouraged subtle dependence on the central government. Provincial governments, when asked for services or help by the minority communities, now directed inquiries to Ottawa. Federal departments referred OLMG's requests to the Social Action Branch, which, with its small budget, could hardly meet the social and economic needs of all minority-language groups in Canada. With multiculturalism policy and a minority government after 1972, the OLMGs felt that the initial commitments of 1968–69 were being displaced if not ignored: "Due to an Anglophone backlash, and for other reasons, there was a discreet but systematic slowdown on minority support programs. Now *multiculturalism* was spoken of as a solution to all problems, but to the French-speaking minorities, it meant the *death sentence for biculturalism.* ... *French-speaking minorities had already provided the justification for Mr. Trudeau's policy, and had helped to assure Ottawa of Quebec's support by showing themselves lively in a renewed Confederation, a sign that they would find it extremely difficult to survive in a broken-down Confederation.*"[59]

The task force also criticized the administrative changes to the Social Action Branch described in chapter 6. "Social Action," with its connotations of commitment and energy, was replaced by the OLMG "program." Now lodged in the Citizenship Branch, this program was simply one of many that addressed "human rights, equal opportunities for women, citizens' organizations, native peoples and multiculturalism, as well as travel and exchange."[60] The groups would lose "their" branch – a demotion, as well as an indication that the OLMGs would no longer receive special action but only be one of many "maintenance" programs administered by the Citizenship Branch. Ottawa's initial support from 1969 to 1973 had made the OLMGs aware of their needs and had enabled them to take action to develop their collective will. They needed more help now in order to progress further. The task force accordingly submitted its recommendations in the form of a manifesto on behalf of the one million French-speaking Canadians outside Quebec.

C'est le temps ou jamais argued that if Canada were serious about preserving and enhancing its OLMGs, it would have to commit efforts to motivating the population toward cultural development, money to ensure cultural vitality, and detailed information to enable the OLMGs to carry out action plans. Cultural programs, social animation, youth programs, development of mass media, and educational opportunities would have to be enhanced. The report praised past support for provincial francophone organizations but emphasized that sustaining grants should be increased. It wanted "branch" status restored to SOS officials responsible for the OLMGs, a new advocacy role for the SOS in representing OLMGs in the federal government, a renewed commitment from the government itself to the OLMGs as a major justification for its national policy of bilingualism, formation of an advisory committee comprising representatives of each provincial francophone organization, and increased budgetary appropriations for the OLMGs and their organizations.

In a fashion similar to women's organizations and particularly the National Action Committee on the Status of Women, which was formed in part to monitor implementation of the recommendations of the Royal Commission on the Status of Women, the FFHQ was established shortly after the submission in November 1975 of *C'est le temps ou jamais*. The nine provincial francophone associations joined in the FFHQ to monitor and, where possible, assist in implementation of the task force's recommendations. As well, however, the FFHQ reflected the provincial associations' disquiet concerning national and provincial commitment to bilingualism and support for francophone minorities.

The four key purposes of the FFHQ were to provide a unified voice articulating the francophone minority situation, to develop common objectives and the means to achieve them, to establish connections with other organizations whose activities might benefit the francophone minorities, and to present a common front of demands for the nine provincial associations.[61] This approach clearly represented a "nationalization" of the francophone minority in response to policy, to Ottawa's encouragement, and to political reality. The Official Languages Act and the national policy of bilingualism that it reflected had situated the OLMGs within a national policy context. These distinct minority communities were encouraged to see themselves as a fact of national life, existing on a national plane, even while rooted in their specific provinces. Ottawa's encouragement had come through the Social Action Branch, and the latter's grants, while small, were unanimously seen as a turning point for the francophone minority in Canada. The reality, however, behind both the policy and the initial encouragement was growing anglophone disgruntlement with bilingualism and realization that many of the key requirements for OLMG's survival – such as minority language education – lay within provincial jurisdiction.

The FFHQ's four major goals reflected its roots in these realities and the analysis presented in *C'est le temps ou jamais*. First, it wanted to see a co-ordinated and comprehensive government policy toward development of the francophone minorities outside Quebec. This would include control of educational institutions ("des moyens d'éducation") and the necessary tools for the community's economic, social, and cultural development. None of these minimal requirements would be met, however, without the concrete recognition of the communities' legitimate rights – the adoption in each province of French as an official language. In addition, the FFHQ demanded that the policy of institutional bilingualism be redirected toward development of francophone communities. Second, it wanted full participation by the francophone minority groups in a tripartite commission that would design a comprehensive and co-ordinated policy. Third, it sought creation of networks and alliances with individuals and organizations across the country that could assist in development of the OLMGs. Fourth and finally, the FFHQ existed to serve the provincial associations and represent their demands.

This list of goals and the more general philosophical position developed by the OLMGs and the FFHQ between 1973 and 1975 served to make them leading critics of Ottawa's language policies, in spite of the federal government's financial support. The FFHQ had its first national assembly on 12–13 June 1976 and within a few months had publicly criticized Ottawa's policy of institutional bilingualism as being wholly inadequate to serve the needs of the francophone communities and the larger interests of a truly bilingual Canada. In April and May 1977 the organization released its two-volume study, Les héritiers de Lord Durham, which documented the circumstances faced by the provincial francophone minorities throughout Canada. The FFHQ used the study as yet another occasion, in light of the gloomy prospects for linguistic-minority survival outside Quebec, to call on the federal government for a co-ordinated strategy of support. The FFHQ also reiterated its demand that the minorities, principally through the FFHQ itself, be consulted in the policy-making process.

The differences between Ottawa and the FFHQ over official languages policy increased with the government's announcement in 1977 of substantially increased aid to OLMGs. John Roberts, secretary of state, announced details of Ottawa's plan in December 1977 and called the francophone organizations to meet with him. The FFHQ refused, complaining that the policy had been determined without its consultation.[62]

The FFHQ had already met with Quebec's premier and his minister of intergovernmental affairs in October and had received a commitment of assistance. The FFHQ submission on which the meeting was based shows that the organization was adopting a militant stand vis-à-vis the language problem. The FFHQ sought Quebec's help as a "natural ally" in its "offensive" against Ottawa and the other provinces. The submission stated that the FFHQ "has no intention of playing the game of 'Canadian unity.' As long as francophones outside Quebec are considered second-class citizens, that is deprived of rights and bereft of essential services in their language, we systematically refuse to let ourselves be dragged into theoretical discussions of national unity."[63] Quebec was being asked to help develop the francophone communities and for assistance in "unmasking and denouncing the bad faith" of the federal and provincial governments. Personnel, expertise, and technical aid, as well as financial support, were requested.[64]

In the ensuing years, the FFHQ emerged as the most articulate and determined national critic of federal and provincial linguistic policies. It condemned, for example, the federal-provincial agreement signed in 1977 that affirmed the right of English- and French-speaking Canadians to receive education in their own language, but which left it to the provinces to determine how that right should be met. It issued more reports (in particular, *Deux poids, deux mesures*) showing the imbalance between rights, services, and institutions enjoyed by the anglophone minority in Quebec and the francophone minorities outside Quebec. It attacked the CMEC, much as CPF had, for inaction on the Bilingualism in Education program. It complained also about the disproportionate funds under formula payments going to Quebec for English-language education. By 1979, however, it appeared that the FFHQ was close to achieving one of its key positional goals – a joint commission consisting of government personnel and representatives of francophone minorities to develop long-term policy for the linguistic communities. The Conservative government of Joe Clark signed an agreement to establish the commission but was defeated in 1980, and the new Liberal government refused, as it had done in the past, to meet the FFHQ's demand.

The FFHQ's central concerns over the next few years continued to be over education, essential services, communications, and economic development. Its larger strategic agenda changed, however, because of developments in the early 1980s. Adoption of the Constitution Act in 1982, with the Charter's provisions on education rights, strengthened the FFHQ's position on minority education. Defeat of the "Oui" side in the Quebec referendum and of the PQ government in 1985 altered the chemistry of nationalism in that province. Election of a Conservative federal government in 1984 encouraged a less confrontational approach, since the Tories had been more conciliatory about consultations with the OLMGs. Finally, the Meech Lake Accord posed fresh challenges, since it proposed to have Quebec sign the constitution and reaffirm federalism but at the same time had the potential of reducing federal and provincial obligations to support official-language minorities throughout the country. The impact of these new developments may be seen in the FFHQ's positions on the 1981 constitutional proposals, the changes in 1988 to the Official Languages Act, and the Meech Lake Accord.

The FFHQ appeared before the Special Joint Committee of the Senate and the House of Commons on the Constitution of Canada on 26 November 1980. Its brief had nine recommendations that together sought to extend and to entrench the language rights of Canada's francophone minorities. The guiding vision behind the FFHQ's recommendations was that francophones outside of Quebec had been the victims of systematic injustice for 113 years and that any constitutional agreement must affirm the principle of two founding peoples and the basic equality of English- and French-speaking peoples in Canada.[65] The FFHQ saw the constitution as a means of binding Ottawa to its linguistic commitments and of enforcing those commitments on provincial governments. The nine recommendations aimed to ensure the right of all citizens to use the official language of their choice in communicating with either federal or provincial governments, as well as the right to French-language education up to the post-graduate level. The FFHQ wanted the constitution to recognize English and French as founding peoples of Canada.[66]

In their testimony before the committee, the FFHQ's representatives reiterated the organization's concern over assimilation of francophone minorities outside Quebec. Their view was that the forces of assimilation were so strong that half measures would no longer suffice. This sense of urgency explains the unequivocal position that the FFHQ took on extension of section 133 of the constitution (making French and English official languages) to *all* provinces and its rejection of numerical qualifications to section 23 rights to official language education. "Nous condamnons le fait que l'on assujettisse le droit à l'instruction dans leur langue maternelle pour les Francophones hors Québec à des considérations numériques. Nous revendiquons pour ces mêmes Francophones hors Québec le droit à l'instruction totalement en français et, ce, dans des écoles homogènes."[67]

The FFHQ's 1980 intervention yielded little. A new section, 16(3), indicated that the constitution did not prohibit creation of new language rights beyond the ones mentioned in the Charter. Section 23 was changed as well, to include a right to official-minority-language education not only for those whose mother tongue was French or English, but also for those who had received their primary education in Canada in either of those languages and who now resided in a province where that language was in the minority. The latter was hardly a concern to the FFHQ, since the section extended these education rights to those who might not actually be "true" members of a province's linguistic minority.

The Meech Lake Accord afforded another opportunity for the FFHQ to address constitutional concerns. The federation took a cautious approach, criticizing some of the accord's key details regarding linguistic minorities but on the whole supporting the document (it refused, for example, to join the Canadian Coalition against the Meech Lake Accord). In August 1987 the FFHQ appeared before the Special Joint Committee of the Senate and of the House of Commons on the 1987 Constitutional Accord to present its brief. The FFHQ criticized the accord on two grounds, while pointedly approving of recognition of Quebec as a distinct society. The first criticism was about a change in the final version of the accord that came about as a result of a second meeting of first ministers on 3 June 1987 (the first meeting was on 30 April 1987). The first version had referred to the existence of "English Canada" and "French Canada" as a fundamental characteristic of the country. The second and final version changed this to "English-speaking Canadians" and "French-speaking Canadians." The FFHQ objected to this because it violated one of the organization's founding principles: that the francophone minorities outside Quebec were not mere collections of individuals but small societies with distinct cultures, of which language was only one, albeit crucial, component.[68] The change in the accord's wording completely removed this collective aspect and made individuals, not communities, the bearers of rights.

The second criticism was predictable: the accord spoke of the role of the Parliament of Canada and the provincial legislatures to "preserve" the fundamental characteristic mentioned above, while the legislature and government of Quebec were to "preserve and promote" its distinctive identity. The FFHQ wanted the other provincial governments to have an obligation to "promote" as well as preserve their communities, particularly since the June version of the accord included subsection 2(4), stating that these new governmental obligations did not affect the legislatures' powers, rights, or privileges relating to language. Even with the obligation to promote, however, the FFHQ was adamant that what was at stake was not merely the right to use official languages but the institutional survival of human communities.[69]

In 1985 the Conservative federal government promised to introduce a new Official Languages Act, but the legislation was not passed until 1988. In this case, the FFHQ was consulted on the changes, and the results show clearly in both the FFHQ's submission before the Commons committee on the bill and the final act itself. The act's preamble, for example, states that the "Government of Canada is committed to enhancing the vitality and supporting the development of English and French linguistic minority communities, as an integral part of the two official language communities of Canada, and to fostering full recognition and use of English and French in Canadian society." Moreover, the legislation states that one of its purposes is to "support the development of English and French linguistic minority communities and generally advance the equality of status and use of the English and French languages within Canadian society." Other sections strengthened and clarified the government's commitment to bilingualism, extended certain provisions, and gave the act primacy in the event of any conflict with other federal statutes or regulations.

Not surprising, the FFHQ complimented the government and on the whole found that the proposed bill was "pour les communautés francophones de l'extérieur du Québec, un nouvel élan dans la politique linguistique du pays."[70] In contrast to its earlier, more strident and more pessimistic views on the Canadian linguistic situation, the FFHQ argued now that bilingualism and linguistic duality were more accepted by the majority of anglophones than ever before. For example, Yvon Fontaine, president of the FFHQ, remarked in testimony on the bill that, despite the assimilation of the past, "il y a encore des communautés avec beaucoup plus de ressources humaines qu'on n'en avait il y a 25 ans. Le niveau d'éducation a augmenté, on a donc des ressources humaines qui sont capables de satisfaire les besoins de ces communautés-là, et je pense qu'il y a un renouveau de dynamisme et de volonté au sein de ces communautés. Et ce projet de loi est une façon, pour nous, de s'assurer qu'il y a aussi des interlocuteurs qui sont prêts à aller faire un bout de chemin avec nous."[71]

Despite the altered and more moderate tone that the FFHQ adopted after the mid-1980s, it was still an organization committed unwaveringly to extension of the rights of francophone minority communities across Canada. In fifteen years its credentials to represent the almost one million francophones who live outside Quebec were firmly established. While the provincial francophone organizations also occasionally intervene at the national level, the FFHQ (and its successor) have primary responsibility for formulating and presenting the views of non-Quebec francophones in Ottawa on issues as diverse as the constitution, official bilingualism, and education. Its publications and interventions have not always yielded immediate results, and its relations with federal and provincial governments have often been stormy, but it has succeeded – in partnership with its own member associations and agencies and organizations such as the commissioner of official languages, the CPF, and AQ – in articulating a unique discourse on linguistic minority rights and grievances.

CHAPTER EIGHT

Multiculturalism

PROGRAM EVALUATIONS

Like OLMG, Multiculturalism underwent several evaluations between 1972 and 1990. The first to assess its impact systematically was conducted in 1976. Preparation of the report *Multicultural Program Granting Activities* was part of a pilot project to "explore the potential usefulness of establishing a computerized statistical information system deal with all grants in the Citizenship Sector of the Department of the Secretary of State."[1] As an "illustrative" exercise, the report did not try to probe specific hypotheses or produce evaluations, instead gathering codable information on the files for all 648 multicultural grants for the fiscal year 1974–75 and running them through a preliminary and somewhat crude statistical analysis.

That year saw $2.65 million spent on grants in four main categories: Multicultural Project Grants, Multicultural Centres, Language Aids, and Citizen Orientation ($6,000 was classed as "unknown").[2] The first category was divided into five "cost centres" consisting of four regions and the national level. The other three categories were completely national. Of the total expended, $2.33 million, or 88 per cent, came under the first category, which covered 621 of the 648 grants, or 96 per cent. Together, Ontario and the Prairies accounted for 36 per cent and 23 per cent, respectively, of the total number of grants awarded. These aggregate data suggest a highly decentralized grants structure wherein the national level awarded only 97 out of 648 grants, for 33 per cent of the total amounts granted.

The report also reviewed some aggregate statistics on the organizational structure of groups supported – "perhaps as much as 14 per cent of all funded groups are not effectively controlled by the membership."[3] Only 83 per cent of the organizations ($n = 483$; 25 per cent missing data) had annual elections of officers. Most organizations (83 per cent) had less than 300 individual members, the average for this group being 84; "typically (45 per cent of the time) organizations funded by multiculturalism which report individual citizens as members have from 20 to 85 members."[4]

Most of the funded groups were at least two years old, and 60 per cent, more than five. This suggested that program support tended to go to "established" organizations, though some of the budgetary data indicated a more precarious existence. The report discussed available data on annual income for 445 files, although the ambiguity of categories on the reporting forms made the findings only tentative. First, the organizations received "at least *one-third (33 per cent) of their income from government sources*, primarily the federal government (24 per cent). The actual figure would be higher (possibly 40 per cent) on the assumption that the label 'social agencies' largely includes indirect government funds and that funds received from a group's national organization may also represent substantial government funds." Second, larger groups tended to be more dependent on government support than were smaller ones. Finally, government monies were highly concentrated among a small number of bodies: 26 per cent received 96 per cent of funds.[5] Groups with annual budgets of less than $10,000 spent 23 per cent of those budgets on salaries and on average ended their fiscal years $250 in debt. The over-$10,000 group spent 41 per cent of budgets on salaries and on average ended the fiscal year with a credit balance of $28,000, or almost one-third of their average income.[6]

What about the range of ethnic groups supported under the program? Application files reviewed in the report contained 74 different ethnic group labels, which the report's authors then collapsed into 24 (for example, "Black," "African," "West Indian," "Haitian," and "Ugandan" became "Black").[7] Ironically, in light of the widely held perception that the program's targets were "other ethnic groups," 13 per cent of funded organizations reported a "membership composed predominantly of Canada's majority cultural groups or native citizens."[8] Almost half (43 per cent) of all monies under the grants program went to five ethnic groups (Ukrainians, Poles, Germans, Italians, and Blacks), with Ukrainians receiving "almost twice as many grants as the next largest group (Poles)."[9] Finally, the data showed that the program had a bias "in favor of multi-ethnic organizations over uni-ethnic organizations, or ... in fostering inter-ethnic group co-operation through its funding practices."[10]

The second section of the report concentrated on funded projects. Once again, original documentation was not designed for this type of data collection, and grant files had to be submitted to a content analysis and grant categories constructed on the basis of textual information. The report eventually decided on nine "macro" categories, five of which were subdivided, yielding a total of 22 project types (see Table 8.1).

The largest single category of grants came under the rubric "Folk Arts," varying from "multicultural festivals, to general performing arts (multi-art-form events) to specific art-form events (primarily folk dancing, singing, theatre and crafts)."[11] Cultural centres involved grants for "some sort of a cultural physical facility."[12] The remaining categories are straightforward, except for "Purchase/Operational Support" – what today we call "core funding." The report defined this category as tending "to be either operational grants to support the general activities of the funded organization rather than a specific project activity or grants to cover capital expenditures such as costumes or musical instruments without reference to up-coming tours, or concerts, or festivals."[13]

In 1981 the Multiculturalism program underwent another review as part of a larger report entitled *A Framework for Cross-Sectoral Evaluation of Core Funding in the Secretary of State*.[14] Rather than focusing on multiculturalism, this report was to develop an evaluative framework for core funding in all three of the sos's key "citizenship" program areas: women, multiculturalism, and official language minorities. As the report pointed out, this type of operational funding was an "astounding phenomenon": these programs provided funds by the mid-1980s to over 3,500 groups, and the activity had commenced only in the 1960s: "In both Official Languages and Multiculturalism, strong and independent organizations have been developed. We now know that organizational support is an extremely effective way of meeting social development objectives. But at the same time, the extent and duration of Government support to organizations is indicative of programming which has become reactive instead of proactive. By the late seventies, Official Language Minority groups and Multicultural organizations had become powerful lobby groups with access to the highest levels of government. In this environment, support was more likely to be based on the strength of an organization's lobbying powers than on assessments of need and rational decisions about the best way to achieve social development objectives."[15] In short order, the organizational support grants had been extended to other disadvantaged groups, partly out of the government's desire to help and partly as a "reaction to the demands of non-funded groups that they receive their fair share of support from Government."[16] The programs had, by the mid-1980s, grown to such proportions that internal sos decision-making was increasingly ad hoc, creating the "perception of continual crisis in some programs."[17]

Table 8.1
Amounts and number of grants by type of project categories, Multiculturalism, fiscal 1974–75

Type of project categories		Number of grants	Amount of grants ($)	Average grant ($000)	Percentage distribution	
Summary	Detailed				By number	By amount
Folk	Festival	94	418,921	4.46	14.69	16.28
Arts	Performing Arts	87	230,202	2.65	13.59	8.94
	Performing Tour	26	113,618	4.37	4.06	4.41
	Theatre	19	70,775	3.73	2.97	2.75
	Dance	31	58,134	1.88	4.84	2.26
	Crafts	7	18,995	2.71	1.09	.74
CULTURAL CENTRES		39	343,851	8.82	6.09	13.36
Conference,	Workshop	41	157,233	3.83	6.41	6.11
etc.	Conference	22	75,523	3.43	3.44	2.93
	Seminar	13	40,828	3.14	2.03	1.59
	Meeting	11	36,105	3.28	1.72	1.40
Media	Publishing	50	174,308	3.49	7.81	6.77
	Media (other)	31	111,632	3.60	4.84	4.34
PURCHASE/OPERATION		21	219,042	10.43	3.28	8.51
Education	Teaching Folk Art	40	109,308	2.73	6.25	4.25
	Educational Program Camps	15	63,238	4.21	2.34	2.46
	Teaching Material	6	12,533	2.09	0.94	0.49
Exhibits	Exhibit – Display	26	67,250	2.59	4.06	2.61
	Library	19	44,785	2.36	2.97	1.74
	Museum – Archive	6	24,644	4.11	0.94	0.96
IMMIGRANT ORIENTATION		25	134,182	5.37	3.91	5.21
RESEARCH		11	48,855	4.44	1.72	1.90
TOTALS		640	2,573,962	4.10	100	100

Source: Secretary of State, Multicultural Program Granting Activities (Ottawa; 1976), Table 9 at p. 78.
Note: n = 640; 1.2 per cent missing data.

The first part of the evaluation entailed canvassing the views on core funding held by departmental managers. There were many definitions and understandings: "Thus, some managers view core funding as a straight-forward tool which allows them to respond to the needs of Canadians. Others view it from the opposite perspective, as an entangled umbilical cord which ties the Department to a plethora of organizations and which it would be dangerous to sever or straighten for the fear of the hue and cry of organizations who feel that their very existence would be threatened by any attempt to rationalize their relationship with the Secretary of State Department."[18]

Some of the irrationalities associated with this situation were discussed. For example, the sos did not have a comprehensive list of groups receiving core funding through its various programs, because of differences in funding criteria and regional discretion in awards. A casual review of the available data suggested that the sos's "peripheral payroll" of core-funded groups was growing at an annual rate of 10 per cent, and that, since departmental policy called for core funding to be made as grants rather than contributions (the latter having stricter reporting requirements), organizations had fewer obligations to report to the sos on the effectiveness and efficiency of their programs.[19] Analysis of the sos's Funding Manual showed that "the Department explicitly recognizes that core funding should be an act of faith."[20] The manual's guidelines varied widely across sub-programs, "from a very articulated perspective on core funding to a completely nebulous view on the matter."[21] Some programs (e.g., Human Rights and the Social and Cultural Development component of the Native programs) left large areas of discretion to program directors or development officers. The report concluded that these flaws in the funding manual were symptomatic of "overall confusion."[22]

Subsequent interviews with thirty-five key sos interviewees produced a long litany of problems. From the departmental perspective, the worry was that the sos, through its funding ties, would become entrapped in providing entitlements to organizations. The sos's priorities would be skewed by group demands, and the groups themselves would become clients (not necessarily co-opted ones), leading to disengagement with their volunteer base and original mission. A whole other category of problems involved difficulties with core funding that arose allegedly from confusion and irrationality in program design. No model guided funding; sub-programs lacked consistency and co-ordination, were inadequately monitored, and had minimal reporting requirements for the groups.[23]

PROGRAM GUIDELINES AND
GRANTING PATTERNS

The Multicultural program in 1988 was divided into several categories at both the national and the regional levels:

Component 4320: Institutional Change:

0813 Cross Cultural Development and Race Relations
0815 Community and Cultural Programs
0816 Cultural and Educational Development
0817 Community Development
0821 Policy, Research and Analysis
Regions

Component 4321: Heritage Enhancement:

0815 Community and Cultural Programs
0816 Cultural and Educational Development
0817 Community Development
Regions

Component 4322: Heritage Language Education:

Regions

Component 4323: Citizenship and Community Participation:

0815 Community and Cultural Programs
0817 Community Development
Regions

Once again, despite the limitations of sos's *Grants and Contributions Manual, 1988*, it is useful to begin there with an analysis of what the various multicultural programs are intended to do. The overriding objective was: "To ensure the full participation of all cultural and racial communities in shaping the nation's social, cultural, political and economic environment."[24] Each of the main sub-programs also had its own specific objectives or expected results. Within Institutional Change, for example, "Respect within Canadian society for the multicultural/multiracial nature of the nation is fostered, and the institutions and decision-making processes have a capacity to serve and to reflect Canadians of all cultures and races."[25] There were several additional categories of results under this general one, but all pointed to stimulation of institutional and attitudinal change. The result of Heritage Enhancement was: "Ethnocultural heritages are promoted and enhanced as integral and evolving forms of the Canadian experience."[26] For Citizenship and Community Participation, "The capacity of new citizens to participate individually or collectively, in Canadian society is enhanced."[27]

Funding guidelines for Multicultural programs are more specific and restrictive than those of Official Language Communities, Promotion of Official Languages, or the Women's Program. This may reflect the longer experience that sos has had with assisting ethnic organizations and the split into a larger number of sub-programs. The general funding guidelines for all grants and contributions, for example, demanded that the organization demonstrate its capacity to complete the activity; submit a report within two months of the project's completion, including an account of the events that took place, number of participants, financial statements, and evaluation of success; and permit public access to resource materials such as publications, films, tapes and slides, and research findings.[28] Applications for sustaining grants had to include as well a three-year program plan with measures of success/failure, as well as an indication of how the organization would sustain itself after the end of federal funding.

The manual also discussed general administrative considerations, stating for example that no projects or activities could receive 100-per-cent financing and that the department had a preference for short-term over long-term projects.[29] There was also a list of budgetary items not considered for funding assistance: salaries and honoraria for elected officers of applicant organizations, capital costs of purchases or improvements that could become real assets, expenses related to annual or regular ongoing meetings (except where overhead assistance has been awarded), expenses incurred abroad, expenses incurred for activities related to the celebration of national days of other countries, and purchase or repair of costumes or related items.[30]

Statistical series for the Multicultural programs are difficult to generate because the categories have changed so frequently. Table 8.2 (expenditures by province from 1976–77 to 1987–88) and Table 8.3 (expenditures by program component for 1982–83 to 1987–88) show steady and incremental growth, punctuated by expenditure surges in 1980–81, 1983–84, and 1984–85. The only real decrease was in 1985–86. Expenditures in 1987–88 under all four main components (Table 8.4) totalled $20,443,678; 1,963 groups received

Table 8.2
Multiculturalism: expenditures ($000) by province for transfer payments, 1976–77 to 1987–88

Year	Nfld	PEI	NB	NS	Que.	Ont.	Man.	Sask.	Alta	BC	Yukon	NWT	Total
1987–88	197.0	120.4	233.4	636.1	3,216.0	8,152.4	2,485.2	652.1	1,899.4	1,914.0	0.0	62.6	19,568.6
1986–87	196.1	153.2	266.2	597.7	3,175.9	7,503.8	1,241.5	660.1	1,497.4	2,470.0	20.5	64.5	17,846.9
1985–86	225.8	129.7	254.1	486.4	2,696.7	7,089.9	1,303.3	539.7	1,336.8	2,019.6	0.0	57.0	16,139.0
1984–85	253.6	143.3	249.4	766.7	3,368.5	7,986.2	1,400.5	747.5	1,497.8	1,924.2	6.3	28.0	18,372.0
1983–84	198.7	162.6	493.1	384.8	2,701.5	6,181.4	1,148.6	524.5	1,078.8	1,452.3	1.9	26.0	14,354.2
1982–83	148.5	141.0	111.3	566.0	1,718.1	3,591.1	758.2	417.5	692.0	984.9	15.0	20.0	9,163.6
1981–82	94.7	98.9	140.6	413.6	1,469.3	3,331.2	722.3	380.8	463.0	958.6	10.1	25.0	8,108.1
1980–81	79.4	39.9	106.2	344.5	1,203.2	3,156.9	640.0	270.0	324.3	902.9	0.0	14.0	7,081.3
1979–80	44.3	43.9	37.5	312.1	256.9	2,500.1	319.7	174.9	287.0	578.9	0.0	47.1	4,602.4
1978–79	37.4	33.4	19.8	160.0	739.3	2,424.7	267.5	136.4	174.6	493.4	0.0	0.0	4,486.5
1977–78	37.6	20.0	25.6	171.1	604.6	1,417.5	250.2	75.9	545.0	334.4	0.0	0.0	3,481.9
1976–77	44.3	20.3	4.3	77.0	345.8	1,256.1	260.0	118.9	92.8	269.1	0.0	0.0	2,488.6
Total	1,557.4	1,106.6	1,941.5	4,916.0	21,495.8	54,591.3	10,797.0	4,698.3	9,888.9	14,302.3	53.8	344.2	125,693.1

Source: Secretary of State, Multiculturalism Directorate, 1989. 1982–83 to 1987–88: Fin. Stat. DSS 9105 and SOSEX; 1978–79 to 1981–82: Micro-fiches Fin. Stat. DSS 9105; 1976-77 to 1977–78; Data bank of those years.

Table 8.3
Multiculturalism: transfer payment expenditures ($000) by component, 1982–83 to 1987–88

	1982–83	1983–84	1984–85	1985–86	1986–87	1987–88
Cultural Enrichment	1,598	3,245	4,001	3,758	3,827	3,847
Performing and Visual Arts	1,240	1,485	1,939	1,570	2,097	1,852
Cultural Integration	1,694	2,586	2,820	2,732	2,960	–
Citizenship and Community Participation*						4,566
Group Development	1,843	2,354	2,818	2,508	2,526	3,288
Intercultural Communications	1,347	2,568	3,475	3,463	3,874	3,891
Writing and Publications	715	956	1,190	765	894	747
Canadian Ethnic Studies	727	1,160	2,129	1,343	1,669	1,377
Total	9,164	14,354	18,372	16,139	17,847	19,568

Source: Secretary of State.
* Introduced in September 1987; absorbs Cultural Integration.

Table 8.4
Multicultural grants programs, Secretary of State, fiscal 1987–88

Program	No. of groups	No. of grants	Total ($)
COMPONENT 4320: INSTITUTIONAL CHANGE			
0813	24	30	764,625
0815	4	4	64,500
0816	72	74	927,282
0817	35	36	897,700
0821	8	8	66,300
Subtotal	432	152	2,720,407
Nfld	2	2	7,000
NS	5	7	90,578
NB/PEI	8	8	215,600
Que.	33	35	637,415
Ont.	61	65	888,565
Man.	19	23	282,300
Sask.	13	14	205,535
Alta	25	27	334,416
BC/Yuk.	26	30	322,450
Subtotal	192	211	2,983,859
Total	335	363	5,704,266
COMPONENT 4321: HERITAGE ENHANCEMENT			
0815	8	9	1,076,000
0816	97	114	1,865,226
0817	11	11	191,000
Subtotal	116	134	3,132,226
Nfld	27	29	122,550
NS	16	16	62,324
NB/PEI	9	10	38,650
Que.	32	34	168,424
Ont.	71	73	443,762
Man.	62	62	368,700
Sask.	27	28	129,160
Alta	38	39	329,714
BC/Yuk.	20	20	133,147
Subtotal	302	311	1,796,431
Total	418	445	4,928,657
COMPONENT 4322: HERITAGE LANGUAGE EDUCATION			
Nfld	5	5	7,950
NS	16	16	33,309
NB/PEI	9	9	12,760
Que.	72	77	456,215
Ont.	376	377	1,772,742
Man.	62	63	250,000
Sask.	60	60	90,902

Table 8.4 (continued)
Multicultural grants programs, Secretary of State, fiscal 1987-88

Program	No. of groups	No. of grants	Total ($)
Alta	122	123	340,456
BC/Yuk.	144	144	434,451
Subtotal	866	874	3,398,785
Total	866	874	3,398,785
COMPONENT 4323: CITIZENSHIP AND COMMUNITY PARTICIPATION			
0815	2	2	110,000
0817	40	43	1,159,827
Subtotal	40	45	1,269,827
Nfld	5	6	57,500
NS	10	11	218,799
NB/PEI	4	4	37,490
Que.	76	78	1,017,900
Ont.	118	138	2,005,148
Man.	24	32	305,000
Sask.	10	13	181,522
Alta	24	30	399,450
BC/Yuk.	31	34	919,334
Subtotal	302	346	5,142,143
Total	344	391	6,411,970
GRAND TOTAL	1,963	2,073	20,443,678

Source: Secretary of State, Grants and Contributions Approved, Fiscal Year 1987–88.
Note: Calculations based on approved grants and contributions.

awards under various categories (though some groups got more than one award). The slight differences between numbers of groups and grants suggest a much wider dispersion of monies than is the case in either the Women's Program or the OLC/POL programs. Table 8.5 draws out some of these data to compare the totals for each component: expenditures and numbers of groups/grants seem evenly spread across the four fields.

Our interest here is, as with the Official Languages and Women's programs, with grants that provide operational support for organizations to represent the constituency (in this case, an ethnic constituency). Of the categories under component 4320, the critical one is 0817, Community Development, under which most national multicultural organizations are funded on an operational basis. In fact, such groups usually also had some additional funding under component 4323: Citizenship and Community Participation Program (see Table 8.6).

Table 8.5
Summary, Multicultural programs, fiscal 1987–88

Component	Number of grants	Expenditures ($)
4320: Institutional Change	335	5,704,266
4321: Heritage Enhancement	418	4,928,567
4322: Heritage Language Education	866	3,398,785
4323: Citizen and Community Participation Program	344	6,411,970
Total	1,963	20,443,678

Table 8.6
Leading multicultural organizations receiving operational funding under Component 4320: Institutional Change/0817 Community Development, Fiscal 1987–88

Organization	A Component 4320/0817 ($)	B % of A	C Component 4323/0817 ($)	D % of C	E Total ($)
Canadian Arab Federation	34,000	3.8	34,000	2.9	68,000
Canadian Ethno-Cultural Council (CEC)	97,500	10.9	102,500	8.8	200,000
Canadian Hispanic Congress	42,400	4.7	42,400	3.7	84,800
Chinese Canadian National Council	38,000	4.2	38,000	3.3	76,000
German-Canadian Congress	65,000	7.2	5,000	0.4	70,000
National Association of Canadians of Origins in India (NACOI)	56,000	6.2	39,000	3.4	95,000
Ukrainian Canadian Committee (UCC)	50,000	5.6	15,000	1.3	65,000
National Congress of Italian Canadians	34,000	3.8	36,000	3.1	70,000
Total	416,900	46.4	311,900	26.9	728,800

Source: Secretary of State, Grants and Contributions Approved, Fiscal Year 1987–88.
Note: Calculations based on approved grants and contributions.

Table 8.6 replicates the pattern from the Official Languages programs. Eight organizations account for almost half (46.4 per cent) of the key funding component that provides operational grants to multicultural groups. If we add the total expenditures under components 4320/0817 and 4323/0817 ($2,057,526), then these eight bodies (10.6 per cent of the total of 75) account for 35.4 per cent of the total expenditures. The concentration, however, is not as great as in Official Languages (or, as we shall see in the next chapter, in the Women's Program), nor are the amounts of grants as large, especially in comparison to organizations such as Alliance Quebec and NAC.

At the provincial level, virtually all funding is project based and very localized. This makes sense because of the local basis of ethnic politics and because two of the four sub-categories of programs are project oriented (heritage enhancement and heritage-language education). As with the national organizations, these two components will be ignored in the review of provincial bodies. We may follow roughly the same procedure and select the leading organization in each region in terms of the proportion of funding. Unlike the other two programs, Multiculturalism does not concentrate so much of its financing on one or two groups. As well, the proportion of groups receiving core funding under this component is much smaller than that in the other two programs (see Table 8.7).

While this program is not as concentrated as the other two, there still is significant "loading" on just a few groups. In Newfoundland, two groups account for all of the grants (though the total is small, only $7,000); in Nova Scotia, one group receives more than half; and in New Brunswick and Prince Edward Island, two groups get 40 per cent. Ontario does not have an umbrella ethnocultural organization, but most of the major "national" ethnic organizations are based in that province and have concentrated membership there. The region is represented through its national organizations (and their Ontario regional branches). Ethnic organizations in Alberta and British Columbia focus almost exclusively on providing services to their constituencies and receive small project grants from the SOS. The single largest BC ethnic group is the Chinese, and they effectively receive representation through their national organization.

Despite the somewhat confusing portrait these data provide of multicultural programs, the broad outlines are clear. First, the range of sub-programs is much wider there than is the case either for Official Languages or for the Women's Program. Second, these sub-programs emphasize project funding for a much wider array of organizations; operational funding is less prominent than for the

Table 8.7
Regional distribution of grants and proportion given to leading grantee,
Multiculturalism program, Component 4320: Institutional Change, fiscal 1987–88

Province/group	$ (province)	$ (group)	% of total
NEWFOUNDLAND			
Ethno-Cultural Association of Newfoundland and Labrador		3,000	42.86
Newfoundland and Labrador Association for Multicultural Education	7,000	4,000	57.14
NOVA SCOTIA			
Multicultural Association of Nova Scotia	90,578	46,280	51.09
NEW BRUNSWICK/PRINCE EDWARD ISLAND			
New Brunswick Multicultural Council Inc.	215,600	40,000	18.55
Prince Edward Island Multicultural Council		47,000	21.86
QUEBEC			
Centre de recherche-action sur les relations raciales	637,415	48,000	7.53
ONTARIO*			
none			
MANITOBA			
Citizenship Council of Manitoba Inc.	282,300	90,000	31.88
SASKATCHEWAN			
Multicultural Council of Saskatchewan	205,535	76,000	36.98
ALBERTA			
none	334,416		
BRITISH COLUMBIA/YUKON			
none	322,450		
TOTAL	2,095,294	354,280	16.91

Source: Secretary of State, Grants and Contributions Approved, Fiscal Year 1987–88.
Note: Calculations based on total recommended grants and contributions.
* There is no provincial umbrella organization in Ontario. The Thunder Bay Multicultural Association was chosen because it received, in addition to $20,000 under the Institutional Change Component, another $55,000 from other components of the Multiculturalism program. That made it the single best-endowed group in terms of operational funding in the region.

other two programs. Third, there is greater regional variation in funding patterns and key recipients. Fourth, there is nonetheless still a discernible tendency to support a limited number of umbrella organizations or key national/provincial organizations representing the interests of different ethnocultural groups.

There are several reasons why Multiculturalism displays these characteristics. The most notable has to do with the sociological reality of Canada's ethnic communities. Even before the immigration wave of the 1970's added significant numbers of non-Europeans to Canada's population, the ethnic mix was complex and variegated. By contrast, provincial francophone minorities are usually concentrated in a few geographical areas and have an incentive to conceive of themselves as a single community united by one overwhelmingly important characteristic, language. Ethnic communities are more dispersed and more numerous, with incentives to maintain in-group solidarity. While from time to time there have been arguments that all of Canada's ethnic communities represent a single national component (e.g., "Third Force Canadians," "visible minorities"), in practice the logic of promoting ethnic identity encourages fragmentation and separateness even while it may invite limited forms of cross-ethnic co-operation. The government's programs have simply reflected this fragmentation in dividing up the available pie into components for each group. Also, government priorities have shifted from time to time, most prominently in the new emphasis after 1980 on race-related issues, which have been added onto existing priorities.

Rather than try to provide a comprehensive analysis of all the groups funded through multicultural programs, the following section provides case profiles of three organizations that reveal different dimensions of the SOS's support to ethnocultural groups. The first is the Canadian Ethnocultural Council (CEC), an umbrella organization founded in 1980 and currently consisting of thirty-eight national organizations of ethnic communities, which in turn claim to represent over 1,000 organizations across Canada. The CEC was formed because of dissatisfaction with the national representation of Canada's ethnic communities. It has lobbied recently on issues as diverse as immigration, the Multicultural Act, and media images of Canada's minorities. The second is one of Canada's oldest ethnic organizations, the Ukrainian Canadian Congress (UCC). The third is the National Association of Canadians of Origins in India (NACOI), formed in 1976, representative of ethnic organizations that focus less on the traditional issues of cultural retention than on the newer questions of race and discrimination.

ORGANIZATIONAL PROFILES

Canadian Ethnocultural Council (CEC)

The CEC was established in 1980 and currently has a membership of thirty-eight national organizations of ethnic communities.[31] Originally titled the Council of National Ethnocultural Organizations of

Canada, it started with thirty groups at a conference in Toronto funded by the sos.[32] In addition to providing a communication forum for Canada's ethnocultural organizations, the CEC was designed to be a vehicle for the co-ordinated representation of ethnic groups' interests in the policy process, particularly around constitutional issues, immigration, race relations, heritage languages, and multiculturalism. According to its statement of aims and objectives, the CEC exists in part to "secure for ethnocultural communities in Canada equality of opportunity, rights, and dignity by making representations to various levels of government, and non-government agencies."[33] The Canadian Consultative Council on Multiculturalism (which was later replaced by the Canadian Multicultural Council) was considered unsatisfactory by many ethnic group leaders because its members were government appointees without any clear mandate to speak for their respective communities. By contrast, the CEC's policies and positions are determined by its Board of Presidents, which consists of the presidents of the member organizations.

The CEC is an advocacy organization that, unlike Canadian Parents for French or the Canadian Congress for Learning Opportunities for Women, does not enjoy charitable status. It is funded almost entirely by the sos. In fiscal 1989–90, for example, the CEC had total revenues of $429,661, of which $343,551 (80 per cent) came from the federal government. The CEC has managed to reduce this dependence on the sos somewhat in recent years. In 1988, for example, it relied on the sos for 90 per cent of its revenues. A truer picture of its financial autonomy is provided by the proportion of revenues coming from sources other than government grants (e.g., membership and registration fees, interest income). In 1989–90 these sources provided the CEC with 2 per cent of its revenue.[34]

Despite a wide range of presentations to parliamentary committees and government commissions, the CEC was still operating on a shoestring four years after its establishment. By 1987, its sos grant support would reach almost $300,00, but in 1984 its total budget was only $17,314 (of which $15,053, or 87 per cent, came from the sos).[35] The CEC had originally received sos operational funding in 1980 and 1981, but this was suspended in 1982. In spring 1983 the CEC made three applications for project funding, and operational funding was restored only in early 1984, at the behest of the minister of multiculturalism, David Collenette.[36] The CEC's outgoing president, Dr. Laureano Leone, noted with some frustration at the 1984 conference that Native and francophone groups, as well as labour organizations, received millions in federal funding. "These are tax dollars and we are tax payers. It is our right."[37] The CEC has used these funds to make representations on behalf of ethnocultural groups on a wide variety of issues, too many to fully review here. Most of its key policy positions in the 1980s have, however, been articulated around four questions: the 1980 constitutional resolution, two House of Commons committee investigations into equality rights, the Meech Lake Accord, and the Multiculturalism Act.

CEC representatives appeared before the Special Joint Committee of the Senate and of the House of Commons on the Constitution of Canada on 9 December 1980. They strongly endorsed entrenchment of a Charter of Rights and Freedoms in light of what they described as Canada's history of discrimination and prejudice against those of non–Anglo-Saxon origins – for example, against Native Canadians, the Chinese, Ukrainians, and Japanese. The CEC argued in favour of the firmest entrenchment of rights possible, criticizing section 1 of the proposed Charter which allowed some restrictions of rights, as long as they were reasonable and consistent with a free and democratic society. The CEC pointed out that past discrimination might well have been justified on precisely these grounds.[38] It also criticized the absence of any statement in the Charter specifying the fundamental multicultural dimension of Canada (the present section 27 of the Charter on Canada's Multicultural Heritage was not in the original October 1980 version). The CEC clearly felt that the Charter's provisions regarding official language education and official-language minority groups implied an unacceptable primacy for the English and French in Canada. "We cannot but view this as a deliberate omission and a sign of overt discrimination of a substantial sector of Canada's population in a document which is to be the yard stick for Canada today and for Canada of the future."[39] In demanding some explicit recognition of Canada's multicultural character, the CEC also requested that the provisions in section 15 on discrimination be broadened to prohibit discrimination based on mother tongue and permit any programs or activities designed to "protect and develop any linguistic and cultural rights in Canada."[40] The CEC's position strongly emphasized the importance of language to a definition of culture, so much so that it also recommended that the Charter include a section giving the provinces the right to extend the status and use of languages other than English and French in their jurisdictions.

The CEC carried the question of equality rights onto a broader policy terrain in its appearances before two parliamentary committees in 1983 and 1985. The first was the House of Commons Special Committee on Participation of Visible Minorities in Canadian Society (chaired by Bob Daudlin), which issued its report, *Equality Now!*, in 1984. The second was the House of Commons Sub-Committee on Equality Rights (chaired by Patrick Boyer), which issued *Equality for All* in 1985. The Daudlin committee focused on the opportunities in Canadian society for non-whites, and its considerations bore directly on the "cutting edge" of multicultural policy. The Boyer committee's mandate was to examine federal laws, regulations, and activities in light of the equality provision in section 15 of the Charter that came into effect on 17 April 1985.

The core of the CEC's recommendations to the Daudlin committee involved affirmative action or equity employment programs for visible minorities.[41] It suggested special training, equity employment through contract compliance, and multicultural broadcasting services as well as regulations to prohibit stereotypes. With respect to political institutions, the CEC had three recommendations. First, it argued that all federal government order-in-council appointments should be made in consultation with the national ethnocultural associations to assure affirmative action for visible minorities. Second, it suggested the same thing for Senate appointments, since it claimed that there were no representatives of visible minorities in the upper chamber. Finally, it suggested a variety of proposals on education to expunge racism in the curriculum and enhance understanding and tolerance.

The CEC's testimony before the Boyer committee in 1985 expanded on these themes. The committee's mandate was to examine application of the Charter's section-15 equality rights to federal statutes, regulations, and practices, though the CEC from the outset urged that these rights had to be viewed in connection with section 27, which guaranteed that the entire Charter must be interpreted in a manner consistent with the "preservation and enhancement of the multicultural heritage of Canadians."[42] As Navin Parekh, president of the CEC put it, "One of the messages we want to convey through our brief to the committee is this, that it is time in Canada now that we look at multiculturalism and the reality of Canada as a country with many different ethnic communities as something beyond merely songs and dances and costumes and food. What in effect we are asking for through this brief is equal participation in all walks of Canadian life: political, economic, social, cultural, and in every other possible way."[43] As in its presentation to the Daudlin committee, the CEC emphasized equity employment and affirmative action appointments to government boards and agencies as a first step to equality.

One of the CEC's key recommendations before the Boyer committee, for which it had lobbied for years, was passage of a separate Multiculturalism Act and establishment of both a distinct Department of Multiculturalism (as opposed to a directorate within the

SOS) and a Commons Standing Committee on Multiculturalism. While the Boyer committee did not mention these demands in *Equality for All*, the government responded in 1985 by appointing the Standing Committee. It also upgraded the Multiculturalism Directorate by appointing an assistant under-secretary of state for multiculturalism and a parliamentary secretary to the minister. The official government position on a Multiculturalism Act was favourable, particularly since the Liberals had introduced a bill in 1984 that had died on the order paper when the 1984 election was called. Introduction of legislation had to wait for appointment of the Standing Committee on Multiculturalism, which finally released a report in March 1987: *Building the Canadian Mosaic*.[44] This report outlined principles to guide Canadian multiculturalism policy, as well as institutional innovations to put those principles into practice. The federal government's response came in Bill C-93, the proposed Canadian Multiculturalism Act, tabled in the House of Commons on 1 December 1987. The CEC's comments on this legislation were affected by its representations on the Meech Lake Accord, presented to the Parliamentary Special Committee in August of that year.

The CEC's position on Meech Lake was that while it was important to bring Quebec into the constitution, this should not be done at the expense of any other sector of Canadian society. The accord's section-16 protection of multicultural rights was not sufficient, from the CEC's point of view, since it was subordinate to the accord's first section, which defined the French and English languages as the "fundamental characteristics" of Canada.[45] The CEC pressed instead for a revised section that would establish multiculturalism as an equally fundamental national characteristic, which could then also enjoy preservation and promotion by Parliament.[46] The CEC recommended, however, that – since the accord appeared to protect ethnocultural communities through section 16 in a way that it did not protect the rights of women and other minorities – it simply be rewritten to exclude any effects whatsoever on the Charter of Rights and Freedoms. The CEC recommended, as a final fillip to the accord's first section, a definition of the "distinct society" clause in regard to Quebec, so as to highlight that province's multi-ethnic character, and addition of a clause affirming Quebec's responsibility to promote and preserve its multicultural heritage.[47] Except for a suggestion that Senate appointments better reflect ethnic diversity and that the Charter's "non obstante" clause (section 33) be repealed, most of the CEC's other recommendations on the accord were minor.

Bill C-93, which was passed as the Canadian Multiculturalism Act in early 1988 before the federal election that fall, was the first formal legislative vehicle for Canada's multicultural "policy" that had been announced in the House of Commons by Prime Minister Pierre Trudeau in October 1971. The original bill fell short of several of the CEC's demands and, after some strenuous lobbying, was partially amended to incorporate them. Section 3(1), for example, originally referred to multiculturalism as only a "basic element" of the Canadian heritage and identity. After the Meech Lake Accord debate, however, the CEC preferred the phrase "fundamental characteristic," which was eventually accepted. Section 3(2) in the original bill declared that all federal institutions "should" ensure, among other things, equal opportunity and promotion of ethnic contributions and understanding. The CEC successfully lobbied for replacing "should" with "shall." The CEC's two main policy recommendations that did not appear in the act were establishment of a separate Department of Multiculturalism and of a commissioner of multiculturalism similar in status and powers to the commissioner of official languages. Up to and shortly after passage of the act, the government persisted in its view that this would isolate multicultural policy; the CEC's view was that it would be a signal of the government's commitment to its multicultural policy and would free officials in the SOS from competing interests such as official languages.[48] The federal government eventually relented and made establishment of a department one of its election pledges in 1988.[49]

The two years following passage of the act in 1988 were turbulent ones for the CEC. Passage of the act and introduction one year later of Bill C-18 to establish a Department of Multiculturalism and Citizenship were clear successes in a long lobbying process extending back to the CEC's founding in 1980.[50] However, the Standing Committee on Multiculturalism was merged with another in April 1989, and a five-year budget increase of $62 million for multiculturalism announced in 1988 was cut to $54 million, including explicit reductions of 15 per cent per year for at least three years to the operational funding of ethnocultural advocacy organizations. The 1990 federal budget also cut $1.4 million from the Heritage Languages Supplementary School Program, which provided student funding for evening and weekend classes in heritage languages. More disturbing still was the apparent rise of racial intolerance across Canada, coupled with a backlash among some prominent editorialists against the policy of multiculturalism.[51]

Despite these setbacks, the CEC continues to play an important role in Canadian ethnocultural politics. Its member organizations usually speak for themselves where and when they have to, but the CEC provides an additional emphasis and enhanced credibility (because of its broader coalition of groups) for often similar positions taken on immigration, constitutional politics, or race relations. Over time and in a distant partnership with government agencies and commissions, the CEC's pronouncements on policy questions have become increasingly sophisticated and wide-ranging. After it was formed in 1980, it focused on what by then were the main areas of ethnocultural concern: multicultural policy, immigration, education, and racial understanding. Through the 1980s it both contributed to and was driven by a broadening discourse on equality rights that rapidly embraced equity employment for visible and other minorities, affirmative hiring programs, and broad educational and communication services.

Ukrainian Canadian Congress (UCC)

The UCC was formed in 1940 to "provide a faction-ridden community with an umbrella organization that could speak for the community while helping to preserve its identity."[52] It was set up as a federation of groups, which in 1990 numbered thirty-two. It has five provincial councils (Ontario, Manitoba, Saskatchewan, Alberta, and British Columbia), thirty local branches in Canadian cities, fifteen standing committees, and two sub-committees. Most of these organizations, however, were created in the early years of Ukrainian immigration to Canada and no longer have many members or a true national presence. The UCC is dominated by its founding members: the Ukrainian Catholic Brotherhood, the Ukrainian Self-Reliance League, and the Ukrainian National Federation. More recent members include the Ukrainian Veterans' Association, the Ukrainian Canadian Professional and Business Federation, and the Canadian League for the Liberation of Ukraine. The UCC has branches in six provinces (Quebec, Ontario, Manitoba, Saskatchewan, Alberta, and British Columbia), as well as provincial councils. Other affiliates are the Ukrainian youth organization and the Ukrainian Canadian Committee Women's Council. The UCC does not represent the entire community,[53] but has become the key spokesperson for Canadian Ukrainian interests.

Those interests have been primarily preservation and enhancement of the Ukrainian fact in Canada, as well as re-establishment of an independent Ukraine, a goal now achieved. The UCC's political lobbying therefore covers a broad range of concerns, from educational policy to immigration and foreign policy. A central domestic issue since the Second World War, however, has been multiculturalism in its various guises and rubrics. It was the Ukrainian community and the UCC in particular that warned the Royal Commission on Bilingualism and Biculturalism against ignoring ethnic Canadians in a dualist vision of the country. It rejected a national policy of bilingualism in favour of territorial unilingualism (French in Quebec and English elsewhere) and even recommended that Quebec decide its future role in Canada in a plebiscite. While official bilingualism prevailed in the government's 1969 policy, affirmation of multiculturalism in 1971 "was seen as a major triumph for the UCC's lobbying skills."[54]

Since then, the UCC has continued to try to foster multiculturalism. In the last decade, that evolution has been powerfully affected by the Charter of Rights and Freedoms, official policies on equity and affirmative action, and the rights of "visible minorities." The UCC is the voice of one of Canada's oldest ethnic groups, moreover one that is not "visible" in an obvious sense. Ukrainian Canadians have readily assimilated into the mainstream and after several generations are often economically and socially well-established. These factors make the UCC's representations on multiculturalism and equality rights different in tone and substance from ethnic groups whose members are racially distinct and less established. Two illustrations of recent positions taken by the UCC are its briefs in 1980 on the constitutional resolution and in 1987 on the Meech Lake Accord.

In 1980 the UCC appeared before the Special Joint Committee on the Constitution, arguing for an entrenched Charter but severely criticizing some of its provisions. The criticism was grounded in the Ukrainian community's experiences in the First World War, when 8,000 Ukrainian Canadians were interned by the government as enemy aliens under the War Measures Act. The UCC did not wish to see any provisions in the Charter for the suspension of rights and so recommended removal of its section 1, which allows limits to rights and freedoms. Referring to the Ukrainian experience in the First World War and the Japanese experience in the Second World War, it argued that "the limitations clause in Section 1 of the Charter is so broad in its application that it would do nothing to prevent a repetition of this kind of systematic abuse of those fundamental rights which the proposed Constitution is supposed to protect."[55] As well, the UCC insisted that the Charter reflect Canada's multicultural character. Despite official federal policy that was supposed to combine and balance bilingualism with multiculturalism, the proposed constitution paid inordinate attention to English-French bilingualism. The UCC was disheartened that the term "multiculturalism" was nowhere in the proposed resolution. It would have preferred a constitutional preamble that affirmed Canada's multicultural character but, in the absence of that, recommended that another sub-section be added to section 15 (equality rights) stating that "everyone has the right to preserve and develop their cultural and linguistic heritage."[56]

One of the most interesting of the UCC's recommendations dealt with educational rights, and it illustrates the tension that exists between official bilingualism and multiculturalism. As we saw in chapter 7, Canada's policy of official bilingualism has been entwined with preservation and enhancement of francophone communities outside Quebec. While the official languages policy is not supposed to lead to an official cultural policy, it obviously must treat the two main linguistic groups, particularly the French, somewhat differently from other ethnic groups. The UCC's submission noted that sections 16 to 22 of the proposed Charter gave English and French equal status and special educational guarantees. It asked for equal treatment of all minorities. "Thus, if the Government of Canada can invade provincial rights in education on behalf of one minority in Quebec and another in the other provinces, we would submit that it can do the same for other ethnocultural minorities whose linguistic and cultural needs are equally pressing."[57] The UCC suggested that the minority-language education rights in section 23 of the Charter be changed so that all Canadians could be educated in the language of the majority in the province in which they reside but would also have the right to be educated in any other language of their choice. This would encourage a variety of bilingual combinations right across the country and ensure a "basic equality of linguistic status" which the UCC identified with true multiculturalism. Guaranteeing educational rights only to French and English gave a "privileged minority status" to those languages and groups and implied that "all cultures are important but some implicitly carry official status."[58]

Similar themes arose in the UCC's submission to Parliament on the Meech Lake Accord. The UCC objected to the accord's assumption that the country's fundamental characteristic was bilingualism, or linguistic duality. It suggested that the opening clauses of the accord be amended to describe both Canada and Quebec as multicultural societies and that Ottawa and the provinces be given responsibility for promoting as well as preserving multiculturalism.[59] The UCC believed that this would ensure that all Canadian governments placed equal and active emphasis on multiculturalism and linguistic duality: "A country that gives greater rights to its citizens based on their belonging to ethnic groups that came to Canada sooner is not our vision of what Canada is or should be. We are all immigrants or descendants of immigrants. We must all be treated equally and fairly." The UCC did not think that section 16 of the accord, which protected multicultural rights, offered enough protection to ethnic minorities. Its own proposals would "reflect the true identity of Canada, will protect the rights of all Canadians no matter what their national origin, and will give governments of all levels a positive duty to protect the equality of all Canadians."[60]

Submissions to parliamentary committees always contain a strong dose of rhetoric, but these remarks are consistent with earlier positions and the broader context of the politics of multiculturalism in Canada. The UCC's submission was marked as well, however, by a measure of mistrust and discontent. It complained, for example, that Canadians of non-British or non-French origins were underrepresented in governing and administrative institutions and demanded that the principles of multiculturalism be more solidly entrenched in the constitution. As well, it announced that these changes could not wait on future constitutional conferences, since in its view Quebec (which it felt had "adamantly refused to recognize the multicultural reality of Canadians in the negotiations") would have no incentives to agree to multiculturalism once the accord were passed. This assessment was disputed by some MPs, but it reflected the mood in ethnic circles. Virtually all ethnic organizations that appeared to comment on the Meech Lake Accord echoed the UCC's criticisms as well as its pessimism over the progress of multiculturalism.

In doing its work, the UCC has been financially supported by the SOS through operational and project grants. In 1987–88 it received $65,000 for community development and institutional change, and in each of the two following years it was awarded $55,300. In 1989–90, this represented 13.6 per cent of a total annual budget of $404,306.[61] It is clear that the national office of the UCC is not dependent on the federal government to the same extent as linguistic-minority or women's groups are. However, the very origins of the organization are entwined with federal efforts in the citizenship field, which from the beginning in the Second World War involved trying to shape the political aspirations of a segment of the political community. In this case, Ottawa worked to unite Ukrainian Canadians through the UCC, and it was successful.

Subsequent government policy used the UCC as a contact point with the Ukrainian-Canadian community for delivery of citizenship programs, particularly important in the 1950s. In the 1960s and 1970s, federal preoccupation with Quebec and language forced ethnic groups to mobilize to ensure that they were not somehow given second-class status in a hierarchy of "official" definitions of citizenship and the Canadian political community. As we have seen in previous chapters, the federal multiculturalism policy was announced in 1971 more to be a foil for the official languages policy than as a bona fide commitment in its own terms. Funding of groups and organizations followed traditional patterns of support for folkloric activities, with some modest operational support for institutional change. But the announcement of a multicultural policy in 1971 and its accompanying administrative structures, however anaemic they may have appeared at the time, did open a new era in ethnic Canadian politics. Much like the linguistic minority groups, ethnic organizations demanded government programs to implement the paper commitment to multiculturalism. Moreover, the policy further encouraged groups to preserve and enhance their distinctiveness, as well as heightening their awareness of unequal treatment. It is not surprising, therefore, that the UCC in 1980 demanded a section in the Charter on multicultural rights, that it was sensitive to the apparent favouritism shown to the linguistic rights of English and French Canadians, or that it wished for an amended section that prohibited discrimination on ethnic grounds. The same logic led the UCC in 1987 to demand that Ukrainian Canadians, like Japanese Canadians, receive an apology and compensation for their sufferings in both world wars.[62]

National Association of Canadians of Origins in India (NACOI)

NACOI was set up in Ottawa in 1976 to provide a national voice for Indo-Canadians on political questions relevant to them. There had been many small, local associations scattered across the country, but they focused on cultural, religious, linguistic, and social issues. The founders of NACOI also felt that "factors such as recurring incidents of friction in a number of cities, and growing inequalities in employment, education, and social participation," demanded the attention of a national body.[63] One of its priorities is to "ensure and protect the rights of Canadians of origins in India."[64]

Its agenda is complicated, however, by two factors that have either no or little impact on Canada's other ethnocultural groups. The first is the diversity within the Indo-Canadian community, reflecting the multicultural, multi-ethnic, and multi-religious character of India itself. As well, many Indo-Canadians, while having ethnic origins in India, actually have emigrated to Canada from third countries in which they have been established for a generation or longer. The second factor is the national security implications of Sikh immigration to Canada, in light of violent conflicts between Sikhs and the Indian government.[65] At the national level, NACOI is thus concerned with activities by the Canadian Security and Intelligence Service, as well as with the refugee determination process. Its local chapters tend to concentrate more on community and cultural affairs. In both 1987 and 1988, NACOI received a grant of $95,000 from the SOS, accounting respectively for 83 per cent and 88 per cent of revenues.[66]

The previous sections on the UCC and the CEC have provided detailed portraits of positions taken on major policy questions by two of Canada's leading ethnocultural organizations. NACOI is a member, as is the UCC, of the CEC, and so there is a great deal of symmetry between its policy positions and those of its sister organizations. The differences reflect the special circumstances of the Indo-Canadian community. The following summary and discussion of NACOI's policy agenda will therefore be abbreviated, since it covers familiar ground.

The most obvious difference between NACOI and the UCC is NACOI's preoccupation with issues that affect visible minorities. Indo-Canadians form a distinct and visible racial group, and so NACOI has had to lobby for policy and program initiatives that address the special problems faced by visible minorities. It has attacked systemic discrimination in the form of height and weight restrictions,[67] and has demanded better protection against hate propaganda and racial slurs.[68] The latter concerns are connected to greater sensitivity to the social perception and presentation of selected groups. In the mid-1980s, for example, NACOI vigorously objected to the way in which the media handled the Air India crash over Ireland and the Sikh insurgency in India.[69] Two other issues that reflect NACOI's special circumstances are immigration and charitable status for ethnocultural organizations. Almost all national ethnocultural organizations criticize Canadian immigration policy for being too restrictive and bureaucratic, but NACOI's view is that Canadian immigration staff and resources are disproportionately sparse for Indian immigrants in comparison with western Europe, leading to delays and frustrations, particularly vis-à-vis family reunification.[70] NACOI has also been frustrated in its attempts to change Revenue Canada's view of who may qualify for charitable status. Regulations prohibit granting of such status to organizations directly involved in political advocacy. NACOI's persistence on this issue in comparison to other ethnocultural organizations reflects the greater divisions within the Indo-Canadian community, which tend to discourage strong financial support for pan-community representation in the form of NACOI.

As a member of the CEC, NACOI has concurred with some of its basic positions. It supports vigorous affirmative action and equity employment, particularly in appointments to government commissions, boards, and agencies. It also agreed with the CEC in demanding a separate ministry of multiculturalism and a commissioner of multiculturalism. Finally, it agreed fully with the CEC's criticisms of the Meech Lake Accord, though it focused its own comments on several key provisions: the distinct society clause, multiculturalism, immigration, and Senate and judicial appointments. NACOI noted that "distinct" means different or unlike and objected to the way in which the accord "confers special status on the French in Quebec and lumps the rest of Canadians as non-distinct persons."[71] Arguing that Canada was now "a nation of minorities," NACOI objected to the granting of special constitutional privileges to Quebec through Meech. Like the CEC, NACOI urged that if Quebec were to be recognized as a distinct society, then Canada's multicultural character should be affirmed also. NACOI, in keeping with its emphasis on immigration matters, attacked the Meech Lake proposal to transfer some immigration powers to the provinces. Finally, like the CEC, it demanded that Senate and judicial appointments reflect Canada's multiculturalism.

NACOI represents the new wave of Canadian ethnocultural organizations. Until the 1960s, most of Canada's immigrants came from Europe, were white, and belonged to the Judaeo-Christian tradition. After 1970 the pattern shifted to include more immigrants from Asia and Africa. These new Canadians, while clearly concerned about cultural survival, also worried about racial and religious discrimination more than did the older ethnocultural communities such as Ukrainians.

CHAPTER NINE

The Women's Program

PROGRAM EVALUATIONS

In 1975 the sos's Policy Branch conducted a statistical study of grants awarded under the Women's Program during fiscal 1974–75 and the first four and a half months of fiscal 1975–76. This was the first review of its type and provides an interesting snapshot of the program at a point when, according to Findlay's analysis,[1] it may have been at the zenith of its influence. The evaluation took the following as the objectives and sub-objectives to be measured:

Objective:
To encourage the development of a society in which the full potential of women as citizens is recognized and utilized.
Sub-objectives:
1. To promote the development, by women's groups, of projects and organizations designed (a) to increase their ability to participate in all aspects of society and, (b) to assist women in bringing about political and institutional change related to the status of women.
2. To promote understanding and awareness of issues relevant to the status of women in Canada.
3. To encourage responsible and affirmative action by those in established institutions to improve the status of women.
4. To encourage existing programs, both within the Department and in other Departments, to fulfill their responsibilities in providing resources for women's activities.[2]

At the time, these objectives were being pursued through two main categories of programs: Support to Women's Groups and Public Education. The combined total cost of these programs for the period under study was $2.9 million, of which 75 per cent was allocated in grants through only two of the six sub-programs, Support Grants and Cultural Grants.[3] The report's statistical analysis focused on monies spent under these two major sub-programs, as well as four minor sub-programs (Native Women, Young Women, International Travel, and Human Rights).

The analysis covered 429 grants with a total value of $1.73 million awarded through the Women's Program during fiscal 1974–75 and the first four and a half months of fiscal 1975–76, as well as eighteen grants co-funded with the Women's Program and some other granting programs in the department. Thus the total value of all the grants reviewed was $2.075 million, of which $1.675 million, or some 81 per cent, came through International Women's Year (IWY) funds. The average amount granted was $4,000, although the regional grant average was $3,000 and the national grant average was $6,350. The Treasury Board's regulations stipulated a maximum of $25,000 per grant, but only four of 429 were at this amount.[4] Of all the grants awarded, the bulk (78 per cent of grants, 65 per cent of expenditures) were "directed at Status of Women's Groups in Canada with a view to supporting and strengthening them"[5] and included conferences, resource projects, and women's centres. The remainder (22 per cent of grants, 35 per cent of expenditures) went to cultural projects aimed at changing public attitudes and awareness regarding women's issues and roles. They included performing arts, graphic and plastic arts, media, and festivals.

The portrait provided is one of a small program doling out relatively small amounts of money. Budget allocations would be set for the fiscal period, and regional directors would negotiate with the program director as to regional allocations. As chapter 6 suggested, without the IWY expenditures, the program would have had an anaemic budget indeed. While the bulk of the funds went for support, that support (in part because of the insistence of the IWY interdepartmental committee) went first to seminars and conferences and then to women's centres. The lobby and advocacy groups that later came to claim large parts of the program (e.g., the National Action Committee on the Status of Women) received a smaller proportional share in the mid-1970s.

Exactly one decade later, the sos's Program Evaluation Directorate commissioned another study of the Women's Program by the DPA Group, Inc.,[6] in response to a Treasury Board directive that all programs be periodically reviewed. Just as the evaluation commenced, however, the government announced, in December 1983, a substantial increase in funding to the program,[7] and so the focus of analysis was shifted from a retrospective to a prospective one. As well, officials chose a qualitative method that emphasized gathering of data from key sources and experts. As a result, the consultants built their report on an open-ended questionnaire filled out by program staff, meetings with regional staff, interviews with ten women's organizations across Canada,[8] lengthy interviews with eight leaders of the women's movement,[9] and observations from attendance at several meetings of program staff and national women's organizations.

The report was divided into five sections, and an appendix reviewed program data. One section reviewed program operations. Noting that the balance of program expenditures for 1983–84 was roughly 60 per cent to the national office and 40 per cent to the regions, the report also pointed out that the director of the Women's Program had no authority over the acceptance or rejection of applications from groups in the regions, nor was she involved in the selection of regional staff members or job descriptions.[10] Moreover, despite an early attempt to balance funding and "social development" activities such as research and information dissemination, and liaison and provision of technical information to groups, what "non-granting activities are being undertaken are ad hoc."[11] Despite using the designation social development officers (SDOs), the program did not have an explicit social development strategy or policy. Yet the SDOs themselves stated that these were among their more important activities.

The SDO role requires considerable judgement, and broad and intensive knowledge about a variety of women's issues and about the technical and psychological aspects of group operations. The SDO in working with a group recommends strategies to the group, makes decisions as to the appropriateness of funding proposals and changes required, and often acts more or less independently in the community. Training for the position is often meagre and the perception of many SDO's is that the district or regional managers are not as involved in the content of Women's Program projects as they may be with other programs. While this allows independence of action it leaves the SDO, in some cases, without the considerable benefit of the support and judgement of her superiors. Finally, the SDO role is challenging because of the inherent conflict of interest that must often exist between the SDO roles of advisor on project form and content, interpreter of the Program, advocate for the group to Government management, and the role and considerable power and control the SDO herself has in recommending or refusing funding, determining the size of grants, etc. The latter role may sometimes undermine her effectiveness with the group, or make her subject to considerable pressure or manipulation.[12]

Problems faced by SDOs were also related to extensive regionalization: "It is evident that there exists considerable variation in how the Program is implemented from one region to another. ... There is a danger that the Program will evolve into essentially 10 or 12 separate Programs, each with its own orientation, policies, funding criteria, priorities, etc."[13]

A statistical appendix analysed approved grant applications for 1983–84 (where data were available, trend analyses were constructed for the 1981–84 period). For example, in 1983–84 the program awarded 451 grants. Almost 90 per cent of these were for amounts less than \$15,000, and close to 40 per cent of all grants and contributions were below \$3,000. This pattern varied little from region to region. Moreover, this pattern, with some minor fluctuations, had been evident in the three preceding years as well. The report noted that SOS guidelines stipulated that organizations have some form of support other than from government, and so the evaluators calculated the proportion of program funding to the total project budget submitted by the applicant. The data showed that "about 60 per cent of the projects receive a grant covering at minimum 50 percent of project costs. From these findings, it can be concluded that the Program is the major source of funds for the majority of the projects undertaken by groups."[14]

PROGRAM GUIDELINES AND GRANTING PATTERNS

The section of the *Grants and Contributions Manual, 1988* dealing with the Women's Program is only a few pages long and considerably less detailed than descriptions of administration of either Official Languages or Multiculturalism. The program's objectives were simply to "increase public understanding" and "promote the organizational development of women's groups."[15] In 1988 the key funding areas were economic equality (employment equity, education and training, childcare, pensions, and women in business), social justice (Charter of Rights and Freedoms, legal equality, family violence, pornography, sexual assault, and portrayal of women in the media), and access and participation (equitable access to services, participation in decision making, and elimination of discriminatory attitudes). The program expected that its results would be "strengthened organizations representative of the broad range of issues and concerns of constituencies" and "appreciation and acceptance of diversity among Canadians."[16]

The program was divided into operational and project funding. The first contributed to "ongoing operational support of organizations" with a proven track record and a primary focus on "women's equality issues." Success of applications for operational funding would depend in part on the organization's previous activities, the views of other community groups and consultants, and whether the organization had a democratic decision-making structure and worked "in concert with other women's groups."[17] Operational funding could be allocated to such costs as staff salaries, rent, office supplies, and administration. Project funding would go to non-profit women's groups "whose primary objective is to improve the equality of women," other non-profit bodies with the same end, and women's committees working within larger organizational structures. Individuals, government agencies, and universities or colleges were not eligible for funding. The manual also listed several activities that were ineligible for project funding: "provision of direct social services; projects whose primary purpose is to promote a view on abortion or sexual orientation; capital costs and travel outside Canada; projects which relate to personal, emotional or spiritual growth and professional development."[18]

The manual stated that the basis of assessment for the contribution of a project or an organization to the amelioration of women's inequality would be the documentation of such inequalities in the 1970 Report of the Royal Commission on the Status of Women. Nonetheless, with the exception of some of the ineligible activities, the manual's section on the Women's Program, like the sections on Official Languages and Multiculturalism, is vague on key terms. "Equality" and "improvement" in the situation of women in Canadian society are certainly laudable goals, but the manual did not provide any clear guidance as to what sorts of organizations and projects would contribute to these goals. The REAL Women imbroglio discussed in chapter 6 shows that while at one level REAL's support of family values, its militantly anti-abortion stand, and its method of applying for funds all violated administrative practices under the program, the group did sincerely believe that its program would contribute to women's equality and improve their lives.

The Women's Program (Component 4250) does not have the subcategories that the Multiculturalism program does. The list is broken down into national (Responsibility Centre 0831) and regional grants, that is, grants to national associations and grants to regionally based ones, and core funding and project funding. The proportions of funding for each of these pairs are fairly even. In 1986–87, for example, 41 per cent ($5,041,337) of grants and contributions went to core funding, and 59 per cent ($7,338,889) to projects. National organizations captured 43 per cent of the core funding avail-

Table 9.1
Women's Program, grants and contributions, 1973–
88

Fiscal year	Budget ($)
1973–74	223,000
1974–75	2,500,000
1975–76	406,000
1976–77	955,000
1977–78	800,000
1978–79	726,000
1979–80	876,000
1980–81	1,286,500
1981–82	2,780,300
1982–83	2,967,200
1983–84	4,245,000
1984–85	9,300,500
1985–86	12,538,000
1986–87	12,426,900
1987–88*	12,467,996

Source: Secretary of State, "Women's Program, Historical Information, Grants and Contributions," 2 April 1987.
Note: These are budgeted amounts, and there is always a minor discrepancy between budgeted amounts and actual expenditures. The only year in which the discrepancy was large was 1985–86, when a government budget freeze reduced expenditures to $10,816,000.
* The 1987–88 figure has been adjusted to reflect calculations based on final list of grants and contributions.

able that year.[19] Most project funding involved small amounts. For example, in 1986–87, 73 per cent of approved projects received $10,000 or less.[20]

Table 9.1 gives the historical profile of funding under the Women's Program. The series shows the massive proportional increase in funding in 1974–75 as a consequence of IWY. Indeed, program funding actually declined in nominal terms between 1976 and 1979. After that, the program enjoyed three subsequent years of growth: 1980–81, when funding increased by 46 per cent (from $876,000 to $1,286,500); 1981–82, in which year it rose by 116 per cent (from $1,286,500 to $2,780,300); and 1984–85, when it grew by 119 per cent (from $4,245,000 to $9,300,500). All these increases occurred under Liberal governments. After the Conservatives won power in 1984, the Women's Program was first frozen and then reduced in a series of federal budgets. Table 9.2 shows the regional and national

Table 9.2
National and regional distribution of grants, Women's Program, fiscal 1987–88

Responsibility centre	Total ($)	No. of groups	No. of grants	% of total
National	4,233,739	43	51	33.96
Nfld	502,650	30	34	4.03
NS	507,147	28	32	4.07
NB/PEI	660,305	39	45	5.30
Que.	1,920,283	150	165	15.40
Ont.	1,205,077	81	86	9.67
Man.	713,000	41	48	5.72
Sask.	612,984	37	40	4.92
Alta	913,550	76	84	7.33
BC/Yuk.	1,199,261	63	73	9.62
Total	12,467,996	588	658	100.00

Source: Secretary of State, Grants and Contributions Approved, Fiscal Year 1987–88.
Note: Calculations based on total recommended grants and contributions.

distribution of grants and monies for fiscal 1987–88: one-third of funding was directed at national organizations, with the remainder disbursed at the regional level.

The Women's Program supports a broad range of activities and projects. For example, there are university chairs, research institutes, small projects, and operating grants. Granting categories allow the same group to get support from more than one source: for example, the National Council of Jewish Women of Canada (Women's Program plus Multiculturalism) or la Fédération des dames d'Acadie (Women's Program plus Language). The Women's Program shows the same type of concentration as Official Language Communities and Promotion of Official Languages. Regionally, for example, the provincial Status of Women Council almost always receives the single largest grant. The top ten national funded groups include advocacy organizations but also groups whose primary purpose is research on women's issues or litigation.

Table 9.2 shows that under the national category (component 4250: Women's Program/Responsibility Centre 0831) for 1987–88, 51 files or projects/grants received $4,233,739. Some groups obtained more than one grant, of course: the Canadian Day Care Advocacy Association, for example, received $213,000 for operations and $50,000 for a report entitled Childcare: Meeting the Challenge. Overall, the 51 national grants were distributed among 43 organizations. The concentration of funding is shown by the proportion of

Table 9.3
Selected women's groups, national grants (Responsibility Centre 0831),
fiscal 1987–88

Group	Operational funding ($)	% of total
Association des femmes collaboratrices	125,817	3.0
Canadian Congress for Learning Opportunities for Women	259,755	6.1
Canadian Day Care Advocacy Association	213,000	5.0
Canadian Research Institute for the Advancement of Women	361,200	8.5
Fédération nationale des femmes canadiennes-françaises (also got $316,406 OLC)	118,059	2.8
National Action Committee on the Status of Women (NAC)	543,701	12.8
National Association of Women and the Law	245,640	5.8
National Watch on the Images of Women in the Media, Inc.	198,414	4.7
Women's Legal Education and Action Fund	268,770	6.3
Women's Research Centre	112,700	2.7
Total	2,447,056	57.7

Source: Secretary of State, Grants and Contributions Approved, Fiscal Year 1987–88.
Note: Calculations based on recommended amount for national-level grants and contributions.

total national grants accounted for by the operational funds disbursed to the top ten organizations (Table 9.3) – 57.7 per cent of total recommended. Five such groups got funding for operations and for a project (Table 9.4). When these groups are added into the sample group total, the amount goes from $2,447,056 to $2,623,556 and the proportion of total grants accounted for by the ten groups rises from 57.8 per cent to 62 per cent.

Usually, the largest single grant went to the provincial Status of Women's council (SOWC) (Table 9.5), though some provinces have an SOWC in more than one city. It is fair to assume that the group with the largest amount of money for operations was implicitly designated by the SOS as the province's lead organization. Supplementary investigations on the mandates of these organizations showed

Table 9.4
Women's groups receiving two or more grants, national grants (Responsibility Centre 0831), fiscal 1987–88

Group	Operations ($)	Other ($)	Total ($)
Canadian Congress for Learning Opportunities for Women	295,755	33,500	293,255
Canadian Day Care Advocacy Association	213,000	50,000	263,000
National Action Committee on the Status of Women (NAC)	543,701	75,000	618,701
National Association of Women and the Law	245,640	10,000	255,640
Women's Legal Education and Action Fund	268,770	8,000	276,770
Total	1,566,866	176,500	1,743,366

Source: Secretary of State, Grants and Contributions Approved, Fiscal Year 1987–88.
Note: Calculations based on total recommended grants and contributions.

that they were indeed at the centre of women's issues in their province. New Brunswick/Prince Edward Island yielded two organizations, as did British Columbia/Yukon.

Table 9.5 demonstrates the concentration of grants/contributions. For Newfoundland, one organization (St John's Status of Women Council) received 12.7 per cent of all funding for the region. Since none of the grants in fiscal 1987–88 to Newfoundland involved "operations," this organization was chosen because it had the largest single grant for a "coordination project." In Nova Scotia, one group (Second Storey Women's Centre) received 9.2 per cent of funding. For New Brunswick and Prince Edward Island combined, the two groups (New Brunswick Women's Network and Women's Network Inc. [PEI]) accounted for 18.7 per cent of the total. In Quebec the single largest grantee (Fédération des femmes du Québec) received only 4.7 per cent of total funding, while in Ontario, the largest grantee (Northwest Ontario Women's Decade Council) received 7.9 per cent. Concentration of funding reaches a high of 23.2 per cent in Saskatchewan (Saskatchewan Action Committee, Status of Women). Nationwide, eleven regional groups (2 per cent) of a total of 545 account for 10.98 per cent of all funding under the Women's Program (excluding grants at the national level).

The total amount recommended for spending under the Women's Program in fiscal 1987–88 was $12,467,996. The top twenty-

Table 9.5
Regional distribution of grants and proportion given to leading grantee, Women's
Program, fiscal 1987–88

Province/group	$ (province)	$ (group)	% of total
NEWFOUNDLAND			
St John's SOWC	502,650	64,000	12.73
NOVA SCOTIA			
Second Storey Women's Centre	507,147	46,763	9.22
NEW BRUNSWICK/			
PRINCE EDWARD ISLAND			
New Brunswick Women's Network	660,305	53,508	8.10
Women's Network Inc.		70,000	10.60
QUEBEC			
Fédération des femmes du Québec	1,920,283	92,000	4.79
ONTARIO			
Northwest Ontario Women's Decade			
Council	1,205,077	96,000	7.97
MANITOBA			
Manitoba Action Committee on the Status			
of Women (Winnipeg)	713,000	120,844	16.95
SASKATCHEWAN			
Saskatchewan Action Committee, Status of			
Women	612,984	142,500	23.25
ALBERTA			
Alberta Action Committee on the Status of			
Women	913,550	115,000	12.59
BRITISH COLUMBIA/YUKON			
Vancouver Status of Women	1,199,261	75,400	6.29
Yukon Status of Women Council		27,700	2.31
Total	8,234,257	903,715	10.98

Source: Secretary of State, Grants and Contributions Approved, Fiscal Year 1987–88.
Note: Calculations based on total recommended grants and contributions.

one national and regional groups (3.5 per cent of the total of 588)
accounted for 28 per cent of the money spent.

As with the analysis in chapters 7 and 8, however, it is more useful
at this point to present profiles of a selected number of national organizations than attempt to generate more aggregate data on either
the full range of women's organizations supported by the program
or even a selected sample. Three organizations that illustrate differ-

ent dimensions of the Women's Program, and also account for a significant proportion of national funding, will be reviewed here: the National Action Committee on the Status of Women (NAC), the Canadian Congress for Learning Opportunities for Women (CCLOW), and the Canadian Day Care Advocacy Organization (CDCAA). The latter two are members of NAC, so the organizations are intertwined. All three are national advocacy organizations and in this respect do not represent the full range of women's groups supported by the SOS. That range includes everything from small community counselling services to large national organizations, but the latter have the most visible and persistent impact on policy in terms of articulating a specific discourse on policy issues related to women.

ORGANIZATIONAL PROFILES

National Action Committee on the Status of Women (NAC)

NAC is an umbrella organization of national and regional women's groups. To qualify for voting membership, a group must be non-governmental, consist of at least ten members, demonstrate that the advancement of the status of women is among its primary concerns, and subscribe to the objectives and purposes of NAC. Group membership is open to community-based, church, union, or political groups, provincial and national associations, and single-issue or constituency organizations. In 1988–89 NAC had 589 members, and it is one of the few women's coalitions in the world of such breadth and scope. Among its seventy-three national organizations, for example, are the Anglican Church of Canada, the Canadian Abortion Rights Action League, the Canadian Federation of Business and Professional Women's Clubs, the Canadian Organization for the Rights of Prostitutes, the National Union of Pakistani Canadians, and the Women's Commission of the Communist Party of Canada. The regional groups include resource and crisis centres, regional wings of political parties, labour groups, various pro-choice organizations, YWCAS, research institutes, and status of women groups. Despite the preponderance of Ontario-based organizations (221, or 42 per cent, of regional associations, as well as the head offices of many national ones), NAC reverberates with regional voices.

NAC strives to be a platform within which women's organizations may articulate and co-ordinate their experiences, as well as the lobbying arm of the Canadian women's movement. The very diversity of organizations and the determination to speak for the interests of more than half of the population has forced NAC to address an agenda much broader and more complex than even those faced by linguistic and multicultural groups. The following passage from the NAC president's report for 1989–90 illustrates this:

We have been involved in several campaigns which have strengthened coalitions between women's groups and with other advocacy groups. At last year's AGM we launched the "Get the Budget on Track" campaign, which involved a broad coalition of groups through the Pro-Canada Network, and initiated a growing cooperation between NAC and the Assembly of First Nations. Since August we have been working with pro-choice groups across the country in a campaign to protect our rights to reproductive choice. We have worked with peace and environmental groups to support the struggle of the Innu people in Labrador against the military base and low level flying. We joined in the CLC-initiated campaign against the GST, and in the coalition opposing the UI bill. We made important links with women's movements in other countries during the preparation of NAC's Parallel Report to the United Nations Committee on the Elimination of Discrimination Against Women and during my attendance at the 34th Session of the UN Commission on the Status of Women.[21]

As described in previous chapters, NAC was formed in the aftermath of the 1970 Report of the Royal Commission on the Status of Women. Its first incarnation in 1971 was as the Ad Hoc Committee on the Status of Women, and its initial purpose was to monitor implementation of the royal commission's 167 recommendations. The first member groups on the steering committee were the Canadian Federation of Business and Professional Women, the Canadian Federation of University Women, the Canadian Home Economics Association, the Canadian Union of Public Employees, the Catholic Women's League of Canada, the Federated Women's Institute of Canada, the Federation of Labour (Ontario), the Federation of Women Teachers Association of Ontario, the National Chapter of Women IODE, the National Council of Jewish Women of Canada, the National Council of Women, the New Feminists, the Women's Coalition, the Women's Liberation Movement (Toronto), and the YWCA.[22] By December 1971, NAC had forty-two member groups, and in 1972 it dropped the "Ad Hoc" from its title "because the government would not otherwise supply the money essential first for the 'Strategy for Change' conference that inaugurated NAC in the spring of 1972, and then for continuing funding."[23] The founding groups represented mainstream, institutionalized feminism, and the challenge for NAC and the entire Canadian women's movement was the development of more grass-roots feminist organizations. This is in fact what happened, as women's centres benefited from grants from the SOS, Local Initiatives, and Opportunities for Youth programs.[24]

As noted in chapter 6, the Women's Program in the SOS had meagre funds for most of the 1970s, beginning with only $200,000 in 1972. The 1975 boost caused by International Women's Year was spent largely on supporting seminars and conferences and initial organization of fledgling groups across the country. In 1977, NAC received only $17,500 in federal funding, though that was more than doubled to $37,000 in 1978. Even in 1980, the entire Women's Program budget was only $700,000. Within two years, however, that had increased to $3.2 million, and another surge followed in 1984–85. The Conservative government began in 1987 to freeze funds and eventually imposed real cuts, so that in 1988–89 NAC faced a 20-percent reduction in its core grant. The organization's heyday therefore was the early 1980s, the years of the last Trudeau government. Although NAC and its member organizations were addressing a wide range of women's issues at the time, a central item on their agenda was the constitutional negotiations in 1981–82, particularly the struggle to strengthen section 15 (equality rights) and insert section 28 into the Charter. During the late 1980s, NAC had to contend with the Conservative government's agenda of free trade, restrictions on abortion, budget restraint, the GST, and the Meech Lake Accord, as well as the rise of groups such as REAL Women. Whereas the early period had been one of relatively abundant resources and strong consensus, the latter has been one of financial strain and internal conflict.

Partly because of tighter finances, in 1987 NAC adopted a new decision-making process whereby the executive would propose annual policy priorities for NAC. The first example of such an approach was the decision by the annual general meeting to concentrate the group's energies on the 1988 federal election. NAC joined the Pro-Canada Network in opposing the Free Trade Agreement, demanded a national childcare program, and fought against recriminalization of abortion.[25] NAC's annual report for 1988–89 contained a list of eight priority recommendations for the coming year:

1. That NAC undertake a country-wide campaign against the proposed implementation of an across-the-board sales tax on goods and services expected in the federal budget.

2. That NAC undertake a cross-country campaign against the erosion of social programs.
3. That NAC campaign to expose the economic, social and ecological effects of the militarization of the economy on women.
4. That NAC be prepared to mobilize against the re-introduction of regressive child care legislation.
5. That NAC be prepared to mobilize against the recriminalization of abortion.
6. That NAC launch a national mobilization campaign to pressure the government to substantially increase the Secretary of State Women's Program budget for the core funding and the project funding of equality seeking women's groups.
7. That NAC undertake a campaign in support of mandatory employment equity legislation.
8. That the Immigrant and Visible Minorities Women's Committee establish a priority campaign for NAC, addressing the needs of this constituency.[26]

This list shows that NAC's priorities by the end of the decade were severely at odds with those of the federal government that funds it. The federal budget's announcement of cuts to the Women's Program was received as an attempt to "silence the women's movement," and NAC found the government's commitment to the priorities of women dwindling in a wide range of recent policy initiatives: failure to introduce a childcare strategy, introduction of a "regressive" abortion law, increased militarization, the GST, attempts to undermine the universality of social programs, privatization, and failed promises of equity employment laws with regard to the working conditions of Native women, visible minority women, and women with disabilities. NAC had always employed forceful rhetoric, but by 1990 its mood was both sour and combative: "The women's movement and NAC are under attack. We must continue to move in ways which strengthen solidarity among women and our allies, and which strengthen our organization. ... We must prepare for a future where we can draw on all the resources available to struggle for our rights and the continued existence of our organization."[27] This mood was powerfully affected in 1990 by the Lépine massacre at the École polytechnique in Montreal, which feminists almost universally interpreted as evidence of deeply rooted and widespread misogyny, but it was also shaped by the sense that the Conservative federal government was even less receptive to NAC's agenda than its Liberal predecessors had been.[28]

By 1990, NAC's tactics showed the continued influence of the organizational review. The policy committees were now more clearly designated as the active arms of NAC's lobbying and other political efforts and were guided by a more coherent set of principles, which included the statement that NAC "emphasizes the concerns of minority and poor women," that the social, economic, and political systems "must change in order to achieve social and economic justice," and that NAC "opposes militarism, and works in ways which are anti-sexist, anti-racist, anti-heterosexist and which preserve feminist principles and the dignity of women."[29]

Action committees were structured to represent the constituencies of Native women, women with disabilities, and visible minority women and were allocated budgets so that they might work more effectively. In 1989, NAC's committees tackled a wide range of issues with an equally wide range of tactics. Employment and the Economy focused on protesting changes to the Unemployment Insurance Act[30] and introduction of the GST. Health addressed cuts in federal transfer payments to the provinces and new reproductive technologies, and it joined with various pro-choice groups to hold meetings, press conferences, and protests and prepare submissions supporting choice.[31] Justice appeared at Commons committee hearings to argue against criminalization of prostitution[32] and organized protests and responses surrounding the Lépine massacre. Social Programs lobbied against the government's inaction on childcare as well as its attempt to place a ceiling on Canada Assistance Plan payments to the provinces.

In the last decade, three of the most prominent issues on NAC's agenda have been the constitutional amendments in 1981, the Free Trade Agreement and election of 1988, and the Meech Lake Accord. Constitutional issues had not been a preoccupation of NAC or other women's groups in the 1970s.[33] Ottawa's announcement in 1980 that it would proceed with constitutional patriation forced feminist organizations across the country to reach a consensus on the question. The first conference to be held by women's groups was sponsored by the Canadian Advisory Council on the Status of Women in September 1980 but was cancelled because of a translator's strike. The nation's first ministers met on 12 September 1980 and failed to reach a compromise; on 2 October 1980 the federal government announced its intention to proceed unilaterally on its own constitutional package which included a Charter of Rights and Freedoms. NAC made representations before the Special Joint Committee of the Senate and of the House of Commons on the package, as did other women's groups.

The Advisory Council planned another conference for 14 February 1981 but cancelled it, allegedly because of pressure by Lloyd Axworthy, minister responsible for the status of women. Doris Anderson, president of the Advisory Council, resigned amid charges that the Liberal government was trying to stifle the voice of women. It was at this point that an Ad Hoc committee was formed to reconvene the cancelled conference in Ottawa. NAC was not officially involved, although many of the key organizers on the Ad Hoc Committee were members of NAC, and the majority of NAC's organizations contributed and participated.[34] NAC later endorsed the resolutions passed by the conference, particularly the recommendation to include a section (what eventually became section 28) that would guarantee all Charter rights equally to men and women. The first ministers met again in November and agreed (with the exception of Quebec) on a constitutional package that made section 28 of the Charter subject to legislative override. This led to fierce cross-country lobbying that succeeded in reinstating section 28's immunity from override.

NAC's position on the constitution and the Charter of Rights was ambivalent in the early stages of the process, since the content of the Charter was unclear and women's groups generally had not fared well before the Supreme Court of Canada on cases grounded in the Canadian Bill of Rights of 1960. Indeed, in November 1980, NAC argued that while a Charter might appear to give women more rights, it was "insidious," given the record of past court decisions.[35] NAC's initial constitutional position, developed for the September 1980 conference of the Canadian Advisory Council, focused more on jurisdictional impediments to effective delivery of a range of social and other services needed by women,[36] but once the proposed Charter was available for discussion, its efforts, like those of most interest groups, focused on rights-related questions. In NAC's case, this focus involved principally section 15, on equality rights, and later section 28. NAC's key concerns were that equality rights be inviolable and not subject to legislative override; that those rights be articulated more clearly, in terms relevant to the needs of women; and that affirmative action be more clearly and positively entrenched in the Charter.[37] In this effort it was largely successful.

NAC's constitutional forays in 1980–81, while they criticized the federal government's proposals, were criticisms of detail, not of substance. The success in sharpening section 15 on equality rights, and then later in reasserting section 28's protection from legislative override, were high points in NAC's lobbying history. By the mid-1980s, NAC's agenda began to diverge in both substance and detail from federal priorities. Some of these differences have been referred to above, but they are most evident in the Mulroney government's two most important initiatives of 1984–90, the Free Trade Agreement (FTA) and the Meech Lake Accord. In the case of the FTA, NAC had already signalled its opposition in presentations before and reactions to the Macdonald Commission.[38] Its principal arguments were that free trade would harm those sectors of the economy that predominantly employ women (i.e., services) and the manufacturing sectors that rely most heavily on female labour (e.g., textiles) and that it would drive down Canadian wages and ultimately erode social programs. These criticisms were incorporated into a more general attack on the FTA when it was finally negotiated and ratified in 1987–88. NAC's 1988 annual general meeting voted to make the federal election its priority and so concentrated much of its efforts on opposing the FTA, since that turned out to be the key campaign issue. NAC joined the Pro-Canada Network and shared its criticisms of the deal.[39]

Whereas NAC was united in its opposition to the FTA, its position on the Meech Lake Accord generated internal debate and division. The challenge was in forging a consensus within NAC between anglophone and francophone women's organizations and between NAC and the main Quebec feminist coalition, la Fédération des femmes du Québec. The consultations were so complex and the range of positions so wide that NAC eventually admitted that no consensus could be forged on the balance between Quebec's status as a distinct society and the protection of women's rights under the Charter.[40] NAC as an organization was happy to recognize the distinct society provision and pointed out that women's organizations in Quebec did not see this as a threat to women's rights. Other groups, however, feared that the entire Charter was threatened by the Meech Lake Accord and demanded that exemptions listed in section 16 of the accord be expanded to include sections 15 and 28 of the Charter. NAC demanded at minimum that section 28 be so included. NAC also expressed concerns about the weakening of the federal spending power, which it saw as a crucial instrument to develop needed national programs for women, such as childcare.

NAC has not been rewarded for its efforts. In 1988 its core SOS grant increased 13 per cent, from $540,071 to $611,387. It rose by only $7,824 in 1989, to $619,211. In 1990 its core grant was reduced by 20 per cent. The organization has been forced to consider new fundraising techniques, but to date these have had virtually no impact, so that the SOS cuts represent real reductions in operating revenue. Despite these setbacks, and perhaps because of them, NAC has become even more vocally opposed to government policy.

This recent hardening of its stand should not obscure the fact that NAC has played a strong advocacy and oppositional role from its very beginning. It has captured the role of spokesperson for women's interests in Canada, so that any parliamentary committee or commission investigating matters of potential import to women will of necessity wish to hear NAC's views. NAC's success in this regard is a result of its remarkable capacity (at least until recently) to bridge the differences among women's organizations and so present a united front on key policy issues. It is a result also of dedicated volunteers (NAC has never had more than a dozen paid staff). But neither of these would have had the same impact without the resources that have, since NAC's founding, come predominantly from Ottawa and the SOS. If NAC has become firmly established in the public's mind as the organizational voice of women, and if it has been able to articulate a feminist perspective that purports to represent the majority of Canadian women and their needs, it is in large part thanks to the SOS and its Women's Program.

The Canadian Congress for Learning
Opportunities for Women (CCLOW)

CCLOW describes itself as a "national, non-profit, voluntary organization which promotes learning opportunities for women."[41] It grew out of the Canadian Association for Adult Education in 1973, as the Canadian Committee for Continuing Education of Women. The committee sponsored several national workshops which culminated in a national conference in 1979 held in Banff, Alberta, at which CCLOW was formally established as a separate organization. CCLOW was incorporated in 1981 and received charitable status in 1982. It was supported from the beginning by project funding from the SOS Women's Program but also received funds from the Ontario government.

The Women's Program began to support CCLOW with core funding in 1983 and has been its major source of financial support. In 1985, for example, its total revenues were $293,520, of which $194,405, or 66 per cent, came from the Women's Program. Membership fees and donations together contributed only $21,337, or 7 per cent, of revenues. CCLOW's annual revenues for 1988 were $355,148, of which $311,255, or 87 per cent, came from the Women's Program. By 1990, successive cuts to the program had reduced revenues from that source to $215,414, causing a decline in overall revenues to $258,803. Even with those cuts, however, the Women's

Program still accounted for 83 per cent of cclow's total revenues (cclow also received project support from the Women's Bureau of the federal Department of Labour, Employment and Immigration Canada, the Ontario government, and the Social Sciences and Humanities Research Council).

cclow, as its name suggests, focuses its efforts on women's education and learning. It does so, however, from a clear political standpoint that gives those efforts much wider application and import. For example, cclow "supports formal, non-formal, lifelong, and experiential learning and adult education based on feminist principles of equality."[42] It is committed to "empowering women through equality of access, equality of participation, and equality of results in education and learning."[43] Its 1985–86 annual report, for example, stated: "cclow recognizes that most women in Canada live in a society where systemic discrimination, especially against women, prevails. ... We strive for the empowerment of women on the personal, social and political levels of their lives."[44] The same report identified specific objectives connected to these larger goals. These included promotion of "feminist education and the empowerment of women" and "feminist principles in education and training by supporting all kinds of learning opportunities."[45] cclow would also work for "redress of the inequities blocking women's access to and experience of learning."[46] More recent mission statements show that these earlier principles continue to guide the organization. For example, a recent document states that cclow "recognizes that progress in education and training must go hand-in-hand with progress in such areas as equal pay for work of equal value, employment equity, and the restructuring of work and family life."[47]

One of cclow's key activities is the commissioning and production of research related to women's learning opportunities. Among the most notable of its studies are *Women's Education and Training in Canada: A Policy Analysis* (by Susan Wismer), *Decade of Promise: An Assessment of Women's Education and Training in Canada, 1976–1985* (by Avebury Research), and *Women and Adult Basic Education: An Exploratory Study* (by Paula De Coito). Once again, however, the organization does not see its research work as completely divorced from advocacy; indeed, there is an intrinsic link among research, advocacy, and information services: "Through our advocacy work, we identify topic areas or policy questions that require more study or response; through information requests we identify what information on any one topic exists, what is not available and what areas deserve further critical analysis."[48]

CCLOW serves also as a central source of information on issues related to women's learning. It responds to requests for information from members, women's organizations, government, and service providers. In 1982 it began production of a quarterly magazine, *Women's Education des femmes*, which still serves as "the primary tool for membership communication on program models, research, and critical areas of theory and comment on women's learning issues."[49] In 1987 this was supplemented by a members' newsletter, *Minerva*, which had to cease publication in 1989 because of lack of funds. In 1983, CCLOW established its Women's Learning Resource Centre, a "vital component of our information services."[50] The centre houses CCLOW reports, briefs, and publications, as well as periodicals, statistics, and government documents.

A final category of efforts includes what the organization describes as networking, communications, and outreach. This is an important if fluid set of activities, in which CCLOW's own resources can be amplified in co-operation with other organizations. The members of CCLOW's board of directors (one from each province and territory) and committees serve as regional and local contact persons for the various networks. CCLOW keeps no list of these networks; they simply develop as members interact with each other and with other organizations and build alliances around several policy issues. In 1987 a provincial/territorial co-ordinator was appointed to assist with network activities and organization, and a special workshop was held in 1989 to further facilitate CCLOW's networking strategies. On joining CCLOW, an individual is linked to the network in that province or territory. These networks consist of individuals and organizations focusing on a wide variety of issues, from childcare to literacy education and rural development. It is at this local level that CCLOW's range of concerns becomes evident, since situations vary widely across the country and call for different interventions.

The preceding suggests that CCLOW is more than a mere research organization, producing technical reports on women's education and learning. Its research and informational activities are grounded firmly in feminist principles similar to those that guide NAC and most of its member organizations. The most important of these principles is equality between men and women. CCLOW has accepted, as a practical benchmark, the definition of equality found in the Charter of Rights (especially in sections 15 and 28),[51] which it helped shape in 1981 when it made its appearance before the Special Joint Committee on the proposed constitution and Charter. Its testimony at that time was consistent with representations made by other feminist groups and provides a useful glimpse of the philosophical underpinnings of the organization's more practical policy advocacy.

While CCLOW supported the briefs presented by the Canadian Advisory Council on the Status of Women and NAC, its own presentation concentrated on education and the "implications for women of the right to learn." While supporting the concept of a Charter, CCLOW urged recognition of adults' fundamental human right to "learning programs as a means to economic independence, meaningful work, and democratic participation in society."[52] The proposed Charter contained democratic rights and freedoms, mobility rights, freedom of expression and assembly and association, and basic political rights. CCLOW claimed that these were empty phrases for the millions of Canadian women who were illiterate, poor, and without access to training or other learning programs.[53] It recommended addition of a clause affirming the right to learn and hence the right of access to learning programs. It also suggested that subsection 15 (2) of the Charter, permitting discrimination in affirmative action programs, specifically name women as a target group.[54]

CCLOW, like NAC and many other women's groups, had its grants first frozen and then cut in 1989–91. Operating grants fell by $38,000 in 1989–90 and $42,000 in 1990–91, forcing a staff reduction of two persons. The national office now consists of the executive director, one support staff member, and a part-time editor. A special appeal to members to make up part of the shortfall in its SOS grant raised only $8,200.[55] The organization has sought the advice of a marketing expert and is currently examining ways in which it might perform some of its research on contract for private firms or government agencies. It is also seeking support from foundations. CCLOW has an advantage in these endeavours over its sister organizations in the women's movement, because of its research orientation, its services, and its concentration on a widely supported policy area. It is clear, however, that CCLOW would not exist in its present form without SOS funding. Its contributions to feminist policy discourse and its representations on behalf of women's learning needs would not exist either. It is difficult to say how crucial CCLOW has been at the local and regional levels. Insofar as it has served as a node for a pre-existing network of feminist organizations, its impact may be minimal. Its special expertise on women's learning and employment, however, has made it a respected voice on "technical" issues, so that it has been able to combine feminist perspectives, policy advocacy, and expert advice.[56]

Canadian Day Care Advocacy Association
(CDCAA)

Up to the end of the 1970s, childcare advocacy focused almost exclusively on the local or provincial level. The 1970 Report of the Royal Commission on the Status of Women did propose national efforts at developing a childcare system and led to the first national conference on the topic, held in 1972 and sponsored by the Canadian Council on Social Development. The 1972 conference did not spawn any national organizations. In 1982, when the Canadian Council on Social Development and Health and Welfare Canada sponsored the Second Canadian Conference on Day Care in Winnipeg, establishment of some sort of ongoing organizational vehicle was a priority.[57] Over 700 delegates from across Canada attended the meeting.

Conference organizers and the session chairs agreed to form a 39-member Interim Steering Committee with a mandate to publish a national newsletter on the status of childcare, lobby politicians and the media, seek support from national organizations such as NAC and the Canadian Advisory Committee on the Status of Women, raise funds, and encourage formation of regional coalitions. The Canadian Day Care Advocacy Association (CDCAA) grew out of this Steering Committee in March 1983, at a meeting funded by Health and Welfare Canada.[58] Its primary mission was to co-ordinate a "cross-Canada public education campaign on how federal government policy can be changed to make accessible, affordable, high-quality care a reality for all Canadian children who need it."[59] An eight-member executive decided to focus its efforts on resolution 19 from the 1982 Winnipeg conference, which called for increased corefunding for daycare. It established three committees (Networking, Communications, and Funding) and resolved to produce a newsletter, set up a network of organizations, and seek funding.[60] The CDCAA applied to the SOS's Women's Program and to Health and Welfare Canada and received support almost immediately. The Women's Program awarded a grant of $15,000, and Health and Welfare, $8,000. This allowed the CDCAA to create a national office in Ottawa. The Women's Program provided project grants for two subsequent years. This money was used "to establish the organization, to hold its first elections, to do public education around the 1984 federal elections, to do outreach to national, provincial and local groups and organizations, to permit the elected Steering Committee to reach out to receive input for the establishment of its policy positions."[61] In 1985, the Women's Program gave the CDCAA a $90,000 operations grant to set up its Ottawa office, and while the organization's financial statistics are confidential, SOS funding has fluctuated between a high of 93 per cent of total revenues in 1988 and a low of 84 per cent in 1990.[62] The CDCAA currently has approximately 1,700 members; 200 are groups, and 1,500 are individuals and families. Group members include women's, community, labour, professional, and daycare groups.

CDCAA is both similar to and different from NAC and CCLOW. It is an advocacy organization, like NAC, but like CCLOW it focuses on a tighter range of policy issues relating to childcare. It produces some research for its briefs, but it is not primarily a research organization. While it is a "women's organization" funded by the Women's Program, and while its policy positions are informed directly by a feminist perspective, it has not considered childcare as purely a women's issue. Nonetheless, it is a member of NAC, and its briefs on economic and social policy issues (e.g., to the Macdonald Commission, the Abella Commission on Equality in Employment, and on the Canada Assistance Plan) show the influence of feminist concerns about adequate support for women who seek employment outside the home (though childcare is broader than that). But unlike CCLOW, which articulates its policy concerns within a distinct feminist discourse, CDCAA steers clear of identifying childcare as an exclusive or even predominantly feminist issue. This reflects the nature of the CDCAA as a coalition of groups and its conscious decision in 1983 to address childcare as a parental/family issue for which women disproportionately bear the burden.

Within a year of its founding, the CDCAA called on Ottawa to appoint a task force to investigate the possibility of a universal program and to pass legislation that would enable the federal government to help finance existing childcare facilities. The first suggestion was taken up with the appointment of the Task Force on Child Care, chaired by Dr. Katie Cooke. The task force issued its report in March 1986 and recommended a system broadly similar to the one envisioned by the CDCAA.[63] A Parliamentary Special Committee was subsequently appointed to study the Cooke Report and hear witnesses on the question, and its April 1987 report differed substantially from both the Cooke and CDCAA recommendations.[64] The committee preferred to deliver federal support primarily through the tax system in the form of childcare credits and deductions and only secondarily through direct support for construction of facilities and operating subsidies. The Cooke Report rejected tax measures of this sort, insisting that financial assistance go only to non-profit

childcare centres. In December 1987 the federal government released its "National Strategy on Child Care," which subsequently became the basis of Bill C-144, the Canada Child Care Act.

The National Strategy on Child Care announced on 3 December
1987 by Jake Epp, minister of national health and welfare, had three
components: enhanced tax measures for parents, a Child Care Special Initiatives Fund, and a new federal-provincial cost-sharing plan
to replace provisions in the Canada Assistance Plan. These measures
were to be phased in over seven years and by the government's estimate would cost $5.4 billion. The CDCAA opposed the tax provisions
as well as the proposed revisions to the Canada Assistance Plan. It
objected to subsidies for commercial centres, the provincial varia-
tions that would result from the plan, and the federal government's
silence on quality standards for childcare services. It was unhappy
with the government's assumption that after seven years the national
need would be met. Indeed, by the CDCAA's calculations, even creation of 200,000 new spaces would leave 1.5 million children in need
of care.[65]

Bill C-144 died on the order paper when the federal election was
called in October 1988. The CDCAA tried to ensure that childcare issues were debated in the campaign. Its special Federal Elections
News Bulletin in October 1988 set out its positions and advised activists on local election strategies; "A New Federal Policy for the 1990's"
outlined what the CDCAA opposed and what it supported. It opposed
income redistribution schemes to provide childcare (e.g., vouchers,
tax provisions), commercial care, limited childcare options, unregu-
lated and informal childcare, inadequate access, and user fees. It
supported a comprehensive, non-profit, licensed, regulated, universally accessible, and publicly supported system.[66] It urged activists to
circulate NAC material on childcare, send postcards, write letters,
make telephone calls, participate in talk shows, develop media campaigns, attend all-candidates meetings, and host childcare forums.

The CDCAA's presentations on the Meech Lake Accord and the
Women's Program, while focused on childcare, addressed it in a
larger context. Its comments on the Meech Lake Accord concentrated on section 7, on national cost-shared programs, whereby the
federal government would compensate provinces that chose not to
participate in national shared-cost programs in areas of exclusive
provincial jurisdiction, as long as the province "carries on a program
or initiative that is compatible with the national objectives." A major
concern had to do with the meaning of "national objectives." Other
parts of the accord (e.g., section 3) used another term, "national
standards and objectives." The CDCAA argued that whatever terms

were used, "the wording must be strong so that the national objectives are set in a way as to ensure program comparability across the
country."[67] The CDCAA provided, as an example, a list of federal objectives that could become the basis of a national childcare program.
These were similar to ones in the Canada Health Act: accessibility to
services, comprehensiveness or universality, quality, portability, and
non-profit administration.[68] The CDCAA was also concerned about
financial compensation for a province mounting a program "compatible with" the national one.[69] "Compatibility" might be defined
very narrowly, and so the CDCAA urged monitoring mechanisms,
systems of redress, and assurances that provinces would not take
federal monies and put them into other, more politically rewarding
programs.

It might appear that the CDCAA is only one player in the field of
childcare policy. The Special Parliamentary Committee on Child
Care, for example, heard over 1,000 witnesses in 1986. One study of
Conservative childcare policy noted that dissenting national organizations (which it termed "child care advocates") formed "a broad
constellation of interest groups, which are diverse in their primary
constituencies but which coalesce around the need for a quality,
government-subsidized system of child care."[71] But most of these
dissenting groups are in one form or another affiliated with or co-
ordinated by the CDCAA. Like CCLOW and NAC, the CDCAA is a node
in a network of organizations and groups. It helps co-ordinate and
mobilize, but, more important, it serves as the key source for a particular point of view on childcare. Its arguments, its positions, and its
vision tend to be echoed in the submissions and positions of other
advocates. Feminist critics of the "mainstreaming" of the childcare
movement note that while "expanded childcare services will improve
many women's lives and make their paid labour more possible, it
leaves gender relations within nuclear families unchanged, does not
challenge the social definition of woman as mother, and does nothing to reorganize the seemingly unbridgeable chasm of 'public' and
'private' realism and responsibilities."[71] But at the same time, the
state has "increased receptivity" to the childcare movement, which
"has successfully convinced the government to initiate policies and
programs to increase state support for childcare."[72]

PART FOUR

Conclusions

CHAPTER TEN

Citizenship and Collective Action

The universe of interest groups in Western democracies changed dramatically in the 1960s. Labour and business organizations, along with traditional philanthropic groups, were supplemented by the civil rights, student, women's, peace, and environmental movements. The organizations that grew from and in turn propelled these movements were different in character and practice from the traditional organizations that preceded them. They had a wider and looser membership, sought goals that did not immediately or materially benefit their members, and championed "life-style" issues, as against the more traditional bread-and-butter agenda of sectoral economic groups.

The identity that underlies group solidarity is not given; it has to be formed and created and maintained. Developments under modern capitalism have loosened the structuring effect of class on identity formation, opening the field to a host of new definitions of an individual's most salient characteristics. And yet, in the mobilization of potentially large groups for diffuse benefits, potential members would be tempted to "free ride." The small membership base of the organizations discussed in this book, and the small proportion of total revenues that they receive from members, confirm the hypothesis. For voluntary organizations, a "soft" membership base could be potentially crippling in many ways, but principally for fundraising. The work of Jack Walker and others seemed to show that one way around this problem was to get financial and technical support from state agencies.

This study has sought to cast some light on these theoretical issues through an examination of three areas of Canadian federal funding for voluntary, non-profit organizations: official language minority groups, multiculturalism, and women. There are at least two crucial differences in this Canadian pattern of funding from the American one. First, federal funding under these programs has been explicitly couched in terms of citizenship development and national unity. The terminology evolved and changed over the first twenty years of these programs, but the central ideas were consistent. There are no parallels in the United States to Canadian policy. There, public support has been given to issue groups without any implication that these groups are prime participants in the development of the American polity or of an enhanced sense of American citizenship. Second, the Canadian programs studied here were often explicitly directed at organizations whose primary purpose was advocacy of a particular political agenda, from universal, publicly funded childcare, to official bilingualism in every province, to affirmative action for visible minorities. American practice on the whole has drawn a line between advocacy and research/service, and pure advocacy organizations have received little or no funding.[1]

The next chapter will examine the role of the state and the political logic of interest-group funding. This chapter will explore some of the implications of this book's findings for our understanding of public interest groups in the larger policy domain of citizenship development.

THE ORGANIZATIONAL UNIVERSE

This study has not attempted to trace the growth of interest groups in each of the three areas covered by the study, or indeed in other areas such as environment or peace. However, the indirect findings from studies and evaluations and comments of policy makers and lobbyists over the last twenty years clearly support the sort of anecdotal evidence that was first offered by Paltiel to the effect that the universe of interest groups changed dramatically after 1970. Robert Presthus's work from the mid-1970s, whatever its other merits, offers a sort of fin-de-siècle portrait of a political system still dominated by elite accommodation among fairly traditional organizations representing the interests of producer groups such as business, labour, and agriculture. Even as Presthus wrote, new forces were on the horizon. The student movement was yielding a new feminist consciousness among female activists, the Royal Commission on the Status of Women was conducting the investigations that would eventually lead it to recommend funding for women's organizations, and minority groups representing linguistic and ethnic communities were emerging and being encouraged to emerge.

By the early 1970s, SOS internal memoranda showed officials overwhelmed by the number of groups forming and coming forward to claim funding. For example, chapter 7 cited a government evaluation of the OLMG program that noted that, of a sample of 325 organizations submitting applications to the program during 1981–82, fully 72 per cent had been established during the life of the program, 40 per cent of them after 1975. Chapter 8 cited a 1975 assessment of the Multiculturalism program that showed that money tended to go more toward established groups, though by the end of the decade organizations had also sprung up to represent new ethnic groups (e.g., the National Association of Canadians of Origins in India) and new dimensions of ethnicity (e.g., immigrant women). Of the three policy areas, women's organizations saw the greatest relative increase in numbers in this decade, and the increase itself was in part responsible for establishment of a separate Women's Program in 1973 to fund emergent organizations. The analysis of the program in chapter 9 showed that the clear intent of funding was to support "non-traditional" women's organizations. Taken together, then, even though precise statistical series are unavailable, the evidence firmly supports the view that the universe of interest groups in all three areas became more complex and more crowded after 1968.

It is also true, however, that the degree of growth and complexity varied across the three sectors. The nature of the social sectors that they represented and the logic of interest representation explain this situation. A first distinction must be made between the OLMGs and ethnic communities, on the one hand, and the "women's community," on the other. OLMGs and ethnic groups were motivated toward preservation of culture and community. French OLMGs in particular faced directly problems concerning assimilation, linguistic retention, and cultural survival. The impetus for preservation varied among ethnic groups depending on how recent was their arrival in Canada, but even here there was general agreement that some things – language, customs, practices – were valuable and required preservation.

OLMGs and ethnic communities usually had some economic base and social organization on which to build interest-group politics. Churches, community clubs, and friendship societies became the sinews from which political representation drew its strength. These living human communities also set limits on the types of new organizations that could spring up to represent their interests. For these reasons, the increase in numbers of groups in the OLMG and ethnic areas was simultaneously more constrained than it was for women's organizations and more viable, because they – particularly some of the traditional ethnic organizations – could draw on pre-existing community resources. Women's organizations were less constrained in form and more precarious in function. Women as a social category do not live in separate communities in the way in which OLMGs or ethnic groups may. In the early 1970s, they did not have a separate economic base. A feminist community remained to be built, and this process presupposed creation of the organizational tools to construct the community. Thus, there was much more organizational ferment as new feminist organizations sprang up to propel the feminist agenda of identity formation. But precisely because these groups were the foundations of a community yet to be, they were both more numerous (less constrained by pre-existing organizations devoted to a central project) and more vulnerable.

Another feature of the organizational universe that emerges from this study is its sheer diversity. While the literature on public interest groups often acknowledges this diversity in the abstract, it tends to treat those groups as variants of a single type. The more detailed empirical evidence presented in this study shows that while these organizations have certain key similarities – most important perhaps, their dependence on government funding – they also vary enormously in size, orientation, and practice. The aggregate data presented in chapters 7–9 showed that by the mid-1980s the sos was funding, in these three programs alone, over 3,500 organizations across the country. Many of these were small service organizations operating at the local level; examples might include an immigrant women's drop-in centre, a francophone club for boys and girls, and an ethnic dance group, although they could also include local branches of large national associations such as Canadian Parents for French (CPF). In sheer number of grants, small organizations of this type accounted for the lion's share of awards made by the SOS. Then there were several research/educational organizations set up rather to compile information of interest to a sector. Such bodies are most prevalent in the women's area and include the Canadian Congress for Learning Opportunities for Women (CCLOW).

Finally, there were the representational, political advocacy organizations that formed the core of this study. Groups such as Alliance Quebec (AQ), the Canadian Ethnocultural Council (CEC), la Fédération des francophones hors Québec (FFHQ), the National Action Committee on the Status of Women (NAC), the National Association of Canadians of Origins in India (NACOI), and the Ukrainian Canadian Congress (UCC) provide research and education services but are devoted largely to lobbying government. Indeed, from a contemporary perspective, it is difficult to conceive of the policy process in any of the three policy areas discussed in this book without the existence of organizations of this type. Government-supported advocacy is a crucial part of the politics of language, multiculturalism, and feminism in Canada.

Finally, though this was not a central part of the analysis in this book, it is clear that organizations in these three areas form networks or broad alliances that cut across their sub-group differences. The FFHQ, for instance, provides an umbrella for provincial francophone associations. And while the organizations must remain distinct, there have been instances (e.g., Meech Lake) where AQ, CPF, and the FFHQ have either joined forces or co-ordinated their responses for maximum effect. The French and English minorities understand that their respective agendas depend on the similar treatment of minorities across the country and on a national policy of official bilingualism. This latter point is the shared ground with CPF.

The same dynamic has operated until recently in the women's area. NAC also acts as an umbrella and has claimed to represent over two million Canadian women. Indeed, NAC has been uniquely able to distil the different priorities of the contemporary women's movement into a single feminist agenda. The provincial Status of Women committees that received the bulk of regional funding under the Women's Program were in effect propelled by the same agenda (they and NAC could trace their origins back to the Royal Commission on the Status of Women of 1970) and hence were NAC's natural allies in the pursuit of women's issues across the country.

The cohesion among ethnic organizations has always been weaker than that in the other two areas, for reasons briefly touched on in previous chapters. Unlike OLMGs or women, who could articulate a theory of their oppression (e.g., assimilation to English, male domination) and focus on a single identity and agenda (e.g., French and its preservation, female and its equality), their raison d'être is the representation of distinct cultures. The maintenance of distinctiveness thus delayed anything more than a loose confederation of groups in this policy field. A mosaic has, by definition, many distinct facets. For reasons developed more fully in the next chapter, there has been an emerging ethnic alliance that now parallels those in the OLMG and women's area. Ethnic political discourse has shifted away from cultural preservation toward such measures as affirmative action and protection against discrimination. Both of these goals are rooted in the change in Canada's ethnic composition in the late 1970s and the emergence of discrimination and racism as matters to be challenged by public policy, and ultimately reflected in the Charter of Rights and Freedoms.

ORGANIZATIONAL PROFILES

It is difficult to present a coherent organizational profile, given such a mix. The nine case studies in chapters 7–9 showed substantial differences in structure and practice in various policy areas. Space did not allow extended analyses of more organizations. Nonetheless, the aggregate evaluation data reported in the three chapters do provide some clues as to the nature of the groups.

All the groups studied in this book are designated as "voluntary, non-profit." Their voluntary character comes from free contributions of time and labour and of money, usually in the form of dues or membership fees, which count for a relatively low proportion of total revenues. Contributions of time and labour are difficult to measure and vary by type of organization. Small, local service groups are labour-intensive and rely most on volunteers; large, national advocacy groups, which receive larger sums of money from the SOS, rely on them least. The differences should not be overemphasized, however. In 1990, for example, NAC had less than a dozen full-time staff; CCLOW less than four. The "national offices" of many SOS-funded advocacy organizations often consist of an executive director, one or two researchers, and a couple of part-time secretaries. The boards of directors and provincial representatives are usually all volunteers. Even a relatively well-endowed organization such as AQ (over $1 million in annual grants from the SOS alone) boasts less than a dozen full-time staff.

Virtually all the groups studied here, except for some of the ethnic organizations which can draw on community financial resources, rely on government for a great deal of their revenue. Though the focus of this book is on funding by the SOS, other federal departments (e.g., National Health and Welfare) and other levels of government, both provincial and municipal, may sometimes provide funding to the same organization and project. The data provided on SOS funding, however, reveal that these organizations do indeed appear to face difficulties in generating financial support from their members or direct beneficiaries. Chapter 7 on OLMGs, for example, showed that from 1970 to 1977, SOS grants contributed 25 per cent of the funds required to implement projects. From 1977 to 1983, however, the proportion rose to 50 per cent. The same study admitted that even while core funding had theoretically been discontinued, "project funding" enabled organizations to engage in general operations. Revenue dependence over the study period (1970–83) in fact had increased for both national and provincial organizations. As well, an increasing proportion of grants was devoted to salaries:

for national organizations it increased from 11 per cent to 37 per cent and for provincial organizations from 28 per cent to 51 per cent. While these data must be interpreted cautiously, they appear to indicate the potential for "rent-seeking" (the pursuit of economic gain for those who run the organizations) and the decline in voluntary labour. The sums going to organizations are usually quite small, however (the majority of the 370 OLMGs received less than $5,900). The three case studies in chapter 7 showed that revenue dependence reached almost 90 per cent.

Similar patterns were revealed in studies of multicultural organizations. A study in 1975 of 483 groups funded through the SOS's Multiculturalism Program found that almost one-quarter of the groups did not appear to have democratic structures (e.g., elections of boards, annual meetings). Over 80 per cent had less than 300 individual members, and the average was 84. An analysis of revenue dependence revealed patterns similar to that for OLMGs: ethnic associations depended on government for as much as 40 per cent of their revenues. Also reminiscent of the case profiles presented in chapter 7, the 1975 study of multicultural groups found that the larger the organization the greater the reliance on federal funding. The same patterns of fiscal dependence emerged in the analysis of women's organizations.

Chapters 7–9 analysed distribution of monies under the three programs and revealed patterns that are broadly consistent within each program over time. The clearest tendency is to concentration. Many relatively small organizations received small grants for projects which they mounted with the assistance of volunteers. Larger operational/project grants went to key national or regional organizations. Thus each program supported hundreds of groups but gave the bulk of its money to a small number of organizations, many of which concentrated on political advocacy rather than service.

The aggregate data showed that even the largest and most prominent of SOS-funded organizations are in fact quite small. The "national" groups in all three fields lack extensive staff and research capabilities, have a small membership base, and are markedly dependent for revenue on government grants, having even in some cases been formed under the auspices of some government agency (e.g., CPF). This inevitably raises the question of representativeness. Pure service organizations – for example, a counselling centre or an ethnic club – do not usually make claims of representation. Their objectives are usually tied to specific needs and categories of people who require their services. Advocacy organizations in a democratic polity operate on different principles: they make claims to governments on behalf of not only their formally registered membership but the larger potential constituency of members interested in the issues that they promote. NAC therefore claims to represent millions of Canadian women because its member organizations have millions of individual members. AQ claims to speak on behalf of Quebec's anglophones, the FFHQ for francophones outside Quebec, and NACOI for Indo-Canadians. Some groups lobby less for a defined constituency than for a cause, although they must present this cause as one that has wide, if concealed support. CPF and the Canadian Day Care Advocacy Association (CDCAA) are examples.

Their limited resources and small membership base mean that these bodies, even many of the ethnocultural ones, are not truly representative. The "millions" of women that NAC allegedly "represents" have never voted on any NAC resolutions; the CDCAA and CCLOW have only a few hundred individual members, and the same is true for ethnocultural groups and OLMGs. These organizations may, however, speak for the latent interests of the people whom they claim to represent. Groups that are themselves the creatures of other organizations (e.g., FFHQ, CEC) can confidently speak for their membership, but this is not the same as representing people. There may be many good reasons for listening to the SOS-funded advocacy, but democratic representativeness is not one of them.

IDENTITY AND CITIZENSHIP

The prominence of advocacy among funded groups points up the emphasis that these SOS programs have continued to place on citizenship development. What precisely do these organizations do? What effect have they on the political system and public policy? The impact of the state on the organizations will be saved for the next chapter; this discussion will focus on organizational practices in the context of citizenship and identity policy.

These areas were at one time intimately related in a policy framework of citizenship development and national unity. More recently, for the organizations at least, the whole field of their endeavour may be seen to involve a discourse on identity, its formation, preservation, and articulation within a national vision. These are grandiose terms, but almost nothing else will do to sum up the original vision and ultimate effect of the programs discussed in this book.

As we saw in chapters 5 and 6, the federal government had established a tenuous foothold in the citizenship policy area immediately after the Second World War. For a number of reasons, that foothold remained weak even while it expanded, and by the mid-1960s the

Citizenship Branch was seriously considering renaming itself the Social Development Branch. We may term this period one of reluctant social mobilization. The political terrain changed dramatically in the mid-1960s, propelled by powerful societal forces. The result was a surge of protest across the developed countries. In North America, the student movement, anti-war protests, and the civil rights campaigns of blacks set the tone for Canadian developments. Policy makers in Ottawa were compelled to respond, but they did so in ways that reflected the particular characteristics of the Canadian social situation and political structure.

In Canada, the pre-eminent political issue of the mid-1960s was the Quebec question, and the main vehicle at the federal level for engagement of that issue was the Liberal party. In that period, the party saw twenty-two years of consecutive power (1935–57) lost to John Diefenbaker and only imperfectly regained in minority governments in 1963–68. It accordingly dealt with social unrest in a special way. The Liberals had shifted to the left after 1957, embracing resurgent democracy to revitalize the party. Pierre Trudeau's own political philosophy, while being an ambivalent blend of populism and statism, was initially receptive to the idea of citizens' participation and development primarily because he saw its usefulness to a national unity agenda. When the Liberal government embarked on citizenship participation in 1969, it did so not primarily to foster a radical regeneration of Canadian democracy but to foster greater allegiance to national institutions through a feeling that those institutions were open to popular forces. The documents and discourse of the time clearly show that citizen participation was considered a matter of both justice and national unity.

These goals were not necessarily inconsistent, but they held separate implications for political action. A pure focus on participation would have encouraged, as it did in the early days, support for the poor, the marginalized, and the otherwise disadvantaged. It would have emphasized individual citizens participating more fully in their own institutions. It implied dissent and occasional confrontation. A pure focus on national unity, however, held completely different implications. National unity encourages a collective orientation rather than an individualistic one. It emphasizes shared characteristics and sublimation of dissent and difference in favour of a larger harmony. It has no necessary implication that the disadvantaged or the poor be accommodated in the political process, unless their dissent threatens national unity.

The practical context of citizenship policy in Canada in that period made national unity a question of French-English accommodation, especially vis-à-vis Quebec. For reasons discussed in earlier chapters, multiculturalism sprang from this policy framework, and the support for OLMGs and ethnic groups formed the templates for support for other citizens' organizations. The Women's Program emerged for other reasons and was fortuitously maintained because of the commitment of activist officials and an unavoidable commitment to the UN's global priority of gender equality. The other citizens' programs which flourished for a time soon disappeared, until by 1975 the Women's Program was the last major non-OLMG, non-ethnic citizens' program left. To be fair, the Liberal government had also pursued the agenda of citizen participation through reforms to Parliament, the use of task forces to elicit public participation, and information strategies to communicate more effectively with the electorate. But the ambitious programs to support citizens' organizations soon were collapsed into the three discussed in this book.

Organizations so supported were all in one form or another devoted to the politics of identity. Chapter 1 discussed some of Alan Cairns's observations of this phenomenon in the contemporary era of the Charter. Cairns points out how the Canadian political landscape is now dotted with organizations that press their claims in terms of rights, rights that hinge on clauses of the Charter and in one form or another touch on the vital question of identity. This book has shown that the progenitors of these groups and this discourse of rights and identity were the programs emanating from the SOS in the early 1970s. OLMGs and Multiculturalism provide the clearest illustrations of the logic at work. Both programs supported organizations that represented or were grounded in collectivities. A francophone provincial organization or one representing an ethnic group was necessarily defined by its relationship to a collective entity or community. It was clearly a matter of public policy that both the linguistic and the ethnic communities in question be considered essential characteristics of Canada. But while the Official Languages Act of 1969 and the prime minister's statement of October 1971 on multiculturalism both upheld these collective aspects of Canadian nationality, neither provided any guidance on the balance that they were to hold. The nervous and sometimes even hostile response of various Canadian ethnic communities in the 1960s to the Royal Commission on Bilingualism and Biculturalism amply demonstrates that these communities recognized the importance of "official" declarations of national character. Such declarations – that Canada was "officially" bilingual or bicultural – could have practical consequences. Moreover, the debates of the 1960s about Quebec's role in Confederation were couched in a discourse of equality and discrimination. This discourse raised issues of justice and injustice and compelled a debate on the formal and practical equality of the two peoples, the two languages, and the two cultures. Thus the entire frame of the debate on this issue encouraged use of terms of equality and rights. Ethnic communities and organizations were not slow to adopt this discourse.

From the outset the discourse of identity therefore concerned collective rights to collective equality in representing something essential about the national character or national mosaic. In practice, the organizations claiming to represent the interests of ethnic or linguistic or racial communities demanded specific policies but cast their rhetoric and symbolic appeals in terms of their communities' collective characteristics. These qualities, often very difficult to define, could be summed in the term "identity": Quebec's identity, the francophone identity, the Italian identity, and so on. In the beginning the concept of identity was central to the articulation of political demands being made by these groups, and for linguistic and ethnic minorities it continued to play an important role. Later, even though rights came to be more important than identity, "distinctiveness" and "identity" remained the basis of their existence.

The same dynamic was evident in the women's movement, though the concept of identity was less obviously central. The contemporary women's movement sought from the outset to generate women's consciousness of their oppression. Whereas for OLMGs and ethnic groups, the community and its identity antedated them and to some extent could be assumed, for feminists community and identity had to be forged. Collective identity can be formed in a variety of ways: struggle, key events that define a direction, articulation of a shared vision by a respected leader, dissemination of research and information that "reclaims" the experience of the group, or creation of what Foucault calls disciplines that ratify the group's identity. All these occurred for the women's movement and were advanced by constituent elements in that movement. The SOS's programs and supported activities – emphasizing conferences, networking, leadership development, "cultural" development through films, women's presses, and creation of Women's Studies Programs at universities – helped create community and identity that could then be capitalized in political terms as demands for recognition or accommodation of that identity and its requirements.

The political practice of the organizations studied in this book and supported by the SOS over the last twenty years was complex and variegated. It was expressed in local community work, in provincial and regional lobbying, and in national action. It cannot be construed as a dominant element; that is, it would be absurd to suggest that well-heeled business associations or lobbyists were somehow frozen out of public policy making by the surge in these groups. All the money spent by government during these years probably never amounted to anything close to what is expended by producers' associations and their lobbies on specific policy demands. Measured in this way, the impact and influence of these organizations has been minimal. Yet the political events of the 1980s and early 1990s reveal the growing prominence of issues championed by organizations in these three areas: official languages, the place of Quebec, equality of and discrimination against women and visible minorities, daycare, language education, and so on. Many of these issues now get discussed in terms of the Charter. Indeed, the centrality of the Charter and the courts has induced many observers to conclude that these changes in the Canadian political process are a result of recent constitutional developments. But the ground was prepared many years earlier with the development of a discourse on collective rights and identity. The influence of programs such as those discussed in this book, and of the groups supported by them, cannot be measured directly. Their strongest impact came through the support that they provided to particular ways of conceptualizing politics, rights, national unity, and the proper claims that can be made by groups on other members of a society.

It would be foolish to try to argue some unique and direct causal impact of the political activity of these groups, if only because the policy process is so complex that few if any issues are determined by a single cause or intervention. It would be equally foolish, however, to abdicate the responsibility of offering some conjectures on impact. What differences do groups like the ones supported by the sos make to Canadian politics and public policy? The answers, tentative at best, can be ranged along a continuum of the most specific to the most general.

(1) Groups do sometimes have a discernible influence on specific policies and programs. Examples abound: CPF's nudging of the CMEC negotiations on official-language education; the FFHQ's demands for different administrative structures in the sos; AQ's suggested amendments to Quebec's social services legislation; the CEC and other ethnocultural groups regarding the Multiculturalism Act and department. The CCLOW is a research organization dedicated to feminist analysis, and it has designed educational programs and innovative strategies for addressing the needs of women in and out of

the work-force. Even when these groups play a largely reactive role, simply appearing before committees or the media to discuss tabled legislation, they can often recommend marginal changes that are implemented. Inclusion of protections for multicultural rights in section 16 of the Meech Lake Accord is an example.

But these organizations, in so far as they are seen as key spokespersons in their policy areas, may also be brought into policy formulation to comment on emerging legislative proposals; this happens regularly in official languages and multiculturalism, less so in the women's field. Their effectiveness at this level is difficult to assess. They can also affect legislation through their perceived role as legitimate spokespersons. When the media seek reactions to policies on childcare, official languages, or multiculturalism, they tend to go to sos-funded groups. The CDCAA, for example, was a highly visible critic of the government's 1988 proposals on childcare and while it was not responsible for their defeat it set the tone for the negative reactions across the country. Finally, the groups have helped protect the sos programs that fund them. Federal governments have on several occasions tried to reduce or redirect funding in the programs discussed in this book, but each attempt has been greeted by vocal resistance from the groups themselves, couched as defence of rights, of citizens, of the weak and the dispossessed, of Canada's core identities.

(2) Despite their often strident criticism (more on this below) of government policy, sos-funded groups are core constituencies of support for government action in the three policy areas. They may not be responsible for the growth in federal and provincial programs in their areas, but they have certainly been consistent defenders of that very growth. Ironically, the groups that grew out of the citizens' movements of the 1960s have become articulate proponents of state expansion. The programs themselves, from official bilingualism to equity employment, have cost the treasury billions of dollars. Groups have demanded expansion of existing programs (e.g., every province officially bilingual, third-language training, mandatory equity employment) as well as new programs (e.g., fully funded childcare). They have called for expanded or new departments and agencies (e.g., multiculturalism and its own ombudsman). In constitutional matters, they tend to seek collective rights that will protect existing programs and compel new ones for the group (e.g., defence of multiculturalism is also a wedge for new language training programs on par with spending for official languages).

(3) It is sometimes said that Canada lives in a perpetual identity crisis. Federal policy since 1970 has institutionalized that crisis. Thus

the sos's funding of groups fragments rather than unifies national identity. This is, of course, ironical and perhaps even a bit perverse, given that the policies devised in 1968–71 were intended to strengthen national unity by making citizens feel that, through their organizations, they could speak for themselves and influence the political system. But reflection on the logic of these citizenship programs shows why this was not to be, and why the opposite was more likely. First, support first provided to OLMGs through the Social Action Branch assisted minority communities that quite rightly felt threatened by current practice and past injustice. These organizations would inevitably begin to press for redress of past wrongs, extension of existing services, and establishment of new programs and services to enable their communities to survive and prosper. They made these claims against governments and society, and thereby became irritants. However just these claims might be, they looked as if they were demands for special treatment. Surely this is the key to the ethnocultural groups' reaction to the Official Languages Act of 1969. Multiculturalism was introduced in part to appease this perception that some groups were winning at the expense of others.

Second, the logic of all three programs, despite their intent to foster national identity, led to the development and emphasis of particularistic identities. The rhetoric of most of these groups pays lip service to a larger political identity and community, as when OLMGs and ethnocultural groups jockey over what makes up a "fundamental" characteristic of the country, but their practice focuses on developing an in-group solidarity. The consequence for the ethnocultural groups is to fragment their separate identities even further, but the same fragmentation occurs among the OLMGs, vis-à-vis their provincial communities and the national "English" community, and among women's organizations, which couch their demands in terms of the very special circumstances and needs of women today.

None of this would have mattered very much had the country possessed some unifying core of symbols or experiences that might have provided a bedrock of national political allegiances. But it did not. The sos's programs did not create division where none had existed before, and neither did they encourage movements and identities that would not have formed in some fashion in the absence of government support. But the programs, by making it possible to organize and articulate demands, did amplify and legitimate a much richer diversity of identities and claims than would normally have been possible. This very diversity has now become enshrined in folk definitions of the Canadian identity: "unified through diversity," "brought together by our differences," "the mosaic." These are banal and sometimes desperate incantations. The reality is a politics over-determined by division and difference. The Meech Lake process reveals this quite well: group after group appeared before committees, conferences, and the media first to applaud cautiously the possibility of constitutional reconciliation with Quebec and then to demand equal status and full protection of their rights.[2]

(4) The fourth effect is tied in a paradoxical way to the previous one of fragmentation. The survey of organizations provided in chapters 7–9 shows that the logic of distinctiveness is fairly quickly joined to another logic of combination and coalition. We might term this effect "recombinant politics," wherein groups informally combine and coalesce as issues demand. At the broadest level, most of the organizations discussed in this book would describe themselves as "equality-seeking" and so tend to adopt roughly similar positions on some core issues. While the specifics differed, for example, on the Meech Lake Accord, most of the national organizations took the view that the document had to be revised more adequately to protect their rights and the process had to be revised to reflect more adequately their participation. The OLMGs pursue separate agendas on language but simultaneously support each other's demands for enhanced services and for constitutional protection. Most SOS-funded women's groups agree on a common core of feminist political principles, and the mainline organizations – NAC being the exemplar – offer virtually identical arguments on a range of policy issues.

Also, many organizations funded through the SOS serve as nodes in broad networks or coalitions of other, non-funded organizations. The labour movement, for example, has links with NAC and with the CDCAA; NAC itself, as befits an umbrella organization, is a vast clearing-house of information and contacts for feminist and social policy groups across Canada. Network-building is the result of the importance of in-group solidarity and the forging of identities: these organizations (particularly in the women's area) forge communities as they create links with other bodies. Another reason to build networks is to establish political legitimacy. As noted earlier, few of these groups are representative in the classical sense. Individual members usually number in the hundreds, rarely in the thousands. Elected politicians place a premium on representation, often demanding to know for whom the organization speaks. The affiliation of organizations to each other maximizes the representational aura that they can cast. It is a mirage, however. Most have little or no mandate to speak on behalf of "linguistic minorities," "Third Force Canadians," or "women."[3]

(5) Recombinant politics in turn is the basis of another effect that balances the fragmenting effect of the programs discussed in this book. The SOS's citizenship development programs served, through

the support that they provided to organizations, to nationalize Canadian politics. First, they helped elevate these policy areas to the national agenda. Canada developed "official" policies on bilingualism and multiculturalism and on women's rights. Second, this in turn encouraged national groups to form (with the aid of the sos) to address these new national policies. All the group profiles (except for the AQ) in chapters 7–9 were of such national organizations. Some groups were the creatures of pre-existing provincial or national associations (e.g., CEC, FFHQ, NAC). Others were formed by a core of activists and then sought organizational affiliations from other groups (e.g., CDCAA, CPF). The evidence presented in chapter 9 showed how many women's groups emerged only after funding became available.

Third, a portion of sos funding goes to purely provincial or local groups, and so the national government's priorities on language, on multiculturalism, and on women get projected into the provincial arena. The logic of OLMGs' survival demands social and educational services that can be delivered only by provincial authority. Ottawa's policy, in other words, demands provincial co-operation. The provincial Status of Women councils exist because of federal support but lobby on behalf of provincial issues and organizations. Again, the point is not that these issues would never get articulated at the local or provincial level. Obviously they would, but quite probably in terms more congruent with local and provincial conditions. The sos's programs "normalized" the politics of official languages, of multiculturalism, and of women. Terms of debate, issues at stake, and demands and claims in almost each broad area and each specific policy within that area are remarkably similar from one end of the country to the other.

(6) This brings us to the most abstract of effects, the level of political discourse. Every country develops its own pattern of political discourse, the language appropriate for public debate of issues – what may be said and what may not, what may be thought and what may not, what the possibilities are and what is unthinkable. It changes over time, varies across policy areas, and is often obscure and inchoate to its users. The existence of a dominant pattern of political discourse does not mean that everyone agrees with it, only that it forms the norm, the benchmark. Nor is the pattern unidimensional: on any single issue there will be many positions and axes of debate, though some will tend to dominate. REAL women's defence of "traditional family values" and various fringe groups' attacks on racial equality and bilingualism are examples of forms of discourse that reject the dominant mode.

sos-funded advocacy organizations in the three policy areas discussed in this book have contributed a particular style of discourse to Canadian politics. The positions and programs that they lobby for and defend differ, of course, but some remarkably strong similarities distinguish these organizations as "citizens" or "equality seeking" groups. Most of the dozens of important briefs, reports, submissions, and pronouncements made by the organizations discussed in the previous chapters emphasize equality. To adopt a metaphor prominent in the Free Trade debate, these groups demand a "level playing field" of rights and public benefits. The equality being championed goes well beyond the traditional or classical liberal vision of equal legal rights. It embraces equality of status and importance, equal right to survival and prosperity, and ultimately equal outcomes and results. The OLMGs, for example, argue their right to survival as coherent and functioning communities; the ethnocultural groups claim the same right. Any attempt at elevation of one group or identity (e.g., the Charter's sections on language rights; Meech Lake's apparent privilege for French and English and Quebec) without safeguards so stringent that they effectively prevent that elevation is universally decried by the groups. Obviously the idea of equality and of special rights to achieve that equality did not get invented by the groups. However, insofar as sos funding supported key organizations in each area, it enabled those organizations to articulate and present on the public stage a coherent set of claims that is based on identity, grievance, and injustice. OLMGs, ethnocultural groups, and women's organizations have been among the most determined Canadian proponents of equality of results and hence of equity and affirmative action through public programs.

Another contribution to Canadian political discourse has come in the way in which these organizations have articulated their grievances. The OLMGs and ethnocultural associations have specialized in articulating the historical dimension of grievance, although women's organizations have also contributed to this style of discourse in uncovering the "herstory" of sexual oppression. Except for Quebec's anglophones and (perhaps) Ontario's francophones, the OLMGs now form relatively insignificant portions of their provincial populations. Moreover, despite twenty years of federal assistance, they are communities in decline. Claims based on numbers and future prospects are therefore doomed. Unsurprising, all the OLMGs, including Quebec's anglophones, have stressed the historical dimension of their importance to the country. For the francophone OLMGs, of course, there are legal grounds for special treatment in the Constitution Act, 1867, and in some provincial statutes, as well as federal language policy. Few OLMG submissions are without some statement on past injustices that now, because they have lingered so long, require redress. The same logic prevails among ethnocultural organizations. After Japanese Canadians successfully lobbied for a formal apology and compensation for their treatment in the Second World War, Ukrainian Canadians and Sikhs sought redress for unjust treatment in the First World War. Ironically, for such an unhistorical people, Canadians are highly sensitized to historical grievances.

The women's movement has added another dimension to the grievance claims in Canadian political discourse. Feminist analysis of women's grievances, while it obviously emphasizes historical injustice, is concentrated on contemporary systems of oppression such as patriarchy and capitalism and the interaction of the two. As befits a perspective that sees oppression rooted in a finely textured array of social systems from family to church to school, feminist analysis has stressed microscopic appraisals of oppression. The women's advocacy organizations sketched in chapter 9 all emphasize the scope and depth of the contemporary challenges faced today by women in their search for equality. Workplace, media, family, sexual relations, social programs, unconscious biases in school curricula – virtually every aspect, however minor or apparently innocuous, is either implicated in sexual oppression or is its symbol. The richness of this analysis has recently dovetailed with claims made on behalf of visible minorities in their struggle against racism, a system that can be seen as equally powerful and pervasive.

A final important contribution to Canadian political discourse arises from the preceding three: the emphasis placed on symbols. If groups seek equal status on a "level playing field" where all rights and privileges and treatment and outcomes are the same; if they stress that distant grievances are the grounds of contemporary oppression; and if finally they see injustice reflected and normalized through a thousand everyday practices, they will, in addition to seeking large and sweeping social and political change, be highly sensitive to their own apparently small symbolic victories. Ironically, some commentators (particularly in the ethnocultural field) have dismissed such victories as "merely symbolic." Adoption of multiculturalism itself is perhaps the prime example of such a victory: apparently hollow, without much monetary commitment, and, ultimately, with little government enthusiasm.

But positive symbols give standing, and "official" adoption of such a policy elevated ethnocultural claims to the same plane as OLMGs' claims. Moreover, from these inauspicious beginnings grew a political discourse of claims that eventually yielded equity employment, legislative commitments in the form of a Multiculturalism Act, and a separate department. The structure of their political discourse encourages advocacy organizations in these three fields to be hypersensitive to status. As "equality seekers" appearing before government for redress, they are forced in a sense to queue for attention and benefits. Position in the queue determines the speed and extent of that redress. If Meech Lake had granted "distinct" status to Quebec, for example, ethnocultural groups would have been bumped further back in order of precedence. Citizens' groups thus specialize in scrutinizing nuances of official pronouncements and acts of government for possible demotions or slights. They specialize in symbols. While all normal politics everywhere is about words and hence demands attention to them, Canadian political discourse appears uniquely attuned to symbols and minute meanings.

If it is true that every country has a pattern of political discourse, then the preceding would suggest that the sos programs discussed in this book helped to establish and maintain organizations whose claims and arguments extended leftward the spectrum of legitimate political debate. By "leftward" I mean support for systematic state expansion, through expenditures and regulations, to ameliorate strongly the effects and workings of a capitalist economy and, more generally, encouragement for a view of the state as a general liability company to which all citizens may turn for compensation for misfortune, whatever its source.

Donald Savoie has diagnosed this situation as being the "Keynesian perspective of the role of government in society": "Before Keynes, regions, communities, and people felt that they were wholly responsible for their own economic well-being. If a community, a business, or an individual fell off the economic ladder, they had no one to blame but themselves. ... The federal government now has numerous government departments and agencies responsible for employment, economic development, regional development, community development, among other things, to which businesses, provincial governments, communities and individuals can turn to for help in climbing the economic ladder or for getting back on the ladder if they should fall off."[4]

The big question, of course, is whether this extension of range makes any difference, or whether it is simply all talk. In fact, it is all talk, and that is precisely why it does make a difference. "Talk" in politics involves defence and attack, justification and rejection on reasonable grounds. Political actors are held accountable as much to public perceptions of what is "reasonable" in terms of political discourse as they are to more obvious concentrations of power. On the Free Trade Agreement, for example, the federal government was constantly badgered to protect Canadian identity and social programs. The agreement was eventually passed, but its text contained the protections that had been demanded by equality-seeking groups and others. Under a conventional assessment of the power of corporations and big business in Canadian politics, this would be difficult to explain.

A related if contradictory effect of the extension of the spectrum of political discourse to the left is a similar, if delayed and attenuated, extension to the right. Unfortunately this phenomenon could not be dealt with in the present study, but anecdotal evidence would suggest that formation of some of the more visible Canadian right-wing advocacy groups is a reaction to the prominence of those on the left. REAL Women was formed in opposition to organized feminism in Canada, various English-rights groups have sprung up recently against "enforced bilingualism," and there have been incidents of strident opposition to the equity employment implications of multiculturalism (e.g., amending the official uniform of the RCMP to permit turbans). These elements remain on the fringes of the political system, in part because they do not and never will enjoy the government funding available to their opponents.

CO-OPTATION

The availability of funding leads to a final reflection, on co-optation. The introductory chapters of this book pointed out that studies of government funding almost always focus on co-optation as its probable consequence. The co-opting may operate at two levels, the organizational and the movement. At the former level, groups that receive funding are allegedly so immersed in fulfilling reporting requirements and meeting program restrictions that they soon lose sight of their original purpose. At the movement level, the left has often argued that government support goes to the less radical, less threatening elements and so validates and legitimizes organizations that do not represent the movement's true nature.

The evidence presented in this book casts doubt on both versions of the co-optation hypothesis, for two key reasons. The first is linked to program administration and the practical impediments placed on groups in accepting funds. The evaluation reports reviewed in chapters 7–9 show that all three programs were loosely administered. Program guidelines were constantly in flux in the early years, and afterward there were so many reorganizations (at least to OLMG and

Multiculturalism) that program staff rarely had time to formulate clear administrative practices. When guidelines did get formulated, as for example in the Grants and Contributions Manual, they were frequently vague. The specific "fit" between an organization's proposal and the program's guidelines and objectives was often obscure and assessment had to be left to the discretion of the social development officer. Other evaluations pointed out that the reporting requirements for each program were very loose and ad hoc. None of the three programs had good statistical series on which to base larger policy judgments. As well, the sos was so regionalized that there was little co-ordination between national headquarters and regional offices. In short, while individual associations from time to time faced reporting and administrative pressures, the evidence would suggest that the sos was rarely organized enough to create difficulties.[5]

Not all applications were funded. Thus the rejections might have been of organizations that represented important but threatening dimensions of these communities. There is some evidence to support this view. Perhaps the most celebrated example concerns REAL Women, discussed in chapter 6. The Women's Program also refused to fund groups that took an official position on either side of the abortion debate (though pro-choice policies have been a key demand of most contemporary feminist organizations). In the language area, interviews with officials of Alliance Quebec suggest that sos funding was forthcoming for that group because it most closely approximated the federal government's position on anglophone rights in Quebec. AQ represented a more accommodative position than that of some other groups, which did not receive funding and which took a more libertarian line on language. The same appeared true for the CDCAA, which represented the less radical elements of the childcare movement. The sos has certainly not funded fringe groups that oppose bilingualism, nor could it be expected to support groups that oppose multiculturalism.

Despite this anecdotal evidence, it is hard for several reasons to credit the co-optation argument as it applies to social movements. First, if one takes the Women's Program, it would appear that it funded organizations whose feminist agenda was well in advance of the views of the majority of Canadian women or the Canadian citizenry generally. Indeed, it could not be otherwise, since the program was deliberately proactive and intended to shift attitudes. Second, even if these groups are middle of the road and somewhat tame, they all engaged in the discourse of rights discussed earlier, which lends itself to more radical interpretations. Governments may (though, as I have argued, in practice they did not) control groups and their funding, but they cannot effectively control the discourse that those groups help to generate and the influence that that discourse has on a country's collective political imagination. Third, the co-optation argument is weak at least in respect to organizations of the type discussed in this book, since these associations have championed the collective identities of their respective communities: linguistic, ethnic, and gender. A collective identity is an exclusionary category: it is shared by a group of people and this sharing sets them apart. One is a member of the community or one is not, and some may claim that this membership (in a primal sense that cannot be learned by outsiders) defines one's understanding of the group's needs – in short, unless one is a francophone, an ethnic, or a woman, one cannot understand precisely the needs of francophones, ethnics, or women. This logic leads to two conclusions: outsiders cannot and should not legislate on behalf of groups defined by a collective identity and hence by unique collective needs, and only insiders can truly represent the community. This logic has protected groups in all three fields, so that despite their dependence on funding, they have always claimed a high degree of autonomy from the state. Were officials to try seriously to compromise the group's autonomy, they would be attacking the group's identity. This has, in some measure, made the state as dependent on its groups as the groups have been financially dependent on the state.

Finally, the co-optation argument assumes some reasonably close commonality and complicity between government and groups. There is evidence for this. Advocacy organizations are often consulted in the formulation of policies and sometimes will publicly defend government initiatives that they find progressive or helpful. In this they may be seen as occasional allies of the government that funds them. However, as chapters 7–9 demonstrated, the most prominent and well-funded organizations are often the government's most strident and articulate critics. The groups may abide by the larger rules of the democratic game, but they are not ciphers. While there are ever-present pressures to accommodate and to agree, there are equally strong if not superior pressures to criticize and attack.

CHAPTER ELEVEN

The State and Collective Mobilization

COLLECTIVE MOBILIZATION

The three programs studied in this book represent examples of the contemporary state's interest in the mobilization of its citizenry. The logic of this mobilization, and the general political interest that all states of all varieties have in it, deserve more attention than they have received in the academic literature. As was discussed in chapter 1, different theoretical orientations have pointed to different bases for this practice. Contemporary Marxist theory has highlighted the unjust distributional structure of capitalism and pointed out that the capitalist state as a result must ensure the legitimacy of the system through devices such as welfare programs and ideological manipulation. Public choice theory arrives at similar conclusions from different assumptions. According to public choice, no state can govern with perfect consensus. The ubiquity of coercion forces officials to consider ways of generating political support, again through programs designed in effect to bribe the citizenry or through information that will stimulate loyalty.

Every modern state requires, at minimum, the forbearance and, at maximum, the loyalty of its citizens. People will not pay taxes if they consider the political system illegitimate, and they will lay down their lives only reluctantly to defend an unjust regime. At the very least, therefore, even the most liberal state will take steps to ensure that citizens understand and accept the basic features of the political system. It can accomplish this goal through measures such as civics courses in schools, state ceremonies, and mild propaganda. Most contemporary states, however, need to generate considerably more than this minimum level of loyalty, since the modern state seeks to implement policies that depend crucially on certain attitudinal variables. Two examples are the attempts to control health care expenditures (which in most advanced countries are heavily subsidized by the state) and to protect the environment. Expenditures on health care depend in part on use rates and personal health habits, so that less frequent use and healthier life-styles should lower costs. But insofar as these become matters of public policy, states are increasingly trying to change those habits. Short of direct controls, this inevitably requires mobilization of sentiments and attitudes. The environment has attracted much more attention in the last decade, and part of the resulting debate has been about what individual citizens can do to deal with the problem. Once again, insofar as this becomes a matter of public policy, governments try increasingly to change "hearts and minds" as a vehicle for ultimately altering behaviour.

While most of the OECD countries are becoming more heavily engaged in citizen mobilization or moral suasion connected to specific public policies, fewer of them need to mobilize deliberately for national unity. Most "mobilization" is usually fairly routine or uncoordinated. It might include civics education or the occasional symbolic manifestation of unity in holidays, the person of the head of state, or national success in some sporting event. The Canadian situation is somewhat different. The country's reliance on immigration in the last thirty years has placed a higher premium on civics education and the integration of immigrants. Linguistic duality, the aspirations of Quebec, and regionalism have made the post-war unity of Canada a more doubtful proposition than would normally be the case in other OECD countries. So while all states are involved in collective mobilization, they will vary in intensity and method.

The three programs analysed in this study are not the sole means that the federal government has had to pursue national unity, but they are among the most important and the most visible. Certainly Pierre Trudeau's Liberals in 1968 left no doubt that citizens' participation was linked intimately to national unity, since only through a rejuvenated sense of political efficacy would Canadians come to appreciate fully and support their national political institutions. Ironically, however, these programs grew out of a much more timid policy framework of immigrant integration, and the ambiguous legacy of this earlier structure hobbled more dramatic policy developments in the 1970s.

As noted in chapter 3, Ottawa developed the concept of citizenship mobilization in connection with the war effort in 1940. The government's experience in the First World War, coupled with the much more extensive war effort in 1940, persuaded policy makers that they needed to ensure the voluntary support of some key immigrant communities. Notably, the administrative agency designed to deal with the problem was called the "Nationalities" Branch and only later, at the end of the war, reconceptualized as an instrument of citizenship policy. The branch was small and disorganized and at one point in 1943 was almost disbanded. Its revival depended on the terms within which it was couched, which emphasized citizenship and the federal government's responsibility to foster and develop it. At the time, citizenship was conceived almost entirely as an issue of integrating immigrants into the "Canadian way of life." Government documents were careful to suggest that the integration was mutual: immigrants were to be integrated into Canada, and settled Canadians, into a readjusted concept of the characteristics of their country.

Neither French-English dualism nor any of the other divisions that conceivably might have plagued the country was addressed through the Citizenship Branch for the first fifteen years of its existence. By the 1960s, however, the branch had gradually expanded its services and its contacts, so that in practice its field of competence now included virtually anything that might impinge on national unity or the integration of citizens into the larger political community. It was this logic that lay behind the branch's new responsibilities in the late 1950s for Native Friendship Centres and later its role in advising the Royal Commission on Bilingualism and Biculturalism on francophone minority groups.

The branch in this period operated with a view that it was engaged in adult education. It had extensive contacts with provincial departments of education, helped produce pamphlets and books and other materials for use in schools, and also provided small grants to a few organizations operating in the citizenship field. Chapter 4 showed how ambivalent policy makers were about such funding for voluntary groups. The review of grants policy conducted during the early 1950s revealed an almost classic liberal perspective on the issue. Officials considered these organizations to exist firmly in the voluntary sector and assumed that as such they should, by definition, be self-supporting. There was strong reluctance to use public funds to support bodies of this type, partly because of the danger that they might become mere instruments of government policy. Strict guidelines were therefore established, and the branch's grants budget, while it grew in the next twenty years, remained modest and limited to a standard list of organizations offering adult education.

Chapter 4 also showed that by the mid-1960s, despite a move back to the sos from Citizenship and Immigration, the branch was uncertain about its mandate and its programs. Senior officials were not sure what the branch was supposed to do, and there was even discussion of disbanding it and absorbing its programs into some other element of the government. The election of the Liberals under Pierre Trudeau in 1968 changed all that, and, as chapter 5 showed, within a year the branch, and the sos more generally, had a mandate from cabinet to force the pace of citizens' participation. What happened?

The explanation hinges on a concatenation of macro- and micro-political forces. At the macro level, Canada suffered the waves of social discontent evident in virtually every OECD country at the time. Contiguity to the United States opened it to special influences from that country's agony over civil rights and over the Viet Nam War. With only short lags behind American developments, Canadians witnessed the rise of an inchoate feminist movement, students' demands for university democratization, and anti-war protests. While Canada had no analogous struggle over civil rights by blacks, one of the most important tracts of that period on the Quebec question, written by Pierre Vallières, was entitled *White Niggers of America*. Some kind of response was necessary, and that response was shaped partly by micro-political forces – in this instance, the party in power.

The Liberal party, after its historic losses in 1957 and 1958 to the Conservatives, revitalized itself sufficiently to win minority governments in 1963 and 1965. It had shifted to the left through adoption of programs to expand the welfare state and acceptance of the value of participatory structures within party and government. Pierre Trudeau, when elected leader of the party and prime minister in 1968, appeared to embrace participation as well. His endorsement of it was qualified, however, since he simultaneously urged more rational government techniques and more efficient administrative and political practices in an age of rapid technological change. Moreover, Trudeau came to office fresh from his battles with Quebec over the constitution, and his thinking was cast against the backdrop of the Royal Commission on Bilingualism and Biculturalism, terrorist incidents in Quebec, and the formation of the Parti Québécois in 1968.

These factors help explain the special character of Ottawa's programs for citizen participation in 1969–70. First, because of the Liberal party's left-wing tinge, it was prepared to respond more generously to social unrest than was the Republican administration of us President Richard Nixon. Second, American unrest and social movements always preceded the Canadian counterparts by a short time, giving officials here a chance to react more calmly and strategically. Good examples of this pattern include the Company of Young Canadians and the Opportunities for Youth program, both of which were designed and announced before any significant pressures were brought on the government by Canadian youth. Third, citizen participation would be framed in Canada as an issue of national unity, and moreover as a question of official languages, bilingualism, and OLMGs. The first programs launched by the SOS were "social action" and were aimed at linguistic minorities. The next significant ones were for multiculturalism, and these again were implicated in the government's larger strategy of dealing with Quebec. Fourth, the SOS and the Citizenship Branch presented themselves as pre-existing instruments that could be used for the government's new policy initiatives. Adult education was de-emphasized in favour of grants to organizations. Fifth, once Ottawa had committed itself to this course of action, officials were put in charge of the SOS and the branch who themselves had a personal commitment to social change and citizen participation. They made the most of what they had and for three years turned the SOS into one of the most exciting places in official Ottawa.

Remarkably, within only a year or so, the entire conceptual framework of government's relation to the voluntary sector had changed. The classical liberal principles that had always kept some distance between government and organizations were jettisoned in favour of a more "proactive" stance. The reasons for this temporary change in attitude deserve some attention. Their brief ascendancy shows the more basic pattern to be the older, classical liberal one. One reason for the change was the argument of necessity: just as in wartime liberal-democratic governments will countenance a degree of manipulation and domination of civil society unthinkable during peace, so the threat to national unity evident in Quebec separatism and general social unrest persuaded some policy makers to set aside their squeamishness. Another reason was the new view of government, popularized to some extent by Trudeau himself, which emphasized its active rather than its reactive component. Technological change, so the argument ran, is so rapid that governments need to be constantly scanning the horizon for problems, anticipating them, and developing solutions before they grow too large. A more proactive stance on national unity seemed to fit quite well with this more vigorous political philosophy. A final reason was general acceptance that organizations in the voluntary sector perform valuable services for the community, irrespective of whether they can generate enough support from members or volunteers to be self-sufficient. In this sense, a role exists for government to assist socially useful bodies.

The new thinking was really an artifact of circumstances. A conjunction of forces had persuaded the Liberals that participation and support for organizations made sense in a fight for national unity, and officials were placed in charge of programs in the sos where they could implement the new agenda. This political practice and the people who put it into effect were not the entire government. The Treasury Board, for example, was a constant thorn in the side of sos officials because it insisted (or tried to insist) that grants programs be "properly" (i.e., conservatively) administered. When the circumstances changed, so too did the forces that had sustained the original initiatives. By 1972 Canada had gone through the October Crisis and weathered the storm of Quebec terrorism; the federal Liberals were almost defeated in the 1972 election, and the prime minister became less interested in the shimmering outlines of a Just Society than he did in political survival. Key officials who had been the backbone of citizen participation drifted away. The exception was the Women's Program, which for separate reasons had an infusion of political commitment and money in 1974 and 1975.

The subsequent histories of the programs are mixed. The country's commitment to official bilingualism has always made it unthinkable that the federal government would ever cut support to OLMGs. For much of the period under review, however, the program languished. First, the logic of the Official Languages Act of 1969 guaranteed individuals access to government services in either language and encouraged individuals to learn the other official language. Canada could be a perfectly bilingual country outside Quebec, even with the complete disappearance of all francophone OLMGs. The OLMGs themselves could not countenance this approach, of course, and pressured Ottawa to substantiate the other dimension of its language policy, which supported the continued survival of francophone communities outside Quebec as the living expression of the country's dual character. OLMGs nonetheless had to fight for this support. The election in 1976 of a PQ government that effectively denied the linguistic duality of Canada outside Quebec forced Ottawa's hand and revitalized the support programs for OLMGs, and eventually for anglophone OLMGs in Quebec as well.

Multiculturalism and the Women's Program evolved quite differently. Support for ethnic organizations was originally considered a way of balancing a perhaps too dualistic vision of the country: emphasis on the Canadian cultural mosaic would counteract any separatist tendencies to argue that the issue was one of francophone Quebec versus anglophone Canada. It was also a clearly political response to ethnic pressures for equal symbolic recognition. Attempts to move away from its patronage aspects of providing small amounts of support for a wide range of cultural organizations met stiff resistance within the ethnic communities themselves. In practice, policy guidelines did change after the mid-1970s to emphasize racial discrimination and rights, but funding grew only incrementally until 1983–84.

The Women's Program, as described in chapter 9, had entirely different fortunes than its companions. It was never conceived within the framework of national unity; rather, its talisman through the period under review was the Royal Commission on the Status of Women. The program emerged almost accidentally under the rubric of Citizens Organizations in the sos in 1973, received a separate designation in 1974 because of the surge of organizations requesting funding, and then had a fortuitous infusion of cash in 1975 because of International Women's Year. The program itself was run for its first three to four years by feminists committed to political action through proactive government programming, and this no doubt explains the special success that the program had in stimulating the growth of "non-traditional" women's groups across the country. Despite some early tensions between the Liberal government and the women's movement in 1980 over patriation of the constitution, it was clear by the end of the process that feminist groups were an important constituency pressing for the "citizens' package" (e.g., the Charter) against provincial recalcitrance.

The Women's Program subsequently saw large proportional jumps in funding in 1981 and again, before the election, in 1984. Unlike official bilingualism and multiculturalism, which have the support of the Progressive Conservatives, the feminist agenda of the Women's Program did not necessarily strike a sympathetic chord with the new government of Brian Mulroney. The REAL Women affair and the Nielsen Task Force hurt the program's credibility with Conservatives, and so after two years of freeze the program was actually cut in the federal budget of February 1990.

STATE AUTONOMY

As Actor

The opening chapters of this book argued that the problem of collective action for some groups was entwined with the problem of the state. Public interest groups face substantial problems of collective action. In order to survive, many of them seek support from public authorities. This is clearly the pattern in the Canadian programs reviewed here. While no one can tell how large the full universe of such organizations might be across all three areas, it is incontestable that the key organizations, the ones that are most critical for policy developments in the three fields, receive indispensable support from the federal government. What impact has the state had in shaping the political landscape? The discussion in chapter 1 pointed out that in large measure this is a question of the state's autonomy, of its capacity to exercise a distinct effect on the political landscape and the flow of political forces. Chapter 2 argued that the state's autonomy must be conceived as operating at three levels: the state as actor, the state as target, and the state as structure.

The state as actor refers to the officials, both elected and appointed, who constitute the governments of the day. To what extent were they simply responding to events and to what extent did they shape those events? It is obvious that any concept of state autonomy that completely isolates it from social forces is inadequate. The Liberal governments during the Second World War and again at the end of the 1960s were not inventing public problems that required attention: the need to mobilize support for the war effort and the threat to national unity and social stability in the 1960s were exogenous variables that forced themselves on policy makers. And yet decisions were being made on types and styles of intervention; these, at least, were chosen, not simply forced. The decision to continue with the Nationalities Branch; the framing of citizenship policy itself; and the housing of the Citizenship Branch first in the sos, then in Citizenship and Immigration, and once more in 1966 in the sos – all of these were made deliberately by political actors.

While the general shape of the national unity crisis of the late 1960s set the stage for the three programs discussed in detail in this book, policy makers themselves had first to agree to the idea of a more proactive policy stance and the use of monies to support organizations. Activist officials within the Citizenship Branch, given favourable circumstances, were able to design a host of new policies and programs. In short, as the public choice literature argues, there is substantial potential for political actors, both elected and appointed, to invent new policies and programs. It is important, however, to gauge the limits of this autonomy.

For appointed officials, the opportunities as well as the limits came in part from the way in which grants were awarded. We have seen the looseness of the grants guidelines throughout the period, and doubtless this enabled administrators from time to time to apply their discretion and support projects and initiatives that they personally favoured. There were several constraints, however. The first was the erosion of political support for these programs after 1972. The programs retained some inertia and so continued to enjoy an

administrative life (their support from the organizational constituencies is discussed below), but the strong political support of the
1969–71 period was gone. The SOS was in constant administrative
turmoil in this period, with almost yearly reorganizations in some
program areas. The second constraint was the rest of the government. While Sue Findlay argues that the muted hostility of non-SOS
officials to the Women's Program reflected sexism, it is less easy to
see how this would explain the Treasury Board's attacks on multiculturalism and OLMGS. In fact, few of the programs in the SOS enjoyed much support among extra-departmental officials, because
they were generally perceived as pure patronage. As well, professional public servants had great difficulty accepting programs with
vague and imprecise goals, for which evaluative data were so difficult to generate.

A third constraint was the nature of grant-giving itself. Kenneth
Boulding's analysis of what he calls the "economy of love and fear"
outlines some of the difficulties.[1] In the last chapter of *A Preface to
Grants Economics: The Economy of Love and Fear,* Boulding talks about
three "traps" that he sees as part of the grants economy. The first is
the "sacrifice trap" – once a grantor makes a grant it becomes part of
his/her identity, definition of self, and it is difficult to say that the
early sacrifices were wrong – one keeps sacrificing anew to validate
the sacrifices of old. This helps explain the longevity of the programs in the face of waning political popularity among politicians
and the public at large. For any government to have completely cut
the programs and grants would have been an admission that the
programs were no longer useful. More important, the nature of this
"trap" meant that the organizations could continually point to past
successes and the work still to be done and could thus demand some
assistance from the government.

The second trap that Boulding identifies is the "dependency trap"
– grants established to deal with a temporary need create adapta-
tions to them that make the need permanent. In a sense, then, the
grants create the need for which the grants are given in the first
place. This may seem an unduly harsh judgment, and perhaps even
slightly absurd. For example, does this mean that the inequality of
women is something created by the Women's Program, which gives
money to women's groups to fight that inequality? Did support for
OLMGS create linguistic assimilation? Did grants to ethnic groups create racism? At this level, of course, the answer must be no.

There are two other ways, however, in which the dependency trap
may operate in connection with the programs discussed in this book.
First, as we saw in chapter 10, monies under these programs were

given in part to help create and promote identities, and this endeavour has involved research and conceptualization of the problems of the various communities to which the support is directed. Women's groups have not created sexism, but they have framed problems in ways (e.g., equity employment) that demand further support for themselves and a broader attack on women's problems. OLMGs did not create linguistic assimilation, but their demands for official bilingualism at the provincial level have framed Canada's language issues in a particular way, one more difficult of resolution than, for example, an administrative and territorial solution.[2] The ethnocultural groups are not responsible for racism, but they have an institutional interest in uncovering every instance and expression of racism in Canada. This diagnosis – made not from malice or bad faith but from heightened sensitivity to questions of race – again demands that groups that make the claims continue to receive support.

Boulding's third category is the "ignorance trap" – the absence of feedback and the extraordinary difficulty of developing information systems that can report the consequences of grants. The ignorance trap afflicted all three of the programs discussed in this book. Virtually every evaluation of every one of the programs, conducted at different times, showed the same problems. Program administrators lacked even the most basic information necessary to gauge the impact of the programs on policy objectives. No clear records were kept of rejection files, monitoring was weak, and few statistical series were kept. It is tempting to ascribe these weaknesses to inefficiency, but Boulding is correct to highlight the problem as a generic one. The granting programs for OLMGs, ethnic groups, and women's organizations were designed not simply to support groups but to deal with issues in the larger policy field. In the most general sense, all three programs were designed to increase tolerance and further the equality of linguistic and ethnic minorities and of women. But how to measure progress toward tolerance and equality? It was virtually impossible to arrive at any clear evaluation, and so ignorance was endemic to all of these programs.

What of elected politicians? They played a crucial role in the story and at certain times acted with remarkable autonomy. The critical period 1968–70 has already been briefly discussed. Certainly there was a backdrop of social forces that presented challenges to politicians, but those challenges were met in ways and with means that reflected individual visions and specific personalities. Prime Minister Trudeau's support for the Official Languages Act, his determination to link bilingualism to social justice, and his partnership with Gérard Pelletier as secretary of state gave the institutional push that the sos's programs needed in their early stages to survive attack from the Treasury Board. There is good evidence as well that federal politicians used these programs creatively against Quebec separatist threats (hence the renewed support for OLMGs in 1976) and to build a pro-Charter coalition in the early 1980s. There are also anecdotal examples of the use of multiculturalism as patronage to gain visibility for local MPs. But we must be cautious. Creative interventions by politicians were the exception rather than the rule. After 1972 most secretaries of state viewed these programs as minor nuisances – not surprising, since they supported groups whose business it was to criticize the government.

These facts, in combination with the points made in chapter 10 on the co-optation thesis, throw some doubt on the degree to which governments can exercise political bias in the favouring of groups through grants and financial support. At the outset of policy making, the shape and nature of the government's priorities certainly set the parameters of which types of groups will receive support and which will not. Obviously in 1969, when these sos programs were launched, and subsequently as they evolved, they would not have provided support to groups that were opposed to official bilingualism, multiculturalism, or a broadly feminist agenda on women's issues. There is also evidence that the programs were used from time to time for partisan advantage, as multiculturalism appeared to be in 1972. In 1981 the Liberals reached out to the women's movement for support of its constitutional proposals, and while this did not involve manipulation of the Women's Program, it was certainly helpful to have a constituency of this type available for mobilization. Individual MPs and even ministers kept a close watch on grants and would try either to claim credit for support provided to groups (often the case in OLMG and Multiculturalism) or to facilitate the granting process. The Conservative attack on the Women's Program is an ambiguous example of partisanship, since David Crombie defended the rejection of REAL Women's grant application, but subsequent Tory budgets inflicted disproportionate cuts on the program.

It should also be clear, however, that there were limits on the exercise of partisanship. As was observed above, the programs, once launched, were ensnared both in the sos bureaucracy and in the proprietary claims made by recipient groups themselves. Politicians in the mid-1970s might very well have wished for different priorities in multicultural and women's grants, but the programs were too brittle and too sensitive to be changed easily at this stage. Program guidelines were often vague, and the notion of fine partisan calibration is simply not believable. The thesis of political bias perhaps models itself after older, more direct and visible forms of patronage, when politicians scooped benefits from out of the pork-barrel and passed them around to supporters. The programs described in this book were to some small degree susceptible to such pressures, but they were heavily insulated as well, merely as a result of being part of a large, rationalistic bureaucracy. The bias that existed is conceived of more properly in terms of structure and discourse, and the programs clearly favoured some forms of political organization and political imagination over others. But the amount of open political bias in the administration and direction of these programs was quite small.

In light of these constraints, it is important to qualify the notion of the state's autonomy as actor. In selected circumstances, when larger social forces were propitious, politicians and officials could and did act to mobilize society in a given direction. But in many respects this mobilization went against the grain of "normal" government, ran the risk of mobilizing too many groups to make too many demands, and was prone to so many administrative weaknesses that the programs were virtually impossible to wield effectively as clean instruments of state power. But why, then, were they not disbanded?

As Target

The previous section addressed the state as an actor, conceptualizing it as made up of politicians and officials with distinct agendas to pursue against other interests in society. The evidence shows that, at least at the point of their initiation, these programs were acts of political leadership, used to mobilize society in a desired direction. While there were broad forces acting on the horizons of policy, there were no explicit demands for programs quite like the ones that were eventually decided on. But the state is more than a mere collection of officials. It is simultaneously an institutional structure that sets the pattern of behaviour of these officials and a repository of powers that these officials use vis-à-vis society. From the perspective of other societal actors, the autonomy of the state exists less as a quality of its officials, doing more or less as they please, than as a set of powers that the state can exercise to effect certain policy goals. Interest groups see the state as a target which, if captured, can then be used to pursue a policy agenda. The public choice literature has conceptualized this strategy as "rent-seeking." The phenomenon is more complex, however, because, as I argued in chapter 10, the organizations that have been supported through these programs represent distinct identities and so have been able to make unique claims for support.

Chapters 2 and 10 discussed the co-optation thesis, but the literature on public interest groups and co-optation rarely admits that groups may, rather than simply be drawn into the government's web, actively seek out grants. In other words, they are willing partners in their own seduction. Groups clearly recognize the possibility of co-optation but prefer being vigilant recipients to pristine paupers. This should be clear from an understanding of their problems in collective action. Given their non-profit status, their only sources of revenue are membership dues or third-party support (any revenue from sales or materials by definition must be small). Third-party support may come from only four sources: private-sector companies, individuals, charitable foundations, and government. Canadian companies and foundations have historically been considerably less generous than their American counterparts, and so the real choices are between small individual donations and government grants. The overhead and per-unit costs of gathering many small donations are probably higher than those required to make a single application to government. Moreover, groups that receive one grant often feel that this creates a putative right to subsequent support (as Boulding points out), and so the long-term pay-off for a single application may be relatively high. The concentration among a few groups and renewals of grants noted for the three programs would appear to support this argument.

The empirical evidence clearly supports the case that groups actively seek government support. During the 1950s, the Citizenship Branch, far from considering an expansion of grants to capture the organizations, was trying to reduce grants. It was the organizations themselves that opposed grant reductions. When the three programs were established in 1969 and 1970, there was in each case an initial surge of applications. None of the programs was ever able to support all the applications made to it. Even successful applicants routinely complained of low funding levels and too many strings. Quite naturally, the bodies active in each area became the program's core constituencies, both demanding more funding and complaining loudly when grant budgets were frozen or cut. The reaction of women's organizations in 1986 to the review of the Women's Program provides the best and clearest evidence that groups come to view the programs as their own, to be tenaciously defended. The state's support for organizations that would otherwise have difficulty in supporting themselves thus becomes itself a target for advocacy groups.

But they seek this support in order to pursue a larger political agenda, to recommend policy choices on some of the most important issues of the day.

As Structure

Conceived as an actor, the state is a government pursuing its policy agendas. Conceived as a target, the state is a bundle of resources that societal actors struggle over and try to capture. Conceived as structure, the state is more a terrain upon which and through which societal issues get addressed, if not always resolved. This structure is distinct from society in that it consists of institutions and practices that, if adopted by actors, force issues down particular channels and not others. Two people arguing in a street will use different terms and logic than if they argue before a judge. The state conceived as structure is autonomous, but not in the sense of action. It does nothing more than provide the framework within which disputes are addressed and resolved. The three programs discussed in this study compel consideration of the state in this sense, for the interests supported by them have increasingly pursued their agendas through the state and sought state action to address the problems that they have identified.

While somewhat abstract, the state as structure has been recognized as crucial by many analysts assessing contemporary politics from a wide variety of perspectives. For example, Habermas and Offe's formulations of legitimation crises point to the internal irrationalities of progressive politicization of class conflict.[3] In the 1970s the concept of "overload" was used to describe political systems beset by surplus demands.[4] More recently, public choice theorists' idea of rent-seeking has captured much the same phenomenon.[5] Most abstractly, perhaps, there is Foucault's concept of normalization and the progressive linkage of systems of power through the mechanisms of political discipline.[6] In Canada, Alan Cairns has argued the importance of the contemporary administrative state for the organization of political and social life.

Despite the obviously wide differences in approach among these authors, several key ideas appear to form the inspirational core of their insights. First, all of them take seriously the institutional distinctiveness of the contemporary state. Institutions and rules are not chimera, nor are they merely rationalizations for pure games of power. Power works in and through the institutions but is nevertheless channelled by them. Second, individual social action may be oriented more or less to those institutions. At its most basic level, this orientation will involve a definition of self that is rooted in those political institutions. The observations cited above seem to coincide on the notion that the state is increasingly complex and large and insulated from social forces, even while larger and larger numbers of citizens appear to orient their behaviour through state institutions. The politicization of family and sexual relations is only one example of the way in which formerly private realms are now regulated by formal rules, legal principles, courts of law, and legislatures. While some may lament the growth of the state as structure, there is no necessarily negative ethical connotation to it. It is simply that social life gets organized in one way as opposed to another.

The story told in these chapters is at one level a tale about political actors who, at a particular moment in Canadian history, mobilized society and helped create a wider range of public-interest organizations. It is also the story of how those groups deliberately sought government support in order to criticize government more effectively. At its deepest level, however, it is a tale of the growth of the state in the structural sense defined above. This growth was only in part intended by politicians, officials, and interest-group leaders. Until the mid-1960s, most government actors accepted the classical liberal ideology that the voluntary sector must remain insulated from government pressures and enticements. The changes during 1968–69 occurred because the federal government felt that it had to make bilingualism an official aspect of the Canadian state. An often forgotten feature of the policy is that it sought to define not only official services but, in some small measure, the official character of the country. The government's rhetoric at the time encouraged OLMGs and individual Canadians to exercise their linguistic rights, and within a few years the linguistic minorities took up that discourse in pressing for renewed government attention to their plight. The designation of "official" languages and an "official" bilingual character to the country made other ethnic groups uncomfortable, and so they pressed for "official" recognition. Although the issue has not been addressed in this volume, the SOS was at the time also creating grant programs to support aboriginal peoples in the pursuit of their political aims.

With the Women's Program, the federal government of Canada was soon engaged in supporting first hundreds and then thousands of organizations across the country. Of these, as we saw earlier, only a handful were engaged in political advocacy, but of what did their advocacy consist? The distinguishing features of the advocacy of these linguistic, ethnic, and women's groups was the emphasis on collective rights and the use of state power to enforce claims made on behalf of those rights. The OLMGs, for example, couched their demands in terms of rights to provincial and federal services and legal demands for the reinstatement of the formerly bilingual status of some provinces (Manitoba, Alberta, and Saskatchewan). Ethnic groups after the mid-1970s pressed for anti-discrimination legislation and tougher human rights codes. Women's organizations have pushed for equity in employment and universal childcare, among other things. Since enactment of the Charter, of which many of these groups were both strict critics and eventually strong champions, the emphasis on rights discourse has increased, but it was there virtually from the beginning.

What Canadians sometimes forget is that problems faced by linguistic minorities, ethnic groups, and women could conceivably be addressed in different ways. On language, for example, Canada might have adopted a territorial approach that would not have made the entire country allegedly bilingual but would instead have provided services as an administrative matter as needed. In Quebec the anglophone minority supported court action against Bill 101 on the basis of its linguistic rights, when in practice that minority has more than ample access to English services, media, and schools. The struggle for adequate childcare has been posed, first, as a women's issue and, second, as a question of a national service demanded as a right linked to the equality of women.

The point is not that Canada organizes its political discourse badly, only that its past practices have contemporary consequences. One is that the discourse of rights, particularly of collective rights, is much more deeply ingrained in the Canadian political process than it is in the American. Most explanations of this focus on lingering cultural legacies (e.g., the "Tory" touch bequeathed Canada in the nineteenth century), but it is equally plausible that federal support of key advocacy organizations over the last decade institutionalized a particular type of political language. Another consequence is that since these rights have to do in part with identity – with the country's official character – the stakes are too high to allow anyone to claim superior status. The manoeuvres over Meech Lake by ethnic groups, women, and aboriginal groups were clearly motivated by the fear that the accord's emphasis on Quebec's distinct (i.e., "French") society and on Canada's linguistic dualism might trump their Charter rights. The manoeuvres and debates over the Charlottetown Accord leading up to the referendum of 26 October 1992 were affected by the same discourse and the same fears.

There is irony in this. Twenty years ago, for interests of state, the federal government embarked on a few relatively modest programs to assist public interest groups in the fight for their visions of Canada. The programs helped sustain organizations whose own interests often forced them to criticize government policy. The groups' pursuit of identity and political rights, as well as the programs' rhetoric of citizen participation and democracy, forced the groups and the government into a sometimes uncomfortable embrace, particularly once the interests of state that had driven the programs evaporated. Neither could easily relinquish the other; neither was wholly dependent on nor wholly independent of its partner. Measured in dollars, the programs were insignificant. Measured in increased tolerance for minorities and women, they were at best marginally successful. Measured in the contours of the country's political imagination, the grooves and folds of its insecurities and its aspirations, these interests of state cut deep and cut long.

Notes

CHAPTER ONE

1 Khayyam Z. Paltiel, "The Changing Environment and Role of Special Interest Groups," *Canadian Public Administration* 25 (Summer 1982): 205.

2 Mancur Olson, *The Logic of Collective Action: Public Goods and the Theory of Groups* (Cambridge, Mass.: Harvard University Press, 1965), 159–60.

3 Sidney Tarrow, *Struggle, Politics, and Reform: Collective Action, Social Movements, and Cycles of Protest,* Center for International Relations, Cornell University, Western Societies Program, Occasional Paper No. 21, 1989, 12.

4 A. Paul Pross, *Group Politics and Public Policy* (Toronto: Oxford University Press, 1986), 127–8.

5 Peter H. Schuck, "Public Interest Groups and the Policy Process," *Public Administration Review* 37 (March/April 1977): 133.

6 Ibid.

7 Ibid., 133–4. The most exhaustive study of PIGs in the United States is Jeffrey Berry, *Lobbying for the People: The Political Behavior of Public Interest Groups* (Princeton, NJ: Princeton University Press, 1977). However, see also Andrew S. McFarland, *Public Interest Lobbies: Decision Making on Energy* (Washington, DC: American Enterprise Institute for Public Policy Research, 1976), and Andrew S. McFarland, *Common Cause: Lobbying in the Public Interest* (Chatham, NJ: Chatham House Publishers, 1984).

8 John D. McCarthy and Mayer N. Zald, "Appendix: The Trend of Social Movements in America: Professionalization and Resource Mobilization," in Mayer N. Zald and John D. McCarthy, eds., *Social Movements in an Organizational Society: Collected Essays* (New Brunswick, NJ: Transaction Books, 1987): 360–1.

9 Jonah Goldstein, "Public Interest Groups and Public Policy: The Case of the Consumers' Association of Canada," *Canadian Journal of Political Science* 12 (March 1979): 142.

10 Ibid., 146.

11 Ibid., 147.

12 Jack L. Walker, "The Origins and Maintenance of Interest Groups in America," *American Political Science Review* 77 (June 1983): 395.

13 Ibid., 402.

14 Ibid., 403.

15 Terry M. Moe, *The Organization of Interests: Incentives and the Internal Dynamics of Political Interest Groups* (Chicago: University of Chicago Press, 1980), 60.

16 Ibid., 100–1. Hugh Helco developed a similar argument a decade earlier; see Hugh Heclo, "Issue Networks and the Executive Establishment," in Anthony King, ed., *The New American Political System* (Washington, DC: American Enterprise Institute, 1978), 92–3.

17 Alan C. Cairns and Cynthia Williams, "Constitutionalism, Citizenship and Society in Canada: An Overview," in Alan Cairns and Cynthia Williams, eds., *Constitutionalism, Citizenship, and Society in Canada*, volume 33 of the research studies prepared for the Royal Commission on the Economic Union and Development Prospects for Canada (Toronto: University of Toronto Press, 1985), 13.

18 Ibid., 42.

19 Robert R. Alford and Roger Friedland, *Powers of Theory: Capitalism, the State, and Democracy* (Cambridge: Cambridge University Press, 1985), 1.

20 Theda Skocpol, "Bringing the State Back In: Strategies of Analysis in Current Research," in Peter B. Evans, Dietrich Rueschemeyer, and Theda Skocpol, eds., *Bringing the State Back In* (Cambridge: Cambridge University Press, 1985), 4.

21 David Easton, "The Political System Besieged by the State," *Political Theory* 9 (Aug. 1981): 303. Easton notes several forces behind the rejuvenation of the concept of the state: a revived Marxism; a longing, after the turmoil of the 1960s and 1970s, for a strong authority and political stability; the rise of economic liberalism, which finds the state a convenient scapegoat for contemporary economic difficulties; and the surge in the policy sciences and policy analysis, which locate the state at the epicentre of public policy.

22 Eric A. Nordlinger, *On the Autonomy of the Democratic State* (Cambridge, Mass.: Harvard University Press, 1981), 3.

23 Alford and Friedland spend five dense chapters reviewing what they call the "class perspective." In passing, they deal with neo-Marxist analyses of feudalism, the rise of the bourgeois state, class, bureaucracy,

imperialism, trade unions, and, of course, the economic imperatives of capitalism. See Alford and Friedland, *Powers of Theory,* chapters 12–16.

24 Perry Anderson notes how the absence of a theory of the state in classical Marxism remains a major item on its theoretical agenda. His description of "Western Marxism" – the heir to the legacy of Marx and Engels – as preoccupied with idealism and aesthetics makes the neo-Marxist rediscovery of the state all the more important. See Perry Anderson, *Considerations on Western Marxism* (London: New Left Books, 1976).

25 Ralph Miliband, *The State in Capitalist Society* (London: Quartet Books, 1973), 55.

26 Poulantzas made these points, with a reply from Miliband, in a debate published by *New Left Review,* nos. 58, 59, and 82.

27 This effort was principally contained in Nicos Poulantzas, *Political Power and Social Classes* (London: New Left Books, 1973).

28 Nicos Poulantzas, *The Crisis of the Dictatorships* (London: New Left Books, 1976), *State, Power, and Socialism* (London: New Left Books, 1978), and "The Political Crisis and the Crisis of the State," in J.W. Freiberg, ed., *Critical Sociology: European Perspectives* (New York: Irvington, 1979), 357–93.

29 Ian Gough, *The Political Economy of the Welfare State* (London: Macmillan, 1979), 11 and 12.

30 Antonio Gramsci, *Selections from the Prison Notebooks* (New York: International Publishers, 1971).

31 A more complex version of this approach may be found in Michel Aglietta, *A Theory of Capitalist Regulation: The U.S. Experience* (London: New Left Books, 1979). Aglietta sees the state as an "institutionalization of social relations under the effect of class struggles." Its role is to manage or regulate the interaction of what he calls the "structural forms" that are linked to the wage relation, such as the money system and collective bargaining.

32 Adam Przeworski and Michael Wallerstein, "The Structure of Class Conflict in Democratic Capitalist Societies," *American Political Science Review* 76 (June 1982): 215–38.

33 An early formulation was Claus Offe and Volker Ronge, "Theses on the Theory of the State," *New German Critique* 6 (Fall 1975): 139–47.

34 Claus Offe, *Contradictions of the Welfare State,* ed. John Keane (Cambridge, Mass.: MIT Press, 1984), 42.

35 Ibid., 43–4.

36 Ibid., 45.

37 Ibid., 48.

38 Ibid.

39 Claus Offe, *Disorganized Capitalism: Contemporary Transformations of Work*

and Politics, ed. John Keane (Cambridge, Mass.: MIT Press, 1985), 236–7.

40 Ibid., 244–7.

41 Fred Block, "Beyond Relative Autonomy: State Managers as Historical Subjects," in Ralph Miliband and John Saville, eds., *The Socialist Register 1980* (London: Merlin Press, 1980), 229.

42 Fred Block, *Revising State Theory: Essays in Politics and Postindustrialism* (Philadelphia: Temple University Press, 1987), 13.

43 For further examples of post-Marxism, see Ernesto Laclau and Chantal Mouffe, *Hegemony and Socialist Strategy: Towards a Radical Democratic Politics*, trans. Winston Moore and Paul Cammack (London: Verson, 1985), and Christopher Pierson, "New Theories of State and Civil Society: Recent Developments in Post-Marxist Analysis of the State," *Sociology* 18 (Nov. 1984): 563–71.

44 Block, *Revising State Theory*, 17.

45 Ibid., 18.

46 Jane Jenson, "Paradigms and Political Discourse: Protective Legislation in France and the United States before 1914," *Canadian Journal of Political Science* 22 (June 1989): 237–8.

47 Nordlinger, *Autonomy*, 1.

48 Ibid., 7.

49 Ibid., 11.

50 Skocpol, "Bringing the State Back In," 31 note 9.

51 For a terse explication of his more recent views, see Eric A. Nordlinger, "The Return to the State: Critiques," *American Political Science Review* 82 (Sept. 1988): 875–901.

52 Theda Skocpol, *State and Revolutions: A Comparative Analysis of France, Russia, and China* (Cambridge: Cambridge University Press, 1979), 25.

53 Ibid., 27.

54 Ibid., chapter 2.

55 Theda Skocpol, "Political Response to Capitalist Crisis: Neo-Marxist Theories of the State and the Case of the New Deal," *Politics and Society* 10 (1980): 155–201; Theda Skocpol and Kenneth Finegold, "State Capacity and Economic Intervention in the Early New Deal," *Political Science Quarterly* 97 (Summer 1982): 255–78.

56 Theda Skocpol, "Bringing the State Back In," 9.

57 Ibid., 14.

58 Ibid., 17.

59 Ibid., 21.

60 Ibid.

61 For an example, which will be discussed at greater length in chapter 2, see Pierre Birnbaum, *States and Collective Action: The European Experience* (Cambridge: Cambridge University Press, 1988).

62 Kim Richard Nossal, "Analyzing the Domestic Sources of Canadian Foreign Policy," *International Journal* 39 (Winter 1983–84): 1–22. For an example of a strong statist orientation to Canadian foreign policy, see John Kirton and Blair Dimock, "Domestic Access to Government in the Canadian Foreign Policy Process, 1968–1982," *International Journal* 39 (Winter 1983–84): 65–98; Thomas Keating, "Domestic Groups, Bureaucrats, and Bilateral Fisheries Relations," *International Journal* 39 (Winter 1983–84): 146–70; and Thomas Keating, "The State, the Public, and the Making of Canadian Foreign Policy," in Robert J. Jackson, Doreen Jackson, and Nicolas Baxter-Moore, eds., *Contemporary Canadian Politics: Readings and Notes* (Scarborough, Ont.: Prentice-Hall, 1987), 356–73.

63 Leslie A. Pal, *State, Class, and Bureaucracy: Canadian Unemployment Insurance and Public Policy* (Kingston and Montreal: McGill-Queen's University Press, 1988); Elizabeth Riddell-Dixon and Gretta Riddell-Dixon, "Seniors Advance, The Mulroney Government Retreats: Grey Power and the Reinstatement of Fully Indexed Pensions," in Robert J. Jackson, Doreen Jackson, and Nicolas Baxter-Moore, eds., *Contemporary Canadian Politics: Readings and Notes* (Scarborough, Ont.: Prentice-Hall, 1987), 277–92.

64 Grace Skogstad, "State Autonomy and Provincial Policy-Making: Potato Marketing in New Brunswick and Prince Edward Island," *Canadian Journal of Political Science* 20 (Sept. 1987): 501–23.

65 Alan C. Cairns, "The Governments and Societies of Canadian Federalism," *Canadian Journal of Political Science* 10 (Dec. 1977): 695–725.

66 Alan Cairns, "The Embedded State: State-Society Relations in Canada," in Keith Banting, ed., *State and Society: Canada in Comparative Perspective*, vol. 31 of the research studies prepared for the Royal Commission on the Economic Union and Development Prospects for Canada (Toronto: University of Toronto Press, 1986), 53–86.

67 Ibid., 57

68 Ibid., 55.

69 Alan C. Cairns, "The Past and Future of the Canadian Administrative State," *University of Toronto Law Journal* 40 (1990): 320.

70 Cairns, "The Embedded State," 83.

71 Cairns, "The Past and Future of the Canadian Administrative State," 341.

72 Ibid., 41.

73 James M. Buchanan, *The Demand and Supply of Public Goods* (Chicago: Rand McNally, 1968), 4.

74 One survey of public choice theory notes, for example, that while the bulk of the literature "is concerned with the positive and normative properties of processes for revealing preferences for public goods," there is a rapidly growing body of work on ways in which preferences

are filtered through institutional processes. Dennis C. Mueller, *Public Choice* (Cambridge: Cambridge University Press, 1979), 148.

75 Albert Breton, *The Economic Theory of Representative Government* (Chicago: Aldine Publishing, 1974), chapter 1.

76 Ibid., 42.

77 Ibid.

78 Ibid., 43.

79 There is a well-developed public choice-grounded literature on electoral cycles and the logic of voting. See James E. Alt and K. Alex Chrystal, *Political Economics* (Berkeley: University of California Press, 1983). Also see Mueller, *Public Choice*, chapter 6.

80 Breton, *Economic Theory*, 144–5.

81 Ibid., 162.

82 Gordon Tullock, *The Politics of Bureaucracy* (Washington, DC: Public Affairs Press, 1965), 32.

83 William A. Niskanen, Jr., *Bureaucracy and Representative Government* (Chicago: Aldine-Atherton, 1971), 15.

84 Ibid., 24.

85 Ibid., 38.

86 Anthony Downs, *Inside Bureaucracy* (Boston: Little, Brown, 1967), 2.

87 Rune J. Sorensen, "Bureaucratic Decision-Making and the Growth of Public Expenditure," in Jan-Erik Lane, ed., *Bureaucracy and Public Choice* (London: Sage, 1987), 66–7.

88 André Blais and Stéphane Dion, eds., *The Budget-Maximizing Bureaucrat: Appraisals and Evidence* (Pittsburgh: University of Pittsburgh Press, 1991).

89 Breton, *Economic Theory*, 157. Breton seems to assume that the government's interest will be in shifting *all* tastes and preferences in a single direction. This is perhaps less likely than its trying to homogenize tastes in "preference sectors" and then use discriminatory policies to appeal to those constituencies.

90 James M. Buchanan, "Rent Seeking and Profit Seeking," in James M. Buchanan, Robert D. Tollison, and Gordon Tullock, eds., *Toward a Theory of the Rent-Seeking Society* (College Station, Tex.: Texas A&M University Press, 1980), 3.

91 Ibid., 7.

92 Roger Benjamin and Raymond Duvall, "The Capitalist State," in Roger Benjamin and Stepen L. Elkin, eds., *The Democratic State* (Lawrence, Kan.: University Press of Kansas, 1985), 28.

93 Ibid., 28.

94 Peter A. Hall, *Governing the Economy: The Politics of State Intervention* (London: Polity Press, 1986), 19.

95 Ibid., 17.

CHAPTER TWO

1 See, for example, Matthew Holden, Jr., "'Imperialism' in Bureaucracy," *American Political Science Review* 60 (Dec. 1966): 943–51; Anthony Downs, *Inside Bureaucracy* (Boston: Little, Brown, 1967); and Harold Seidman, *Politics, Position, and Power: The Dynamics of Federal Organization*, 3rd ed. (New York: Oxford University Press, 1980).

2 Robert A. Alford and Roger Friedland, *Powers of Theory: Capitalism, the State, and Democracy* (Cambridge: Cambridge University Press, 1985), 436.

3 Theodore J. Lowi, "The Welfare State: Ethical Foundations and Constitutional Remedies," *Political Science Quarterly* 101 (1986): 220.

4 Paul Sabatier, "Social Movements and Regulatory Agencies: Toward a More Adequate – and Less Pessimistic – Theory of 'Clientele Capture'," *Policy Sciences* 6 (Sept. 1975): 301–42.

5 James T. Bennett and Thomas J. DiLorenzo, *Destroying Democracy: How Government Funds Partisan Politics* (Washington, DC: Cato Institute, 1985), xi.

6 Ibid., 385.

7 Ibid., 391.

8 Ibid., 392.

9 Ibid., 393.

10 Ibid., 395.

11 Ibid., 397–401.

12 Martin Loney, "A Political Economy of Citizen Participation," in Leo Panitch, ed., *The Canadian State: Political Economy and Political Power* (Toronto: University of Toronto Press, 1977), 446.

13 Ibid., 448.

14 Ibid., 454.

15 Ibid., 456.

16 Ibid., 463–4.

17 Roxana Ng, *The Politics of Community Services: Immigrant Women, Class and State* (Toronto: Garamond Press, 1988), 26–7.

18 Ibid., 27.

19 Jeffrey Simpson, *Spoils of Power: The Politics of Patronage* (Toronto: Collins, 1988), 19.

20 Ibid., 372.

21 Ibid., 372–3; also see Reg Whitaker, "Between Patronage and Bureaucracy: Democratic Politics in Transition," *Journal of Canadian Studies* 77 (Dec. 1983): 895–910. For a more tortuous version of this argument, see Gerard S. Vano, *Neo-Feudalism: The Canadian Dilemma* (Toronto: Anansi, 1981).

22 Myrna Kostash, *Long Way from Home: The Story of the Sixties Generation in Canada* (Toronto: Lorimer, 1980), 5.

23 Ibid., 28.

24 John Meisel and Vincent Lemieux, *Ethnic Relations in Canada: Voluntary Associations*, vol. 13 of the Studies of the Royal Commission on Bilingualism and Biculturalism (Ottawa: Queen's Printer, 1972), 310.

25 Sandra Gwyn, "The Great Ottawa Grant Boom (and How It Grew)," *Saturday Night* 87 (Oct. 1972): 23.

26 Ian Hamilton, *The Children's Crusade: The Story of the Company of Young Canadians* (Toronto: Peter Martin Associates, 1970). See also Cyril Levitt, *Children of Privilege: Student Revolt in the Sixties* (Toronto: University of Toronto Press, 1984).

27 Gwyn, "The Great Ottawa Grant Boom," 24.

28 Doris Shackleton, *Power Town: Democracy Discarded* (Toronto: McClelland and Stewart, 1977).

29 David Milne, *Tug of War: Ottawa and the Provinces under Trudeau and Mulroney* (Toronto: James Lorimer, 1986), 212.

30 Sally M. Weaver, "The Joint Cabinet/National Indian Brotherhood Committee: A Unique Experiment in Pressure Group Politics," *Canadian Public Administration* 25 (Summer 1982): 211–39.

31 J. Hugh Faulkner, "Pressuring the Executive," *Canadian Public Administration* 25 (Summer 1982): 248.

32 J. Rick Ponting and Roger Gibbins, *Out of Irrelevance: A Socio-Political Introduction to Indian Affairs in Canada* (Toronto: Butterworths, 1980), 124.

33 Paul Malvern, *Persuaders: Influence Peddling, Lobbying and Political Corruption in Canada* (Toronto: Methuen, 1985), 29.

34 Ibid., 132–9.

35 Ibid., 190.

36 Ibid., chapters 9 and 10.

37 Eric Waddell, "State, Language and Society: The Vicissitudes of French in Quebec and Canada," in Alan Cairns and Cynthia Williams, eds., *The Politics of Gender, Ethnicity and Language in Canada* (Toronto: University of Toronto Press, 1986), 69.

38 Conrad Winn, "Department of the Secretary of State: Potpourri or Cultural Mandate," in G. Bruce Doern, ed., *Spending Tax Dollars: Federal Expenditures 1980–81* (Ottawa: School of Public Administration, Carleton University, 1980), 159.

39 Betty Steele, *The Feminist Takeover: Patriarchy and Matriarchy in Two Decades* (Richmond Hill, Ont.: Tercet, 1987).

40 Nancy Adamson, Linda Briskin, and Margaret McPhail, *Feminist Organizing for Change: The Contemporary Women's Movement in Canada* (Toronto: Oxford University Press, 1988), 150–1.

41 Ibid., 153–4.

42 Ibid., chapter 7.

43 Angela R. Miles and Geraldine Finn, eds., *Feminism in Canada: From Pressure to Politics* (Montreal: Black Rose Books, 1982).

44 Sandra Burt, "Women's Issues and the Women's Movement since 1970," in Alan Cairns and Cynthia Williams, eds., *The Politics of Gender, Ethnicity and Language in Canada* (Toronto: University of Toronto Press, 1986), 138.

45 Sandra Burt, "Canadian Women's Groups in the 1980s: Organizational Development and Policy Influence," *Canadian Public Policy* 16 (March 1990): 21.

46 Sandra Burt, "Legislators, Women, and Public Policy," in Sandra Burt, Lorraine Code, and Lindsay Dorney, eds., *Changing Patterns: Women in Canada* (Toronto: McClelland and Stewart, 1988), 148.

47 See Michèle Miville Blanchard, "La femme et les mouvements féministes," *Canadian Women's Studies* 1 (Winter 1978–79): 94–5; Nicole Laurin-Frenette, "On the Women's Movement, Anarchism and the State," *Our Generation* 15 (Summer 1982): 27–39; Helen Maier, "We Will Survive," *Kinesis* (June 1984): 7; Joni Miller, "Living without Government Money," *Kinesis* (June 1984): 8–9; Susan O'Donnell, "Our Taxes Are for Us," *Kinesis* (June 1984): 8, 13; and Sally Hunter, "Government Strategies," *Priorities* 5 (May 1977): 9–10.

48 Sue Findlay, "Facing the State: The Politics of the Women's Movement Reconsidered," in Heather Jon Maroney and Meg Luxton, eds., *Feminism and Political Economy: Women's Work, Women's Struggles* (Toronto: Methuen, 1987), 31.

49 Ibid., 39.

50 Ibid., 39–40.

51 Raymond Breton, "Multiculturalism and Canadian Nation-Building," in Alan Cairns and Cynthia Williams, eds., *The Politics of Gender, Ethnicity and Language in Canada* (Toronto: University of Toronto Press, 1986), 45.

52 Ibid., 48.

53 Ibid., 52.

54 Ibid., 53.

55 Raymond Breton, "The Production and Allocation of Symbolic Resources: An Analysis of the Linguistic and Ethnocultural Fields in Canada," *Canadian Review of Sociology and Anthropology* 21 (1984): 125.

56 Norman Buchignani, "Canadian Ethnic Research and Multiculturalism," *Journal of Canadian Studies* 17 (Spring 1982): 17.

57 Alan B. Anderson and James S. Frideres, *Ethnicity in Canada: Theoretical Perspectives* (Toronto: Butterworths, 1981), 323.

58 B. Singh Bolaria and Peter S. Li, eds., *Racial Oppression in Canada*, 2nd ed. (Toronto: Garamond Press, 1988), 39.

59 Daiva K. Stasiulis, "The Political Structuring of Ethnic Community

Action: A Reformulation," *Canadian Ethnic Studies* 12 (1980): 20.
For another example of an exploration of the thesis that the state and
its structre determines the anatomy of ethnic organizations, see
Richard Henry Thompson, "The State and the Ethnic Community: The
Changing Social Organization of Toronto's Chinatown," PhD dis-
sertation, University of Michigan, 1979.

60 Stasiulis, "Political Structuring," 35.

61 Daiva K. Stasiulis, "The Symbolic Mosaic Reaffirmed: Multiculturalism
Policy," in Katherine A. Graham, ed., *How Ottawa Spends: 1988/89:
The Conservatives Heading into the Stretch* (Ottawa: Carleton University
Press, 1988), 98.

62 Evelyn Kallen, "Multiculturalism: Ideology, Policy and Reality," *Journal
of Canadian Studies* 17 (Spring 1982): 59.

63 Manoly R. Lupul, "The Political Implementation of Multiculturalism,"
Journal of Canadian Studies 17 (Spring 1982): 93–102.

64 Lance W. Roberts and Rodney A. Clifton, "Exploring the Ideology of
Multiculturalism," *Canadian Public Policy* 8 (Winter 1982): 88–94;
and Howard Brotz, "Multiculturalism in Canada: A Muddle," *Canadian
Public Policy* 6 (Winter 1980): 41–6.

CHAPTER THREE

1 Norman Wilding and Philip Laundy, *An Encyclopaedia of Parliament*,
4th ed. (New York: St. Martin's Press, 1971), 676–9.

2 *The Oxford English Dictionary*, 2nd ed., vol. xiv, (Oxford: Clarendon
Press, 1989), 846.

3 Wilding and Laundy, *Encyclopaedia*, 676.

4 Ibid., 679.

5 The following brief history of the Secretary of State is drawn from
annual reports for the period.

6 Adam Shortt and Arthur G. Doughty, eds., *Canada and Its Provinces*,
vol. 6, *The Dominion: Political Evolution* (Edinburgh, 1914), 323.

7 Ibid., 321.

8 J. L. Granatstein, *Canada's War: The Politics of the Mackenzie King Government, 1939–1945* (Toronto: Oxford University Press, 1975), 20.

9 The treatment of West Coast Japanese went well beyond the more benign instruments of citizenship policy for two reasons and so will
not be addressed here. First, British Columbia put strong pressure on
Ottawa to deal harshly with its Japanese population, pressures that
had no analogy among other provinces. Second, it was only in 1934
that Japan and Canada signed an agreement that allowed Japanese
immigrants to Canada to renounce their allegiance to the emperor and
become naturalized Canadians. This prior allegiance fuelled per-

ceptions that the Japanese were somehow "unloyal" and led to further repressions. For details, see Ken Adachi, *The Enemy That Never Was: A History of the Japanese Canadians* (Toronto: McClelland and Stewart, 1976), 200.

10 N.F. Dreisziger, "The Rise of a Bureaucracy for Multiculturalism: The Origins of the Nationalities Branch, 1939–1941," in Norman Hillmer, Bohdan Kordan, and Lubomyr Luciuk, eds., *On Guard for Thee: War, Ethnicity, and the Canadian State, 1939–1945* (Ottawa: Canadian Committee for the History of the Second World War, Directorate of History, Department of National Defence, 1988), 4.

11 National Resource Mobilization Act, 1940, SC 1940.

12 National Archives of Canada (NA), RG 35/7, National Records Committee Files, vol. 5, History of Department of National War Services: Organization and Administration, Part I, p. 2.

13 The National Resources Mobilization Act received royal assent on 21 June 1940, and the national registration regulations were approved by PC 3156 on 12 July 1940. The transfer was effected on 21 March 1942 and 26 September 1942 by PCs 2253 and 8800, respectively.

14 PC 4748, 13 September 1940. NA, RG 35/7, National Records Committee Files, vol. 5, History, p. 2.

15 Ibid., p. 6. The transfer was effected by PC 2031, 24 March 1941.

16 NA, RG 35/7, National Records Committee Files, vol. 5, History, p. 10. The transfer was effected by PC 4215, 11 June 1942, and also included the adminstration of the Canadian Travel Bureau. National War Services thus had control of the CBC, the National Film Board, and the Canadian Travel Bureau. The latter was involved in overseeing travel across the border, principally from the United States to Canada, but tourism was effectively nonexistent after late 1942. Nonetheless, about 50,000 inquiries were received by the Bureau between 1943 and 1945 and had to be answered; they covered travel regulations, food and gas rationing, use of cameras under war conditions, and so on.

17 Ibid., p. 15. The transfer was effected by PC 2253, 25 March 1942.

18 NA, RG 35/7, National Records Committee Files, vol. 16, Department of National War Services: Organization and Administration, Part II, n.d., but probably 1945–6, p. 2 and 1–2.

19 Ibid., p. 2.

20 Ibid., p. 9.

21 NA, RG 35/7, National Records Committee Files, vol. 16, Advisory Committee on Co-operation in Canadian Citizenship (Nationalities Branch), n.d., but probably 1945–6, p. 1.

22 Ibid., p. 2.

23 Ibid, p. 3.

24 Ibid., p. 3.

25 N.F. Dreisziger, "The Rise of a Bureaucracy," 19.

26 PC 105/9400, 3 December 1941.

27 PC 104/9400, 27 November 1941. Tracy Philipps was a British adventurer, soldier, and linguist born to minor nobility in 1890. During the First World War he fought in Africa and Italy. He was an administrative officer in some of the conquered European territories, crisscrossed equatorial Africa several times, and spoke nine African languages. In 1920–23 he worked in the Caucasus and Ukraine on famine relief, thereby qualifying as something of an expert on Ukrainians. He was enticed to Canada while attending a Ukrainian congress in the United States and asked to "enter into discussion with Ukrainian organizations in Winnipeg with a view to developing a body which would unite the various Ukrainian organizations for war purposes." NA, RG 35/7, National Records Committee Files, vol. 16, Advisory Committee, p. 4.

28 NA, RG 6, Department of Secretary of State, ACC 86–87/319, file 1–1–1, Thorson to England, 4 Dec. 1941.

29 NA, RG 35/7, National Records Committee Files, vol. 16, Advisory Committee, p. 6.

30 Ibid., p. 5.

31 Ibid., p. 6.

32 Ibid., p. 7.

33 NA, RG 35/7, National Records Committee Files, vol. 16, Advisory Committee on Co-operation in Canadian Citizenship (Nationalities Branch), Part II (Confidential), p. 2.

34 NA, RG 6, Department of Secretary of State, ACC 86–87/319, file 1–2, memorandum from C.H. Payne to LaFleche, 24 Sept. 1943, p. 2.

35 Canada, Parliament, House of Commons, *Debates*, 27 April 1944, pp. 2395–423.

36 Ibid., p. 2412.

37 NA, Robert England Papers, MG 30, C181, vol. 3, Report of the Reorganization of the Nationalities Branch, Department of National War Services, 12 June 1944, p. 6.

38 Ibid., p. 8.

39 Ibid., p. 9.

40 Ibid., pp. 11–12. Only those items in quotation marks are actually quotes; the remainder is paraphrased from the report.

41 Ibid., p. 23.

42 NA, RG 35/7, National Records Committee Files, vol. 16, Advisory Committee, p. 18.

43 The transfer was effected by PC 6689, 26 October 1945, and became effective on 1 November.

CHAPTER FOUR

1 NA, RG 6, Department of Secretary of State Files, ACC 86–87/319, file 1–1, "Canadian Citizenship Branch," 1 Nov. 1945.
2 Ibid., p. 1
3 Ibid., pp. 2–4.
4 Ibid., p. 7.
5 Carty and Ward are mistaken when they allege that there really was no concept of Canadian citizenship before 1947. In fact, the Canadian Nationals Act and the Immigration Act, both of which antedated the Second World War, referred to Canadian citizenship, but in very limited ways. See R. Kenneth Carty and W. Peter Ward, "The Making of Canadian Political Citizenship," in R. Kenneth Carty and W. Peter Ward, eds., *National Politics and Community in Canada* (Vancouver: University of British Columbia Press, 1986), 68–9.
6 Canada, Parliament, House of Commons, *Debates*, 20 March 1946, p. 131. Martin had been a proponent of a citizenship act since 1942 and had adopted it as a "crusade" after visiting the military cemetery at Dieppe. See Paul Martin, *A Very Public Life*, vol. 1: *Far from Home* (Ottawa: Deneau, 1983), 437.
7 Canada, Parliament, House of Commons, *Debates*, 2 April 1946, p. 505.
8 NA, RG 6, Department of Secretary of State Files, ACC 86–87/319, file 1–1, "Tentative Programme of the Canadian Citizenship Branch," 1949.
9 "Tentative Programme."
10 Canada, Parliament, *House of Commons Debates*, 26 Nov. 1949, p. 2284.
11 Ibid., p. 2285.
12 Canada, Department of Citizenship and Immigration, *Annual Report 1950*.
13 NA, RG 6, Department of Secretary of State Files, ACC 86–87/319, file 1–1–1, "Memorandum to Deputy Minister," 9 Sept. 1950.
14 NA, RG 6, Department of Secretary of State Files, ACC 86–87/319, file 1–1–1, "Confidential Memorandum to Miss Hayward, Mr. Haugan and Dr. Black," 3 Oct. 1950.
15 NA, RG 6, Department of Secretary of State Files, ACC 86–87/319, file 1–1–1, "Memorandum to Deputy Minister," 19 Oct. 1950.
16 NA, Robert England Papers, MG 30, C181, vol. 3, file 3, "First Annual Conference of the Canadian Citizenship Branch," 20–25 Aug. 1951.
17 Ibid., p. 6.

18 NA, RG 6, Department of Secretary of State Files, ACC 86–87/319, file
   1–1, "Statement of the Aims and Objectives of the Canadian Citizenship Branch," 15 Oct. 1951.
19 Ibid.
20 W.H. Agnew, "Historical Review of the Canadian Citizenship Branch"
   (Ottawa: Secretary of State, 1967), 30.
21 NA, RG 26, Department of Citizenship and Immigration Files, vol. 85,
   file 1–24–119, "Memorandum to Colonel Fortier," 30 Oct. 1953.
   The Canadian Citizenship Council and its Quebec counterpart, La Société canadienne d'enseignement, had been supported for some
   years. Camp Laquemac offered a bilingual program, managed jointly
   by Laval and McGill universities, for the training of community
   leaders and senior officers of voluntary organizations.
22 This chapter's focus on the Citizenship Branch should not obscure
   the fact that the question of the state's relation to voluntary organizations was also being addressed in other parts of government. The
   Massey Commission Report (1951), for example, argued that its focal
   point had been "the relation of voluntary effort to governmental
   activity," and it made several seminal recommendations for state support of the arts. See Canada, Royal Commission on National Development in the Arts, Letters and Science, *Report* (Ottawa: King's
   Printer, 1951), 73.
23 NA, RG 26, Department of Citizenship and Immigration Files, vol. 85,
   file 1–24–119, memorandum from Minister of Citizenship and Immigration to Governor-General in Council, 15 Jan. 1951.
24 NA, RG 26, Department of Citizenship and Immigration Files,
   vol. 85, file 1–24–119, "Grant to Canadian Citizenship Council," 19 Dec.
   1951, p. 1.
25 Ibid., p. 2.
26 Ibid.
27 NA, RG 26, Department of Citizenship and Immigration Files, vol. 85,
   file 1–24–119, Laval Fortier to Hugh Wallis (President of the Canadian Citizenship Council), 23 Jan. 1952.
28 NA, RG 26, Department of Citizenship and Immigration Files,
   vol. 85, file 1–24–119, Eugène Bussière (Director, Citizenship Branch)
   to John Kidd (Executive Director, Canadian Citizenship Council),
   13 Jan. 1954.
29 NA, RG 6, Department of Secretary of State Files, ACC 86–87/319,
   file 1–1, "Memorandum to Director of Canadian Citizenship," 16 Dec.
   1953.
30 NA, RG 26, Department of Citizenship and Immigration Files, vol. 84,
   file 1–24–106, Minutes of the Meeting of the Board of Directors
   of the Canadian Citizenship Council, 14 Jan. 1954, p. 1.

31 Ibid., p. 1.

32 NA, RG 26, Department of Citizenship and Immigration Files, vol. 84, file 1–24–106, Walter Harris to Frank Patton, 16 July 1954, p. 1.

33 Ibid., pp. 1, 2.

34 NA, RG 26, Department of Citizenship and Immigration Files, vol. 84, file 1–24–106, "Memorandum to Deputy Minister Re Grants," 28 Dec. 1954, p. 1.

35 Bussière also mentioned that the Canadian Citizenship Council was "relatively new and not too well established." The council's new and lesser fortunes under the revised policy may have reflected a change of leadership in the branch. Frank Foulds, the first director of the branch and Bussière's predecessor, was a member of the council's executive and had in fact approved the use of grant money to cover some portion of the council's modest staff salaries.

36 This strategy also had its liabilities, however. A study undertaken earlier in the year by the Advisory Committee on Citizenship had agreed that grant requests were increasing and that it would be unadvisable for the branch "to offer financial assistance in the general support of organizations." Some groups were taking advantage of project-based funding by going to several departments for support for the same project. NA, RG 26, Department of Citizenship and Immigration Files, vol. 66, file 2–18–1, part 2, "Grants and Funds for Research Projects in Citizenship Matters," 17 May 1954, p. 1.

37 NA, RG 6, Department Secretary of State Files, ACC 86–87/319, file 1–1, "Memorandum Re Statement on Branch Policy," 10 Aug. 1955, p. 1.

38 NA, RG 6, Department Secretary of State Files, ACC 86–87/319, file 1–1, "Canadian Citizenship Branch: Statement on Policy," n.d. (but c. summer 1955), p. 2.

39 Ibid., p. 3–4.

40 Ibid., p. 6.

41 NA, RG 6, Department Secretary of State Files, ACC 86–87/319, file 1–1, R. Alex Sim (Acting Director of Citizenship Branch) to R. J. Nichols (Technical Services, Department of Citizenship and Immigration), 18 July 1956, p. 3. Some of these groups are more properly considered religious than ethnic (e.g., Jewish and Doukhobor). The descriptive terms are the ones current at the time, thus accounting for the use of "Negro" rather than "Black."

42 Ibid., p. 3.

43 NA, RG 6, Department Secretary of State Files, ACC 86–87/319, file 1–1, "Memorandum to Deputy Minister Re Liaison Division – Canadian Citizenship Branch," 24 Oct. 1957, p. 1.

44 Ibid., p. 2.

45 Ibid., p. 5. Some years later, R. Alex Sim, the chief of the Liaison Division, wrote to Robert England and mentioned the branch's growing activities with Natives, particularly in the establishment of urban "Friendship Centres": "Thus we are moving into a new phase where the skills that were applied to immigrant groups can be used with Indians who migrate to the city." NA, Robert England Papers, MG 30 C181, vol. 2, file on Citizenship Division Report 1937–62, 14 Aug. 1962, p. 2.

46 John G. Diefenbaker, *One Canada: Memoirs of the Right Honourable John G. Diefenbaker: The Crusading Years, 1895–1956* (Toronto: Macmillan, 1975), 140–1.

47 Ibid., 225.

48 See comments of various ministers in Peter Stursberg, *Diefenbaker: Leadership Gained: 1956–62* (Toronto: University of Toronto Press, 1975), 216–19.

49 Peter C. Newman, *Renegade in Power: The Diefenbaker Years* (Toronto: McClelland and Stewart, 1963), 228–9.

50 J.L. Granatstein et al., *Nation: Canada Since Confederation* (Toronto: McGraw-Hill Ryerson, 1990), 467.

51 Freda Hawkins, *Canada and Immigration: Public Policy and Public Concern* (Montreal and London: McGill-Queen's University Press, 1972), 96.

52 Ibid., 96–7.

53 Ibid., 97.

54 NA, RG 26, Department of Citizenship and Immigration Files, volume 85, file 1–25–7, part 1, J.H. Gordon (Acting Director, Citizenship Branch) to H.M. Jones (Acting Deputy Minister, Department of Citizenship and Immigration), 10 Oct. 1963.

55 NA, RG 26, Department of Citizenship and Immigration Files, vol. 85, file 1–25–7, part 1, John Fisher (Commissioner, National Centennial Administration) to C.M. Isbister (Deputy Minister, Department of Citizenship and Immigration), 4 Dec. 1963.

56 NA, RG 26, Department of Citizenship and Immigration Files, vol. 65, file 2 – 2–4, C.M. Isbister (Deputy Minister, Department of Citizenship and Immigration) to George F. Davidson (Secretary, Treasury Board), 8 Oct. 1964.

57 W.H. Agnew, "Historical Review of the Canadian Citizenship Branch" (Ottawa: Secretary of State, 1967), 49–50.

58 NA, RG 6, Department of Secretary of State Files, vol. 661, file 2–2–4, "A New Focus for the Citizenship Branch," attached to a memorandum from Jean Lagassé (Director of the Citizenship Branch) to Charles A. Lussier (Assistant Deputy Minister for Citizenship), 6 May 1965, p. 3. Lussier passed the paper on to Isbister, the deputy minister, on

the same day, noting that the search for a new focus for the branch
had been under way for a year.

59 Ibid., pp. 3, 4.

60 Ibid., p. 5.

61 Gérard Pelletier, "1968: Language Policy and the Mood in Quebec," in Thomas S. Axworthy and Pierre Elliot Trudeau, eds., *Towards
a Just Society* (Toronto: Viking, 1990), 207.

62 Bernard Ostry, *The Cultural Connection: An Essay on Culture and Government Policy in Canada* (Toronto: McClelland and Stewart, 1978),
100.

63 NA, RG 6, Department of Secretary of State Files, vol. 661, file
2–2–4, "The Citizenship Branch in Its New Function," Aug. 1966,
p. 1.

64 NA, RG 6, Department of Secretary of State Files, vol. 661, file 2–2–4,
"Memorandum to the Secretary of State," 20 Sept. 1966.

65 NA, RG 6, Department of Secretary of State Files, vol. 661, file 2–2–4,
"Memorandum to Cabinet: Confirmation of Citizenship Branch
Role," Feb. 1968, p. 1.

66 NA, RG 6, Department of Secretary of State Files, vol. 661, file
2–2–4, memorandum from G.G.E. Steele to J.H. Lagassé, 15 Feb. 1968.

67 NA, RG 6, Department of Secretary of State Files, vol. 661, file
2–2–4, J.S. Hodgson (Principal Secretary to the Prime Minister) to
G.G.E. Steele (Under Secretary of State, SOS), 19 March 1968.

68 Ibid.

CHAPTER FIVE

1 NA, RG 6, Department of Secretary of State, vol. 661, file 2–4–8,
vol. 1, "Report of SLO's Staff Conference May 18–20, 1965," p. 1.

2 Canada, Royal Commission on Bilingualism and Biculturalism, *Preliminary Report* (Ottawa: Queen's Printer, 1965), Appendix III, 177–84.

3 Royal Commission on Bilingualism and Biculturalism, *Report*,
vol. 5, book 1 (Ottawa: Queen's Printer, 1970), 128.

4 As pointed out in the last chapter, the SOS was drawn into the linguistic area largely as a consequence of the Royal Commission on Bilingualism and Biculturalism. Until 1963, the branch had not
differentiated its human relations activities between Native Indian,
multi-ethnic, and French-English relations. Until the commission
demanded its services, the branch had seen its role as integrating immigrants and (after 1960) Native Indians into either of the two
major linguistic groups. See Canada, Secretary of State, Citizenship
Branch, "Programme Memoranda: Citizenship Branch Total Programme" (Ottawa, 1967), 7.

5 Secretary of State, Social Action Branch, "General Outline of the Social Action Branch Programme" (Ottawa, 1970), 1.

6 Secretary of State, *Annual Report 1970*, 4.

7 Ibid.

8 Ibid.

9 Ibid., 5.

10 Secretary of State, Social Action Branch, *Director's Report*, 1970, 5.

11 Social Action Branch, "General Outline," 3.

12 Ibid.

13 Ibid., 4.

14 Ibid., 6.

15 Social Action Branch, *Director's Report*, 1970, 2.

16 NA, RG 6, Department of Secretary of State, ACC 86–87/320, vol. 1, file 10–1, part 1, "Some Thoughts on the Application of the 'New Concept of Ministry Organization' to the Portfolio of the Secretary of State and the Responsibilities of the Minister 'without Portfolio' for Citizenship and Information Canada," Appendix B, 3 March 1971, p. 1.

17 John Jaworsky, "A Case Study of the Canadian Federal Government's Multiculturalism Policy," MA thesis, Carleton University, 1979, 61.

18 Joseph Wearing, *The L-Shaped Party* (Toronto: McGraw-Hill Ryerson, 1981), 16–17; Christina McCall-Newman, *Grits* (Toronto: Macmillan, 1982), 14–17.

19 Richard Stanbury later became a senator. His younger brother, Robert Stanbury, was appointed minister without portfolio responsible for citizenship and Information Canada in 1969.

20 Wearing, *The L-Shaped Party*, 24–5.

21 McCall-Newman, *Grits*, 40–1.

22 Lorna Marsden, "The Party and Parliament: Participatory Democracy in the Trudeau Years," in Thomas S. Axworthy and Pierre Elliott Trudeau, eds., *Towards a Just Society* (Toronto: Viking, 1990), 271.

23 Stanbury was less successful in remodelling the party. He was part of a Pearsonian faction whose efforts culminated in the Liberal party's 1970 convention. While some reforms were implemented, the convention's policy proposals were rejected by cabinet and were unsupported by Trudeau and his own entourage. Wearing, *The L-Shaped Party*, 171.

24 The issue of Native organizations and their participation in the policy process was specifically and carefully addressed in H.B. Hawthorn, ed., *A Survey of the Contemporary Indians of Canada*, two vols. (Ottawa: Information Canada, 1967–8), especially in vol. 2. The analysis focused on the nature of the democratic state, the autonomy exercised by

public officials, and the need to support Native organizations to ensure their participation and a mechanism for policy makers to address the Native community more effectively.

25 See Michael Clague, "Citizen Participation in the Legislative Process," in James A. Draper, ed., *Citizen Participation: Canada: A Book of Readings* (Toronto: New Press, 1988), 39.

26 Ian Hamilton, *The Children's Crusade: The Story of the Company of Young Canadians* (Toronto: Peter Martin Associates, 1970), 2.

27 Sandra Gwyn, "The Great Ottawa Grant Boom (and How It Grew)," *Saturday Night* 87 (October 1972): 22.

28 Ibid., 23. For a similar assessment, see Doris Shackleton, *Power Town: Democracy Discarded* (Toronto: McClelland and Stewart, 1977), 87. A flavour of what most partisans at the time meant by "participating citizens" can be gleaned from Canada, Task Force on Government Information, *To Know and Be Known* (Ottawa: Queen's Printer, 1969), 44.

29 NA, RG 6, Department of Secretary of State, vol. 661, file 2–4–8, vol. 1, memorandum from Jean H. Lagassé (Director of Citizenship Branch) to C.A. Lussier (Assistant Deputy Minister – Citizenship), 23 March 1966.

30 The Departmental Estimates for 1967–68 noted the doubling of expenditures under "Grants for Citizenship Promotion" (from $236,000 to $480,000) and explained it partly as a result of the branch's increasing involvement in Youth Services.

31 NA, RG 6, Department of Secretary of State, ACC 86–86/319, file 2–14–2, vol. 2, "Minutes, Policy Committee Meeting," 30 June 1969, p. 1.

32 Ibid., p. 2.

33 Bernard Ostry, *The Cultural Connection: An Essay on Culture and Government Policy in Canada* (Toronto: McClelland and Stewart, 1978), 115.

34 Ibid., 117–18.

35 Interview with Stewart Goodings, 22 March 1989, Ottawa. Goodings was assistant director and acting director (for nine months) of the Company of Young Canadians between 1965 and 1969. He joined the Citizenship Branch in 1971 and was made "Chairman" of Citizens Organization Program in 1972.

36 Interview with Stewart Goodings, 22 March 1989, Ottawa.

37 Interview with Robert Nichols, 30 March 1989, Ottawa. Nichols joined the Citizenship Branch in 1971, at Bernard Ostry's invitation.

38 The Cabinet Committee on Priorities and Planning first approved of the objectives in April 1970. The proposal was contained in Cabinet document no. 440.70.

39 Bureau of Management Consulting, "Organization Study of the Sec-

retary of State Citizenship Organization" (Ottawa: Department of
Supply and Services, Jan. 1971), 4–7.

40 Ibid., 21.

41 Ibid., 25.

42 Ibid., 25.

43 Ibid., 25.

44 Canada Consulting Group, "Improving the Management Effectiveness of Citizenship Branch, Department of the Secretary of State" (Ottawa, Nov. 1971), I-4.

45 Ibid., I-11.

46 Ibid., I-12.

47 See Nancy Adamson, Linda Briskin, and Margaret McPhail, *Feminist
Organizing for Change: The Contemporary Women's Movement in Canada*
(Toronto: Oxford University Press, 1988); and Alison Prentice et al.,
Canadian Women: A History (Toronto: Harcourt Brace Jovanovich,
1988).

48 Naomi Black, "The Canadian Women's Movement: The Second
Wave," in Sandra Burt, Lorraine Code, and Lindsay Dorney, eds.,
Changing Patterns: Women in Canada (Toronto: McClelland and
Stewart, 1988), 83. Also see Sylvia B. Bashevkin, *Toeing the Lines: Women
and Party Politics in English Canada* (Toronto: University of Toronto
Press, 1985), 23–5.

49 Prentice et al., *Canadian Women*, 355.

50 Ibid., 345.

51 Ibid., 348.

52 For Bird's own story of the commission's work, see Florence Bird, *Anne
Francis: An Autobiography* (Toronto: Clarke, Irwin, 1974), 262–318.

53 Canada, Royal Commission on the Status of Women, *Report* (Ottawa:
Information Canada, 1970), 51.

54 Ibid., 49.

55 Howard Palmer, "Reluctant Hosts: Anglo-Canadian Views of
Multiculturalism in the Twentieth Century," in *Multiculturalism as
State Policy: Conference Report*, Second Canadian Conference on
Multiculturalism, Ottawa, 13–15 Feb. 1976 (Ottawa: Canadian
Consultative Council on Multiculturalism, 1976), 101–2.

56 Raymond Breton, "Multiculturalism and Canadian Nation-Building,"
in Alan Cairns and Cynthia Williams, eds., *The Politics of Gender, Ethnicity and Language in Canada* (Toronto: University of Toronto Press,
1986), 47.

57 Canada, Parliament, House of Commons, *Debates*, 8 Oct. 1971, 8,545.

58 Ibid., 8,546.

59 Jaworsky, "A Case Study," 59.

60 Secretary of State, *Annual Report 1972*, 5.

61 Ibid.

62 Secretary of State, Citizenship Branch, "Evaluation Report on Citizenship Participation Activities Supported by the Citizenship Branch, December 1971 – December 1972" (Ottawa, 1973), 5. The total requested amount was $4.9 million over the period.

63 Secretary of State, *Annual Report 1971*, 4–5.

64 Citizenship Branch, "Evaluation Report," 2.

65 Ibid., 4.

66 Ibid., 9.

67 Ibid., 10.

68 Secretary of State, *Annual Report 1974*, passim.

69 Interview with Stewart Goodings, 22 March 1989, Ottawa. Goodings became the "Chairman" of the Citizens' Organizations program in 1972, and it was in part through his efforts that "new and emerging groups" and "womens' groups" were given priority. Goodings also agrees that the OLMG core funding set the pace for the other Citizenship programs.

70 Ostry, *The Cultural Connection*, 118.

71 Ibid., 224–5 note 5.

72 Lorna Marsden, "The Party and Parliament: Participatory Democracy in the Trudeau Years," in Thomas S. Axworthy and Pierre Elliott Trudeau, eds., *Towards a Just Society* (Toronto: Viking, 1990), 274.

73 Canada, Parliament, House of Commons, *Debates*, 17 May 1973, 3,863.

74 Interview with Robert Nichols, 30 March 1989, Ottawa.

75 Jaworsky, "A Case Study," 110–11.

76 Interview with Stephen J. Jaworsky, 20 Feb. 1990, Ottawa. Jaworsky joined the Citizenship Branch in 1959 and became national liaison officer for ethnic groups in 1966. He was a key adviser on ethnic issues in the development of multicultural policy and worked in the branch until 1974.

CHAPTER SIX

1 Interview with Dan Iannuzzi, 27 Sept. 1988, Toronto. Iannuzzi is chair and publisher of *Corriere Canadese*.

2 Department of the Secretary of State of Canada, *Annual Report 1975*, 24.

3 Ibid., 25.

4 Secretary of State, *Annual Report 1978*, 63.

5 The following is taken from Secretary of State, *Annual Report 1980–81*.

6 Ibid., 2.

7 A copy of the submission is attached as an appendix to Secretary of

State, "Structural Changes in the Department of the Secretary of State from 1969–70 to 1984–85" (Ottawa, n.d., but c. 1985). The submission candidly admitted that the SOS "has for many years been divided into multiple programs with little relationship between their objectives. ... The Department has lacked the capacity to develop overall strategies and policies that provide a more global approach to assisting the diversity of client groups covered by the various programs of the Department."

8 Jean Marchand (20 April 1968–5 July 1968); Gérard Pelletier (6 July 1968–26 Nov. 1972); Hugh Faulkner (27 Nov. 1972–13 Sept. 1976); John Roberts (14 Sept. 1976–3 June 1979); David Mac-Donald (4 June 1979–2 March 1980); Francis Fox (3 March 1980–21 Sept. 1981); Gerald Regan (22 Sept. 1981–30 Sept. 1982); Serge Joyal (6 Oct. 1982–17 Sept. 1984); Walter McLean (17 Sept. 1984–19 Aug. 1985); Benoît Bouchard (20 Aug. 1985–29 June 1986); David Crombie (30 June 1986–30 March 1988); Lucien Bouchard (31 March 1988–30 Jan. 1989); and Gerry Weiner (from 30 Jan. 1989).

9 Stanley Haidasz (27 Nov. 1972–7 Aug. 1974); John Munro (8 Aug. 1974–20 April 1977); Joseph-Philippe Guay (21 April 1977–15 Sept. 1977); Norman Cafik (16 Sept. 1977–3 June 1979); Steve Paproski (4 June 1979–2 March 1980); James Fleming (3 March 1980–11 Aug. 1983); David Collenette (12 Aug. 1983–16 Sept. 1984); Jack Murta (17 Sept. 1984–19 Aug. 1985); Otto Jelinek (19 Aug. 1985–29 June 1986); David Crombie (30 June 1986–30 March 1988); Lucien Bouchard (31 March 1988–30 Jan. 1989); and Gerry Weiner (30 Jan. 1989–).

10 Secretary of State, Social Action Branch, "Policies and Regulations" (Ottawa, 1969), 1.

11 Ibid., 3.

12 Ibid., 4.

13 Ibid., 4.

14 Ibid., 7.

15 Secretary of State, *Annual Report 1970*, 5.

16 Secretary of State, Social Action Branch, *Annual Report, 1970* (Ottawa, 1970), 5.

17 Secretary of State, *Annual Report 1975*, 24, 31.

18 Canada, Official Languages Commissioner, *Annual Report* (Ottawa, 1976), 9.

19 "Francophone Federation Wants Bigger Share of Funds," *Globe and Mail*, 8 Jan. 1977, 5.

20 "'Moral Responsibility' Vow Good Omen for Francophones," *Montreal Star*, 19 April 1977, B8.

21 Official Languages Commissioner, *Annual Report* (Ottawa, 1977), 22.

22 Ibid., 24.

23 Canada, Parliament, House of Commons, *Debates*, 18 Oct. 1977, 3.

24 "English-Speaking Quebecers Promised Funds from Ottawa," *Vancouver Sun*, 28 Oct. 1977, A15.

25 House of Commons, *Debates*, 27 Oct. 1977, 333 and 334.

26 Official Languages Commissioner, *Annual Report* (Ottawa, 1977), 22.

27 "Minority Groups Get New Program in Ottawa Shuffle," *Globe and Mail*, 11 Nov. 1977, 8.

28 Paul Malvern, *Persuaders: Influence Peddling, Lobbying and Political Corruption in Canada* (Toronto: Methuen, 1985), 205.

29 Secretary of State, *Annual Report 1980–81*, 15–16.

30 Secretary of State, *Report of the Task Force on Improving Certain Aspects of the Administration of the Official Languages and Citizenship Programs* (Ottawa, 1980), 4.

31 Official Languages Commissioner, *Annual Report* (Ottawa, 1980), 19.

32 FFHQ, *La fédération des francophones hors Québec: son origine, son orientation, ses membres, ses objectifs, ses programmes* (Ottawa, 1981), 1.

33 Ibid., 6–7.

34 Secretary of State, *Grants and Contributions Manual, 1988* (Ottawa, 1988), v.1.1.

35 Ibid., v.1.4.

36 Statistics Canada, *Dimensions: Language Retention and Transfer* (Ottawa: Minister of Supply and Services, 1989), Table 1.

37 Secretary of State, Program Evaluation Directorate, *Evaluation Report of the Official Language Minority Groups Program (OLMG), 1970–82* (Ottawa, 1983), 47–8.

38 The focus of this section, and indeed of this book, is on federal policy. Several provinces have undertaken initiatives in all three areas of interest, but they cannot be treated here. On the multiculturalism front, Ontario, Alberta, and Nova Scotia have distinct provincial policies to address the area. Alberta created its Cultural Heritage Council in 1972, and Ontario set up an Advisory Council on Multiculturalism in 1973. In Nova Scotia, the Department of Tourism and Culture has a cultural affairs division that is responsible for multiculturalism.

39 Secretary of State, *Annual Report 1975*, 31.

40 John Jaworsky, "A Case Study of the Canadian Federal Government's Multiculturalism Policy," MA thesis, Carleton University, 1979, 109.

41 Ibid., 104.

42 Ibid., 115–16.

43 "Ottawa Places Emphasis on Fight against Discrimination in Altering Multicultural Program," *Globe and Mail*, 26 Nov. 1975, A1–2.

44 Interview with Stephan J. Jaworsky, 20 Feb. 1990, Ottawa.

45 Secretary of State, *Annual Report 1980*.

46 Secretary of State, *Annual Report 1980–81*.

47 Daiva K. Stasiulis, "The Symbolic Mosaic Reaffirmed: Multiculturalism Policy," in Katherine A. Graham, ed., *How Ottawa Spends: 1988/89: The Conservatives Heading into the Stretch* (Ottawa: Carleton University Press, 1988), 90.

48 Secretary of State, *Annual Report 1982–83*, 15.

49 "The Political Two-Step" *Globe and Mail*, 22 Jan. 1984, A6.

50 Secretary of State, *Annual Report 1984–85*, 36–7.

51 Canada, Parliament, House of Commons, Standing Committee on Multiculturalism, *Multiculturalism: Building the Canadian Mosaic* (Ottawa: Queen's Printer, June 1987).

52 "New Multiculturalism Bill Gets Mixed Reviews," *Toronto Star*, 2 Dec. 1987, A2.

53 This clause is paralleled by two others: "(g) assist ethno-cultural minority communities to conduct activities with a view to overcoming any discriminatory barrier and, in particular, discrimination based on race or national or ethnic origin," and "(h) provide support to individuals, groups or organizations for the purpose of preserving, enhancing and promoting multiculturalism in Canada."

54 "Boost in Funding for Ethnic Programs Draws Mixed Reviews," *Vancouver Sun*, 31 May 1988, A8; and "MPs Vote 100–0 to Approve Bill Promoting Multiculturalism,"*Toronto Star*, 13 July 1988, A8.

55 Naomi Black, "The Canadian Women's Movement: The Second Wave," in Sandra Burt, Lorraine Code, and Lindsay Dorney, eds., *Changing Patterns: Women in Canada* (Toronto: McClelland and Stewart, 1988), 96.

56 Rita Cadieux, assistant director of operations, Citizenship Branch, at the time, recalls that another stimulus to the development of the Women's Program in 1970–71 was a request by Bernard Ostry to find ways to spend some unallocated monies in the branch before the end of that fiscal year. The report of the Royal Commission on the Status of Women had just been released, and so money for women's groups was a new priority. Interview with Rita Cadieux, 21 Feb. 1990, Ottawa.

57 Sue Findlay, "Facing the State: The Politics of the Women's Movement Reconsidered," in Heather Jon Maroney and Meg Luxton, eds., *Feminism and Political Economy: Women's Work, Women's Struggles*, (Toronto: Methuen, 1987), 39.

58 Ibid., 39–40.

59 Secretary of State, "The IWY Program at Secretary of State: An Assessment," (Ottawa, 1976), 26.

60 Ibid., 35.

61 Ibid., 104.

62 Of the nine, six were delivered directly by the Women's Program, and three by other programs in the Citizenship Branch. The seminars were on the following themes: Women in Politics, Rural Women, Women and Human Rights, Women and the Media, Native Women, Women in Canada's Minority Cultures, Learning for Transition, Women and Voluntarism, and Women and Alternatives. There was a total of 244 invited participants in the entire series, with an average of 27 attending each seminar. The Women's Program invited 76 women's organizations to a consultation on 19–20 October 1974 to discuss the IWY. Several resolutions were passed to censure the Privy Council's use of its portion of the IWY money to run conferences. Secretary of State, Citizenship Branch, Women's Program, "Summary of Consultation with Representatives of Women's Groups on the Department of Secretary of State's International Women's Year Program" (Ottawa, 1974), 6.

63 Hosek's description of the key women's groups that lobbied around the Charter shows a preponderance of federally funded organizations; see Chaviva Hosek, "Women and Constitutional Process," in Keith Banting and Richard Simeon, eds., *And No One Cheered: Federalism, Democracy and the Constitution Act* (Toronto: Methuen, 1983), 280–300. Romanow, Whyte, and Leeson argue that the Joint Parliamentary Committee hearings on Ottawa's unilateral constitutional proposal in 1980 "helped the federal government strategy. The presentations and concerns of a large number of special interest groups supporting the charter created a large reservoir of support for the resolution"; Roy Romanow, John Whyte, and Howard Leeson, *Canada Notwithstanding: The Making of the Constitution, 1976–1982* (Toronto: Carswell/Methuen, 1984), 121. David Milne, *Tug of War: Ottawa and the Provinces under Trudeau and Mulroney* (Toronto: James Lorimer, 1986), 50, agrees with this assessment. For a more critical view of special-interest bargaining before the Joint Committee, see Edward McWhinney, *Canada and the Constitution, 1979–1982* (Toronto: University of Toronto Press, 1982), 54–5.

64 "Group Vague on Funding, Membership," *Calgary Herald*, 8 March 1984, C11.

65 Danielle Crittenden, "REAL Women Don't Eat Crow," *Saturday Night* 103 (May 1988): 31. Gwen Landolt, one of the founders of REAL, also helped launch Campaign Life. Grace Petrasek, the group's first president, had also been active in the anti-abortion movement. Crittenden's article tells some of the same story told here but is seriously mistaken about the sequence of events and dates. For example, the application for $92,000 that she claims was made in 1985 was actually

submitted in 1984. She also accuses the Women's Program of not responding to requests from REAL for application forms, which is false, according to the documentation. Her story, as a consequence, puts the Women's Program in an unfavourable light.

66 Grace Petrasek to Serge Joyal, 25 July 1984. The information on which this section of the chapter is based was obtained through the Access to Information Act in 1989.

67 Grace Petrasek (President of REAL) to Tamara Levine (National Projects Officer, Women's Program), 9 Nov. 1984.

68 Lyse Blanchard (Director, Women's Program) to Grace Petrasek (President, REAL), 14 Dec. 1984.

69 Ibid.

70 Telephone memorandum, Secretary of State, Women's Program, 26 Nov. 1985: "[REAL] would like an application form/sent a proposal already and does not want to go through that 'rigamorale' again. She wants it sent immediately – special delivery – 'unless we want difficulty/there are MPs waiting to assist them'. Took address but did not promise an application form."

71 Grace Petrasek (President of REAL) to Lyse Blanchard (Director, Women's Program), 9 Dec. 1985.

72 Joanne Linzey (Chief, Program Delivery, Women's Program) to Grace Petrasek (President, REAL), 30 Dec. 1985.

73 Sue Hierlihy (REAL) to Judy Wright (Chief of Program Delivery, Women's Program), 13 April 1987.

74 House of Commons, Standing Committee on Secretary of State, *Fairness in Funding: Report on the Women's Program*, 26 May 1987, 16.

75 Secretary of State, *Response to the Standing Committee on Secretary of State, Fairness in Funding*, 30 Nov. 1987.

76 Crittenden, "REAL Women," 27–35.

77 Interview with Gwen Landolt, 27 Sept. 1988, Toronto.

78 "Ottawa Promises Cash, Anti-Feminist Group Says," *Winnipeg Free Press*, 28 Feb. 1989, 10.

79 "Ottawa Puts Squeeze on Feminists," *Toronto Star*, 25 Feb. 1989, H1.

80 *Maclean's*, 6 March 1989, 7.

81 "Tories to Break Tradition by Boycotting Women's Lobby Sessions," *Globe and Mail*, 13 May 1989, A7.

82 "Funds Reduced or Ended for Outspoken Women's, Native Groups," *Globe and Mail*, 23 Feb. 1990, A9.

83 For example, see Secretary of State, *Report of the Task Force on Improving Certain Aspects of the Administration of the Official Languages and Citizenship Programs* (Ottawa, 1980), for citations of lack of consensus about citizenship programs and friction between regional offices and national headquarters.

CHAPTER SEVEN

1 In 1979 the sos also conducted an evaluation of grants given to the private and voluntary sector for translation and provision of services in minority languages (known as bilingualism development). The report found it difficult to assess whether the program had in fact encouraged provision of services in English and French that might not otherwise have occurred: "Many associations offered some services and materials in English and French before applying for a grant. Insufficient data exist to determine whether these associations subsequently expanded the range of services and materials available in English and French to clients or members. On the basis of those data which are available for recipients of more than one grant, most associations which offered services and materials in English and French continued to do so in the interval between grants." Secretary of State, Language Programmes Branch, "The Program of Aid to Associations: An Evaluation" (Ottawa, 1979), 40.

2 Secretary of State, Program Evaluation Directorate, "Evaluation Report of the Official Language Minority Groups Program (OLMG), 1970–82" (Ottawa, 1983), x.

3 Ibid., 7.

4 Ibid., 41.

5 Ibid., 44.

6 Ibid., 45.

7 Ibid.

8 Ibid., 46.

9 Ibid., 49.

10 Ibid., 51.

11 Ibid.

12 Ibid., 52.

13 Ibid., 69.

14 Ibid., 72.

15 Ibid., 73 and 82–83.

16 Ibid., 86.

17 Ibid., 117.

18 Ibid., 141.

19 Secretary of State, *Grants and Contributions Manual, 1988* (Ottawa, 1988), v.1.1.

20 Ibid., v.1.3.

21 Ibid., v.1.4.

22 Ibid., v.2.1.

23 Ibid.

24 CPF, *Annual Report 1988–1989*, 36.

25 CPF, *Annual Report, 1982–83*, n.p., table entitled "Canadian Parents for French, Statement of Revenues and Expenditures for the Fiscal Period Ended March 31/83." These figures are for the previous nine months.

26 Commissioner of Official Languages, *Parents Conference on French Language and Exchange Opportunities*, March 1977, 1.

27 Ibid., Appendix I, 1.

28 Canadian Parents for French, *Newsletter*, no. 2, Jan. 1978, 2.

29 Ibid., 3.

30 Canadian Parents for French, "A Message from the National Chairman – Janet Poyen," *Newsletter*, Dec. 1978.

31 Canadian Parents for French, *Newsletter*, Dec. 1979, 1.

32 Janet M. Poyen, "Canadian Parents for French: A National Pressure Group in Canadian Education" MA thesis, University of Calgary, 1989, 96, note 7.

33 Canadian Parents for French, *Chairman's Newsletter*, Aug. 1980, 2.

34 Canadian Parents for French, "Funding for Bilingualism in Education – Meetings with Ministerial Assistants held in Ottawa, November 21, 1980."

35 For example, Janet M. Poyen (Chairman, CPF) to Jean Chrétien (Chairman, Social Development Committee), 30 Sept. 1981; Monique Bégin (Minister of Nationnal Health and Welfare) to Poyen, 27 Oct. 1981. Poyen also corresponded with Marc Lalonde (Minister of Energy, Mines and Resources), Gerald Regan (Secretary of State of Canada), John Roberts (Minister of Environment), Yvon Pinard (President of the Privy Council), and Francis Fox (Minister of Communications).

36 Canadian Parents for French, *Federal-Provincial Agreement on Bilingualism in Education Funding*, March 1981.

37 Canadian Parents for French, *Brief to the Council of Ministers of Education, Canada*, Jan. 1981, 2.

38 Poyen, "Canadian Parents for French," 83–84.

39 This figure has been cited by AQ since 1982. Current estimates put the anglophone population of Quebec at 800,000.

40 Alliance Quebec, Draft Budget 1989–90.

41 Interview with Michael Goldbloom, 26 Feb. 1990, Montreal.

42 "Eric Maldoff, Alliance Quebec's Founding President, Steps Down," *The Quebecer*, Summer 1985, 8.

43 Ibid.

44 Alliance Quebec, "Presentation to the Joint Committee of the Senate and the House of Commons on Official Languages," 1983.

45 Alliance Quebec, "A Policy for the English-Speaking Community in Quebec," May 1989, 1.

46 Ibid., 31.

47 Ibid., 41.

48 Ibid., 60.

49 Ibid., 62.

50 Ibid., 61.

51 Alliance Quebec, "Brief Submitted to the Standing Committee on Privileges and Elections of the Manitoba Legislative Assembly on the Proposed Amendments to the Manitoba Act, 1870."

52 Alliance Quebec, "Brief by Alliance Quebec to the Special Joint Committee of the House of Commons and the Senate on the Constitutional Accord," 17 Aug. 1987, 2.

53 Interview with Michael Goldbloom, Montreal, 26 Feb. 1990.

54 Fédération des francophones hors Québec, *Rapport Annuel, 1986–1987*, 18. Since member organizations receive the lion's share of their own funding from the SOS, their contributions to the FFHQ are really for the most part SOS money by another name. This would boost the SOS's proportion of FFHQ's revenues above 90 per cent.

55 La Fédération des francophones hors Québec, "La Fédération des francophones hors Québec: son origine, son orientation, ses membres, ses objectifs, ses programmes" (March 1981), 1.

56 Ibid.

57 For ease of reference, quotations from *C'est le temps ou jamais* will be made to the English translation, *It's Now or Never* (Ottawa: SOS, 1975), 12.

58 Ibid., 16.

59 Ibid., 19.

60 Ibid., 20.

61 La Fédération des francophones hors Québec, "La Fédération," 2–3.

62 "Government Adds Another $45 Million to Support Minority Language Groups," *Globe and Mail*, 21 Dec. 1977, 9.

63 "Francophone Group Would Expose 'Scandals' Weighing against French outside Quebec," *Globe and Mail*, 2 March 1978, 10.

64 Ibid., 10.

65 Special Joint Committee of the Senate and of the Hosue of Commons on the Constitution of Canada, *Minutes of Proceedings and Evidence*, no. 13, 26 Nov. 1980, 27.

66 Ibid., 30–1.

67 Ibid., 29.

68 Special Joint Committee, no. 3, 5 Aug. 1987, 6.

69 Ibid., 15–16. Testimony by Yvon Fontaine, president of the FFHQ.

70 House of Commons, Legislative Committee on Bill C-72, An Act Respecting the Status and Use of the Official Languages of Canada, *Minutes of Proceedings and Evidence*, no. 7, 20 April 1988, 4.

71 Ibid., 29–30.

 1 Canada, Secretary of State, *Multicultural Program Granting Activity,
     Fiscal 1974–75* (Ottawa, 1976), 6.
 2 Ibid., 7.
 3 Ibid., 12.
 4 Ibid., 14. Emphasis removed from original. The report also dis-
     cussed the 11 per cent of organizations that listed other groups rather
     than individuals as members, but for reasons of brevity this section
     is not discussed here.
 5 Ibid., 20–2.
 6 Ibid., 25.
 7 *N* for analysis was 553 groups, with 14 per cent of data missing.
 8 Secretary of State, *Multicultural Program Granting Activity, Fiscal
     1974–75*, 29.
 9 Ibid., 31.
10 Ibid., 32.
11 Ibid., 35.
12 Ibid., 36.
13 Ibid., 37.
14 Secretary of State, Program Evaluation Directorate, *A Framework for
     Cross-Sectoral Evaluation of Core Funding in the Secretary of State*
     (Ottawa, March 1986).
15 Ibid., 8–10.
16 Ibid., 12.
17 Ibid., 13.
18 Ibid., 15–16.
19 Ibid., 19.
20 Ibid., 23.
21 Ibid., 24.
22 Ibid., 33.
23 The sos programs were reviewed more publicly and even more
     critically in 1984–85 as part of the Conservatives' Program Review Task
     Force. See Canada, Task Force on Program Review, *Culture and
     Communications* (Ottawa: Minister of Supply and Services, 1985). The
     sos was reviewed in this volume, although the Women's Program
     was discussed as well in another volume detailing citizenship initiatives;
     see Canada, Task Force on Program Review, *Citizenship, Labour and
     Immigration: A Plethora of "People" Programs* (Ottawa: Minister of Supply
     and Services, 1985).
24 Secretary of State, *Grants and Contributions Manual 1988* (Ottawa, 1988),
     IV.1.1.

25 Ibid., IV.1.1.
26 Ibid., IV.1.2.
27 Ibid., IV.1.2.
28 Ibid., IV.1.3.
29 Ibid., IV.1.5.
30 Ibid., IV.1.5.
31 In 1990 the CEC's members were Armenian National Federation, Bye-
    lorussian Canadian Coordinating Committee, Canadian Arab Fed-
    eration, Canadian Federation of Vietnamese Associations, Canadian
    Hispanic Congress, Canadian Jewish Congress, Canadian Polish
    Congress, Chinese Canadian National Council, Council of Muslim Com-
    munities in Canada, Croatian Peasant Society, Cypriot Federation
    of Canada, Czechoslovak Association of Canada, Estonian Central
    Council of Canada, Federation of Danish Associations, Federation
    of Korean Associations in Canada, Federation of Lao Associations of
    Canada, Federation of Sikh Societies in Canada, Finnish-Canadian
    Cultural Federation, First Portuguese Canadian Congress, German-
    Canadian Congress, Hellenic Canadian Congress, Icelandic Na-
    tional League, Latvian National Federation in Canada, Lithuanian
    Canadian Committee, National Association of Canadians of Origins
    in India, National Association of Japanese Canadians, National Black Co-
    alition of Canada, National Congress of Italian Canadians, National
    Council of Barbadian Associations of Canada, National Council of Gha-
    naian Canadians, National Council of Jamaicans and Supportive
    Organizations in Canada, National Federation of Pakistani Canadians,
    Russian Canadian Cultural Aid Society, Serbian National Shield So-
    ciety, Slovak Canadian National Council, Slovenian National Federation,
    Ukrainian Canadian Congress, and United Council of Filipino As-
    sociations in Canada.
32 For ease of presentation, this chapter will refer to the CEC even
    when it used its original designation.
33 Canadian Ethnocultural Council, *Constitution and By-Law No. 1*
    (1989).
34 Canadian Ethnocultural Council, *Annual Report 1989–90*, 26.
35 Canadian Ethnocultural Council, *Building the Consensus*, National Con-
    ference Report, June 1984, 22.
36 Ibid., 14.
37 Ibid., 17.
38 Canada, Parliament, Special Joint Committee of the Senate and of the
    House of Commons on the Constitution of Canada, *Minutes of Pro-
    ceedings and Evidence*, no. 22, 9 Dec. 1980, 77.
39 Ibid., 78.
40 Ibid., 79.
41 Canada, Parliament, House of Commons, Special Committee on

Participation of Visible Minorities in Canadian Society, *Minutes of Proceedings and Evidence*, no. 9, 12 Oct. 1983, 27–42.

42 Canada, Parliament, House of Commons, Subcommittee on Equality Rights, *Minutes of Proceedings and Evidence*, no. 7, 7 May 1985, 5. The CEC made two appearances before the Boyer Committee – the first in May, when it stated its preliminary thoughts on section 15 rights, and the second in September, when it presented a more substantial brief, the research for which was funded in part by the minister of justice.

43 Ibid., no. 28, 26 Sept. 1985, 5.

44 After passage of the Multiculturalism Act, the government decided in 1989 to merge the Standing Committee on Multiculturalism with the one on Communications and Culture. After lobbying by the CEC and other ethnocultural associations, the separate committee was re-established.

45 Section 16 of the accord read: "Nothing in section 2 of the *Constitution Act, 1867* affects section 25 or section 27 of the *Canadian Charter of Rights and Freedoms*, section 35 of the *Constitution Act, 1982* or class 24 of section 91 of the *Constitution Act, 1867*." The enumerated sections dealt with aboriginal and multicultural rights.

46 Canada, Parliament, Special Joint Committee of the Senate and of the House of Commons on the 1987 Constitutional Accord, *Minutes of Proceedings and Evidence*, no. 7, 13 Aug. 1987, 42.

47 Ibid., 43.

48 Canadian Ethnocultural Council, *Ethno Canada*, vol. 8, no. 1 (Winter 1988): 9.

49 Bill C-18, to establish a Department of Multiculturalism and Citizenship, was introduced in the Commons on 18 May 1989.

50 Bill C-18 was a bittersweet victory, however: the proposed department did not meet the CEC's criteria of an effective administrative instrument; from the CEC's perspective, the government appeared unresponsive to ethnocultural groups' demands for amendment.

51 See, for example, Keith Spicer, "Ottawa Should Stop Money for Multiculturalism," *Gazette* (Montreal), 9 March 1989: B-3.

52 For the early history of the UCC, see Oleh W. Gerus, "The Ukrainian Canadian Committee," in Manoly R. Lupul, ed., *A Heritage in Transition: Essays in the History of Ukrainians in Canada* (Toronto: McClelland and Stewart, 1982), 195, and Michael H. Marunchak, *The Ukrainian Canadians: A History*, 2nd ed. (Winnipeg: Ukrainian Academy of Arts and Sciences, 1982), 806–14.

53 Marunchak, *The Ukrainian Canadians*, 818–19.

54 Gerus, "The Ukrainian Canadian Committee," 206.

55 Canada, Parliament, Special Joint Committee of the Senate and of the

House of Commons on the Constitution of Canada, *Minutes of Proceedings and Evidence*, no. 14, 27 Nov. 1980, 54.

56 Ibid., 560 Section 15 was not amended along these lines, but a new section 27 was added to the Charter that reads: "This Charter shall be interpreted in a manner consistent with the preservation and enhancement of the multicultural heritage of Canadians." According to Hogg, the section "may prove to be more of a rhetorical flourish than an operative provision." See Peter W. Hogg, *Canada Act 1982 Annotated* (Toronto: Carswell, 1982), 72.

57 Special Joint Committee, *Minutes*, no. 14, 27 Nov. 1980, 56.

58 Ibid., 58.

59 Special Joint Committee on the 1987 Constitutional Accord, *Minutes*, no. 7, 13 Aug. 1987, 98.

60 Ibid., 99.

61 Financial data were kindly provided by B. Werbeniuk of the national office of the UCC. The financing picture is a little more complicated than these figures might suggest. For example, in 1988 the UCC received $1 million from the SOS, but half of this was for college programs in Ukrainian studies and the rest went to special Ukrainian cultural and information projects. Moreover, the member organizations and provincial chapters of the UCC apply for funds from the SOS as well. The $55,300 referred to in this paragraph is for the national office only.

62 Canada, Parliament, House of Commons, Standing Committee on Multiculturalism, *Minutes of Proceedings and Evidence*, no. 11, 8 Dec. 1987 and no. 21, 14 June 1988.

63 National Association of Canadians of Origins in India, *Thirteenth Annual Conference*, 1988, 1.

64 Ibid., 1–2.

65 Canadian politicians have also sometimes faced a dilemma in attending public functions hosted by some Sikh organizations in their ridings, since the Canadian government's official position supports the Indian government's rejection of the creation of an independent Sikh state, known as Kalistan. For example, Joe Clark, minister of external affairs, wrote to provincial premiers in 1988 advising them not to participate in activities of three Canadian Sikh organizations devoted to a Kalistan state.

66 National Association of Canadians of Origins in India, *Thirteenth Annual Conference*, 1988, 35. Membership dues and donations dropped 38 per cent between 1987 and 1988.

67 Canada, Parliament, House of Commons, Sub-Committee on Equality Rights, *Minutes of Proceedings and Evidence*, no. 19, 15 July 1985, 101.

68 Ibid., 102.

69 For example, see ibid., 103, and Canada, Parliament, House of Commons, Standing Committee on Multiculturalism, *Minutes of Proceedings and Evidence*, no. 8, 16 June 1987, 13.

70 For example, see Sub-Committee on Equality Rights, *Minutes*, no. 19, 15 July 1985, 101–2, and Standing Committee on Multiculturalism, *Minutes*, no. 8, 16 June 1987, 9.

71 Special Joint Committee, *Minutes*, no. 7, 13 Aug. 1987, 81.

CHAPTER NINE

1 Sue Findlay, "Facing the State: The Politics of the Women's Movement Reconsidered," in Heather Jon Maroney and Meg Luxton, eds., *Feminism and Political Economy: Women's Work, Women's Struggles*, (Toronto: Methuen, 1987), 31–50.

2 Canada, Secretary of State, Policy Branch, "Women's Program Granting Activities: Interim Statistical Review, Fiscal 74–75 and 75–76" (Ottawa, 1975), 1.

3 Ibid., Figure 1 at 2. Support to Women's Groups had three sub-programs (Support Grants, Resource Development, Consultation), as did Public Education (Cultural Grants, Seminars, Promotion).

4 Ibid., 16.

5 Ibid., 17.

6 DPA Group Inc., "Evaluation of the Women's Program," prepared for the Program Evaluation Directorate, Secretary of State (March 1985).

7 The cabinet directive called for an almost four-fold increase over four years, from $4 million in 1983–84 to over $15 million in 1987–88.

8 The groups were Second Storey Women's Centre (Bridgewater, Nova Scotia), the Canadian Research Institute for the Advancement of Women (Halifax, Nova Scotia); la Riposte des femmes contre la violence (no place listed); Comité provincial des femmes en agriculture (Longueuil, Quebec); Women's Continuing Education Committee, United Theological College of the United Church (Montreal); National Action Committee on the Status of Women (Toronto); Political Action Women (Hamilton); Single Mothers against Poverty (Hamilton); Alberta Status of Women Action Committee (Edmonton); and Women's Coordinating Committee for Celebration of Non-Violence (Edmonton).

9 The interviewees, with the positions they occupied at the time, were Dr. Margaret Fulton (president, Mount St Vincent University); Mme Danielle Hébert (directrice, Comité de condition féminine, Conseil

des syndicats nationaux); Mme Michèle Jean (sous-ministre adjointe à la formation professionnelle, ministre main-d'oeuvre et sécurité du revenu, Gouvernement du Québec); Ms. Maureen O'Neil (co-ordinator, Status of Women Canada); Ms. Monica Townson (economist); Ms. Patricia Cooper (past president, Calgary YWCA); Dr. Sheila Wynn (director, Women's Secretariat, government of Alberta); and Ms. Eileen Hendry (acting president, Canadian Advisory Council on the Status of Women).

10 DPA Group, "Evaluation of the Women's Program," 32.

11 Ibid., 34.

12 Ibid., 36.

13 Ibid., 44 and 45.

14 Ibid., Appendix E, 23.

15 Secretary of State, *Grants and Contributions Manual 1988*, II.12.1.

16 Ibid., II.12.2.

17 Ibid., II.12.2.

18 Ibid., II.12.3.

19 Secretary of State, "Core Funding by Region, 1986–87," n.d.

20 Secretary of State, "Women's Programme, Fiscal Year 1986–87, Number of Projects Approved," 2 April 1987.

21 National Action Committee on the Status of Women, *Annual Report 1989–90* (Ottawa, 1990), 2.

22 Nancy Adamson, Linda Briskin, and Margaret McPhail, *Feminist Organizing for Change: The Contemporary Women's Movement in Canada* (Toronto: Oxford University Press, 1988), 52.

23 Alison Prentice et al., *Canadian Women: A History* (Toronto: Harcourt Brace Jovanovich, 1988), 350.

24 Adamson, Briskin, and McPhail, *Feminist Organizing for Change*, 55.

25 National Action Committee on the Status of Women, *Annual Report 1988–89* (Ottawa, 1989), 6.

26 Ibid., 7.

27 National Action Committee, *Annual Report 1989–90*, 2–3.

28 Ibid., 3–4.

29 Ibid., 4.

30 Bill C-21 was to eliminate government contributions to the Unemployment Insurance Account and thereby have the entire program funded through employer and employee premiums.

31 Women's Program funding guidelines prohibit support for "projects whose primary purpose is to promote a view on abortion or sexual orientation," and so NAC's prominent pro-choice position on abortion appears anomalous. However, pro-choice lobbying is only one of NAC's activities and as such is not a "project."

32 In the absence of social service programs to help young people get out of prostitution, NAC feels that criminalization only makes prostitutes' work more dangerous.

33 Chaviva Hosek, "Women and Constitutional Process," in Keith Banting and Richard Simeon, eds., *And No One Cheered: Federalism, Democracy and the Constitution Act* (Toronto: Methuen, 1983) 281.

34 Penny Kome, *The Taking of Twenty-Eight: Women Challenge the Constitution* (Toronto: Women's Press, 1983), 51.

35 "Charter Would Enshrine Bias, NA Says," *Globe and Mail*, 21 Nov. 1980, 9.

36 "Overlapping Jurisdictions: A Pitfall in Supplying Services to Women," in Audrey Doerr and Micheline Carrier, eds., *Women and the Constitution* (Ottawa: Canadian Advisory Council on the Status of Women, 1981), 149–64.

37 Canada, Parliament, Special Joint Committee of the Senate and of the House of Commons, *Minutes of Proceedings and Evidence*, no. 9, 20 Nov. 1980, 57–76.

38 Marjorie Cohen, *The Macdonald Report and Its Implications for Women* (Toronto: NAC, 1985).

39 For a discussion of the FTA and the politics that surrounded it, see G. Bruce Doern and Brian Tomlin, *Faith and Fear: The Free Trade Story* (Toronto: Stoddart, 1991).

40 National Action Committee, "Brief on the 1987 Constitutional Accord," Feb. 1988, 4.

41 Canadian Congress for Learning Opportunities for Women, *Annual Report, 1985–86*, 1.

42 Canadian Congress for Learning Opportunities for Women, "The Organization: Structure and Program Descriptions for 1989–90," 1.

43 Ibid.

44 Canadian Congress for Learning Opportunities for Women, *Annual Report, 1985–86*, 1–2.

45 Ibid., 2.

46 Ibid.

47 Canadian Congress for Learning Opportunities for Women, "The Organization: Structure and Program Descriptions for 1989–90," 1.

48 Ibid., 5.

49 Ibid., 7.

50 Ibid.

51 See testimony by the CCLOW on funding of the Women's Program in Canada, Parliament, House of Commons, Standing Committee on Secretary of State, *Minutes of Proceedings and Evidence*, no. 9, 17 Feb. 1987, 63.

52 Canada, Parliament, Special Joint Committee of the Senate and of the

House of Commons on the Constitution of Canada, *Minutes of Proceedings and Evidence*, no. 24, 11 Dec. 1980, 61.

53 Ibid., 72.

54 The October 1980 version of the subsection read as follows:
"(2) This section does not preclude any law, program or activity that has as its object the amelioration of conditions of disadvantaged persons or groups." The April 1981 version read: "(2) Subsection (1) does not preclude any law, program or activity that has as its object the amelioration of conditions of disadvantaged individuals or groups including those that are disadvantaged because of race, national or ethnic origin, colour, religion, sex, age or mental or physical disability."

55 Interview with Aisla Thomson, executive director of CCLOW, 16 July 1990.

56 For example, CCLOW was consulted on the Canadian Jobs Strategy and claims that it helped redefine the criteria for eligibility for re-entry and job development programs. In 1990, CCLOW was one of only three community-based organizations, and the only women's group, asked to participate in task forces to examine Ottawa's new Labour Force Development Strategy. Correspondence from Aisla Thomson, executive director, CCLOW, 16 Aug. 1990.

57 Canadian Day Care Advocacy Association, "History of the Canadian Day Care Advocacy Association" (Ottawa, 1990), 5. This is a confidential draft document kindly loaned by the CDCAA.

58 Ibid., 8.

59 Canadian Day Care Advocacy Association, *The CDCAA Story* (Ottawa: 1984), 4; as cited in Denise Guichon, "Agenda-Setting and Child Care Policy in Canada," MA thesis, University of Calgary, 1987, 80.

60 Canadian Day Care Advocacy Association, "History," 8.

61 Canada, Parliament, House of Commons, Standing Committee on Secretary of State, *Minutes of Proceedings and Evidence*, no. 13, 17 March 1987, Appendix "Secy-11," 6.

62 These figures were kindly provided on request by the CDCAA. Membership fees have never been more than 5.8 per cent of revenues (1985), and while donations accounted for 3.8 per cent of revenues in 1985, they have never topped 1 per cent since then.

63 Canada, Task Force on Child Care, *Report* (Ottawa: Status of Women Canada, 1986), Appendix B, "Task Force Recommendations."

64 Canada, Parliament, House of Commons, Special Committee on Child Care, *Sharing the Responsibility* (Ottawa: Queen's Printer, 1987), Appendix A, "Recommendations." The committee urged a tax approach based on a childcare expense deduction and a refundable childcare tax credit, along with continued use of subsidies through the Canada Assistance Plan.

65 Canadian Day Care Advocacy Association, *Vision*, no. 6, Dec. 1987, 7.
66 Canadian Day Care Advocacy Association, "News Bulletin: Federal Elections," Oct. 1988.
67 Canada, Parliament, Special Joint Committee of the Senate and of the House of Commons, *Minutes of Proceedings and Evidence*, no. 7, 13 Aug. 1987, 10.
68 Ibid.
69 Ibid., 11.
70 Susan D. Phillips, "Rock-a-Bye, Brian: The National Strategy on Child Care," in Katherine A. Graham, ed., *How Ottawa Spends, 1989–90: The Buck Stops Where?* (Ottawa: Carleton University Press, 1989), 172.
71 Susan Prentice, "The 'Mainstreaming' of Day Care," in Sue Findlay and Melanie Randall, eds., *Feminist Perspectives on the Canadian State*, an issue of *Resources for Feminist Research* 17 (Sept. 1988): 61.
72 Prentice, "'Mainstreaming'," 62.

CHAPTER TEN

1 A related issue that has not been addressed directly in this book is the rules governing charitable status. CPF and CCLOW, for example, are registered charities: donations made to them are tax-deductible. In exchange for this status, they must refrain from certain political activities. Until 1985, they had to refrain from them completely. Since then Revenue Canada has allowed a small percentage of the resources of charitable organizations to be directed to ancillary and incidental non-partisan political activities as long as the organization devotes substantially all of its resources to charitable activities. Some activities, such as oral and written presentations to elected representatives and relevant government bodies, commissions, or committees, are viewed as benign within the general ambit of charitable activities. While charities may not endorse or oppose candidates, parties, or politicians, they may engage in activities (e.g., advertisements, publications, conferences) which try to sway public opinion. No more than 10 per cent of their revenue can be directed to these incidental and ancillary activities.

Charitable status does not restrict an organization from conducting open lobbying, and in practice a wide range of "political" activity is still open (e.g., networking, issuing research reports that define and redefine issues). Moreover, charitable status is no panacea, as the financial fortunes of the CCLOW and CPF attest. Charitable status or not, these two organizations would probably disappear without federal funding. See Canada, Revenue Canada, Taxation, "Registered Charities

– Ancillary and Incidental Political Activities," Information Circular 87–1, 25 Feb. 1987.

2 No judgment is being made here on the validity of claims or identities. Diversity and fragmentation may be good things in some larger, democratic sense. My point is simply that fragmentation is not the same as unity, implying different political processes as well as demanding different political skills.

3 Once again, no judgment is being made here. The "free-rider" problem for organizations of this type means that they are likely to have low ratios of membership to affected population. Hypothetically, if given a chance, the affected population might indeed support the organization's stand.

4 Donald J. Savoie, *The Politics of Public Spending in Canada* (Toronto: University of Toronto Press, 1990), 347.

5 Groups themselves constantly lament the time and effort that must go into the application and reporting process. The relevant consideration is not whether resources are expended this way and consequently drawn from other activity, but whether in the absence of grants similar if not greater resources would have to be devoted to fundraising. Only if the alternative is almost-automatic, multi-year, no-strings-attached public funding does the lament have force.

CHAPTER ELEVEN

1 Kenneth E. Boulding, *A Preface to Grants Economics: The Economy of Love and Fear* (New York: Praeger, 1981).

2 Kenneth McRoberts, "Making Canada Bilingual: Illusions and Delusions of Federal Language Policy," in David P. Shugarman and Reg Whitaker, eds., *Federalism and Political Community: Essays in Honour of Donald Smiley* (Peterborough, Ont.: Broadview Press, 1989), 141–71.

3 Jürgen Habermas, *Legitimation Crisis* (Boston: Beacon Press, 1973).

4 Michel J. Crozier et al., *The Crisis of Democracy* (New York: New York University Press, 1975).

5 James M. Buchanan et al., eds., *Toward a Theory of the Rent Seeking Society* (College Station: Texas A&M, 1980).

6 Leslie A. Pal, "Knowledge, Power and Policy: Reflections on Foucault," in Alain-G. Gagnon and Stephen Brooks, eds., *Social Scientists and the State* (New York: Praeger, 1990), 139–58.

Index